TWENTY ALL-TIME GREAT SCIENCE FICTION FILMS

KENNETH VON GUNDEN
STUART H. STOCK

ARLINGTON HOUSE
Distributed by Crown Publishers, Inc. New York

To Donna and Tammy—who put up with it.

Published simultaneously in Canada by General Publishing Company Limited

Printed in the United States of America

Library of Congress Cataloging in Publication Data

Stock, Stuart H.
    Twenty all-time great science fiction films.

    1. Science fiction films—History and criticism.
I. Von Gunden, Kenneth.   II. Title.
PN1995.9.S26S77   791.43'09'09356   81-3451
ISBN: 0-517-548283   AACR2

Editorial and Production Services by Cobb-Dunlop, Inc.
Manufactured in the United States of America

10 9 8 7 6 5 4 3 2 1

First Edition

NOTE: The photographs used in this book were issued by the original producing companies at the time of the films' releases and belong to the collections of the authors, unless otherwise noted.

CONTENTS

INTRODUCTION

Poster from *This Island Earth.*

Poster from *Forbidden Planet.*
Notice how the poster distorts the
content of the film.

Poster from *Invader from Mars.*
Notice the Martian leader in the
upper left corner.

Most people interested in science fiction realize that SF films present moviemakers with unique problems—problems which result in films that range from embarrassing self-parodies to splendidly flawed masterpieces. Science fiction readers have continually demanded movies that capture the intellectual scope and excitement of written science fiction, but the peculiar demands of the film medium, including financial limitations, often force complex ideas aside in favor of strong visual images. And the necessity for films to earn mass-market profits requires plots understandable to the mass non-SF reading public. Production values, including special effects, are stressed at the expense of intellectual content.

When filmmakers with limited budgets attempt SF movies, the results are often uneven—and sometimes laughable. Filmmakers with larger budgets are usually more successful, but there is frequently a three-way "tug-of-war" amongst the intellectual, visual, and commercial elements of big-budget SF films. Low-budget films like *Robot Monster* turn out to be unintentionally hilarious, but a more carefully produced movie like Don Siegel's *Invasion of the Body Snatchers*—though still made on a limited budget—is nightmarishly effective, and a gigantic effort like *2001: A Space Odyssey* achieves a mysterious, uncertain brilliance.

But as SF film budgets grow, so does the scrutiny of the moneymen, whose only interest is to supply a "product" suitable for mass consumption. Creative control may slip from the writer and director to the studio hacks willing to meet the requirements of the people with the money: to make more money for them and offend no one.

Poster from *The Day the Earth Stood Still*. Notice how the poster distorts the film's content.

Poster from *2001: A Space Odyssey*.

Poster from *Invasion of the Body Snatchers*.

Still, good science fiction films *have* been made. And between the extremes of laughable and excellent is a vast collection of films whose quality and importance are hotly debated by fans of science fiction and film alike.

Books dealing with SF films usually take the form of surveys, treating each film at greater or lesser length—the depth and quality of the treatment depending solely on the whims of the author, though this is rarely made clear. Such surveys necessarily overlook important information, since their main intention is to list as many films as possible, and what information they do provide is often inaccurate. Films of interest may receive only cursory treatment, or they may be ignored altogether. Fans of science fiction films have nowhere to go for complete information and thorough examinations of individual movies. Our intention in this book is to begin to remedy that situation.

By limiting ourselves to twenty films, we hope to provide information on each film chosen that is as complete and accurate as we can make it, considering them as both science fiction and works of cinema. We want to make clear that the word "great" in the title of this book does not mean "best." We have chosen twenty films that

represent to *us* the wide range of quality in science fiction films, and that we believe we can treat in the complete and accurate manner we have described. Some are well known; some are obscure. For those that are well known we hope to provide greater background information and deeper understanding. For those more obscure we hope to make SF and film fans more aware of the contributions of these films and the people who made them.

We do not wish to swamp the reader with facts. When we have information that is only marginally relevant or simply interesting, but which does not seem to belong in a particular film's chapter, we will refer the reader to an appendix at the back of the book. An example of such material might be the "mainstream" films of a director who has worked in both SF and the mainstream. Robert Wise, director of *The Day the Earth Stood Still*, for instance, is best known for his mainstream films.

One thing we will not do in this book is to define science fiction. We believe it makes more sense to suggest some of the things science fiction does and to see how SF film has dealt with these things—for better or worse. Science fiction may celebrate science and technology, or it may warn of their frightening consequences. It may offer us serious or satirical insights into the nature of reality or the structure of society. It may provide a pleasant diversion or lead us to the brink of startling horror. Or it may do all these things.

Film, too, may do all these things. When the power of film is combined with science fiction, the two have the potential to take us beyond ourselves to confront those places and things, and ask those questions, that in our narrow daily concerns we so often only wonder about.

The authors would like to extend special thanks to the following people for their assistance: Forest J. Ackerman, Bob Casto, Roger Ebert, Linda Friend, Steve and Nancy Gould, William Hepfer, Charles Mann, Philip Klass, Ib Melchior, Evan Philips, Fred Ramsey, Jim Roth, Caroline Meredith, Kathy Shields, Curt Siodmak, Theodore and Jane Sturgeon, Bill Spangler.

The authors would also like to acknowledge the assistance of Jerry Ohlinger's Movie Material Store and The Memory Shop.

THINGS TO COME

Great Britain, 1936. American running time: 100 minutes (9,000 feet). Black and White. A London Film Production, released by United Artists. English title: The Shape of Things to Come. Running time: 113 minutes

PRODUCTION CREDITS

PRODUCER	(Sir) Alexander Korda
DIRECTOR	William Cameron Menzies
SCREENPLAY	H. G. Wells
PHOTOGRAPHY	Georges Perinal
SETTINGS DESIGNED BY	Vincent Korda, Moholy-Nagy
SPECIAL EFFECTS DIRECTED BY	Ned Mann
SPECIAL EFFECTS PHOTOGRAPHER	Edward Cohen
EXTERIOR PHOTOGRAPHY	Osmond Borradaile
ASSISTANT TO SPECIAL EFFECTS	Lawrence Butler
SPECIAL EFFECTS TECHNICIAN	Harry Zech
MUSIC	(Sir) Arthur Bliss
MUSICAL DIRECTOR	Muir Matheson
PRODUCTION MANAGER	David B. Cunynghame
EDITOR	William Hornbeck
ASTRONOMICAL ADVICE	Nigel Tangye
COSTUMES	John Armstrong, Rene Hubert
ASSISTANT ART DIRECTOR	Frank Wells
RECORDING ENGINEER	A. W. Watkins

CAST

JOHN CABAL, OSWALD CABAL	Raymond Massey
"PIPPA"/RAYMOND PASSWORTHY	Edward Chapman
RUDOLPH: THE BOSS	(Sir) Ralph Richardson
ROXANA BLACK/ROWENA CABAL	Margaretta Scott
THEOTOCOPULOS	(Sir) Cedric Hardwicke
DOCTOR HARDING	Maurice Braddell
MRS. JOHN CABAL	Sophie Stewart
RICHARD GORDON	Derek DeMarney
MARY (HARDING) GORDON	Ann Todd
CATHERINE CABAL	Pearl Argyle
MAURICE PASSWORTHY	Kenneth Villiers
MORDEN MITANI	Ivan Brandt
THE CHILD	Anne McLaren
THE AIRMAN	John Clements

H. G. Wells was one of the few giants of literature —let alone a major science fiction writer—to write the screenplay for a science fiction film and to have a hand in its making.

To [*The Shape of*] *Things to Come* Wells brought not only his strengths as a writer but also his weaknesses. The early Wells, the Wells of *The Time Machine*, was a writer of dark, pessimistic novels and short stories. The aging Wells, the sixty-eight-year-old Wells of *Things to Come*, was a Fabian socialist and an optimistic believer in man's ability to scale utopian heights and conquer base instincts.

Things to Come soars above the petty plot devices of the average science fiction film by presenting serious ideas in fictional form—that war will be the end of mankind if man does not end war; that technology, properly utilized by the finest minds, can bring about worldwide prosperity; and that mankind is destined always to strive for a better life, for adventure, for the stars themselves.

Things to Come suffers from its author's blind spots as well as benefiting from his vision. Wells's utopia of 2036 looks distressingly like a fascist state run by a benevolent dictator. John Cabal and his fellow airmen, dressed in their all-black uniforms, resemble stormtroopers when they subdue brigands with the Orwellian-sounding "gas of peace."

Wells's longtime friend and fellow member of the socialist Fabian Society, Beatrice Webb, found the scenes of civilization crumbling before the onslaught of war "vividly impressive; without H. G.'s expansive imagination and artistic talent it could not have been conceived." But she found the new society that replaced the old distressing. "Restless, intolerably restless, is this new society of men: ugly and depressing in its sum total. . . . As an attempt to depict *a new civilization*, the film is a disastrous failure."

The scenes of the Christmas Eve 1940 air attack on Everytown (London) were received in several ways— each to have a profound impact on the Second World War that was to follow. British audiences were horrified at the destruction from the air, although the shots of hundreds of enemy bombers flying over the White Cliffs of Dover provoked laughter, not fright —no bombers could cross France, bomb England, and then return to their bases inside Germany! France itself, of course, was protected from invasion by the Maginot Line. It was, everyone knew, impenetrable.

The scenes of a ruined Everytown (again read London) so impressed the appeasers in the British government that they redoubled their efforts to buy peace by allowing Hitler to satisfy his territorial demands in eastern Europe without fear of retaliation.

Winston Churchill and the Air Ministry were convinced by *Things to Come* that the heavy bomber would play an important role in the coming war and acted to increase production. Prime Minister Neville Chamberlain, however, believed the film presented a devastating argument for "peace in our time" at all costs.

In Germany, Adolf Hitler saw *Things to Come* and ordered the Luftwaffe's Göring to show the film to his generals. Hitler wanted the German air command to be capable of duplicating the total destruction wrought by bombing in the film.

Things to Come cost £350,000 or nearly $1,400,000 to produce. Although the film opened February 21, 1936, in London to excellent reviews, it died at the box office, especially in the United States, and never earned back its cost. Wells himself was keenly disappointed with the result. "My film is a mess of a film and Korda ought to be more ashamed of it than I am," he wrote to Beatrice and Sidney Webb in 1936.

Wells was too hard on *Things to Come*. It is a magnificent failure, a glorious attempt to present unusual, even unpopular, ideas in the guise of science fiction. That it fell short of its lofty goals is no surprise; that it aspired to such goals is.

Until the release of Stanley Kubrick's *2001: A Space Odyssey* more than thirty years later, *Things to Come* stood alone as the most ambitious and expensive SF film ever undertaken.

> . . . a day will come, one day in the unending succession of days, when beings, beings who are now latent in our thoughts and hidden in our loins, shall stand upon this earth as one stands upon a footstool, and shall laugh and reach out their hands amidst the stars. [H. G. Wells, *The Discovery of the Future*, 1902]

The movie opens in "Everytown" at Christmas time in 1940. The people of the city are bustling about the streets, buying toys and other presents. Christmas carols fill the air, and someone writes a Christmas greeting in the freshly fallen snow. But war headlines are juxtaposed with the cheer, and a placard reading "War Scare" moves toward the camera until it fills the screen with its ominous message. Everywhere there are newspaper headlines and signs warning of the imminence of war; the people pay them no mind.

John Cabal is entertaining two friends, Harding and Passworthy, at his house. The men stand in front of a large picture of an airplane, discussing the war talk. Kneeling under a Christmas tree, Passworthy's sons inspect their new toys—rifles and other war toys —while grandfather Cabal extols the blessings of progress. Cabal and his two companions discuss the merits of the progress that war brings.

Outside, searchlights pierce the night sky as an air raid begins. The radio tells of bombers crossing the Channel, and calls for immediate mobilization. A flyer, Cabal will be pressed into service. Grimly, he tells Passworthy he has his stimulus to progress!

In Everytown motorcycles race through the streets as anti-aircraft guns are wheeled into position and loudspeaker trucks warn everyone to return home. "Heavenly peace" is forgotten as the shoppers panic. Alone in their home, Cabal and his wife look down on their sleeping children and worry about what the future will bring them.

As Passworthy marches off to war, his son Horrie marches back and forth in front of his house beating a toy drum. He beats for war while shadows of marching soldiers appear behind him.

Gas masks are distributed in the streets amid panic, and the anti-aircraft guns are readied and fired. As Everytown dims its lights, the bombs begin to fall. Buildings collapse as a car overturns and a top-hatted gentleman shakes his fist at the unseen enemy overhead. The camera pans over a pile of rubble, revealing little Horrie Passworthy's body half buried in it.

A montage of war scenes details the extent of the war. The tanks of 1940 give way to streamlined models, soldiers fight and die, ships wage furious sea battles, and wave after wave of bombers cross the English Channel on their way to bomb [London]

Cabal, now a fighter pilot, shoots down an enemy plane that has just released poison gas. After the airman crashlands in a field, Cabal pulls the dying man from his plane. When a little girl appears, the dying airman gives her his gas mask to protect her from the gas that is slowly approaching. Cabal takes the girl to his plane, returning long enough to leave a revolver for his gallant foe to shoot himself with.

The war continues. The years 1945—1955—1960 flash on and off the screen, revealing a never ending war. A soldier's body, caught on barbed wire, melts away, leaving only the tatters of his uniform behind. A newspaper dated 1966 and costing four pounds sterling (about nine dollars today) tells of the Wandering Sickness that is sweeping across the world.

Everytown is in ruins, and the Wandering Sickness still strikes down those who contract it. Harding, now much older, is the only local doctor—and he's running out of even the most basic medical supplies. As he tells young Gordon, an aircraft mechanic who loves his daughter, "There's nothing to make anyone comfortable anymore." Gordon's sister, dazed by the Wandering Sickness, stumbles outside, where she is shot down by Rudolph, an emerging strong man.

1970. The disease is gone after killing half the world's population. Everytown is again bustling, if primitive. Horses are used to pull automobiles, and Gordon is struggling to find parts and gas for the deteriorating airplanes of the Chief, as Rudolph now calls himself.

John Cabal emerges from his futuristic aircraft.

The Chief and his mounted warriors return triumphantly from a raid against the Hill people. While the Chief berates Gordon for being unable to get his planes airborne, a modernistic propeller plane is spotted overhead. When it lands it disgorges a white-haired John Cabal in an all-black uniform with a strange apparatus on his head—a gas mask.

Cabal is now part of Wings Over the World, a world organization of engineers and scientists dedicated to bringing back civilization and ending warfare. Cabal speaks briefly with Dr. Harding in his quarters, but the Chief's men take him to see their leader. Cabal informs the swaggering Chief that he represents law and sanity in the form of World Communications.

With Cabal locked up, the Chief's woman, Roxana, pressures him to do more. As a result, the Chief wars on neighboring shale pits for oil for his planes and is victorious. This grand success prompts him to plan more warfare in the name of ending all war. To this end, the Chief puts Gordon, Dr. Harding, and Cabal together to work for him.

Roxana visits Cabal and tells him he excites her; she is able to read and wants to see more of the world. When Cabal spurns her advances, she threatens him. Cabal coolly informs her that even if he is killed his hopes will carry on—"the human things go on—We —forever."

Cabal plots with Gordon, who escapes and flies to Cabal's base to report. The black-uniformed Airmen prepare giant bombers, loading them with the gas of peace. The Chief sends his men aloft when they appear, but the puny biplanes have no chance and are shot down (off screen) or routed. People fall as the gas wafts into Everytown. The Chief, defiant to the end, shoots into the air helplessly, then collapses. The parachutists land, marching into Everytown in exactly the same way as the Chief's victorious horsemen.

Cabal is freed as the residents of Everytown awaken from their sleep. Told that the gas has inexplicably killed the Chief, Cabal grimly notes that he died with his world of eternal warfare. Cabal and his Airmen vow that the ruined world will be rebuilt.

The reconstruction begins. Great machines dig into the earth. There is a montage of scenes of machines/men/construction. Technology is recreating the world, replacing what it destroyed.

It is now 2036, and Everytown has been rebuilt as an underground city. A sculptor, Theotocopulos, speaks against the new ways—including the Space Gun, which is to send men and women to the moon.

An old man views scenes from the past with his great-granddaughter. Theirs is a world without windows, and he tells her of the time of windows and of seeing John Cabal as a boy. The old man tells the little girl that it is John Cabal's great-grandson, Oswald Cabal, who rules Everytown now.

Oswald Cabal, steely-visaged and strong, learns that Maurice Passworthy and his own daughter Catherine wish to be the first people to circumnavigate the moon when the Space Gun is ready.

While Cabal ponders his daughter's decision, Theotocopulos goes on worldwide television to argue against the Space Gun. Sounding remarkably like a sixties' liberal, he asks rhetorically, "What good is all this progress?"

Cabal's friend Passworthy doesn't want his son to go, but the decision to do so is quickly reached when Cabal and the others learn that a mob is marching to the site of the Space Gun.

Cabal and the others reach the Space Gun ahead of the mob by helicopter. The Gun is monstrously huge; people seem like less than ants beside its bulk. As Maurice Passworthy and Catherine Cabal are lowered down its barrel, the Space Gun is readied for firing. Cabal warns Theotocopulos and his followers away, telling them to beware of the Gun's concussion. Paying no heed to his warning, the mob surges forward as the Gun fires.

Standing in an observatory, Cabal and Passworthy spot the tiny projectile among the stars as it heads for the moon.

Passworthy asks, "Is there never to be an age of happiness? Is there never to be any rest?"

Cabal responds: "Rest enough for the individual man. Too much of it and too soon, and we call it death. But for man no rest and no ending. He must go on—conquest beyond conquest. This little planet and its winds and its ways, and all the laws of mind and matter that restrain him. Then the planets about him, and at last out across immensity to the stars. And when he has conquered all the depths of space and all the mysteries of time—still he will be beginning."

"But we are such little creatures. Poor humanity. So fragile, so weak."

An example of things *not* to come: this publicity shot of Ernest Thesiger was produced before he was replaced by Cedric Hardwicke in the role of Theotocopulos—who is seen addressing Everytown via worldwide television.

The model of the massive space gun and the miniature landscape surrounding it. A gantry is about to place the projectile in the gun's barrel. If you look closely, you'll see the space gun has a sight on the end of the barrel.

"Little animals, eh?"

"Little animals."

"If we are no more than animals, we must snatch at our little scraps of happiness and live and suffer and pass, mattering no more than all the other animals do, or have done. It is that—or this? All the universe—or nothingness? Which shall it be, Passworthy? Which shall it be?"

Herbert George Wells was born September 21, 1866, the son of a shopkeeper. Young Bertie, as he was called, briefly attended Bromley Academy, leaving to become a draper's apprentice (the basis for his novel *Kipps*). In short order he was a pupil-teacher at Wookey (yes, Wookey), a chemist's assistant in Midhurst, a draper, and a pupil-teacher at Midhurst School. Wells then won a scholarship to enter the Normal School of Science in South Kensington, where one of his teachers was the famous T. H. Huxley, an early proponent of evolutionary theory.

Influenced by Huxley, Wells joined a debating society and won a teaching post at Holt Academy. It was about this time that Wells began to make money from the writing he was doing at night. His first scientific romance (as SF was then called) was *The Time Machine*, published in 1895, when he was nearly thirty.

A Victorian and a young man fighting his way up the ladder of success in a society built on class distinctions, the young Wells wrote novels and short stories that reflected his pessimism about the world.

One of the first great science fiction writers, along with Jules Verne, Wells established many of the principles of speculative fiction that later writers were to follow. In nearly all his science fiction the characters are vehicles; the idea, the concept, or the society is the hero, the focal point. Wells knew that in science fiction the characters make clear the society or the time—the reverse of the mainstream novel form. If one remembers this, it's clear that Menzies, often singled out for his awkward direction of the people in *Things*, was really being true to Wells's intent by presenting the movie's characters as symbols rather than as flesh-and-blood human beings.

(For more on Wells, see the chapter on *War of the Worlds*.)

Alexander Korda (1893–1956), eldest of the three talented Korda brothers, was born Sandor Kellner in Hungary.

Alex made the best grades in school of the three brothers and became a journalist for a Budapest newspaper when he was twenty. After writing an essay for his newspaper on motion pictures, he was considered an expert in the young and blossoming field. He was asked to translate the German, French, and English subtitles into Hungarian, since he, like his brothers, was fluent in several languages. Soon, with the aid of a secondhand movie camera, he was writing, producing, and directing his own modest productions.

The young Hungarian became a director for Sascha Films in Vienna and moved to the UFA Studios in Berlin in 1923. By 1926 Korda was ready to try

Hollywood. First National Pictures hired him, and he made *The Private Life of Helen of Troy,* his only film for the studio. Warner Bros. acquired First National in a merger, so Korda jumped over to Fox Studios when his contract expired.

Korda soon tired of Hollywood. He didn't like the life or the way Fox was treating him, so he packed up and returned to Europe, settling in London.

With an old friend, writer Lajos Biro, and Stephen Pallos, a French movie salesman, Korda created London Films. After making a few forgettable films to put money in the till, Alex sent for his brother Vincent, who joined the company as an art director.

The persuasive Korda tracked down Charles Laughton and proposed that the actor portray Henry VIII in a London Films production. Staking his time and work against future box office profits, Laughton and many of the other actors and technicians worked for almost nothing. United Artists agreed to distribute the film. When the movie appeared, it was an immediate success, earning a half million pounds for London Films and making the homely Laughton an even bigger international star, as well as winning him an Academy Award as Best Actor. Korda's London Films was firmly established, and its success encouraged a new wave of British filmmaking. Korda is credited with single-handedly creating the British film industry.

In 1929 H. G. Wells wrote a screenplay that was never produced. *The King Who Was a King* was openly hostile to warfare and probably could not have been filmed, given its many sets, characters, and immensely grand scenes.

Wells was determined to make a film of one of his books, however, and through his secretary, Russian refugee Moura Budberg, he met Alexander Korda. Korda was fascinated by the English writer and resolved to make a film with him. Surprisingly, their first choice was *The Shape of Things to Come,* which Wells hoped would popularize his private scientific elitism.

Korda did all he could to assure Wells's participation. He asked Wells to write the screenplay and hired his son, Frank Wells, as an assistant art director. Frank Wells also worked on Korda's production of H. G.'s *The Man Who Could Work Miracles.*

For the many conferences between Wells and the Korda brothers, Moura Budberg served as interpreter, since Wells spoke English and the Kordas French.

After Korda told Wells that his first draft of the screenplay was virtually unfilmable, Wells began a second draft. H. G. (as his friends called him) was assisted by Hungarian writer Lajos Biro, once Korda's boss, a Hungarian diplomat, and a co-founder of London Films.

Raymond Massey, in his autobiography *A Hundred Different Lives,* recalls that Wells's authority in the making of *Things* was unprecedented for a writer: he had complete control of the screenplay, the direction, design, cutting, and even the promotion of the film. But, Massey notes, since Wells's only film experience "consisted of a visit to Walt Disney's studio in Hollywood," he soon discovered that he needed help in bringing his vision to the screen.

Massey, who was to portray both John and Oswald Cabal in *Things,* recalled reporting to work on the first of July, 1934. As Wells watched a number of scenes being shot, he knew the script needed more work. "Many of the sequences," he later admitted, "which slipped easily from my pen when I wrote the scenario were extremely difficult to screen, and some were impossible." As Wells wrote of the experience:

> ... An earlier treatment was made, discussed, worked upon for a little and discarded. It was a 'prentice effort and the Author owes much to the friendly generosity of Alexander Korda, Lajos Biro and Cameron Menzies, who put all their experience at his disposal during the revision.
>
> They were greatly excited by the general conception, but they found the draft quite impractical for production. A second treatment ... was made into a scenario of the old type [and] set aside for a second version, and this again was revised and put back into the form of the present treatment. Korda and the Author had agreed upon an innovation in film technique, to discard the elaborate detailed technical scenario altogether and to produce directly from the descriptive treatment.... We have found this worked very well in practice—given a competent director. But this time, however, the author, now almost through the toils of his apprenticeship, was in a state of fatigue towards the altered, revised, and reconstructed text, and, though he had done his best to get it into tolerable film prose, he had an uneasy sense that many oddities and awkwardnesses of expression that crept in during the scenario had become now so familiar to him, he was blind to them and unable to get rid of them.

The screenplay was finally finished after production had already begun. If *Things to Come* seems somewhat dated to us today, it is the fault of Wells's heroic dialogue and labored constructions. Wells, born during the Victorian era, was then sixty-eight years old and his romantic-sounding dialogue is a product of the time in which he grew up.

Raymond Massey writes of being disappointed by the version of *Things* that was released, believing that cutting the film by one third jumbled the continuity and harmed the story line. Massey, too, was talking about the original British version, which ran 130 minutes, cut to 113 minutes, not the 100-minute version released in the United States on April 17, 1936, at the Rivoli Theater in New York City. A number of stills and publicity shots document scenes apparently filmed but edited from the film before release, at least for the U.S. There were also several sequences that survive in stills for which the necessary model and special effects work was probably deemed too expensive or complicated.

The credits for the U.S. version have Margaretta Scott, playing not only Roxana Black, the Chief's woman, but also Rowena Cabal, the wife of Oswald Cabal. Rowena does not appear, although there are stills showing her with her husband and dramatically posed publicity shots.

The screenplay for the film, the final draft, is longer and contains more scenes than the finished film, scenes presumably filmed before being cut.

Major sequences in Wells's script but not in the film include:

—Cabal expressing disgust for walking into the Chief's hands so blithely (cutting this scene makes Cabal more a superman but makes his intentions—to create a dictatorship of Airmen—less clear).

—Roxana's offer of herself to Cabal and his rejection of her—although the beginning and ending of the scene remain intact.

—Cabal's monologue over the unconscious Roxana, when he calls her an eternal adventuress.

—Oswald Cabal's scene with his wife Rowena, in which he calls her a "love-huntress" and wonders why they could not work together.

Also missing is a scene in which young Horrie Passworthy wars upon brother Timothy's toy rail-

The man on the left is producer Alexander Korda. He's seen talking to the author of the screenplay and a giant of literature, H. G. Wells.
Seemingly bemused, Cabal (Raymond Massey) listens to the boasts of Everytown's "Boss" (Sir Ralph Richardson) while a somewhat apprehensive Roxana Black (Margaretta Scott) looks on.

THINGS TO COME

road only to end up wrestling with him on the floor. This missing scene blunts the ironic impact of seeing Horrie lying dead in the rubble after Everytown is bombed.

The female Airmen (Airpersons?) may have been cut from the film, but Wells offered us something very rare in SF and SF film in their place—the first humans to go to the moon and back are a man and a *woman*. Wells, though he once told W. Somerset Maugham that he couldn't write unless he had sex with a woman after lunch and before dinner every day, was in many ways an early feminist. Certainly he knew that women had minds equal to those of men and that women, just as well as men, could put aside sexual biology and work toward a common goal.

The segment hit hardest by cuts and changes is the final third of the film, set in the Everytown of 2036. Here a number of scenes detailing life in the modern underground city were either cut or not filmed at all. Theotocopulos's speech is longer and more impassioned in the script, touching upon matters of religion and science not mentioned in the film. Also missing are scenes of citizens debating what he has to say. As the film has it now, all Theotocopulos does is give one speech and everyone immediately rebels against progress and the Space Gun.

Perhaps the kindest cut of all was the one that removed a sequence which had the Airmen writing SURRENDER in the sky with their airplanes. Today it would too quickly bring to mind the Wicked Witch writing SURRENDER DOROTHY with her broomstick in *The Wizard of OZ!*

Early press releases announced that Alexander Korda's new film, *One Hundred Years to Come,* would be directed by Lewis Milestone, who had won an Academy Award for his direction of the classic antiwar film, *All Quiet on the Western Front.* But Korda chose William Cameron Menzies to take up the director's reins when Milestone decided instead to direct two less complex films, *The Captain Hates the Sea* and *Paris in Spring.*

William Cameron Menzies (1896–1957), who is best remembered as a production designer rather than as a director, created a stupendous castle for the 1922 silent *Robin Hood.* Because of this achievement, Menzies was chosen to design the sets for Douglas Fairbanks's 1923 production of *The Thief of Bagdad,* a task he repeated for Korda's 1940 remake starring Sabu.

Menzies dominated the world of art direction in Hollywood throughout the thirties and early forties; in 1928 he won the first Academy Award for Best Art Direction (or "Interior Decoration" as it was then known) for *The Dove.*

For *Gone With the Wind,* Menzies drew nearly three thousand detailed, perfectly composed sketches for the camera to follow, every shot on paper, right down to the lighting effects. Because *GWTW* went through several directors, many people in the film industry credit Menzies's sketches for providing the

visual blueprint that held the Oscar-winning movie together. Menzies even served as a second-unit director for *GWTW,* shooting battle scenes between the North and the South.

Seeking a way to describe Menzies's contribution to *GWTW,* art director Lyle Wheeler and producer David O. Selznick devised the term "production designer."

"When Menzies worked as a director," Lyle Wheeler recalled, "I used to tell him, 'You're no damn good as a director.' The first thing he would ask for when he came on the set is, 'Dig me a hole in here,' and that's where he would put his camera. He wanted to photograph ceilings and didn't give a damn what the actors were saying."

Menzies, for all his faults—indeed, perhaps because of them—was probably a wise choice as director of *Things to Come.* Anyone else, a director unused to giving up so much control, would have rebelled at allowing the novice Wells to dominate the creative process as he did. Korda most likely saw in Menzies a compliant artist, more concerned with the film's look than its substance.

Portrait of John Cabal (Raymond Massey).

Moholy-Nagy, a fellow Hungarian, to design a number of back projections, notably for the scenes showing the ruined world being rebuilt by huge machines. Moholy-Nagy's work was acceptable. Ned Mann was hired to handle the film's special effects. He was a Hollywood friend of Menzies who had also worked on *The Thief of Bagdad*. Mann was responsible for outstanding special effects for Cecil B. De Mille's *Madam Satan*. Since special effects work was almost unknown in England, with Mann came other Hollywood professionals: rear projection expert Harry Zech, optical effects man Jack Thomas, model builder Ross Jacklin, traveling matte expert Paul Morell, effects cameraman Eddie Cohen, and Lawrence Butler, an expert on providing "full-sized mechanical effects."

Since Korda had allowed Wells such a large hand in the production, Wells was also able to choose the person he wanted to write the musical score for the film. Wells decided on Sir Arthur Bliss.

"I continue to be confident and delighted," Wells wrote to Bliss on June 19, 1934. "But I am not so sure of the Finale. Perhaps I dream of something superhuman, but I do not feel that what you have done so far fully renders all that you can do in the way of human exaltation. It's good dash—nothing you do can fail to be good—but it is not yet the exaltant shout of human resolution that there might be—not the marching song of a new world of conquest among the atoms and stars."

Korda wanted to add Bliss's music after the film was shot and edited, the normal way of scoring a film. Wells would have none of it. "I says Balls!" Wells wrote to Bliss in October. "I say a film is a composition and the musical composer is an integral part of the design. I want Bliss to be in touch throughout. I don't think Korda has much of an ear, but I want the audience at the end not to sever what it sees from what it hears. I want to end on a complete sensuous and emotional synthesis."

Much of the finished score was recorded before the scenes it was to accompany were shot. Further, the rebuilding of the devasted Everytown by the giant machines was shot and edited to correspond to Bliss's music.

When Wells saw the finished rebuilding section with Bliss's appropriately ponderous and machinelike music, he turned to Korda and said, "Very good machines. Very good, but the machines of the future will make no noise!"

Wells's domination of the early story conferences was a burden Korda gladly bore to insure the great man's participation. But at times his patience wore thin. Wells would lecture in his high, squeaky voice while the Kordas would gently point out why one of his ideas was impossible to film. Korda had had such battles with Charles Laughton during the making of *The Private Life of Henry VIII*, and one day was heard to mutter that "H. G. is a second Laughton!"

Bliss's music is one of the best things about *Things to Come*, and Wells's choice of him to write the score was a wise one. In the war scenes Bliss's martial music

Standing beside a giant telescope, Oswald Cabal (Raymond Massey) and Passworthy (Edward Chapman) stare into the heavens after their children have embarked on a journey to the moon. "All the universe—or nothingness," says Cabal. "Which shall it be, Passworthy? Which shall it be?"

Publicity poster for *Things to Come*.

is stirring and evocative, its drumbeat intensity all-too-clearly underscoring the appeal such sounds have for the human soul. It is the soaring finale, however, as Cabal and Passworthy contemplate the vastness of the universe, that sweeps the listener along with its promise of greater things to come. Certainly, the final scene is theatrical, but its combination of undying human aspiration and indomitable will captures man at his best. Massey's craggy face, seen in close-up as he delivers Wells's message of hope and conquest, is matched by Bliss's musical shout of exaltation. Man is tentatively reaching out for the stars, all the universe, and he will make it his or die trying.

Wells was correct in predicting the Second World War in *Things*, along with the use of the heavy bomber to terrorize and demoralize civilian populations. In addition, he foresaw the use of worldwide television and the special problems it would bring by instantaneously linking the homes and offices of everyone in the world. But some of the other futuristic or scientific predictions or expectations of the film are off mark, such as the continuing use of poison gas—mainly a phenomenon of World War I.

The Space Gun is an error of enormous proportions. Here Wells has reverted to Verne's nineteenth-century prediction of space travel by means of a gun-fired projectile. An anonymous scientist, writing in *The Journal of the British Interplanetary Society*, assumed the Gun to have a barrel a half mile in length. He wrote: "To obtain a muzzle velocity of 7 miles per second—the minimum velocity required by the projectile—would necessitate an acceleration up the barrel of 49 miles per second. Assuming the weight of either of the space travellers as 120 pounds, and using the equation $p = m \cdot F$, we see that the force on either person would be about 435 tons!" And if you look closely, you'll see that the Space Gun has a *sight* on the end of the barrel.

In a time facing an oil shortage of its own, we can only marvel at Wells's making the goal of the Chief's war against the Hill people their oil-bearing shale, from which he hoped to extract gas for his airplanes.

Things to Come is not an actors' picture, despite the many monologues Wells put into his characters' mouths. Raymond Massey disliked the formalized dialogue and lamented that "the picture was fantastically difficult to act. A benign big brother was bound to be a bore. He was the fellow I played in the futuristic part of the film. I could only act Oswald Cabal as calmly and as quietly as possible...."

Massey holds the three sections of the film together, his lean face and frame embodying the will and determination of a man who has seen too much war and wants to put an end to it forever. His final speech, to Passworthy, is flawlessly delivered and one of the great moments in science fiction film.

Raymond Massey (1896–) was born in Toronto, Canada, into a family that owned a worldwide farm implements business. His mother, an American, took him to the theater when he was young, and he soon vowed to become an actor. A soldier in the war, he tried his hand at acting in England and soon became a hardworking actor/manager/director much in demand. He even appeared in a play or two with a younger fellow named Laurence Olivier.

Massey is best remembered for his portrayals of Abraham Lincoln on stage and in film, and for his role as Doctor Gillespie in the television series *Dr. Kildare* (1960–66). His last appearance as an actor was in Tennessee Williams's *The Night of the Iguana* in Los Angeles in 1975–76. Crippling arthritis had made it impossible for him to work, and he was feeling his age in other ways. Sadly, as he concluded in his autobiography, "I had the sense to know that my working years in the theater were over."

Massey's first film role was as Sherlock Holmes in *The Speckled Band* (1931). He made his first of several films for Alexander Korda, *The Scarlet Pimpernel*, in 1934. *Things* was followed by *The Prisoner of Zenda* (1937), *Abe Lincoln in Illinois* (1939), *East of Eden* (1955), and his last movie, *MacKenna's Gold* (1968). (For a fuller listing of Massey's films, see the Appendix.)

Sir Ralph Richardson played the role of Rudolph, the Chief of Everytown who holds Cabal captive. Now one of the grand old men of British theater and screen, Richardson was a vigorous thirty-four when *Things* was shot. His Chief, though a villain, is the most vital and compelling character in the film. Richardson captures the Chief's uncertain mixture of bravado and insecurity, and one feels sorry for him when Cabal announces that he is dead.

A great eccentric, Ralph Richardson (1902–   ) is not only one of the finest stage actors of our time but also a marvelous screen actor who has made many films, beginning with *The Ghoul* in 1933. His other films include *The Man Who Could Work Miracles* (1936), *The Four Feathers* (1939), *The Wrong Box* (1966), and Richard Lester's outrageous SF black comedy, *The Bed Sitting Room* (1969). (For his other films, see the Appendix.)

Sir Cedric Hardwicke's role of Theotocopulos offers him little chance to show his acting ability, since Wells wrote it at one pitch. Cedric Hardwicke (1893–1964) became a classic stage actor in England, and made his first motion picture, the silent *Nelson*, in 1926. He had a marvelous speaking voice, and George Pal chose him as the narrator of his production of *The War of the Worlds*. Hardwicke's career was erratic, since he too often chose inferior material.

Among his many films are *Stanley and Livingston* (1939), *A Connecticut Yankee in King Arthur's Court* (1949), *Richard III* (1955), and *The Ten Commandments* (1956) (For further information, see the Appendix.)

Things to Come is unique for not having a mad scientist at its core and for not expressing tired clichés about things "Man was not meant to know." *Things* is instead closer to the SF magazines of the time, which foresaw the future as a breathtaking series of technological advances, from domed cities to moving sidewalks.

H. G. Wells knew that the future he predicted in *Things* was not a real projection of events, not the way things would really be. But he was concerned with getting people at least to think about the future and to see that it is a direct result of the decisions we make today.

Because Wells had larger-than-life statements and themes to present in *Things*, the movie's human side suffers, although not as severely as some critics would have us believe, since Wells does show the effects of war and progress on individuals and their families.

Wells saw that the greatest danger to progress was war and warns that conflict will destroy us. When Harding and Passworthy present the argument that war stimulates progress, Wells has Cabal warn us that war may mean an end to man.

Progress. The grandfather in the Cabal household argues for it while the grandfather in the world of 2036 wonders if progress is not sometimes too rapid for man's good. More than forty years later we're still debating the merits of progress. Unlike Theotocopulos, we don't want to halt all progress, but we do want more from it than the sterile and ordered lifestyle of the Everytown of the future.

The visionary Cabal and the frustrated and worried Theotocopulos are both aware, in their own ways, that life must offer Man more than comfort and enough to eat; it must offer challenges and something to fight for. For Theotocopulos that means destroying science and technology; for Cabal only the stars will do.

If *Things to Come* has about it an air of innocence for us today, a belief that man can shape the future and make it his, perhaps we are too cynical. For if we do not move forward, solving our problems of energy, population, hunger, pollution, and global conflict, moving out into the solar system and beyond, we face an end to our species.

Wells was wrong about one thing: It is not a choice between "all the universe—or nothingness," the Earth *or* the stars; we can have them both.

DESTINATION MOON

Eagle-Lion Films. Running Time: 92 minutes. Technicolor. Loosely based on the novel Rocketship Galileo *by Robert A. Heinlein. Early titles:* Journey to the Moon, Operation Moon. *Opened in New York City on June 27, 1950, at the Mayfair.*

PRODUCTION CREDITS

PRODUCER . . . . *George Pal*
DIRECTOR . . . . *Irving Pichel*
SCREENPLAY . . . . *Robert Heinlein, Rip Van Ronkel, & James O'Hanlon*
CINEMATOGRAPHER . . . . *Lionel Lindon*
PRODUCTION DESIGNER . . . . *Ernst Fegte*
SPECIAL EFFECTS . . . . *Lee Zavitz*
ANIMATION DIRECTOR . . . . *John S. Abbott*
EDITOR . . . . *Duke Goldstone*
SET DECORATION . . . . *George Lawley*
ASSISTANT DIRECTOR . . . . *Harold Godsoe*
MUSIC . . . . *Leith Stevens*
CARTOON SEQUENCE . . . . *Walter Lantz Studio*
SOUND . . . . *William Lynch*
MAKEUP . . . . *Webster Philips*
TECHNICAL ADVISER . . . . *Robert A. Heinlein*
TECHNICAL ADVISER ASTRONOMICAL ART . . . . *Chesley Bonestell*
PRODUCTION SUPERVISOR . . . . *Martin Eisenberg*
COLOR CONSULTANT . . . . *Robert Brower*

CAST

JIM BARNES . . . . *John Archer*
DR. CHARLES CARGRAVES . . . . *Warner Anderson*
GENERAL THAYER . . . . *Tom Powers*
JOE SWEENEY . . . . *Dick Wesson*
EMILY CARGRAVES . . . . *Erin O'Brien Moore*
BROWN . . . . *Ted Warde*

Believe it or not, *Destination Moon* is a controversial movie. Among science fiction fans it is generally taken as a matter of faith that the film is one of the few authentic pieces of SF ever brought to the screen. Yet even among fans today there are those who consider the film hopelessly dated and insufferably boring.

SF writer Arthur C. Clarke looks back on *Destination Moon* (hereafter referred to as *DM*) with fondness, as does director Robert Wise, who would film *The Day the Earth Stood Still*, *The Andromeda Strain*, and *Star Trek: The Motion Picture*. Richard Hodgens, in his *Short, Tragical History of the Science Fiction Film*, calls *DM* "a good, semi-documentary film," but also says that "today its optimism is rather depressing."

James Robert Parish and Michael Pitts, in their book *The Great Science Fiction Pictures*, describe *DM* as "technically mediocre and never really very exciting." John Baxter measures it as "tepid," and French critic Pierre Kast refers to *DM* as "stupid, dull, and puerile."

Yet at the time of *DM*'s release critics found it generally praiseworthy. *Newsweek* complained the film got off to a slow start, but suggested it would "provide satisfaction for the admirers of the scientific type of adventure story." *Time* said it "speculates entertainingly . . . on what may happen when man takes his first . . . flight . . . to the moon." Kenneth Heuer, of the Astronomy Department of the Hayden Planetarium, writing in *Films in Review*, liked the film, but complained it didn't have enough information about the moon in it.

Bosley Crowther, in the *New York Times*, said that the film "makes a lunar expedition a most intriguing and picturesque event." But in the time-honored tradition of mainstream reviewers of SF films, he urged people to go strictly for the special effects.

Crowther went on to say: "Even though Mr. Pal [the producer] assures us . . . everything . . . has been checked . . . for what you might technically expect, this corner withholds its opinion of the voyage's plausibility." Some twenty years after the first successful moonflight, Crowther's doubts seem rather quaint.

Whether *DM* is really dated, boring, puerile, and other things it's been called remains a matter of opinion. It did, however, start the fifties' cycle of SF films (see Appendix), though many of those later films lacked the effort put into *DM*. Whatever one thinks of it today, its place in the history of SF film is assured.

DM begins at an army testing station where Dr. Charles Cargraves and General Thayer observe the takeoff of an atomic-powered rocket designed by Cargraves, and built to put a satellite into Earth orbit. But the rocket crashes soon after takeoff. Cargraves suspects sabotage but it doesn't matter. Both he and Thayer know the failure will mean the end of government support for the project.

Two years later Thayer arrives at Barnes Aircraft to see its owner, Jim Barnes. Thayer implies there is evidence proving Cargraves's rocket was sabotaged. Stressing the military importance of a base on the moon, Thayer convinces the initially skeptical Barnes to supervise the construction of a spaceship to fly to the moon.

Barnes organizes a meeting of leading industrialists to describe the moon project. The government, he tells them, isn't capable of handling such a job in peacetime; only U.S. industry can do the job. Barnes uses a Woody Woodpecker cartoon to explain the principles of spaceflight, but the businessmen remain unconvinced. Finally, Thayer details the importance of the moon as a strategic outpost and suggests "others" realize this also. Unless the U.S. gets there first, he implies, there may some day be no U.S. Impressed by this argument, the businessmen agree to support the project.

A montage of shots showing the planning and construction of the ship follows. Some time later, with the ship nearly completed, Brown, the ship's electronics man, talks to his assistant, Joe Sweeney. Sweeney doubts the ship will ever get off the ground, but Brown hardly notices—his stomach has been bothering him.

Barnes and Thayer arrive at the desert launch site, where Cargraves shows them a letter from the Atomic Energy Commission denying them permission to test the rocket's atomic engine. They appear beaten, but Barnes suggests they take off at the next favorable time—seventeen hours from then—with him, Cargraves, Thayer, and Brown, as crew.

Working feverishly, they prepare spaceship LUNA for takeoff. At the last minute Brown is rushed to the hospital with appendicitis. Only Sweeney can replace him, and he doesn't want to go. The other three succeed in persuading him.

As final preparations are made and Cargraves says good-bye to his wife, an official arrives at the gate with a court order to prevent the takeoff. Barnes defies the order, and the ship blasts off.

The massive acceleration at takeoff rams the crew into their couches, their faces contorted by the terrible pressure. When the engines finally cut off, the travelers find themselves floating in the weightless conditions of space. Barnes hands out magnetic-soled boots, designed to keep the crew from floating about the ship.

Suddenly, the explorers realize they've made it into space. Looking through the aft porthole, they observe the rapidly retreating Earth, picking out cities.

The men settle into life aboard ship. Some time later, Barnes tries to extend the antenna for the piloting radar needed for the moon landing. It refuses to budge. Sweeney admits to greasing it before takeoff, unaware that conditions in space would make the grease freeze. Cargraves, Barnes, and Sweeney go outside the ship in spacesuits to free the antenna, anchoring themselves to the ship with safety lines.

Barnes and Sweeney work on the antenna while

Barnes (John Archer) uses an oxygen tank like a miniature rocket to propel himself out to Cargraves—who has drifted away from the ship after taking off his safety line.

Cargraves goes aft to inspect the rocket tube. Leaning over for a better look, Cargraves releases his safety line—and suddenly finds himself drifting free of the ship.

Barnes and Sweeney rush to his aid. They throw Cargraves a rope, but the distance is too far. Barnes quickly tells Thayer to bring out an oxygen tank. Using the tank like a miniature rocket, Barnes propels himself out to Cargraves and brings him back.

The rest of the trip is without incident. But as they prepare to land on the moon, Barnes misses their exact landing site and is forced to expend extra fuel during the touchdown.

Once on the surface, Cargraves and Barnes go outside to inspect the moonscape. Cargraves claims the moon in the name of the United States of America for the benefit of all mankind.

Exploration begins. Cargraves and Sweeney set up a large, telescopic camera, lifting it easily in the moon's lighter gravity. Thayer prospects for minerals and finds traces of uranium.

Meanwhile, Barnes has contacted Earth. Because of the error in landing there's some question about the LUNA's chances of taking off again. The crew jettisons as much nonessential material from the ship as they can to lighten it. Even after this, however, calculations show they must get rid of another thousand pounds.

The four men tear out most of the ship's equipment, cutting every unnecessary item out of it. They plan to discard three of the spacesuits, keeping only the one needed to get rid of the other three. Yet they are *still* 110 pounds short.

With only eighteen minutes till takeoff, Barnes, Cargraves, and Thayer realize one of them must stay behind. Each tries to persuade the others why *they* should go back. Sweeney, who appears selfishly concerned with his own safety, suggests they draw lots. Then, while the others are occupied, Sweeney slips outside and prepares to sacrifice himself by staying behind.

Barnes pleads with him to return, but Sweeney

refuses. With less than fifteen minutes left, Barnes hits on a solution that convinces Sweeney to come back. First, they junk the radio, which weighs fifty pounds. Then Sweeney enters the airlock and files a notch in its seal, ties a rope to his empty spacesuit—weighing seventy pounds—and weights it with an oxygen tank. With Sweeney safely in the control cabin, Barnes opens the airlock, and the spacesuit is dragged out.

Minutes later, with all aboard, the spaceship LUNA takes off—headed for home.

DM began in the mind of science fiction writer Robert A. Heinlein. In 1948, at the top of his profession, Heinlein arrived in Hollywood with the dream of writing a screenplay for a solid, factual SF film. SF fan and literary agent Lou Schorr brought Heinlein and screenwriter Alford "Rip" Van Ronkel together, and the two came up with a story about a moon trip loosely based on Heinlein's novel *Rocketship Galileo*, tentatively titled *Journey to the Moon*.

But Heinlein and Van Ronkel couldn't sell their idea to any of the major studios. In 1948, hard science fiction was a property no one was buying, and without studio money *Journey to the Moon* would never get off the ground.

Van Ronkel finally met independent producer George Pal. (For information on Pal, see the chapter on *The War of the Worlds*.) Pal became interested in *Journey to the Moon*, and he too tried marketing the script to the studios—without success.

Pal eventually got Peter Rathvon, a former chief at RKO and then head of independent Eagle-Lion Pictures, to back the film. Pal made a two-picture deal with Rathvon for his own film, *The Great Rupert*, to be followed by the Heinlein-Van Ronkel screenplay. Nevertheless, he had to use at least some of his own money to finance the films. The title was changed first to *Operation Moon* and finally to *Destination Moon*. Shooting began in November 1949 at the General Service Studio in Hollywood, with location work in the Mojave Desert.

From the start of filming to the movie's wrap-up in April 1950, making *DM* became something of a trial for those involved. Aside from the problems of just shooting the film, the filmmakers faced studio interference, and for a while it looked as though *DM* might wind up a combination of musical comedy and pseudoscientific nonsense. But the filmmakers held out. In the end, it was worth it. *DM* cost $586,000 to make and earned $5.5 million. It was Eagle-Lion's top grosser for the year, and the film won an Oscar for its special effects.

One of the people who fought hard for the integrity of *DM* was Robert Heinlein, who became the film's technical adviser. One could expect no less from one of the top writers in the field of science fiction.

Heinlein was born in Missouri in 1907. He was educated at the University of Missouri and the U.S. Naval Academy at Annapolis, serving as a naval officer for five years before retiring for health reasons.

He enrolled in UCLA to study mathematics and physics, dropping out after a year, again because of his health.

Between 1934 and 1939 Heinlein worked in silver mining, real estate, and even in state politics. During World War II he served as an engineer at the Naval Air Experimental Station in Philadelphia.

In 1939, Heinlein, a longtime reader of SF, decided to try his hand at writing. His first story, "Life-Line" (*Astounding*, 1939), was minor but his career soon took off, and he became one of the foremost authors in John W. Campbell's *Astounding*.

Today, Heinlein is one of the most respected figures in SF. He has produced more significant SF writings than can be mentioned here, winning four Hugo awards (the Oscar of science fiction), and the first Grand Master Nebula Award presented by the Science Fiction Writers of America. His work has never failed to stimulate thought as well as controversy.

Nearly every article on *DM* mentions its origins in Heinlein's novel, *Rocketship Galileo*. But *DM* bears no relationship to that book except for the trip to the moon and the name of the scientist involved. Actually, *DM* has more in common with Heinlein's 1950 novelette, "The Man Who Sold the Moon." Both suggest private industry would be the moving force behind the first moon trip, and both capture the frantic energy of making the trip a reality.

Most sources also ignore his novelette, "Destination Moon," which appeared in *Short Stories Magazine* in September 1950 (see Appendix). The story isn't elaborate and reads like a treatment for the film, but there are definite differences.

The story opens with a quote from a future history, outlining the problems faced by the first space pioneers. The first scene is set at the rocket launch site, where news of the AEC's denial of permission for the test has just arrived. Only Barnes has the same name as in the film; the scientist here is named Corley, and the military man is an *Admiral* Bowles. Sweeney is called Manny Traub, and though he is a last-minute replacement, he isn't reluctant to join the crew.

There is more emphasis in the story on sabotage and the danger of allowing the Soviets—named quite clearly—to establish a base on the moon. Also, just before takeoff Barnes is forced to use the rocket-jet to scare off a band of thugs trying to interfere in the launch. The early takeoff and use of fuel later endangers the ship's safe arrival on the moon. The rescue of the scientist in the film is missing from Heinlein's story.

After landing, the crew finds evidence that could indicate an already established Russian base—or even an alien visitation. The story's final dilemma is similar to the film's. The solution of one man remaining comes up, but the problem is solved without Traub (or Sweeney) trying to sacrifice himself, simply by discarding the oxygen tanks and other unnecessary equipment from the final spacesuit. Even then the ship's ability to take off is in question, and the story ends ambiguously with another quote from the future history, applauding the efforts of the space pioneers.

Despite its skeletonlike structure, the *DM* novelette is pure Heinlein. It's an interesting companion piece to the film, showing the gap between what is envisioned in the writer's mind and what finally reaches the screen (see Appendix).

Producer George Pal chose Irving Pichel, who had also worked on *The Great Rupert*, to direct *DM*. Pichel is really the forgotten man of the film. It has been suggested that Pal overshadowed Pichel's work on *DM*, but it seems unlikely that a professional like Pichel, with over thirty films to his credit, would step aside so easily. In fact, Pichel fought hard for the film's scientific and dramatic integrity.

Pichel's direction of *DM* has often been panned—one critic called it "arthritic." But Pichel must have faced the classic problem of all SF film directors—how to balance the human elements of the script with the idea behind the story. In *DM* the problem was especially acute, since the emphasis had to be on the trip to the moon.

As an editor of *Hollywood Quarterly*, Pichel wrote frequently on the craft of the director, analyzing what many directors took for granted—and what many didn't. In one of these, "Seeing with the Camera," he wrote:

> A skillful craftsman, regardless of his general philosophy concerning the use of the camera, will be governed by one fundamental consideration—that in every shot the content shall be more important than the manner in which it is transmitted.

With that stricture in mind, perhaps, Pichel chose to emphasize the story of *DM* and keep his craftsmanship in the background.

There's no doubt that the details of the moon trip dominate the plot and characters of *DM*, and this weakens the film by conventional standards. Cargraves's relationship with his wife is handled rather heavily, but the film's final dilemma—deciding who will stay on the moon and Sweeney's attempt to sacrifice himself—is genuinely tense and dramatically convincing.

Pichel kept his direction sincere and to the point. Nowhere in *DM* is there a moment when the characters take the action less than seriously (some might call this a fault). There is never any doubt that Thayer, Barnes, and Cargraves really believe in what they're doing.

Evidence of Pichel's close collaboration with the writers is everywhere. When we first see Jim Barnes, for example, he's working on a jet engine in the factory with his men. The scene quickly establishes Barnes as not just an executive, but a man willing to tackle a problem and get his hands dirty.

Later, when Thayer tries to convince Barnes to build the rocket, Barnes tells him not to get comfortable, or even light his cigar; they're going to lunch, since Barnes isn't interested in Thayer's pitch. But Thayer makes his speech anyway. "Well, Jim," he asks finally, "do we go to lunch—or do we go to the moon?" For an answer, Barnes lights the general's cigar. It's a smooth piece of direction that makes its point with subtlety and humor.

But *DM* has a special quality going for it beyond simple drama, and Pichel made the most of it. Part of the film's goal was to establish a real feeling for space travel, to evoke what science fiction readers call the "sense of wonder," and it's in conveying this feeling that Pichel shows his real strength, backed up by superb special effects, art direction, and the magnificence of early technicolor.

When the astronauts get their first look at the retreating Earth through the aft port, there is a poignancy hard to ignore as they pick out cities and Barnes humors the naive Sweeney, pointing out "Brooklyn" for him.

There is a similar moment of wonder when the men leave the ship, standing before the emptiness of space, the globe of Earth hanging majestically in the sky. When Barnes says the sight is "more beautiful than I ever dreamed" and Cargraves sadly echoes him, "We'll never be able to describe it to anyone," the awe in their voices is totally convincing.

The actual moon landing provides another awesome moment as the astronauts realize they are the first men ever to set foot on another world. The bleak lunar surface, seen through their eyes, conveys the sense that what we are seeing is unlike anything we have seen before.

Today, in the post-Apollo era, jaded perhaps as we are by a series of largely uneventful moonflights, the moments of wonder in *DM* may seem unexciting. But to the audiences of 1950, and to all those who dreamed of spaceflight before the NASA program—and who continue to dream of it—the sense of wonder at strange, new things in *DM* remains powerful and affecting. Part of that sense of wonder depends on Pichel's ability to make us believe the actors believe, and at this he succeeds admirably.

Irving Pichel was born in Pittsburgh, Pa., in 1891. After taking a degree in English at Harvard, he became interested in the theater. In 1927 he became a writer for MGM, but soon began directing, working on *The Most Dangerous Game* (1932, with Ernest B. Schoedsack) and the 1935 version of *She* (with Lansing S. Holden). Pichel also acted during this period, appearing in such films as *Oliver Twist* (1933), *Cleopatra* (1934), and *Dracula's Daughter* (1936).

Pichel moved up at 20th Century-Fox during World War II, becoming firmly established as a director. Among his later films of interest are *The Pied Piper* (1942), *The Moon Is Down* (1943), the mature *O.S.S.* (1946), and the delightful *Mr. Peabody and the Mermaid*. Pichel died in 1954, and at his death the *Hollywood Quarterly* ran a memorial to him in which he

Cargraves (Warner Anderson) and Barnes (John Archer), the fast-approaching moon behind them, stand on the outer skin of the spaceship LUNA. (The "stars" behind them are auto headlight lamps.)

drew praise from such notables as screenwriter Dudley Nichols, actor Paul Muni, and director Josef von Sternberg.

A large part of the effectiveness of *DM* is the result of the technical artistry of cinematographer Lionel Lindon, special effects director Lee Zavitz (the man who burned "Atlanta" in *Gone With the Wind*), animation director John Abbott, art director Ernst Fegte, and artist Chesley Bonestell. Making *DM* posed a multitude of problems for these people in every respect.

The spaceship LUNA, for example, was part studio mock-up, part location mock-up, and part animation. The ship, supposedly 150 feet tall, was actually a 4-foot model. A full-size model of the ship's tail was built in the Mojave Desert for the necessary scenes at the launch site. For the close shots of the actors walking on the ship's surface in space, the studio mock-up was used, with the camera turned upside down to show the men in a similar position.

The ship's takeoff was a masterpiece of animation, using a miniature launching site, complete with gantry and tiny floodlights. Other shots of the ship in space, including the long shots of the men walking along the hull and the moon landing, made use of animation, performed by John Abbott and his techni-

cians, who had cut their teeth working for Pal on his Puppetoons.

One of the major problems for the special effects crew was building a realistic control room for the LUNA that could be used to show the weightless conditions of space and also accommodate the technical equipment necessary for making a movie. Technical Adviser Heinlein made sketches for a control room, which were expanded by Chesley Bonestell. But a model built to their specifications proved impractical. A model constructed to meet the needs of the cameraman was rejected by Heinlein as unrealistic. Finally, after some wrangling, a practical compromise was found.

To allow the camera inside the control room, the entire set was built so that every panel could be removed. This, plus the man-hours involved in bolting and unbolting panels, rigging and rerigging lights, drove costs up enormously.

In the cramped area of the control room it was impractical to show weightlessness by attaching wires to the actors vertically; in some cases it would have demanded "floating" around corners. To solve this problem, a device something like a huge drum was designed to enclose the entire control room set—at a cost of $35,000—allowing the control room to turn in any direction. With this device the actors could "float" realistically, and even appear to walk on the walls (see Appendix).

But the drum was three stories high, requiring that the camera be mounted on a giant boom just to reach the action. It's said that Cecil B. DeMille came to see this monster boom. The camera also had to rotate to follow the action, but this meant removing its sound-proof outer casing, which in turn meant dubbing the actors' voices in many of the control room scenes.

To show the crushing force of takeoff acceleration on the crew, their couches were constructed with cushions that could be inflated or deflated with compressed air. During takeoff, air was slowly released from the cushions to make the men appear to be pushed down by a tremendous weight (see Appendix). To add to the effect, a thin membrane that could be stretched by a device offscreen, was glued to the actors' faces, resulting in their painful grimaces during blast-off.

Another problem arose in the design for the spacesuits. Heinlein wanted to use actual pressure suits in the film, but to show the effects of low gravity on the moon it was necessary to attach wires to the suits, making actual pressurization impossible. To show

pressurization in these scenes, lamb's wool padding was used, making the actors very uncomfortable under the hot lights. Actual pressurization, however, was used whenever possible. The wires also dictated the design of the spacesuits, with an inner pressure suit and outer "chafing" suit to absorb punishment. The design hid the wires and harnesses needed to suspend the actors in various scenes.

One more difficulty with the suits occurred in filming the scene in which the crewmen first don them. When the spacesuit locker was opened, the suits hung straight down, though the ship was supposedly in a weightless condition. Filming was stopped, and a hasty threading job done to simulate the weightless effect.

The rescue of Dr. Cargraves in space also required a complicated solution. A shotgun was proposed first as the propellant to be used by Barnes in the rescue, but no reason could be found for taking a shotgun to the moon. Then a flare pistol was suggested, but it didn't *look* realistic and proved dangerous on the set as well.

An oxygen bottle was finally chosen as meeting all the requirements. Then the scene had to be filmed.

Dr. Cargraves (Warner Anderson) takes a souvenir photograph of Joe Sweeney (Dick Wesson). Note Sweeney's hand is upraised for the next shot, in which he appears to be supporting the Earth like "a modern Atlas."

The actors were handled like marionettes by huge block-and-tackle devices controlled by several men, with the wires attached by harnesses under the spacesuits. Thin, almost invisible threads suspended the safety lines, and one member of the film crew had nothing to do but go back and forth keeping the wires "invisible" by covering them with black paint. The scene itself was hard for the actors, since they were suspended in the air for up to two hours at a time for only a few minutes of film.

According to an article in *The American Cinematographer* published prior to *DM*'s release, part of the rescue was filmed by seating John Archer on a camera dolly covered by black velvet and shooting from a low angle to avoid any trace of the dolly. For other shots, Archer sat on an extension from the camera boom, with the action again shot from below to miss the boom. The angle from which Archer is seen as he jets out to Cargraves and the smoothness of his movement seems to support this, as does a picture from the article.

The oxygen tank was made of balsa wood for lightness and easy handling, with a smaller tank of CO_2 of the type used inside fire extinguishers. The CO_2, however, produced a falling "snow" which ruined the illusion of the scene. Careful editing finally eliminated the "snow," and the scene is thoroughly convincing.

To simulate the look of star-filled space, it took between 1,500 and 2,000 auto headlight bulbs strung on a backdrop of 400 feet of black velvet with some 70,000 feet of wire. Astronomical expert Chesley Bonestell objected to the headlamps, however, pointing out that real stars vary in brightness while the headlamps were all the same. But with limitations on time and money, the headlamps were accepted as the best that could be done under the circumstances.

Although perfectly acceptable to the naked eye, the bulbs produced a red halo on Technicolor film, requiring that they be covered with green plastic screens (called "gels") to remove the red. But the gels melted easily near the hot lights and had to be replaced twice a day. The bulbs themselves burned out regularly and had to be replaced.

Several obstacles had to be overcome to create the lunar surface on a Hollywood soundstage. Light on the moon is intense and the atmosphere completely clear. Smoking was restricted on the set and blowers ran constantly to get rid of the blue smoke that formed around the arc lights. To get the smoke out, the stage doors had to be kept open, letting in noise that got on the soundtrack, later requiring expensive redubbing.

Duplicating light on the lunar surface was also difficult because of the need for a single, intense light-source resembling the sun. Some time was spent searching for such a light, but when none proved available, massive arc lights (known as "brutes") were used, with smaller lights filling in the gaps for the closest approximation of sunlight possible.

It was in designing the actual lunar surface that the talents of astronomical artist Chesley Bonestell came into play. Heinlein had chosen the crater Aristarchus for the spacecraft's landing site, but Bonestell opted for the crater Harpalus for that area's greater visual effect, including the Earth's position as seen from this spot, where the camera could capture it as well as the moonscape.

To construct the lunar scene, Bonestell first built a model of the area based on a photo taken at Mt. Wilson Observatory. He then photographed the model, enlarged the picture, and produced a twenty-foot-long by two-foot-high oil painting from it. Next came a photographic enlargement of the painting, then another, larger painting. This, in turn, was painted on a twenty-foot backdrop and connected to a floor and sky also designed by Bonestell. It was Bonestell's painstaking attention to detail here and in *DM*'s other astronomical paintings that give the film its distinctive look.

Chesley Bonestell began his career studying architecture, though he never received a degree in the subject. Despite this, he worked for several architectural firms in San Francisco and helped design the Golden Gate Bridge. Bonestell eventually became a matte and background artist in movies, working on such films as *The Hunchback of Notre Dame* (1939) and *Citizen Kane* (1941).

But Bonestell is best known for his astronomical art, which graced the covers of *Astounding* and *The Magazine of Fantasy and Science Fiction*, as well as appearing in such magazines as *Life* and *Coronet*. Bonestell also provided artwork for three other George Pal films: *When Worlds Collide* (1951), *The War of the Worlds* (1953), and *The Conquest of Space* (1955). This last film was partly inspired by a book of the same title which Bonestell worked on with science writer Willy Ley in 1949. Bonestell has illustrated some ten books, and his work has appeared at the National Air and Space Museum in Washington, D.C. In 1974 he was awarded a Hugo for special achievement.

The lunar surface took a hundred men about two months to build. Art director Ernst Fegte made one change in Bonestell's design, putting huge cracks in the lunar surface. Bonestell objected, pointing out that such cracks could never occur on the waterless moon. But there was a reason for Fegte's decision. Placing larger cracks in the foreground and smaller ones toward the rear gave a sense of perspective to the set, making it look bigger. To further enhance the illusion of depth, midgets in proportionally sized spacesuits were used in some shots. The mistake of the cracks is unfortunate, but merely emphasizes the difficulties inherent in making an earthbound film about a body in space.

Leith Stevens's score for *DM* set a pattern for nearly every SF film to follow it. Stevens even talked to scientists in an effort to get a feel for space that he could communicate in the music. The score is strong

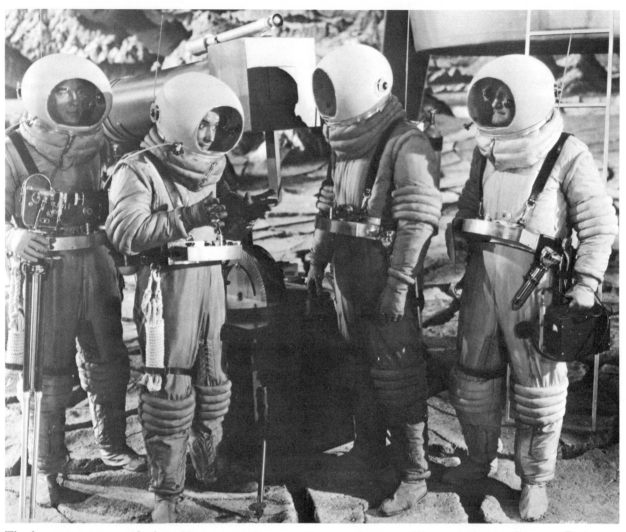

The four astronauts outside their ship LUNA on the moon. They are Cargraves (Warner Anderson), Sweeney (Dick Wesson), Barnes (John Archer), and Thayer (Tom Powers).

and dramatic, emphasizing the strangeness of the moon and of outer space as well as their majesty. Later SF film composers would seize on the eerier elements of Stevens's music, using them more to convey foreboding and uncertainty.

The decision to cast *DM* with relative unknowns was deliberate. Pal felt that well-known actors would distract from the story (one suspects financial considerations might also have been involved). Critics usually ignore the actors in *DM*, yet it is worth noting again that there's a sincerity in all the performances.

Despite the fact that he won the Jesse Lasky "Gateway to Hollywood" contest, John Archer never rose beyond second-string roles in films. He made his debut in *Flaming Frontiers* (1938) and appeared in various films throughout the forties, fifties, and sixties.

Warner Anderson had a long career as a character actor until his death in 1976, usually in staunch, "official" roles as military men, judges, or doctors. His films include *Destination Tokyo* (1944), *The Caine*

Mutiny (1954), and *The Blackboard Jungle* (1955). Anderson also appeared in three TV series: *The Doctor*, *The Line-Up*, and *Peyton Place*.

Tom Powers, who died in 1955, appeared in character roles in nearly every type of film imaginable. Some of his credits include *Double Indemnity* (1944), *Two Years Before the Mast* (1946), *Donovan's Brain* (1953), and *Julius Caesar* (1953). His last film, *UFO* (1956, released after his death), was a documentary-like treatment of the then current interest in flying saucers.

Dick Wesson began his career as a nightclub comedian and made his film debut in *DM*. Wesson went on to play character parts in such films as *Inside the Walls of Folsom Prison* (1951), *About Face* (1952), and *The Desert Song* (1953). Wesson also appeared as Jackie Cooper's sidekick on the fifties' TV series *The People's Choice*.

Critics have sometimes complained about Wesson's role as the stereotypical "Brooklynite," his ignorance, which requires the other cast members to be constantly explaining things to him, and about his rather broad attempts at humor. In 1950 movies were full of such stereotypes, left over in part from so many World War II films in which the crews of bombers or battleships were supposed to represent a cross section of America, with one Italian, one Jew, one Texan, one playboy, *ad nauseum.*

As for Sweeney's "ignorance," it is important to remember that *DM* wasn't made just for critics or SF fans, but for a general audience. To make the story work it was necessary to have someone in the crew ask the questions the audience wanted to ask. Unfortunately, the device of Sweeney's ignorance has grown ponderous to those who have seen the film over and over, and the jokes have become stale. Viewed objectively, however, in terms of the fifties' audience (or anyone seeing *DM* for the first time), Wesson's role not only provides some comedy relief, but is also important to the film's development.

With the few exceptions noted, every effort was made to make *DM* scientifically accurate. Ley and Bonestell's *The Conquest of Space* (1949) was practically required reading on the set. The one imaginative leap in the story was the development of a workable atomic engine to power spaceship LUNA—and that

leap wasn't very far even in 1950.

Of course, care was taken to show all the important elements of a trip to the moon: the design of practical spacesuits, the method of landing on Earth by parachute (which would become a reality), the weightless conditions in space, the astronomical and lunar details, and even the radio delay between distant objects in space (in the moon's case about two-and-a-half seconds) that some SF films still ignore today.

Perhaps the most amazing part of the effort to make *DM* scientifically convincing involved things not seen in the film. All the calculations for the trip —speeds, trajectories, mass ratios, etc.—were worked out as if the ship were really going to the moon, with some of the calculations done by well-known astronomer Robert S. Richardson. Robert Heinlein came to Hollywood in 1948 to make an SF film that would be scientifically convincing. At the very least, he succeeded at that (see Appendix).

The fifties (or maybe the late forties) echo subtly in *DM*. The first rumblings of the Cold War can be felt in the film. After all, the driving force behind this moon trip isn't just Dr. Cargraves's visionary fervor, but also General Thayer's warnings that an attack from space cannot be stopped—and that "others"

A shot of the astronauts setting up their scientific equipment outside the base of the LUNA on the moon. The cracks, while scientifically incorrect, gave the set perspective.

know this as well. "Others," of course, refers to the Soviet Union, and *DM* contains a number of veiled references to foreign sabotage and propaganda aimed at stopping the moon project.

Thayer's warning still has some validity, though it wasn't clear in 1950 that guided missiles would make an attack from the moon unnecessary. Yet in Thayer's urgency there are hints of the space race between the U.S. and Russia that would become a reality in the late fifties.

Perhaps the scene in *DM* that raises the most eyebrows today—and even provokes some chuckles—is that in which American industry unselfishly assumes the burden of sending a rocket to the moon. It is sometimes hard these days to imagine American industry being unselfish about anything, though such an extreme view is as absurd as the opposite one.

Of course, self-interest is also involved. Barnes warns the businessmen that if they want to stay in business they'd better get behind the project—or a Soviet base on the moon will end the capitalist system. There's *nothing* like the profit motive to send American industry roaring into action. The problem with

the scene in the movie is that it's played with such deadly seriousness that it becomes a bit hard to take.

Yet we are all victims of what science fiction writer William Tenn calls "temporal provincialism" —the tendency to interpret history from our own position in it. It *was* American industry, collaborating with science and government, that helped win the Second World War. After the war, the sense of a threat to the "American way of life" posed during the war and after it by the growing power of communism must have seemed very serious, perhaps more than we fully appreciate today. And when the U.S. did embark on a space program, it was with the help of private industry. It is only with our historical perspective that *DM*'s treatment of American industry comes across as naive.

The optimistic attitude toward science displayed in *DM* is somewhat ironic in retrospect, since *DM* began the fifties' cycle of SF films, in which science wasn't always treated so well. Throughout the 1950s science fiction films would question scientific progress over and over, supporting it in some cases, condemning it in others. But *DM* has almost no such

Long shot of spaceship LUNA on the moon's surface.

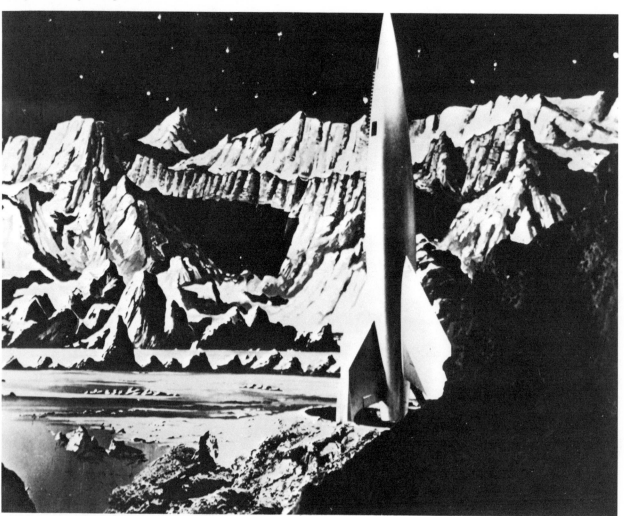

questions. Only Sweeney expresses some uneasiness when uranium is found on the moon. "Then you could blow up the moon, too," he says. "Ain't *that* dandy?"

DM clearly belongs to the school of science fiction that celebrates science and technology. Its description of a trip to the moon closely resembles the kind of science fiction appearing in magazines such as *Amazing* or *Wonder* in the twenties or thirties in which technology by itself was often enough to make a story.

By its end, however, *DM* has become a scientific problem story more typical of the Campbell era of *Astounding*. These stories stress the ability of the human mind to solve any problem by a combination of reason, technology, and sheer determination. (For a full discussion of the scientific problem story, see the chapter *Robinson Crusoe on Mars*.)

Heinlein, of course, was one of the top writers to emerge from *Astounding*, and it's no accident that this philosophy celebrating the human mind is reflected in *DM*'s ending. It might have been more aesthetically satisfying for Sweeney to die on the moon, sacrificing himself for the others. But that's not the philosophy this kind of SF tries to convey. For Heinlein, what's important is not only Sweeney's *offer* to sacrifice himself, but that the tragedy—any tragedy—is avoidable *if* we use our intelligence.

This is the optimistic message *DM* puts across so strongly. It is reflected even in the sequence where Cargraves photographs the illusion of Sweeney holding up the Earth like "a modern Atlas." The scene is played for laughs, but it's a powerful symbol of how one school of science fiction regards humanity's relation to the world—as holding it in its hands, supporting it. It's an image of the human race larger than any world and as big as the universe itself.

Destination Moon remains a landmark in the history of SF film. The sincerity of its direction and acting, the strength of its special effects, the integrity of its screenplay—indeed that of George Pal, Irving Pichel, Robert Heinlein, and all the others who worked on it—make *DM* stand out as one of the most memorable SF films ever made.

The admittedly clichéd final statement of *Destination Moon*, that this is "The End—of the Beginning," is perhaps part of what made critic Richard Hodgens remark that the film's optimism is depressing today—though it is hard to see how optimism can be depressing. Perhaps what Hodgens meant is that the film's innocence makes us uncomfortable as we watch it today.

Yet its optimism remains fresh. To those who grew up with the dream of space travel, *Destination Moon* remains a stirring, dramatic, and stimulating film that reaches to the core of our sense of wonder about the universe. If we sometimes find ourselves reacting to its optimism about man's ultimate destiny a little wryly, or with embarrassment, perhaps the fault is not in the film, but in ourselves.

THE THING

An RKO/Winchester Pictures Release. Running Time: 86 minutes. Black and White. Based on the story "Who Goes There?" by John W. Campbell (writing as Don A. Stuart). Full title: The Thing From Another World. *Opened May 2, 1951, at the Criterion Theater, New York City.*

PRODUCTION CREDITS

PRODUCER . . . . *Howard Hawks*
DIRECTOR . . . . *Christian Nyby (& Howard Hawks, uncredited)*
SCREENPLAY . . . . *Charles Lederer*
CINEMATOGRAPHER . . . . *Russell Harlan*
ASSOCIATE PRODUCER . . . . *Edward Lasker*
ART DIRECTION . . . . *Albert D'Agostino & John J. Hughes*
SET DECORATION . . . . *Darrell Silvera & William Stevens*
SPECIAL EFFECTS . . . . *Donald Stewart*
SPECIAL CAMERA EFFECTS . . . . *Linwood Dunn*
EDITOR . . . . *Roland Gross*
MAKEUP . . . . *Lee Greenway*
MUSIC . . . . *Dimitri Tiomkin*
SOUND . . . . *Phil Brigandi & Clem Portman*

CAST

CAPTAIN PAT HENDRY . . . . *Kenneth Tobey*
THE THING . . . . *James Arness*
NIKKI NICHOLSON . . . . *Margaret Sheridan*
DR. ARTHUR CARRINGTON . . . . *Robert Cornthwaite*
NED SCOTT (SCOTTY) . . . . *Douglas Spencer*
LT. ED DYKES . . . . *James Young*
BOB (THE CREW CHIEF) . . . . *Dewey Martin*
LT. MACPHERSON . . . . *Robert Nichols*
SERGEANT BARNES . . . . *William Self*
DR. STERN . . . . *Eduard Franz*
DR. CHAPMAN . . . . *John Dierkes*
MRS. CHAPMAN . . . . *Sally Creighton*
DR. VORRHEES . . . . *Paul Frees*
REDDING . . . . *George Fenneman*
GENERAL FOGERTY . . . . *David McMann*

In 1951 the Earth received two messages from space. One came from Klaatu, the friendly alien of Robert Wise's *The Day the Earth Stood Still.* Klaatu's message to us was complex: Learn to live in peace, and you may join in a great community of peoples among the stars. Fail in this task, and you face obliteration.

The other message, delivered by a creature not half as magnanimous as Klaatu, was simpler: There may be many beings among the stars, and some of them may be hostile to man—some of them may even be *things.*

If *Destination Moon* set a pattern for space exploration films to come, then Howard Hawks's *The Thing (from Another World)* was certainly the model for the "monster-on-the-loose/invasion" movies which came to dominate the fifties. Few of those films, however, would be able to match the high standard set for them by *The Thing.*

The Thing drew excellent reviews from nearly every critic of the time. The *New York Times* said it was "Generous with thrills ... with just enough light, bantering dialogue ... so the film does not appear to take itself too seriously." Arthur Knight, in *The Saturday Review,* acknowledged the film's scientific flaws, but praised it for its conviction, calling it "close to a horror masterpiece."

Manny Farber, in *The Nation,* described it as "a slick item ... better than ordinary entertainment." *Films in Review* called it "the best thriller since *King Kong.*" The only dissent came from *Time* and *The New Republic,* both of which found the film a bit juvenile.

The minority view didn't seem to matter. *The Thing* was a box office smash and was rereleased in 1954 and 1957, again with remarkable success. Today, the film works as well as it did in 1951. It has restraint, intelligence, and, perhaps most important, a *style* sorely lacking in many of today's SF films.

A heavily bundled figure fights its way through a driving snow toward a doorway. As the figure passes we see this is the entrance to the Officers' Club at the Air Force base at Anchorage, Alaska.

Inside, the cold and darkness give way to warmth and light. The bundled form unwraps to reveal Ned Scott, a reporter sent to Anchorage to get a story. So far, he's been unsuccessful.

Scott (known, of course, as Scotty) is introduced to Captain Pat Hendry by Hendry's copilot, Lt. Ed Dykes. In the course of their conversation Scotty hears about Polar Expedition Six, a group of scientists camped near the pole studying arctic conditions, and led by Nobel Prize-winner Dr. Arthur Carrington.

Scotty and the scientists and soldiers leave the saucer crash site after their attempt to melt the alien craft out of the ice that somehow caused it to catch fire and explode.

The military men and scientists at the polar base stare silently at the block of ice, now empty, that contained the body of the alien. From left to right: Bob (Dewey Martin), Dr. Chapman (John Dierkes), MacPherson (Robert Nichols), Hendry (Kenneth Tobey), Carrington (Robert Cornthwaite), Dykes (James Young), and Scotty (Douglas Spencer).

Hendry is suddenly called to the office of the base commander, General Fogerty. Carrington has sent a message about a possible plane crash near the expedition. It could be Russians, and Fogerty orders Hendry and his crew to fly out and investigate, with Scotty along for the ride.

At the polar base Hendry goes looking, not for Carrington, but for Nikki Nicholson, the doctor's secretary. Some time earlier, it seems, Hendry tried a little "romance" on Nikki—but she got the better of him. Now, he'd like to start all over, but Nikki takes a wait-and-see attitude and escorts him to Carrington.

Carrington shows Hendry photos of something streaking across the sky, something containing the equivalent of 20,000 tons of steel. Hendry guesses it's a meteor, but when other pictures show the object moving *upward* in a manner impossible for a meteor, Hendry agrees they'd better take a look.

With the scientists aboard, Hendry and his men fly to the scene of the crash. The object has apparently melted into the ice, which has refrozen around it. The

only evidence of its presence is a long skidmark and a stabilizing fin sticking up through the ice. And the Geiger counter is picking up radioactivity.

The party spreads out around the dark object in the ice in an effort to get some idea of its shape, and the men find themselves standing *in a perfect circle*. There is a moment of stunned silence as they grasp that what they've found is a *flying saucer*. Scotty is frantic to radio back the news, but Hendry stops him, knowing he can't release the story without permission from higher authority—much to Scotty's annoyance.

The expedition decides to melt the ship out with thermite bombs, but somehow the ship catches fire, and the saucer is destroyed in a tremendous explosion.

Discouraged, the party starts back to the plane, but one of them spots something in the ice that looks like a man. Using axes, the men chop out a block of ice with the survivor in it and bring it back to camp, placing it in a storeroom.

Carrington and several others are eager to thaw the alien, but some of the other scientists disagree; the alien might harbor microorganisms dangerous to humans. But Hendry isn't taking any chances—he's lost the saucer and he doesn't intend to lose its occupant. He denies Carrington access to the alien and posts a guard in the storeroom, where the frigid air from a broken window will keep the ice from melting.

Hendry radios Anchorage for instructions, but a heavy storm is blocking communications. Until it clears they can only sit tight.

Some time later, Sergeant Barnes takes over the watch in the storeroom. Barnes doesn't like what he can see of the alien through the ice—it's some seven feet tall, hairless, with long, taloned fingers—and the eyes are open and staring. Barnes covers it with a blanket left by his predecessor, but it is an electric blanket and is still on. Unnoticed by Barnes, the ice begins to melt.

A shadow looms up behind Barnes. He spins to see the alien behind him, pulls out his pistol, and fires wildly, but the shots have no effect. Barnes rushes frantically to find Hendry.

Weapons ready, Hendry and his men return to the storeroom, but the alien is gone. From the window they see it locked in combat with the sled dogs. Hurl-ing one dog away, the giant alien races off into the darkness, but under one of the dead animals Hendry finds a severed arm.

Inside, the scientists examine the arm, discovering it's actually plant tissue. The alien is some kind of vegetable creature. Carrington displays seedpods taken from the hand. He begins to speculate on the superiority of this kind of emotionless reproduction.

Suddenly, *the hand begins to move*. Carrington suggests the plant tissue has absorbed nourishment from the dead dog. "You mean it *lives* on blood," Scotty says balefully.

Hendry organizes a search for the alien. Carrington pleads with him not to harm it, to allow him a chance to communicate with it. Hendry agrees—so long as the alien is locked up in a safe place.

The searchers find nothing in the base greenhouse, but Carrington notices some of the plants have wilted, as if from a blast of cold air. He remains behind in the greenhouse with three of his associates. They find traces of blood on a large bin. When they open it a sled dog falls out, drained of its blood by the alien. Realizing the greenhouse is the most likely place for a plant creature, Carrington organizes a watch, but

Dr. Carrington (Robert Cornthwaite) and his colleagues examine the "offspring" of *The Thing from Another World*.

warns the others not to tell anyone about it.

Hendry and the others return from a fruitless search of the area around the camp. Moments later, one of the scientists, Dr. Stern, staggers into the mess hall and collapses. Stern manages to tell how he and two others were in the greenhouse when the alien entered, knocking him down. Somehow he crawled out, but not before seeing the other two men hanging over a beam, their throats cut by the alien.

Hendry races to the greenhouse and opens the door—to find himself face-to-face with the alien. It lashes out at him, but he slams the door on its arm—an arm that's regrown—sending pieces splintering in all directions.

Hendry orders the greenhouse doors blocked. Learning that Carrington was aware of the alien's presence, he angrily restricts the scientist's movements. For the moment, the alien is trapped in the greenhouse.

Carrington calls a meeting of his supporters in his lab, including Nikki. He claims he's been searching for a way to stop the alien "scientifically," but he's tired and drawn from lack of sleep, and his actions seem to contradict his words.

Using blood plasma, Carrington has been growing seeds from the alien's severed arm in a box of soil. The tiny plants pulsate as they feed on the plasma. One of the scientists points out the alien is doing the same thing in the greenhouse with blood from the dead men. For the first time, the others speculate that the alien may be the vanguard of an invasion, but Carrington doesn't seem to care.

Hendry visits Nikki, who is typing Carrington's notes. Frightened, she shows him what Carrington has been doing. Hendry takes a party to the lab to destroy the plants, but a new radio message from General Fogerty orders him not to harm the alien.

Stymied, Hendry radios for new orders. In the meantime, he and the others try to figure out some defense against a creature invulnerable to bullets.

"What do you do with a vegetable?" Scotty asks. "Boil it," Nikki answers abruptly. "Boil it, stew it, bake it, fry it." Suddenly, they realize they have a weapon.

Almost simultaneously, the Geiger counter begins to chatter. The alien is out of the greenhouse and coming closer. Buckets are quickly filled with kerosene.

The Geiger counter goes crazy, Nikki cuts the lights, and suddenly the alien is in the room. The men douse it with kerosene, and one fires a flare pistol at it. The alien bursts into flame, slashing wildly at everything around it. It dives through a window and flees into the night.

Hendry prepares to go after the alien with kerosene and fire, but one of the scientists suggests electricity would do a better job of burning the creature, and a plan takes shape.

Nikki points out it's getting colder. The alien has cut off the oil supply to their heating system. Soon the arctic cold will overcome them. Realizing the alien may try to cut their electricity next, Hendry herds the whole group into the generator room and prepares for a last ditch stand in the corridor outside it.

Fogerty radios again that the alien should not be harmed, but Hendry ignores the message. Carrington tries to protest, but Hendry has no time to listen.

The plan is to catch the alien in the corridor in an electric "flytrap." With the corridor wired, the defenders wait tensely as the clicking of the Geiger counter begins to build once more.

The door at the corridor's end is yanked open, and the alien smashes through the flimsy barrier there, advancing steadily down the hall. Then the lights go out.

Carrington has shut down the generator and is keeping everyone away at gunpoint. Hendry rushes to the generator room, but Carrington warns him back. In the darkness, someone tears the gun from Carrington's hands.

Power returns, and Hendry and his men wait for the alien to step squarely into the trap. Carrington suddenly races out and tries to reason with the alien, but it brushes him aside like an insect and keeps on coming.

Three arcs of crackling electricity trap the alien between them. It begins to smoke, and before the eyes of the defenders it slowly dwindles away to ashes.

Shortly after, the defenders assemble in the radio room. Every trace of the alien has been destroyed. With the airwaves finally clear and the battle over, Scotty is allowed to send his story.

"I bring you a warning," he says. "Every one of you listening to my voice. Tell the world. Tell this to everybody wherever they are. Watch the skies, everywhere. *Keep* looking, *keep* watching the skies."

For if one Thing could come from the stars, perhaps there may be others.

The Thing was adapted from the novelette "Who Goes There?" written by the man who is often regarded as the figure most responsible for changing the course of modern science fiction. The story appeared in the August 1938 issue of *Astounding Stories* under the name Don A. Stuart, but the author's real name was John W. Campbell, Jr.

Born in 1910, John Campbell sold his first SF stories while still studying physics at MIT and Duke University. Campbell's earliest efforts were in the then popular area of wild space adventure (or "Space Opera"). Later, when his stories became more complex and thoughtful, Campbell adopted the pen name Don A. Stuart to prevent confusion between his new writing and the old. Many of the stories from his "Stuart" period, such as "Twilight" (1934) and "The Machine" (1935), would set a tone for later SF and influence a generation of writers to come.

By 1937 Campbell was sharing editorial duties on *Astounding* with F. Orlin Tremaine. In May 1938, Campbell took full control of *Astounding* and his en-

Menaced by The Thing, soldiers and scientists prepare to use a roll of wire to set an electrical trap for the giant alien.

ergies from then till his death in 1971 would be devoted to running that magazine (later called *Analog*). Except for a few stories after it, "Who Goes There?" marked the end of Campbell's writing career. But his editorial policies would have a profound impact on science fiction, leading to greater maturity and a whole "school" of science fiction thought (see the chapter on *Robinson Crusoe on Mars*).

The relationship between *The Thing* and "Who Goes There?" is relatively slim. While both stories are set at isolated outposts, Campbell chose the South Pole, while *The Thing* takes place at the North Pole. In "Who Goes There?" a scientific expedition discovers the frozen survivor of a spaceship buried in Antarctic ice for twenty million years.

As in the film, the explorers accidentally destroy the ship while trying to free it from the ice. The frozen survivor is brought back to camp, and the scientists debate whether the alien should be thawed out. The creature seems to radiate a kind of evil:

It was face up there on the . . . table. The broken half of the ice axe was still buried in the queer skull. Three mad, hate-filled eyes blazed up with a living fire, bright as fresh-spilled blood, from a face ringed with a writhing loathsome nest of worms, blue mobile worms that crawled where hair should grow . . .

Despite the danger, the creature is allowed to thaw

—and suddenly it's loose in the camp. But unlike the plant creature of the film, this alien is a shape-changer, capable of duplicating any living being right down to its thoughts, as well as reproducing itself by consuming the flesh of the original.

"Who Goes There?" now becomes a classic suspense story, as the men try desperately to determine which of them is still human, and which are monsters. But "Who Goes There?" also sets a pattern for the scientific problem story, in which reason, science, and determination combine to solve a problem. This type of story would appear in *Astounding/Analog* over and over in the years to come (see the chapters on *Robinson Crusoe on Mars* and *Destination Moon*).

Campbell's reaction to *The Thing* was generous. While he felt his original idea was more suspenseful, he couldn't argue with the film's success and its status as a classic in the field. Yet Campbell never stopped hoping someone would remake "Who Goes There?" as he wrote it (see Appendix).

Despite many years of Hollywood mythology, Orson Welles had nothing to do with filming *The Thing*. Christian Nyby is credited as the film's director, but it's been more than convincingly established that the real credit belongs to producer/director Howard Hawks.

Nyby was Hawk's film editor and wanted to move

THE THING

This behind-the-scenes shot of Arness and a midget also dressed and made up as The Thing shows how the alien was "fried away" in the film's climax—the midget (and later a small model) were substituted for the 6' 6" Arness.

into directing, so Hawks gave him a chance with *The Thing*. Nyby's work after *The Thing*, however, never lived up to that film's promise. His five films, *Hell on Devil's Island* (1957), *Six Gun Law* (1962), *Young Fury* (1964), *Operation CIA* (1965), and *First to Fight* (1967), are all ably done, but none comes close to *The Thing*. Nyby has also done extensive work in TV, proving himself an excellent director of action shows.

Hawks never admitted directing any part of *The Thing*. He read Campbell's story while in Germany, working on *I Was a Male War Bride* (1949), and thought it "an adult treatment of an often infantile subject," but he used only some four pages from the novelette.

After the film was in production, according to Hawks, Nyby came to him and admitted having some problems. Hawks agreed to help out, and was present for every important scene, supervising and making

suggestions whenever he felt it necessary. One imagines a "suggestion" from Hawks at this point carried quite a bit of weight.

The Thing really has all the marks of a Hawks film: tough, competent men, facing overwhelming odds; the humorous, overlapping dialogue; Nikki, the Hawksian woman, able to give as good as she gets from any man; the swift pacing; and the straightforward yet riveting camerawork.

All these things can be seen in such Hawks movies as *Bringing Up Baby* (1938), *The Big Sleep* (1946), *Red River* (1948), and many, many others. In fact, the situation of a group of people caught somewhere with someone or something trying to get at them was one Hawks used several times, as in *Rio Bravo* (1959), *El Dorado* (1966), and *Rio Lobo* (1970).

There are some truly memorable moments in *The Thing*. Hawks sets the mood right from the beginning as the heavily bundled figure moves through the icy darkness. Is this the horrible "thing" we've been prepared for? But when Scotty enters the Officers' Club the sense of menace evaporates. Hawks fools us in similar ways throughout the picture.

The scene at the crash, as the men stand in a circle, arms extended, realizing they've found a flying saucer, is almost viscerally exciting, backed up by Dimitri Tiomkin's hard, *threatening* score, which is effective all through the film. Tiomkin, incidentally, was one of the first film composers to use a theramin—an electronic device which produces high frequency vibrations—to add an especially eerie quality to many of the scenes (see also the chapter on *The Day the Earth Stood Still*).

Hendry's encounter with the alien in the greenhouse is also one of the film's highlights. Even though we know the alien is in the greenhouse, we hardly expect to come face-to-face with it—the first time we've done so, incidentally—when Hendry opens the door. It's the way Hawks sets us up for the surprise that still makes audiences gasp at the scene today.

The sequence in which the defenders first use fire against the alien is also beautifully constructed. The clicking of the Geiger counter starts slowly, then builds rapidly. The men rush around the room furiously, preparing to meet the creature. The fast, overlapping dialogue increases the tension. Suddenly, the lights go out, the door springs open, and the seven-foot Thing is framed in the lighted doorway before it enters the room, collides with the flare, and bursts into flame.

The scene is almost surrealistic (with credit due to cinematographer Russell Harlan), since all we can see in the dark is the creature's flaming body, flailing about, roaring madly amidst the shadowy figures of the men until it dives out the window—and the director allows us to breathe again.

Hawks showed an intelligent restraint throughout the film. As students of the thriller know, what is unseen or half-seen is often more terrifying than the goriest details. Earlier plans called for more direct shots of the alien, including one of his biting the neck of one of the men in the greenhouse. This and other scenes showing the alien more clearly were cut before the film's release to good effect.

Howard Hawks was born in Goshen, Indiana, in 1896. After receiving a degree in mechanical engineering at Cornell University, he went to Hollywood and began his film career as an assistant property man at Paramount, and later as an assistant director.

Hawks served as a fighter pilot in World War I, and held a variety of jobs until returning to Hollywood in 1922 as an independent producer/director of short comedies. He moved up into bigger productions for Jesse Lasky's Famous Players Corporation, then went to MGM as head of their story department, and then to Fox, where he directed his first full-length picture, *The Road to Glory* (1926). That was the start of a directorial career that ended only with his death in 1977 (see Appendix).

Strangely enough, part of *The Thing*'s success is due to its humor, its almost tongue-in-cheek attitude. The genuinely funny dialogue keeps the audience constantly off guard. Just when we are most relaxed by the humor, Hawks hits us with the unexpected, and the contrast heightens the effect enormously. In 1975 Stephen Spielberg used a similar technique to underline the tension in *Jaws*.

There are so many fine comic moments in *The Thing* it would be cheating the viewer to mention too many. Perhaps the film's most famous line is Scotty's, after Carrington has finished describing the alien's vegetable nature. "An intellectual carrot!" he exclaims. "The mind boggles!"

One moment which rarely fails to get a laugh occurs near the film's climax, as the soldiers wait for the alien to appear. Lieutenant MacPherson suddenly gets an idea. "What if he can read our minds?" he asks. "Then he's gonna be real mad when he gets to me," answers one of the others.

Perhaps the most striking example of humor in the film involves the very mature byplay between Hendry and Nikki. Watching Nikki rake Hendry over the coals about their first date is delightful. One scene often cut from prints (especially for TV) shows Hendry seated, his hands tied behind him for Nikki's "protection," while she feeds him a drink. Finally, she kisses him, he frees himself and reciprocates, much to her surprise. Their sparring crops up throughout the movie, but never distracts from the main thrust of the film.

Credit for *The Thing*'s superb combination of action and humor belongs to Hawks, who was adept at directing both, and to writer Charles Lederer, whose film career went back at least as far as his 1931 screen adaptation of *The Front Page*. Lederer had worked with Hawks on *His Girl Friday* (1940) and on his previous picture, *I Was a Male War Bride*, and was clearly a natural to write the screenplay for *The Thing*.

According to Hawks, the script for *The Thing* was written with Lederer in about four-and-a-half days. There's also evidence that writer/director Ben Hecht, another frequent collaborator of both Hawks and Lederer, had a hand in the script as well (see Appendix).

Special effects for *The Thing* were not a major problem. The expediency of having the saucer crash into the ice removed the necessity of showing it. The real challenge was to makeup man Lee Greenway. Greenway took the already six-foot, six-inch James Arness and added four inches to his height with built-up shoes.

The Thing's makeup was sculpted between twelve and eighteen times over a period of three months before Hawks was satisfied—considering how little of it was seen—and was said to cost some $40,000. The alien's "voice" was actually the screeching of a cat, slowed, amplified, or distorted as required. For the alien's final destruction in the electric "flytrap," a series of smaller and smaller actors in "Thing" makeup was used, ending up with a small model.

Hawks submitted the script for *The Thing* to the Air Force, hoping for cooperation on the use of planes and facilities, but was turned down. At the time, the Air Force had just finished its first investigation of UFO's: "We've just spent half a million dollars proving there are no such things as flying saucers," they said. "Why should we help you make a picture about one?" Hawks did without official help, filming the "polar" sequences in the Rockies, near Cut Bank, Montana, and using standard Hollywood facilities and equipment for the rest. The picture does not suffer from it.

SF fans often have the feeling that Kenneth Tobey was in almost every SF film of the fifties. Actually Tobey appeared in only three, *The Beast from 20,000 Fathoms* (1953), *It Came from Beneath the Sea* (1955), and, of course, *The Thing*. He also showed up in one horror film, *The Vampire* (1957).

Tobey's professional career goes back at least as far as a small part in a New York stage performance of *As You Like It* in 1941. He's played everything from bit parts to starring roles in over thirty-five films, often playing military men. His films include *I Was a Male War Bride* (1949, where Hawks may have first noticed him), *Twelve O'Clock High* (1949), *Davy Crockett* (1955, as Jim Bowie), *The Man in the Gray Flannel Suit* (1956), *Gunfight at the O.K. Corral* (1957, as Bat Masterson), *The Candidate* (1972), and many others.

Tobey also starred in the fifties' TV series *The Whirlybirds* (also known as *Copter Patrol*), as well as doing other TV work, including a stint in the sixties as Bill Cosby and Robert Culp's boss on *I Spy*. He is still very active today in films and TV. (For a list of his films, see the Appendix.)

Tobey is excellent in *The Thing*. Manny Farber described his work as a "fine, unpolished performance of a nice, clean, lecherous American Air Force Officer." That comes off as a slightly left-handed compliment, but in *The Thing*, and most of his other films, Tobey conveyed a kind of clean-cut competence and masculinity that audiences always enjoyed—a kind of John Wayne-like strength without the physical height or swagger.

In *The Thing* Tobey is tough when necessary, but convincingly bemused by Nikki's aggressiveness and the antics of his crew. More important, *The Thing* demanded a kind of ensemble acting, where all the players had to work together. Tobey never dominates the other actors, but his performance makes it clear that *he* is the leader, the Hawksian Hero.

Douglas Spencer (Scotty) was an all-purpose Hollywood actor with more than twenty-five films to his credit, such as *A Place in the Sun* (1951), *Houdini* (1953), and *Shane* (1953). Spencer also had a brief role as "The Monitor" in *This Island Earth* (1955). He

really shines as the wisecracking reporter in *The Thing* and has some of the film's best lines—another case of a character actor who showed what he could do when given the chance. Spencer died in 1960.

Margaret Sheridan portrays Nikki in the style that's come to be known as the "Hawksian Woman": strong, determined, sexy even in a bulky sweater and pants, and able to dish it out at least as well as she can take it. She belongs to a long line of Hawksian heroines that included Rosalind Russell, Ann Sheridan, and Katharine Hepburn.

The size of Sheridan's role in *The Thing* doesn't compare with those of the actresses mentioned above in their films for Hawks. On the other hand, it's Nikki who supplies the idea for the weapon which stops the alien. Sheridan made only four other films before fading into obscurity: *One Minute to Zero* (1952), *Pride of the Blue Grass* (1953), *I, The Jury* (1953), and *The Diamond Wizard* (1954).

From the moment Robert Cornthwaite appears on the screen as Dr. Carrington, the audience feels uncomfortable with him. "I dislike being vague," he says to Hendry with such condescension that we *know* there's going to be trouble between them. As Carrington becomes more and more obsessed with the alien, Cornthwaite plays him with a growing wildness in his eyes, yet with a dignity and restraint that makes it hard to dislike him totally.

Cornthwaite is another longtime character actor. He was considerably younger than he looked as Carrington, and is still active in films and TV. Some of his films include *Monkey Business* (1952, another Hawks film), *Kiss Me Deadly* (1955), and *Day of the Outlaw* (1959). Cornthwaite also played more benevolent but less noticeable scientists in *The War of the Worlds* (1953) and *Colossus—The Forbin Project* (1970).

James Arness really got his role in *The Thing* because of his height and build. He made his film debut in *The Farmer's Daughter* (1947) and spent most of the fifties making westerns and war films, until landing the lead role in the TV series *Gunsmoke* in 1955. (For more on Arness, see the chapter on *Them!*, and for a note on some of the other familiar faces in *The Thing*, see the Appendix.)

The same Cold War fears which appear throughout the SF films of the fifties surface vaguely in *The Thing*. The multitude of invasions by creatures from space, giant insects, dinosaurs, and the like seemed to symbolize the era's anxieties about Communist aggression and nuclear destruction.

At least part of the reason for the presence of an Air Force base in Alaska, as shown in *The Thing*, was the common belief that if a Russian attack came, the polar route would be the most likely one for it. Of course, when news of the mysterious crash reaches the base, the first thought is that it could well have something to do with the Russians.

The flying saucer craze of the fifties was at least partly another sign of Cold War anxiety. The strange

One of the advertising posters for the film, including both scenes from the movie and the publicity shots. Nikki Nicholson (Margaret Sheridan), as shown here, was the film's love interest.

lights or objects in the sky that appeared and disappeared so quickly seem to reflect the instantaneous mass destruction represented by the atomic bomb.

We know Hawks got the idea for *The Thing* from Campbell's story, yet he couldn't have been unaware of the cold war implications in the final script. Mentioning the Russians and the choice of a "flying saucer" as the alien's vehicle suggests a deliberate and subtle attempt to heighten the film's tension by playing on some very real subconscious fears of the audience.

Hawks wanted it clear that he didn't consider *The Thing* to be just another horror movie. He said:

> . . . an out-and-out horror thriller [is] based on that which is impossible. The science fiction film is based on that which is unknown but is given credibility by the use of scientific facts which parallel that which the viewer is asked to believe.

Actually, there wasn't much in the film which required a scientific rationalization. The scientists' discussion of carnivorous and communicating plants as an explanation of the alien's vegetable nature passes very quickly—so quickly that the audience has little time to notice the holes in the logic, and perhaps that's all that's really required (see Appendix).

The Thing is clearly infected with the antiscientific attitude which appears throughout the SF films of the fifties. Like so many of its postwar cousins, the alien bears the taint of radioactivity, and at least one disparaging remark about splitting the atom is made. Yet the attitude toward science and scientists expressed in *The Thing* is more complex than just simple paranoia.

When the alien is first brought back to camp, the scientists are split about thawing it out, with one camp led by Dr. Carrington and the other by Dr. Chapman. Chapman's group backs Hendry all the way. Even Carrington's supporters begin to have doubts when he starts growing the alien plants in his lab.

Carrington's degeneration is central to the view of science we eventually get from *The Thing*. Carrington is anxious to examine the alien. He and the other scientists are described as being like "kids with a new toy," a statement that implies a certain lack of maturity, but also a healthy scientific curiosity.

Carrington's stiffness makes him a bit hard to take at first, but this is a mere eccentricity. It's when he begins to speculate on the "neat and unconfused" method of the alien's reproductive system, without "pain or pleasure as we know it," that we start to become really suspicious of him, and the sexual implications behind his statement add to our uneasiness (see Appendix).

Yet Carrington's defense of the alien seems convincing. He suggests the alien's violence is only a reaction to the various attacks made on it. Carrington only wants to communicate with the alien and straighten things out. Even Hendry doesn't dismiss the idea; he says Carrington can do whatever he likes, so long as there isn't any danger.

But as Carrington's anxiety builds, his judgment becomes clouded. He's had no sleep since the discovery of the alien, and it's his fault two men are dead. He begins to retreat into the psychological safety of "emotionless" science. "There are no enemies in science," he says, "only phenomena to study."

Carrington's ability to balance rational self-interest against scientific curiosity eventually snaps completely. As Hendry prepares for the showdown with the alien, Carrington tries to talk him out of it:

> You're robbing science of the greatest secret that's ever come to it. Knowledge is more important than life. We've only one excuse for existing—to think, to find out, to learn. It doesn't matter what happens to us; nothing counts except our *thinking*.

Carrington's speech is a classic argument in favor of scientific curiosity and makes a good deal of sense if we don't stop to consider what's coming down the hall. But then he goes too far. "We owe it to the brain of our species," he says, "to stand here and die, without destroying a source of wisdom." This is scientific curiosity pushed beyond the limits of all common sense, and it's this kind of insensitivity which characterizes the scientist in so many SF films of the fifties.

Throughout his films, Howard Hawks displayed little affection for people whose ideals were rooted in the abstract rather than in a solid reality. His preference was for men of ideals who were also men of action—practical men. In *The Thing* it's the "Scientist," as symbolized by Carrington, who bears the brunt of Hawks's impatience with those who refuse to face what he at least considered the realities of life.

The Thing is less anti-science than it is anti-Carrington, really anti-stupid. We should remember that by the film's end everyone—even Carrington's supporters—have recognized the alien menace. *The Thing* ultimately stands against any attitude which places intellectual needs over human ones. It's a theme repeated again and again in both filmed *and* written science fiction, and one we probably shouldn't forget.

Whether one cares to delve into the deeper implications of *The Thing* or not, one point remains true; it's one of the most exciting, purely *enjoyable* SF films ever made. The superb film "sense" of Howard Hawks in guiding his cast and crew could produce no less.

Some SF fans may complain that *The Thing*'s portrayal of the scientist, and its image of what lies beyond the stars, is neither pleasant nor fair. But we know nothing about what kind of life may exist in other parts of the universe. When the day finally comes that we encounter an alien form of life, we can only hope it more closely resembles the friendly spaceman of *The Day the Earth Stood Still* than the menacing creature of *The Thing*—and that whichever it is, we have the knowledge and wisdom to deal with it.

THE DAY THE EARTH STOOD STILL

Based on the story "Farewell to the Master" by Harry Bates. A 20th Century-Fox Production and Release: September 1951. Black & White. Running time: 92 minutes (8,235 feet).

PRODUCTION CREDITS

PRODUCER	*Julian Blaustein*
DIRECTOR	*Robert Wise*
SCREENPLAY	*Edmund H. North*
MUSIC	*Bernard Herrmann*
DIRECTOR OF PHOTOGRAPHY	*Leo Tover, A.S.C.*
ART DIRECTION	*Lyle Wheeler and Addison Hehr*
SET DECORATIONS	*Thomas Little and Claude Carpenter*
EDITOR	*William Reynolds, A.C.E.*
WARDROBE DIRECTION	*Charles LeMaire*
COSTUMES	*Perkins Bailey*
MAKEUP	*Ben Nye*
SPECIAL PHOTOGRAPHIC EFFECTS	*Fred Sersen*
EFFECTS TEAM (UNCREDITED)	*Ray Kellogg, L. B. Abbott & Emil Kosa*
SOUND	*Arthur H. Kirbach, Harry M. Leonard*

CAST

KLAATU/MAJOR CARPENTER	*Michael Rennie*
HELEN BENSON	*Patricia Neal*
TOM STEVENS	*Hugh Marlowe*
PROF. BARNHARDT	*Sam Jaffe*
BOBBY BENSON	*Billy Gray*
MRS. BARLEY	*Frances Bavier*
GORT	*Lock Martin*
DREW PEARSON	*Drew Pearson*
H. V. KALTENBORN	*H. V. Kaltenborn*
ELMER DAVIS	*Elmer Davis*
COLONEL	*Carleton Young*
MR. HARLEY	*Frank Conroy*
MAJOR GENERAL	*Fay Roope*
MRS. CROCKETT	*Edith Evanson*
MAJOR WHITE	*Robert Osterloh*
BRADY	*Tyler McVey*
GOVERNMENT AGENT	*James Seay*
MR. BARLEY	*John Brown*
HILDA	*Marjorie Grossland*

An unidentified flying object, which turns out to be a saucer, lands on the Mall in Washington, D.C. Klaatu, an alien in a space suit, emerges and is shot. A giant robot, Gort, appears and destroys all weapons. Klaatu halts him with a command and is then taken to Walter Reed Hospital, where his alienness is confirmed. While there, Klaatu seeks a meeting with *all* the world's leaders. He is told by a Presidential secretary that this is impossible—and that he is not free to leave. Amused, Klaatu escapes and takes a room as a "Mr. Carpenter." He meets and likes Earth people, especially Helen and Bobby Benson. To complete his mission, Klaatu seeks out an Einstein-like scientist and arranges for a demonstration of his alien powers. But even as he stops all electricity on Earth for thirty minutes, he is being betrayed. And his nonviolent display incites even greater hostility and fear toward him by official Washington and the military. With xenophobia at its peak, the troops are told that he need not be taken alive. On his way to deliver his message to Earth's scientists, he is shot and killed. Dying, he gives Helen Benson a message for Gort that will prevent a rampage by the robot. Gort retrieves Klaatu's body and restores it to life. Klaatu reveals his message to the assembled scientists—part matter-of-fact explanation, part dire warning—that mankind will be destroyed if it carries its warlike ways into space. His warning delivered, Klaatu expires and leaves us to decide.

The Day the Earth Stood Still begins with excited news reports from around the world. Elmer Davis and H. V. Kaltenborn, well-known newscasters of the time (the 1940s), report an unidentified object flying over the East Coast, seen by average Americans in bars and outside radio and television shops. The object, now clearly a saucer, flies over Washington, D.C., past such landmarks as the Smithsonian Institution and the Mall as people scatter in fear.

Columnist Drew Pearson, wearing a hat (which never fails to elicit titters from modern audiences), is seen talking to a television camera. His face appears on sets in use around the country. "Just a minute, ladies and gentlemen . . . I think something is happening!" What is happening is that a ramp has come out of the saucer. The watching soldiers, some in tanks, nervously touch their weapons for reassurance.

Klaatu appears in his spacesuit and says, "We have come to visit you in peace, and with good will." He walks down the ramp, bringing out something that looks like a weapon to the watching troops.

What happens next is put this way in Harry Bates's original story, "Farewell to the Master":

And then occurred the thing which shall always be the shame of the human race. From a treetop a hundred yards away came a wink of violet light, and Klaatu fell.

In response to this act of aggression, the giant robot Gort appears from the ship. The onlookers panic and run. Gort, slowly and deliberately, melts the weapons and tanks with a beam of energy from his visor. A word from Klaatu halts him and the soldiers cautiously approach. The "weapon" Klaatu brandished turns out to be "a gift for your President . . . with this he could have studied life on the other planets."

Fear of the unknown, of the *different*—it is this that marks Man's first encounter with an alien intelligence. Klaatu comes in peace, bearing gifts, and our response is an act of violence. This is the theme of *The Day the Earth Stood Still* (hereafter *Day*). It is a message carefully and entertainingly woven into ninety-two minutes of fast-paced escapism. As its producer, Julian Blaustein, has noted: "People don't buy tickets to listen to lectures. You defeat yourself if you try to say something in terms of purely politically oriented statements. It becomes a bore."

Day is many things, but never a bore. It is fondly remembered as one of the best science fiction films of the fifties—indeed, of any decade. What made the film so appealing at the time of its release, a time when science fiction was viewed as junk or kiddy fare, was its adult approach to the SF themes it addressed.

Despite the lurid posters 20th Century-Fox's advertising department concocted, *Day* was not intended to shock or titillate its audiences; nor was it made to showcase the talents of its special effects crew. Instead, at a time of mounting hysteria over Communists and "One-Worlders," *Day* dared to suggest what might seem obvious: peace was possible only when no one had the means to wage war. This was a bold idea for any film to espouse in 1951. The nation was just one year into the polarizing Korean War, and hard looks were being cast in the direction of Hollywood. There was a very real fear that Communist-controlled producers and screenwriters were secretly inserting party propaganda into movie scripts.

If there was a saving grace in presenting important ideas in science fictional guise, ideas sometimes criticized as "pink" or "leftist," it was that no one paid any attention to "that Buck Rogers stuff." Science fiction writer William Tenn (who teaches English and ethnic humor at Penn State under his real name, Philip Klass) tells his classes of wanting to leave science fiction for other forms of writing. But this was just as the McCarthy period was beginning, and he found he was free to write whatever he wanted in science fiction and SF magazines because the establishment neither read nor paid any attention to science fiction. Important work could be done in the genre.

In 1949, Julian Blaustein, a staff producer for 20th Century-Fox, decided to find a science fiction story suitable for filming. Blaustein's challenge was to choose a story that production chief Darryl F. Zanuck would not reject as too expensive to film. To insure that the project would not be shelved because of high production costs, Blaustein decided to consider only earthbound stories—complicated special effects and alien sets were out. Blaustein also wanted to make an entertaining film that would say something of importance, so he told his assistant story editor, who was looking for suitable material, "Our theme is that peace is no longer a four-letter word."

Finally, Blaustein unearthed a ten-year-old science fiction magazine, the October 1940 issue of *Astounding.* There he found former editor Harry Bates's "Farewell to the Master." (Other notable stories in that issue were "Butyl and the Breather," by Theodore Sturgeon and the second installment of A. E.

A publicity photo. Typical of the 1950s, it makes the film more action-oriented than it really is—and Patricia Neal, while she may have been carried in Gort's arms—is not a blonde!

THE DAY THE EARTH STOOD STILL

Van Vogt's classic, "Slan.") Blaustein had read no further than the wounding of the peaceful Klaatu when he realized he had the germ of the film he wanted to make.

Zanuck read the story and was not particularly impressed with its potential, but allowed Blaustein to purchase the screen rights anyway *if* the film stayed totally on Earth. With Zanuck's reluctant blessing, Blaustein bought the script rights from the owners of *Astounding*, Street & Smith Publications, for a mere thousand dollars. Half of that, or just $500, went to Harry Bates. Bates, in his seventies now, is still resentful that he didn't get more money, but a realistic appraisal of the market for short SF stories, especially one under fifteen pages in length, at that time would probably show that the sum was not below marketplace norms.

At Blaustein's request, Edmund H. North, a writer working at 20th Century-Fox, read the story and accepted the assignment to write the screenplay for the film. Starting work on the script in July 1950, North finished a thirty-five-page plot outline in four weeks. By then two events had occurred which would affect Zanuck's decision to go ahead with the film.

On June 27, 1950, George Pal's *Destination Moon* opened to good reviews in New York City and was an instant success. Drawing crowds across the country, *Destination Moon* proved to Blaustein—but, more importantly, to Zanuck—that people would pay to see good science fiction. At a time when television was eroding movie profits this was good news.

The second event was sobering for any studio about to produce a "peace" film: the Korean War (or "police action") broke out on June 25, 1950. However, buoyed by *Destination Moon*'s continuing success at the box office, Zanuck gave Blaustein the green light to proceed with *Farewell to the Master*, as the film was tentatively titled.

Edmund North now began in earnest to turn his plot outline into a complete script. After going through several revisions, North's final screenplay was completed on February 21, 1951. In adapting "Farewell to the Master" to the screen, North retained the heart and soul of Bates's story while dropping or changing those elements that seemed dated or irrelevant to the basic story he and Blaustein wanted to tell. Gnut, as he was called in the story, became Gort. Bates's use of a bird and a gorilla—as part of the "resurrection" procedure Gort employs to revivify Klaatu—were eliminated to simplify the plot and keep it credible for a general audience.

North also changed Gort/Gnut's role. While Gnut was the "master" referred to in the story's title, Gort is the master (a word not used in the final screenplay) only in matters relating to aggression. Perhaps his thinking was that filmgoers were not prepared to accept mankind's putting its fate into the hands of an all-controlling outside force or authority. It may have been a wise decision, since the United Nations concept itself was not fully accepted in 1951.

Gort and Klaatu stand on the ramp outside the saucer. Note the line running down the robot's arm revealing where the two halves of his "suit" come together.

Still, North's screenplay has Klaatu willing to speak only to all mankind, not just to the politicians and military men of one nation, however powerful. It is clear that only an effort by *all* men can bring true and lasting peace. In this way *Day* is a fable, a cautionary tale, much as are *1984*, *A Clockwork Orange*, and *Fahrenheit 451*.

Day's screenplay and the resulting film can be read as reflecting the values, hopes, and fears, and the realities of life in the United States in 1951. When Klaatu lands in Washington, our response is typical of the times: we rush tanks and soldiers to surround the saucer. As if all that firepower isn't enough, many of the officers draw and brandish their handguns. Even though Klaatu waits two hours before descending from the saucer, to let the initial panic subside, he is still shot for the first "suspect" move he makes. "Shoot first and ask questions later" was the order of the day.

After Klaatu neutralizes all the electricity on Earth for thirty minutes, the sequence that gives the film its name, General Cutler, in charge of apprehending Klaatu, tells his staff that the missing alien *must* be taken, alive or dead, despite conceding that hospitals, planes in flight, and the like were not affected by the blackout.

Helen Benson's boyfriend, Tom Stevens, who eventually betrays Klaatu, represents a certain type of mentality of the late forties and early fifties. When we first meet him, he seems full of charm and is both understanding and appreciative of Klaatu's offer to watch Bobby so that he and Helen can have a day in the country together. Slowly and painfully, layer by layer, his insurance salesman's veneer of charm is peeled away to reveal a desperately macho and emotionally stunted figure. Tom *knows* he is right about turning Klaatu in to the authorities and that Helen is wrong, because, after all, he's a man, while she's merely a woman. Tom pays little attention to Helen's arguments, and when she pleads with him not to call General Cutler because the rest of the world is involved, he says, "I don't *care* about the rest of the world."

When Tom realizes Helen is repulsed by his selfishness, he makes matters worse by insisting, "You'll feel different when you see my picture in the papers.... You wait and see. You're going to marry a big hero." Helen replies, "I'm not going to marry anybody," and walks out, leaving him alone to complete his call to General Cutler and fulfill his Judas role.

It is interesting to note the reception accorded Klaatu on his arrival on Earth in *Day,* because the treatment of the alien in science fiction and horror films is often an accurate reflection of the mood of the country at the time a film is produced.

In many SF films—perhaps too many—the alien arrives bringing death and destruction and seeks to dominate or eliminate mankind. This is true of H. G. Wells's Martians in his Victorian-era science fiction novel, *The War of the Worlds,* and of George Pal's fifties movie version of the 1898 book. Wells intended his invasion of tentacled Martians—who "glistened like wet leather"—to symbolize the "alien" invasion of foreign cultures by the industrially advanced white man, specifically the British. Intent upon extending and exploiting an empire on which the sun would never set, the British felt few compunctions about dominating their weaker and less technologically advanced neighbors; it was their "white man's burden." Wells reasoned that if man had no reservations about killing and enslaving his fellow-man on almost any pretext, why wouldn't a scientifically superior alien race act the same toward the whole of mankind?

Science fiction film is, of course, primarily a visual medium. Invading aliens, attacking our cities and homes from flying saucers, are arguably more visual than aliens who come in peace. While it may not be intellectually challenging, it's surely exciting to see Hollywood's special effects wizards destroy the Capitol dome or topple Tokyo into the sea.

Movies also voice fears that exist in our subconscious and which we are afraid to confront consciously. It may be that we are fearful that aliens might do to us what we've done to the black, red, and yellow man, or torture and butcher us as we do the animals of the world.

The great fear of the early 1950s was a fear of the atomic bomb, which had just fallen into the hands of the Communists. Given this justifiable paranoia, it's easy to see why so many SF films of the fifties present the alien as invader. A man runs down the street in *Day* after the saucer lands, shouting, "They're here. They've landed on the Mall!" Whoever *they* are, surely they mean us no good. It's all the more remarkable, then, that in *Day* the alien Klaatu offers us a gift and comes in peace.

After being told he is being held in "protective" custody, Klaatu merely smiles. Later, a man is seen reading a newspaper whose headline proclaims: "Man From Mars Escapes From Hospital!" Other reactions include a terrified mother dragging her two children in from their play in the street.

This scene dissolves to a shot that follows a man with a suitcase walking down an atmospheric residential street at night. The man is Klaatu and, as he passes by houses, we overhear excited voices from radios inside; one radio voice says, "There's no denying there's a monster at large," pretty much summing up the hysterical attitude taken toward the escaped Klaatu.

This scene, as well as the one that follows, shows just how much director Robert Wise owes to horror film producer Val Lewton. A film editor before he became a director, Wise edited and took over the direction of Lewton's 1943 classic, *The Curse of the Cat People.* Wise remarked of *Day,* perhaps with Klaatu's appearance at Mrs. Crockett's boarding house in mind, that "it stressed the very elements emphasized by Lewton in the early forties—fear of the unknown and horror based on legitimate psychological reaction."

Fear of the unknown. Seeking a room for rent, Klaatu enters the boarding house as the boarders watch another report about the missing alien on television. Unaware of his entry, they turn, startled, when Bobby, wide-eyed, nudges his mother and asks, "Hey, Mom, who's that?" All they can see is a figure standing in the shadows, its face unclear. It is a moment of extreme tension, broken only when one of the men snaps on a light and the menacing figure is revealed to be a well-dressed man who steps forward and says, "My name is Carpenter. I'm looking for a room." The tension is punctured and everyone glances about guiltily, ashamed for having been alarmed.

One of *Day*'s key scenes, which shows not only the general attitudes of the time and the reaction to the missing alien—the "monster" at large—but also the sensitivity of one of the main characters, is the "breakfast scene," which occurs shortly after Klaatu has moved into the boarding house on Harvard Street. Since a detailed examination of the scene is rewarding, we've reproduced a bit of Edmund H. North's revised final script, dated February 21, 1951:

Mrs. Barley is a middle-class ... lady, firm and unrelenting. Her husband is a born complainer. Mr. Krull is a

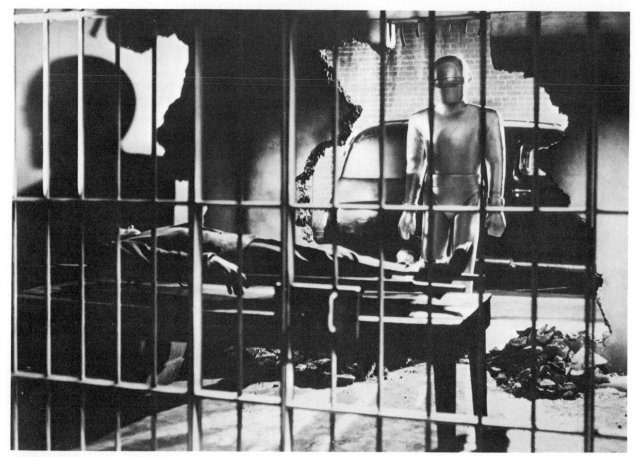

Having melted the wall of the jail cell in which the body of Klaatu lies, Gort prepares to retrieve Klaatu and restore him to life.

shriveled little accountant, precise and finicky.... From a portable radio on the table comes Gabriel Heatter's voice.

GABRIEL HEATTER'S VOICE: ... and so, on this Sunday morning, we ask the question that's been plaguing the entire nation for two days now: "Where is this creature and what is he up to?" If he can build a space ship that can fly to Earth—and a robot that can destroy our tanks and guns—what other terrors can he unleash at will? ... Obviously we must find this monster. We must track him down like a wild animal and destroy him.

Not exactly the voice of reason and moderation. As Heatter continues to excoriate the alien—a "monster" whose only crime was the destruction of a few tanks and guns, injuring no one—Mrs. Barley is seen reading a newspaper showing giant Gort-like robots attacking humans with killer rays while the paper's caption asks, "Are We Long For This World?"
North's screenplay continues:

Mr. Barley reaches out and snaps off the radio.

MR. BARLEY (snorting, he tosses his paper down): Why doesn't the Government do something. That's what I want to know.

MR. KRULL (mildly): What can they do? They're only people—just like us.

MR. BARLEY: People my foot! They're Democrats!

MR. KRULL: It's enough to give you the shakes. He's got that robot standin' there—ten-foot tall—just waitin' for orders to destroy us.

HELEN (thoughtfully): This space man—or whatever he is. We automatically assume he's a menace ... Maybe he isn't one at all.

MR. BARLEY (glaring at her for this silly notion): Then what's he hiding for? Why doesn't he come out in the open?

MR. KRULL (indicating the radio): Like the fella says: "What's he up to?"

HELEN: Maybe he's afraid.

MRS. BARLEY (with a derisive snort): He's afraid!

HELEN: After all, he was shot the moment he landed here. (She pauses for a moment thoughtfully.) I was just wondering what I would do.

KLAATU (to Helen, helpfully): Perhaps, before deciding on a course of action, you'd want to know more about the people here—to orient yourself in a strange environment.

MRS. BARLEY *(sharply)*: There's nothing strange about Washington, Mr. Carpenter.

KLAATU *(quietly, tongue in cheek)*: A person from another planet might disagree with you.

MRS. BARLEY: If you want my opinion, he came from right here on Earth, And *(with significant emphasis)* you know where I mean.

MR. KRULL: *They* wouldn't come in a spaceship. They'd come in airplanes.

As we can see, the reactions to the missing Klaatu range from the near-hysteria of Gabriel Heatter's radio commentator to Helen Benson's thoughtful identification with the problems he would have as a stranger in a strange land. Helen, with the exception of her son Bobby and Dr. Barnhardt, is the only human who thinks of the alien visitor as a *person* rather than as a *thing*. Her simple humanity makes her a rare standout in SF films dealing with close encounters of the third kind.

The moviegoer sees the story from the alien's point of view, and is manipulated somewhat into feeling sympathy for, and identifying with, Klaatu because he is essentially human in all respects. Yet, he is also a superior, a "good," human being, morally as well as technologically. In this respect, Klaatu resembles Superman. Klaatu must become Mr. Carpenter, as Superman must become Clark Kent, to pass unnoticed among Earth people. In assuming human identities, both superior aliens can learn the ways of the planet Earth while escaping the unrelenting pursuit of those who seek to destroy them.

This is what makes the alien as savior so appealing to us: A man appears from the heavens who is man but who is also more than man. *Day* is a modern retelling of the Christ story and, as such, has enormous appeal for a troubled world. In this manifestation the alien is a messiah, not an invader. THEY are still out there in their spaceships, but now they are only waiting for the right time to land and solve our earthly problems: to cure cancer, to tell us the true meaning of life, and to take us to a higher plane of existence.

But, as always, there are those who oppose this, those who control and run the world as it is now: the

The revived Klaatu speaks briefly with Helen Benson before going out to speak to a gathering of the world's top scientists.

military, the establishment, the international conspirators, and Satan's forces. Just as they crucified the son of God, so too do they wish to kill Klaatu.

If this seems a little farfetched, Edmund H. North himself admitted that the parallels between the story of Christ and *Day* were intentional: from Klaatu's earthly name of Carpenter, to the betrayal by Tom Stevens, and finally to his resurrection and ascent into the heavens at *Day*'s end. "It was my private little joke. I never discussed this angle with Blaustein or Wise because I didn't want it expressed. I had originally hoped that the Christ comparison would be subliminal."

The analogy is incomplete, however, because the Breen Censorship Board objected to Gort's bringing Klaatu back to life, insisting that "only God can do that!" When the board remained adamant in the face of North's argument that the movie was science fiction and dealt with legitimately unearthly powers, a compromise was reached. In the film, Helen Benson tells Klaatu that she thought he was dead and he replies that he was. Helen looks at Gort in awe and says, "You mean he has the power of life and death?" Klaatu replies gravely, "No, that is a power reserved to the Almighty Spirit." Klaatu's resurrection is only temporary; he will live, but no one can say for how long. Only the Almighty Spirit and the Breen office have that power.

As pure "cinema," *Day* is outstanding. Its production values attest to its relatively high budget of $960,000 (which, admittedly, included inflated studio "overhead costs" unrelated to the filming) and the fact that the men and women who made the film were Hollywood professionals in the best sense of the word.

Leo Tover's black-and-white photography is gorgeous and crisp, clearly showing why so many film purists lamented the almost total changeover to color. In a strange way, a film like *Day* is superior *because* it is B/W. Pinpoint lighting allows B/W movies a full visual range: from brilliant white to an utterly stark

While Gort stands motionless, Klaatu explains to the scientists and soldiers that the robot is the real master, who has the power to stop all acts of aggression. Klaatu offers us a choice between peace and destruction.

black, with delicate shadings between those poles. The sets of early color films had to be flooded with light, and this tended to limit the depth of focus (the camera's ability to see both near and far objects clearly) and the uses of shadow. In a carefully conceived film like *Day* the director and the photographer use the interplay between light and shadow to manipulate the mood of scenes: Klaatu stepping out from the shadows into the light at the boarding house; Gort slowly turning in response to a flashlight signal from Klaatu, his visor then bathed in a bright pulsating light; and the dimly lit elevator that traps Klaatu and Helen for thirty minutes.

An editor himself once, Wise worked closely with editor William Reynolds. Fast-paced and yet still somehow deliberate, *Day*'s editing is dramatic and concise. One of Reynolds and Wise's most effectively cut sequences occurs when Bobby Benson, after following Klaatu to the ship, watches first in curiosity and then terror as Gort knocks out the two guards standing watch. The camera follows Gort's approach to the two men, and then Reynolds cuts back to Bobby's face for his reaction. We see Bobby's eyes widen in fear as we simultaneously hear a cymbal clash to indicate Gort's crashing together of the men's heads. Reynolds cuts back to Gort, now seen standing over the fallen soldiers.

Much of the movie's tension and impact comes from director Wise's camera placement and movement. To emphasize Gort's size and strength, Wise shoots him from below, making him appear even more impressive. All the shots of Gort imbue him with power and mystery. An alien force all the more awesome because of his silence and immobile face, Gort is given majesty because of Wise's careful shot selection. There is never a scene in *Day* when Gort appears less than frightening or, which is more important, unintentionally funny. Wise is also adept at placing his actors so that the relationships between them are subtly reinforced; all the shots of Klaatu, Helen, and Tom Stevens together suggest the emotional tensions just below the surface as Helen is gently pulled between the two men.

While the movie practically gallops at times, North and Wise are also able to have deliberately moving, character-exploring scenes, too. They accomplished this by using newsmen, soldiers, doctors, and newspaper headlines to pass on information the audience needs and to keep the story moving ahead. With the "plot" then well in hand, they had the freedom to explore the human aspects of the movie.

While *Day* makes some attempts to maintain scientific accuracy, it is, on the whole, unsuccessful. Klaatu claims to have traveled 250 million miles through space. At that distance, the only planet he could really be from is Mars.

Venus, as well as Mars, is postulated as a likely candidate for Klaatu's home planet by the scientists in the film. In reality, both Mars and Venus are unlikely to harbor any life as we know it, though less was known about the two planets at the time of the film's production. Still, enough *was* known of them for it to be unlikely that a humanoid race such as Klaatu's could have evolved there, especially one so advanced. Arguing further against Mars (and Venus) is the fact that the doctors who examine Klaatu acknowledge that his atmosphere is quite similar to ours.

Not only is Klaatu virtually human, he is 78, of a life expectancy of 130, and speaks English—and other languages—from monitoring our radio and television broadcasts.

Perhaps the strongest bit of scientific verisimilitude in the movie is Professor Barnhardt's problem in celestial mechanics that Klaatu corrects—it was the work of the film's technical advisor, Dr. Samuel Herrick of UCLA.

Producer Blaustein assigned Fred Sersen the job of devising *Day*'s special photographic effects, most of which were completed after the principal photography had been shot. The members of Sersen's (uncredited) effects team included Ray Kellogg, L. B. Abbott, and Emil Kosa.

The task of designing the giant robot Gort fell to art directors Lyle Wheeler and Addison Hehr. After reading Harry Bates's original story and his description of Gnut, Hehr decided to use foam rubber to duplicate Gort's metallic-looking yet flexible "skin." Hehr patterned the foam rubber into a suit and painted it silver. Once Gort's "bioplasmic insert"—actor and former doorman at Grauman's Chinese Theater, Lock Martin—had climbed into the suit, full-length lacing up and down each arm and down the back was pulled tight. To shoot the robot from the back, walking away from the camera, a second suit with lacing up the *front* was devised. The seven-foot, six-inch actor's hands and feet were covered by individual gloves and boots, and his head was fitted with a helmet that made him well over eight feet tall. Although Blaustein and Wise were concerned that audiences might giggle when they saw Gort's "fluid metal" suit bending and creasing as he walked, it was never a real problem due to careful editing. Gort's presence in the film is ominous, not laugh-provoking, so the illusion is accepted.

Since the helmet Lock Martin wore was just that and nothing more, it was necessary for Hehr to create a mock-up head that could execute the many things called for in the script. The mock-up had a visor capable of opening and closing, and a pulsating electronic "eye." Whenever Gort's head is shown in close-up, it is Hehr's mock-up we're really seeing.

When Gort used his destructive ray to disintegrate a tank, the helmet mock-up, shot against a special background, was used. The heat ray was matted in by Fred Sersen, and the destruction of the tank was accomplished by using a series of matte paintings by Ray Kellogg and Emile Kosa. The matte paintings (a *matte* is an element of a movie scene or shot which blacks out unwanted portions of a picture; a *matte*

Klaatu (Michael Rennie) stands in his blue spacesuit to the right, while veteran character actor Harry Lauter stands at the far left.

This was a rare color shot, a publicity photo, that convinced many people that the production was originally planned for color instead of black and white—something those involved with the film now deny.

painting is the artistic replacement for the blacked-out portion; the live-action portion of the picture is the *plate*) hid the replacing of the tank by a melted one. Similarly, it was matte paintings by Kellogg and Kosa which simulated Gort's disintegration of the plastic block the army had enclosed him in.

For scenes where Gort's size was to be emphasized, the studio's art department built a nine-foot fiberglass mock-up. It is this oversize mock-up that is seen in most long shots of Gort, not only to underscore Gort's proportions but also to hold to a minimum the time Lock Martin had to spend in the claustrophobic and extremely hot foam rubber suit he wore as the robot.

Klaatu's evocative spaceship, one of the screen's first and best flying saucers, was really two-foot and three-foot miniatures used by Fred Sersen's special effects unit, and a three-fourths full-size mock-up used by director Wise and crew. The mock-up, 100 feet high and 25 feet wide, was the model from which Klaatu and Gort emerged upon landing on the Mall. The hidden one-fourth was given over to the men and machinery which operated the ramp that emerged from the saucer's hull. The mock-up was built on 20th's backlot, where the studio's Century City complex of office buildings and shops now stands.

The music for *Day* was composed by Alfred Hitchcock's favorite composer, Bernard Herrmann. Herrmann was requested by director Wise, who had met him while both were working on *Citizen Kane,* Wise as an editor and Herrmann as composer. Herrmann was shown a cut of the completed film and liked it very much. Since it was science fiction, Herrmann had no intention of writing an ordinary score. As he recalled working on the film, shortly before his death in 1975, Herrmann said, "I felt we should do it by taking advantage of using electronic instruments, which hadn't been done then." (This was, of course, before Louis and Bebe Barron gave *Forbidden Planet* its eerie electronic score.)

Left alone by the studio to produce the score, Herrmann replaced 20th's string section with electronically amplified instruments. He made extensive use of electronic violins and electronic bass, and the theramin, which is played by waving one's hands back and forth in front of it. It was the theramin that Herrmann settled on to convey *Day*'s unearthliness and to achieve a strangeness of sound that was both musical and ominous. "Today," explained Herrmann to an interviewer, "we get pretty near the same sounds from synthesizers, which are much simpler to operate, but somehow it lacks the weirdness of it."

Herrmann completed scoring the film in five weeks and recorded the sound track with the Fox Orchestra in Hollywood. It remained one of Herrmann's favortie scores—and pictures.

The pivotal role of Klaatu went to British actor Michael Rennie (1909–1971). Studio head Zanuck had at first wanted Spencer Tracy to play Klaatu, but producer Blaustein convinced him that an unknown actor would be best for the role. Robert Wise initially wanted Claude Rains, but he was busy with a stage play, so the part went to Rennie, who had already appeared in 20th Century's 1950 production, *The Black Rose,* filmed in England. Michael Rennie's first film role was in the British production *Secret Agent* (1936). Most of his later films were for 20th Century-Fox as well as *Day* and included *The Lost World* (1960) and *The Power* (1967). Never a star of the first magnitude, Rennie worked steadily and gave strong performances. While *Day* remains the film he is most remembered for, many more people know him best for his role as Harry Lime in the television series *The Third Man.*

As Klaatu, Rennie brought to the man from outer space an air of quiet dignity and self-assurance. Blaustein said, "Rennie's voice is marvelous," and the hint of English accent gave Klaatu an extra dimension; to American ears his accent was foreign yet somehow familiar and reassuring.

Contract player Patricia Neal (1926–   ) was given the part of Helen Benson. The twenty-year-old Miss Neal's first film had been *John Loves Mary* (1949) and was quickly followed by one of her best-known features, *The Fountainhead* (1949). Other notable films she appeared in include *A Face in the Crowd* (1957) and *Hud* (1963), for which she won the Academy Award for Best Actress and the British Film Academy Award (BFA). A stroke, followed by a strenuous recovery, caused her semiretirement. Her husband is Roald Dahl, a Norwegian-born but English-by-choice writer of films and children's books *(Willy Wonka and the Chocolate Factory).*

Miss Neal's Helen Benson projects a winsome mixture of intelligence, sensitivity, and mature sexuality. When Klaatu's message must be gotten to Gort, so that he will not go on a murderous rampage of revenge, it is Patricia Neal's capable Helen who has the daring and strength to get the job done. It was this inner strength that enabled Miss Neal to overcome the stroke she suffered in real life; not only did she have to learn how to talk again, she also decided she would have to learn how to be an actress again. She was successful and appeared in the two-hour made-for-television movie *The Homecoming,* which became the basis for the series *The Waltons.*

Hugh Marlowe (1914–   ) was chosen to play Helen Benson's boyfriend Tom Stevens. Born Hugh Hipple, he was a radio announcer who turned to acting and has been in motion pictures since 1937. He has appeared in *Twelve O'Clock High* and *All About Eve,* both 1950, and in *Earth Versus the Flying Saucers* (1956). His later roles have been predominantly in SF and horror movies.

As Tom Stevens, Marlowe was able to use his radio announcer's voice to good effect; smooth and well-modulated, it is the voice of a snake oil salesman. Marlowe's Tom Stevens is slick and shallow, a man who will drop any pretense of charm if it means there's a buck or a promotion in it for him.

For the Einstein-like Professor Barnhardt, Blaustein cast veteran actor Sam Jaffe (1897–   ). On stage since 1916, Jaffe went to Hollywood in 1933 and appeared in several of the thirties' most memorable films, including *Lost Horizon* (1937), in which he played the beatific High Lama, and *Gunga Din* (1939). Jaffe played the title role in the latter film, portraying Kipling's loyal and courageous water-bearer. Television viewers remember him as Dr. Zorba in the medical series *Ben Casey*.

Jaffe was perfectly cast as Professor Jacob Barnhardt. He had the unruly hair of an Einstein, and the quiet dignity of a man of deep moral convictions. And audiences always responded to his on-screen portrayal because he was likable—he seemed more like a favorite uncle than an actor. As Barnhardt, Jaffe makes us believe man can learn from Klaatu, that men of good will exist and do make a difference. It is no small achievement in a film where almost everyone else is incapable of seeing beyond his or her small personal interests.

The role of Bobby Benson went to Billy Gray (1938–   ). An actor since the age of six, he had a previous film role in producer Blaustein's comedy-drama *Mr. 880*. Most Americans remember him as Bud Anderson in *Father Knows Best*, the long-running family television series starring Robert Young. Today he remembers *Day* as a fun experience, and adds, "My mother and Michael Rennie had a little thing going on the side. I also wanted to keep some of the 'diamonds,' but I couldn't get away with it."

An accomplished actor for one so young, Billy Gray gave Bobby Benson a believability not in the screenplay. As the role was written, Bobby Benson was too good to be true. When his mother told him to run along to bed, he would reply, "Okay." What kid worth his salt gives in so easily? And yet Billy Gray made it work because you could tell that while he might be a good boy, he was a good boy with a sense of adventure. He horse-traded two dollars for two of Mr. Carpenter's diamonds and asked him not to tell his mom because "she doesn't like me to steal from people." He has grit too. When Helen and Tom make fun of his tale of seeing Mr. Carpenter go into the spaceship, he says, "I'd never call *you* a liar," striking a blow for kids everywhere.

Like any film over twenty-years old, *Day* is somewhat dated today, but perhaps less so than many more recent SF films. The clothing styles (Drew Pearson's hat again!), the cars, the scientific knowledge, and the social milieu of *Day* are relics of the past, but not its theme and its message. Peace in a troubled and armed world is still an elusive goal, perhaps unattainable unless we are forced by some outside agency to ac-

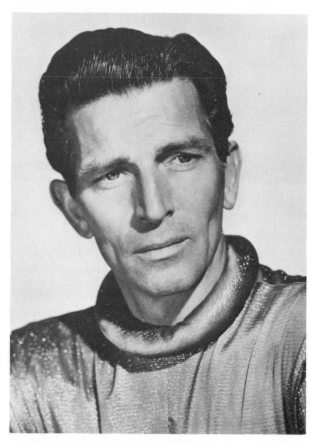

Portrait of Michael Rennie as Klaatu.

cept the fact that we are all passengers on spaceship Earth.

Klaatu's and Bobby's visit to Arlington National Cemetery has as much meaning for us today as it did for those who saw it in 1951; its message is as clear as it was then, and it is the same: war is waste.

The best-remembered line from *The Day the Earth Stood Still* is Klaatu's message for Gort, given to Helen Benson: "Klaatu barada nikto." But it is Klaatu's reply to the radio interviewer at the saucer site that resonates with meaning for us today as much as it did nearly thirty years ago. Asked if he was afraid of the saucer and its missing inhabitant, Klaatu replied, "I *am* fearful when I see people substituting fear for reason." That was all he could say before he was cut off.

If Gort were to return alone, without the now-deceased Klaatu, would we react any differently today? And would Gort make good Klaatu's warning, reducing our planet to a handful of burned-out cinders?

Have we learned from our mistakes of the past hundreds—or even thousands—of years? Are we ready to listen and to learn ... or are we still cutting off those who speak what we don't want to hear?

It's something worth thinking about.

THE MAN IN THE WHITE SUIT

An Ealing Studios Release (released in the U.S. by the Rank Organization and Universal-International). Running Time: 85 minutes. Black and White. British Release: 1951. Opened in New York City on March 31, 1952, at the Sutton Theater.

PRODUCTION CREDITS

PRODUCER	Michael Balcon
DIRECTOR	Alexander Mackendrick
SCREENPLAY	Roger MacDougall, John Dighton, A. Mackendrick
CINEMATOGRAPHER	Douglas Slocombe
ART DIRECTOR	Jim Morahan
EDITOR	Bernard Gribble
SPECIAL EFFECTS	Sidney Pearson
SPECIAL PROCESSES	Geoffrey Dickinson
ASSOCIATE PRODUCER	Sidney Cole
SOUND EDITOR	Mary Hubberfield
ADDITIONAL PHOTOGRAPHY	Lionel Banes
COSTUME DESIGN	Anthony Mendleson
MAKEUP	Ernest Taylor & Harry Frampton
SCIENTIFIC ADVISER	Geoffrey Myers
MUSIC	Benjamin Frankel
PLAYED BY	The Philharmonia Orchestra
CONDUCTED BY	Ernest Irving
PRODUCTION SUPERVISOR	Hal Mason

CAST

SIDNEY STRATTON	Alec Guinness
DAPHNE BIRNLEY	Joan Greenwood
ALAN BIRNLEY	Cecil Parker
MICHAEL CORLAND	Michael Gough
SIR JOHN KIERLAW	Ernest Thesiger
CRANFORD	Howard Marion Crawford
BERTHA	Vida Hope
WILSON	John Rudling
FRANK	Patric Doonan
HARRY	Duncan Lamont

The Man in the White Suit is a classic example of the science fiction film that isn't considered science fiction, at least outside the SF field. When it was released in the U.S., critics had nothing but praise for it, but not one said anything that might suggest *The Man in the White Suit* was science fiction.

The *New York Times* called it "a deft and sardonic little satire" and "a most ingenious fable." Comparing it to *The Lavender Hill Mob*, the previous film from Britain's Ealing Studios, Hollis Alpert remarked in *Saturday Review* that the film was "so clever in its story and filled with so much whimsical invention . . . I was unable to decide which I liked better."

Variety hailed it as a "new comedy winner." *Time* described it as "top-grade movie material with the quality of good British woolen, the frothiness of fine French lace," and *Newsweek* described it as "a choice piece of movie foolery and effervescent philosophizing."

The key words here are "satire," "fable," "whimsical invention," and "philosophizing." Over the years critics have adapted words like these to describe books and movies with science-fictional premises such as *Brave New World*, *1984*, *Fail-Safe*, *Slaughterhouse-5*, *Dr. Strangelove*, *Shikasta*, and a multitude of others which don't fit specific critical definitions of SF.

Because *The Man in the White Suit* (hereafter referred to as *MWS*) has no spaceships, monsters, or lavish special effects—perhaps because it is satirical and serious—critics have been unable, or unwilling, to accept the basic science-fictional premise that lies at its core.

Like much science fiction, *MWS* asks the question "What if—?" (see the *Dr. Strangelove* chapter). In this case, however, the question isn't "What if we could send a spaceship to Mars?" or "What if the Earth were invaded?" *MWS*'s "What if—?" is more subtle, more down to earth, and because of this it emerges as one of the most mature, enjoyable, and intelligent SF films ever made.

Michael Corland, owner of a textile mill in the north of England, is anxious to impress Alan Birnley, one of the largest textile manufacturers in the country. Corland hopes to marry Birnley's daughter, Daphne, as well as get Birnley to invest in his mill.

With this in mind, Corland gives Birnley a tour of his mill, but Birnley is singularly unimpressed. Corland is showing Birnley his research lab when Daphne arrives. While Birnley inspects the lab, Corland tells Daphne things aren't going so well. Daphne encourages him, but as he starts to kiss her, Corland is hit from behind when the lab door is pushed open by a laborer's cart. The laborer is Sidney Stratton.

In Corland's lab Birnley notices an odd-looking apparatus making a noise something like the cross between a gurgle and a belch. Birnley asks what the device is, but no one seems to know, much to Corland's displeasure.

In the midst of the confusion, Sid comes in, but when he sees what's happening, he quickly backs out again. Corland orders his assistant to find out what the device is and to whom it belongs.

At lunch Corland nearly chokes when his assistant brings word the mysterious device has cost 4,000 pounds. There's still no clue as to who's responsible. Soon Corland is questioning everyone in the lab. Looking for her father, Daphne enters the lab and notices a very guilty-looking Sid.

In the next scene Sid appears to be making a full confession to Corland. When the camera pulls back, however, we see Sid is actually talking to the washroom mirror. When someone else comes in, Sid slips quietly away.

Sid gets another laborer's job, this time at Birnley's mill. He meets Bertha, a young woman who works at the mill and is a staunch member of the textile workers union. Bertha befriends Sid and is clearly attracted to him.

While emptying the trash one day, Sid gets a look at Birnley's lab. It's twice the size of Corland's, and Sid is obviously delighted. By now it's clear Sidney Stratton is no ordinary worker, but a man with something on his mind.

Sometime later, Sid helps deliver an electron microscope to the lab. Like Sid, the men from the microscope company are wearing overalls. While the company men wander away, Sid displays an obvious knowledge of the microscope's workings to Hoskins, who runs the lab.

Believing Sid is from the microscope company, Hoskins asks if he'll stay on a few days to supervise the microscope's use. Thinking fast, Sid agrees, provided he's given some space to work on his own projects.

Bertha shows up at Sid's rooming house to find out why he's left his job. An excited Sid tries to explain things to her, including the fact that he's not getting paid any longer but Bertha doesn't understand.

Sid asks Mrs. Watson, his landlady, if he can owe her the rent for a few weeks, and the old woman agrees. Bertha offers to lend him some money, but although he thanks her, it's clear Sid isn't really listening, and Bertha's feelings are hurt.

Birnley decides not to invest in Corland's mill. Daphne suggests to Corland that they get married anyway, but Corland refuses to marry her unless his prospects are better.

Daphne argues with her father, saying he's against Corland simply because of the incident with the mysterious device in the lab—and that, says Daphne, could happen anywhere. Birnley, however, denies it could ever happen at *his* mill.

Daphne storms out. In the hall she spots Sid and recognizes him. Thinking that if she can expose him to her father she'll have made her point, Daphne follows Sid into the lab.

Sid hides, and Daphne fails to catch him. When she sees his apparatus, however, she knows she's got her

Sid (Alec Guinness) ponders a chemistry text when he's supposed to be working.

man and hurries off to find her father.

Sid goes after her and persuades her to listen to him. As he explains his project to her, Daphne finds herself fascinated, not only with the project, but with the man. That night she astounds her father by taking two volumes of the *Encyclopaedia Britannica* to bed with her.

Next day, with the lab deserted during lunch, Sid readies his device for its first test. He strings a long detonator into the corridor, and, steeling himself, pushes the button. The solution in the apparatus turns white.

Hoskins enters. Sid is delirious with joy and races off to see Birnley, but Hoskins won't permit it—one doesn't just barge in on the owner of the mill! Hoskins has Sid restrained, and when Sid admits he doesn't even really work at Birnley's, he's quickly ejected and the liquid poured down the drain.

That night Sid goes to Birnley's home. The butler refuses to admit him. Upstairs, Birnley is trying to explain to his board of directors where 8,000 pounds of factory money disappeared, not knowing it went for Sid's experiments.

Sid convinces the butler to take Birnley a note. Meanwhile, Daphne discovers Sid outside and lets him in. She hurries upstairs to tell her father about him. The butler spots Sid hiding behind the stairs and chases him while Daphne pleads with her father to give Sid a hearing.

Birnley finally confronts Sid who is then thrown out of the house. Daphne angrily explains Sid's invention to her headstrong father—a cloth that will never wear out and repels all forms of dirt. Daphne leaves her father sputtering on the stairs.

Next day Sid reappears at Birnley's lab. Hoskins is just about to take him to task when Birnley enters and informs him Sid is working there now.

Sid tries to create the white liquid again, but his apparatus blows up. He tries again, and again it explodes. Soon, everyone at Birnley's is setting his watch by Sid's explosions.

Birnley starts to worry; Sid's experiments are costing him money. He goes to the lab, not knowing Sid is about to try again. Huddled behind sandbags, Sid punches the detonator button, and this time the process works—the liquid turns white. Birnley nearly faints when he discovers how close he's come to being killed.

The liquid is swiftly turned to fibers and woven into cloth. Sid is measured for a suit, instructing the tailor to send him paper patterns, since the only way to cut the material is with an acetylene torch. Soon Sid has a weirdly luminous white suit.

Sid displays the suit to Daphne, who suggests it makes him look like a knight in shining armor. The whole world, she says, will bless him for his discovery.

Corland hears of the new cloth from a spy he's

planted at Birnley's. Corland and the other major textile manufacturers, headed by the infamous Sir John Kierlaw, descend on Birnley's mill, where Birnley is about to announce the discovery to the press. But the mill owners want the cloth suppressed, fearing it will ruin them and everyone else in the clothing business, and Birnley is forced to go along with them.

The mill owners confront Sid with a new contract. He starts to sign it, then hesitates, suspecting their intentions. They offer him a quarter of a million pounds for control of the fiber. Sid refuses and tries to leave.

The mill owners, however, have no intention of letting Sid get away, and a brawl takes place. Sid escapes from the office, and the others give chase. When Sid accidentally knocks himself out, he's taken to Birnley's home and locked in the attic.

Rumors of the new cloth leak to the press, and the bottom drops out of the textile market. The mill owners are frantic; they must get control of the cloth. When Daphne enters, they hit on the idea of using her to persuade Sid. Even Corland, her supposed fiancé, endorses the plan. Daphne, no fool, demands 5,000 pounds for her trouble. Sir John Kierlaw agrees.

Daphne attempts to "seduce" Sid into giving in, but Sid holds firm. Daphne is delighted; she has only been testing him.

Daphne suggests Sid go to the newspapers and make the whole story public. Sid reminds her they're locked in the attic. With Daphne's help, Sid uses a spool of his unbreakable thread to let himself down the side of the house and escape. Meanwhile, the mill owners learn the workers have gone on strike as a protest against the new cloth.

At the railroad station, Sid finds he doesn't have enough money for a ticket. He races back to his rooming house for more money and runs into Bertha. Sid is glad to see her until he discovers she is against him too. Bertha manages to lock him in his room, posting her friend Harry as guard.

The union Works Committee arrives at Birnley's home to state its grievances. But even though labor and management agree Sid's invention must be suppressed, their natural suspicion toward each other keeps them from getting together.

Back at the rooming house, Sid gets a little girl to distract Harry and escapes. When the news reaches Birnley's home, labor and management finally unite

Labor confronts management. The old man seated in the chair behind the desk is Sir John Kierlaw (Ernest Thesiger).

Daphne (Joan Greenwood) prepares to "seduce" Sid.

to find Sid and stop him.

Sid is chased all over town, his luminous white suit making him easy to spot. He runs into his landlady, Mrs. Watson, returning with her laundry basket. Sid asks her for something to cover his suit, but instead she accuses him: "Why can't you scientists leave things alone?" she asks. "What about my bit of washing when there's no washing to do?" She walks away.

A sudden awareness of all the implications behind his discovery creeps across Sid's face. Yet there's a kind of determination there also.

Sid is surrounded by the mob. He tries to push his way through, but angry hands reach out for him— and his suit comes apart. The fibers, it seems, are unstable. The crowd goes wild, ripping Sid's suit to pieces, leaving him finally in only his shirt and shorts.

The crowd suddenly quiets, as if the meaning of their actions has finally sunk in. The camera lingers on Daphne a moment, her face a mixture of concern and disappointment. Someone steps forward and gives Sid a coat.

Next day Sid leaves Birnley's mill for good. As he walks away reading his notes, he pauses, and a look of comprehension lights up his face. "I see!" he says, and takes off purposefully down the street. Somehow, we know this is not the end of Sidney Stratton.

MWS was a product of Ealing Studios, a small British film company that got its start in 1931, but which really blossomed in the late forties and early fifties. Ealing developed a distinctive style of satirical comedy, making use of such writers as Roger Mac-Dougall, John Dighton, T. E. B. Clarke, and directors Robert Hamer, Charles Crichton, and Alexander Mackendrick.

Part of Ealing's success was due to the influence of producer Michael Balcon. Balcon was a pioneer in the British film industry, and responsible for many advances in it. Balcon, for example, was the first producer to recognize the talents of Alfred Hitchcock. In 1938, Balcon joined Ealing and supervised many of their most successful achievements. Some of his other films are *Dead of Night* (1945), *Saturday Night and Sunday Morning* (1960), and *Tom Jones* (1963).

MWS benefits enormously from the pointed direction of Alexander Mackendrick. His style in *MWS* is deliberate and subtle, with meticulous attention to detail in every scene. Yet Mackendrick manages to take a film which is essentially intellectual in nature and keep it moving so the viewer is never bored.

The film is marked by Mackendrick's strong sense of composition. The viewer often gets the feeling he's looking at a painting in which the painter/director has carefully measured the relationship between the characters and objects on his canvas.

Mackendrick spent long hours setting up the scenes for *MWS*, rehearsing his actors until he felt each scene was exactly right. To aid in his setups, Mackendrick worked from sketches he made himself and pasted into the script.

Mackendrick's almost uncanny sense of composition does more than just give *MWS* a distinctive look. The director seems unusually aware of how a scene's structure contributes to its overall effect, as in the sequence where the mill owners try to trick Sid into giving up his rights to the cloth. The actors are carefully placed to reveal their attitudes and create maximum tension. Sid is seated facing Sir John Kierlaw, who is behind a huge desk. Two of the mill owners stand on either side of Sid, forming an almost perfect

Sid (Alec Guinness) displays his miraculous suit to Frank (Patric Doonan) and Bertha (Vida Hope).

triangle. Birnley, the unwilling conspirator, stands near Kierlaw, but off to one side.

There is a sense of oppression in the scene, a feeling that Sid is surrounded, as if the mill owners were ready to pounce on him—which they are. Birnley's placement conveys clearly his ambivalence toward the events. The composition of the scene contributes almost subconsciously to the way we feel about the people in it.

The use of composition to show relationships is also evident in the scene where labor and management confront each other. Mackendrick places labor on one side of the room and management on the other, with a clear *visual* gap between them, emphasizing their mutual animosity. Interestingly, when the two sides hear Sid is on the loose, they stream out of Birnley's house in a group, united finally by mutual greed and self-interest.

Alexander Mackendrick, born in Boston in 1912, is an American of Scottish descent. Mackendrick eventually went to Britain, where he became involved in making industrial documentaries, experience which shows up in *MWS*'s depiction of the textile industry. During World War II Mackendrick made films for British Intelligence.

After the war Mackendrick entered commercial films as a screenwriter and graduated to directing, with *Whiskey Galore* (*Tight Little Island*, 1948). His other films include *The Ladykillers* (1955), *The Sweet Smell of Success* (1957), *A Boy Ten Feet Tall* (*Sammy*

Going South, 1962), and *A High Wind in Jamaica* (1965). Mackendrick made one more movie, *Don't Make Waves* (1967), before dropping out of films to accept a post at the California Institute of the Arts (see Appendix).

No plot summary can really give a sense of the humor in *MWS*. Much of it is pure slapstick: the chemist who keeps swallowing the contents of his pipette; Corland nearly choking when he finds out how much Sid has cost him; the comic brawl in Birnley's office; the butler who ends up falling on the valuable vase he's been trying to protect.

But the bulk of the humor in *MWS* is satiric. The film's comedy is aimed squarely at the greed and pomposity of the mill owners at least at first. Later, the focus expands to include the workers. They are shown to be just as greedy and self-interested as the mill owners.

Yet there are few belly laughs in *MWS*. The humor is dry, often biting. Even the physical humor fails to elicit much more than a chuckle. Perhaps this is because beneath the film's comedy there's a very unpleasant view of humanity. It's hard to forget the amoral self-interest of Sir John Kierlaw, or the look of absolute horror that passes over Sid's face when he finds Bertha is against him too.

No one comes off very well in *MWS*. One gets the feeling that if the mob had not ripped Sid's suit to pieces, they would have gladly done it to him. *MWS* is ultimately a satire on human greed. If it has one specific message, it's that when the individual pocketbook is threatened, the public welfare be damned—a theme with an uncomfortable ring of truth to it.

Credit for *MWS*'s mixture of humor and seriousness belongs to Mackendrick, John Dighton, and Roger MacDougall. The original idea came from an unpublished play of MacDougall's, and the screenplay was nominated for an Oscar in 1952. MacDougall would later script another science-fictional satire, *The Mouse that Roared* (1959). Dighton had already worked on another of Ealing's classic comedies, *Kind Hearts and Coronets* (1949).

MWS belongs to the long tradition of satire in SF. Lucian of Samosata's *True History* (A.D. 2nd Century), one of the first works of SF cited by literary historians, is a satire. Other early satires involved trips to the moon, lost continents, or other imaginary worlds. Best known, perhaps, is Jonathan Swift's *Gulliver's Travels* (1726).

Science fiction allows writers to comment on society by distancing the reader from it in time or space, by exaggerating current trends, or by speculating on the effects of technology on society. SF satire flourished particularly during the 1950s in the SF magazine *Galaxy*, edited by H. L. Gold.

SF satire has proven a fertile ground for many writers, among them Kurt Vonnegut, Jr., William Tenn, Fredric Brown, Robert Sheckley, and Ron Goulart. The most famous SF satires are probably those of Frederick Pohl and C. M. Kornbluth, whose novel *The Space Merchants* about an Earth controlled by advertising agencies, stands as a classic of the genre.

While not precisely satire, the most interesting analogue to *MWS* is the story "Let There Be Light" (1940) by Robert Heinlein. In it two scientists find a cheap way to convert sunlight into electricity, and find themselves opposed by the power industry.

Heinlein's story also includes a reference to "Breakages, Ltd.," a corporate entity mentioned in George Bernard Shaw's *The Apple Cart* (1930), which is devoted to suppressing discoveries that threaten

Sidney Stratton (Alec Guinness) confronts Sir John Kierlaw (Ernest Thesiger, with back to camera) while Cranford (Howard Marion Crawford, left), Corland (Michael Gough, right), and Birnley (Cecil Parker, far right) look on.

THE MAN IN THE WHITE SUIT

established industries. Both "Let There Be Light" and *MWS* have some of the flavor of Shaw's writing.

Special effects are not a major part of *MWS*, but they do play a role in making the film convincing. To show the cloth repelling ink a sequence was filmed in which mercury was poured on a piece of black material. Naturally, the mercury beaded and ran. To produce the effect, the sequence was printed in the film as a negative, so the black cloth appears white, and the silvery mercury looks like black ink.

At one point Sid brushes dirt off his sleeve, leaving his suit spotless. Accomplishing this effect required some careful editing. As Sid starts to brush the dirt off, filming was stopped and another white jacket substituted. Another shot of Sid brushing his sleeve was made. When the beginning of the first "brushing" was combined with the end of the second, the illusion was complete.

Showing Sid walking down the side of the house required a mock-up of the outer wall built parallel to the floor. Then, Alec Guinness simply walked backward on it, holding onto a taut spool of white thread, while the camera filmed the scene tilted on its side.

Equally important are the film's efforts to convince us of the reality of Sid's fiber. In one scene this involves showing us how the weaver cuts her finger when she tries to pluck the thread from the loom. Shortly after, the unique properties of the thread are demonstrated when it succeeds in breaking the machine designed to test its tensile strength—before the machine can break it!

Benjamin Frankel's score for *MWS* is unusual for its almost symphonic quality. The music ranges from stirring to whimsical. Most noticeable is its brassy, metallic quality, which seems to reflect the workings of modern industry. Strangely enough, while Frankel's score has never been released as a recording, the belching, gurgling noises of Sid's chemical apparatus were seized on by some enterprising (?) musician, and set to music as "The White Suit Samba."

From left to right: Cranford (Howard Marion Crawford), Sid (Alec Guiness), and Michael Corland (Michael Gough).

Since satire deals largely with ideas, individual characterization is often neglected. This is at least partly true in *MWS*, but Mackendrick works hard to give his characters some sense of identity beyond stereotyping. A great deal of his success, of course, comes from the remarkable company of actors assembled for *MWS*.

Sir Alec Guinness is one of the most versatile actors ever to appear on the screen. Born in London in 1914, Guinness joined Britain's Old Vic Repertory in 1936, enjoying a long and successful stage career before making his film debut as Herbert Pocket in *Great Expectations* (1946).

During his time at Ealing, Guinness undertook a series of bizarre roles. In *The Lavender Hill Mob* (1951) he was a quiet bank teller who plans a big heist. In *The Ladykillers* (1955) he was a mad criminal genius, and in *Kind Hearts and Coronets* (1949) Guinness played *eight* different roles.

Guinness has appeared in all kinds of films and has rarely repeated himself. He won an Oscar for his role in *The Bridge on the River Kwai* (1957). His films include *Tunes of Glory* (1960), *Lawrence of Arabia* (1962), *Doctor Zhivago* (1966), and *Hitler—The Last Ten Days* (1973).

More recently, Guinness appeared as Obi-wan Kenobi, Luke Skywalker's mentor, in *Star Wars* (1977) and its sequel, *The Empire Strikes Back* (1980), receiving an Oscar nomination for his performance in the first film. Guinness was knighted in 1959 and awarded a special Oscar in 1980 in recognition of his career.

Guinness brings a marvelous innocence and vulnerability to Sidney Stratton. Yet while he's innocent, he isn't stupid, catching on quickly to what the mill owners want from him. Sid's dedication and idealism make him easy to identify with, but that same dedication makes him insensitive to Bertha. Interestingly, when Daphne shows a similar insensitivity by laughing at him, Sid is hurt himself.

Joan Greenwood is known for her unmistakable voice and her portrayals of intelligent, independent women. She began her stage career at seventeen, making her film debut in *John Smith Wakes Up* (1940). Her other films include *Whiskey Galore* (1948), *Kind Hearts and Coronets* (1949), *Tom Jones* (1963), and *The Moon Spinners* (1964).

Daphne is a typical role for Greenwood—attractive and feminine, but with a hard-edged toughness and intelligence. She faces off with the fearsome Sir John Kierlaw and comes out on top. Daphne quickly grasps the essentials of Sid's ideas and is thoroughly sympathetic with his goals.

But there's another side to Daphne. She's anxious to leave the small mill town she's grown up in and sees Corland as her ticket out. When he fails her, she turns to Sid. It's Daphne who labels Sid "a knight in shining armor," but when the suit falls apart and the knight fails, she is obviously disappointed. When Sid leaves Birnley's, he leaves alone.

Cecil Parker was a long time character actor, on screen from 1933, often in snobbish roles of one sort or another. Parker appeared in such films as *Father Brown* (1954), *The Admirable Crichton* (1957), *A Tale of Two Cities* (1958), and *Oh What a Lovely War* (1969). He died in 1971.

Birnley is one of Parker's more rounded portrayals, stuffy but no fool. While his reaction to Sid is negative at first, he's eventually persuaded to come around. He is reluctant to join the schemes of the other mill owners, and shows a surprising fatherly concern for Daphne when he learns his colleagues plan to use her as a weapon against Sid.

The late Vida Hope had a long career in British films as a character actress, often in roles similar to her portrayal in *MWS*. Like Daphne, Bertha is a tough, self-sufficient woman, although she represents a kind of unthinking, automatic response to the mill owners. Whatever *they're* for, *she's* against. Hope's character is especially interesting, since her attraction to Sid doesn't stop her from turning against him, and then rationalizing it's for his own good.

Michael Gough has been acting since 1936. He may be familiar to SF/horror fans for his roles in several British horror films, such as *Horror of Dracula*, (1958), *Konga* (1961), *Dr. Terror's House of Horrors* (1965), and others. *MWS* misleads us, since Gough at first looks like the hero of the film, but his greed and hypocrisy soon emerge, and he becomes one of the film's villains.

It's sometimes hard to believe Ernest Thesiger was ever young. By the time of his film debut in *The Old Dark House* (1932), Thesiger had been acting for nearly twenty-five years. SF fans will best remember him as "Dr. Praetorius," the crazed scientist who makes miniature people in *The Bride of Frankenstein* (1935).

Thesiger's portrayal of Sir John Kierlaw is one of the most interesting in *MWS*. At first, all we see of him is his huge car and a dark figure in a massive fur coat. Birnley trembles at the mention of his name. Kierlaw is carefully made to seem mysterious and all-powerful.

When we finally see Kierlaw, he turns out to be a wizened old man, barely capable of getting around on his own. But there is something utterly sinister about him. When the other mill owners voice concern about the rest of the clothing industry, Kierlaw demands they get back to the point—the effect Sid's discovery will have on *them*. He's ready to use force to get what he wants from Sid, ready to pay any price, human or otherwise.

Yet Kierlaw seems to have a knowledge the other owners lack. He exchanges looks with Sid and Daphne that suggest a common understanding. But Kierlaw's understanding makes no difference—his self-interest comes first. He is a totally unprincipled, amoral representative of the modern industrial world.

Howard Marion Crawford (Cranford) may also be familiar to film fans. Crawford specialized in playing bluff, hearty Englishmen in many films, such as *Lawrence of Arabia* (1962), but he also turned up as Dr. Watson in the fifties' *Sherlock Holmes* TV series with Ronald Howard, and as Dr. Petrie in several of the Dr. Fu Manchu films produced by Hammer Studios in the sixties.

Like any good SF film, *MWS* tries to provide a convincing scientific background for its speculations. A chemist was hired as scientific adviser for the film, and it was his job not only to check for accuracy, but also to come up with impressive but harmless chemical reactions for the camera.

To reinforce the scientific basis for Sid's material, hints are dropped that he's using "heavy hydrogen" (or deuterium) and radioactive thorium in his work. As in much early SF, the suggestion that the mysterious properties of radioactivity are involved allows for an easier suspension of disbelief by the audience.

Sid also gives Daphne a long explanation of his work, which she elaborates on later to her father. No matter that most of it is nonsense; it's the scientific rationalization that counts.

Like most satires, *MWS* makes us laugh, but it also makes us think. *MWS* uses humor to ask some important questions about science and the desirability of progress.

Sidney Stratton represents a kind of exaggerated scientific ideal, a man totally dedicated to progress. His love for science is evident in the delight we see in his face when he examines Birnley's lab, in the awe with which he regards an electron microscope, and in the persistence which keeps him working in a series of miserable jobs so he can continue his scientific quest.

Yet the image of the scientist in *MWS* isn't too different from the one we find in dozens of other SF movies—not mad necessarily, but at least a little crack-brained. Overall, however, Sid is a likable fellow, and we're meant to sympathize with his commitment to scientific progress.

The mill owners appear to be the villains, wanting to suppress Sid's discovery for their own benefit. But they express a very real concern when they point out that Sid's invention will affect the livelihood of everyone from sheepherders to tailors, indeed, anyone even remotely connected with the clothing business.

The benefits of a material that repels dirt and never wears out are obvious, but there's no denying that such an invention could disrupt the lives of hundreds of thousands of people. Suddenly, the issue is not so clear-cut, and we find ourselves caught between Sid's idealism and the greed of Sir John Kierlaw.

The value of scientific progress is questioned more directly by Sid's landlady, who asks him why scientists always have to meddle in everything. His invention threatens even the washing she does to supplement her income.

Sid is stunned by her attitude. He has no desire to hurt this woman who's been kind to him, and he's suddenly forced—as we are—to reconsider the ideals he's believed in for many years. Perhaps unchecked scientific progress isn't always such a good idea.

On the other hand, Sidney Stratton isn't defeated at the end of *MWS*. It is implied that he will try again, perhaps with the same chaotic results. The important thing is that he *will* try, no matter what the results, and keep on trying until he reaches his goal.

Sidney Stratton, like progress, can't be stopped. Technology is no genie to be tricked back into the bottle and sealed up forever. And if the genie won't go back in, *MWS* asks, what are the consequences?

The real issue at the heart of *MWS* is whether or not the human race is prepared to pay a price for technology. Are we willing to live with pollution? Can we face the risks of nuclear power? Are we ready to deal with the social implications of so-called "test-tube babies"? How much are we prepared to spend—or lose—and how much disruption in our lives will we accept to ensure the greatest good for everyone? Though *MWS* takes a lighthearted approach to this issue, beneath the humor there are serious questions waiting to be answered.

Thanks to a remarkably literate script, incisive direction, and a truly marvelous cast, *The Man in the White Suit* succeeds as a delightful example of both science fiction and satire. SF satire is a particularly useful medium for social commentary because it lets us see our society from a different perspective. As in *The Man in the White Suit*, SF satire forces us to confront our ideas, our traditions, and ourselves—and in doing so we often discover we're not really comfortable with what we see.

DONOVAN'S BRAIN

A United Artists/Dowling Productions Release. Running Time: 83 minutes. Black and White, 35 mm. Based on the novel by Curt Siodmak. Opened in New York City at the Criterion Theater, January 20, 1954.

PRODUCTION CREDITS

PRODUCER	Tom Gries
DIRECTOR	Felix Feist
SCREENPLAY	Felix Feist
ADAPTATION	Hugh Brooke
PRODUCTION DESIGNER	Boris Leven
CINEMATOGRAPHER	Joseph Biroc
SPECIAL EFFECTS	Harry Redmond, Jr.
EDITOR	Herbert L. Strock
MUSIC	Eddie Dunstedter

CAST

DR. PATRICK CORY	Lew Ayres
JANICE CORY	Nancy Davis
DR. FRANK SCHRATT	Gene Evans
HERBIE YOCUM	Steve Brodie
CHLOE DONOVAN	Lisa K. Howard
ADVISER	Tom Powers
TOM DONOVAN	Michael Colgan
RANGER TUTTLE	Kyle James
MR. WEBSTER	Peter Adams
W. J. HIGGINS	Stapleton Kent
NATHANIEL FULLER	Victor Sutherland
BANK MANAGER	John Hamilton

Curt Siodmak's novel, *Donovan's Brain*, has been filmed three times. The book itself has sold over five million copies in ten languages. Orson Welles even adapted it for the 1940s' radio series *Suspense*. While Siodmak was certainly not the first in science fiction to write about the concept of a brain divorced from its body, *Donovan's Brain* set a pattern for the countless imitations that would follow it. The popularity of Siodmak's novel—and the idea behind it—suggests there is something about this image of the brain freed from the confines of the body that captures and holds the imagination.

In 1944 Republic Pictures released a version of Siodmak's novel called *The Lady and the Monster* with Eric von Stroheim, taking massive liberties with the original story. The 1962 Stross-CCC production, *Vengeance* (see Appendix), with Peter van Eyck, also altered Siodmak's plot.

Of the three film versions of *Donovan's Brain*, the one which most nearly captures the spirit of Siodmak's novel—though it too made changes—is the 1953 United Artists/Dowling Production, which bears the novel's title and stars Lew Ayres.

At the time of its release, *Donovan's Brain* (hereafter referred to as *DB*) attracted very little attention. Of the major newspapers and periodicals of the time, only the *New York Times*—doing its duty—bothered to review it, calling the film "a limp and artificial thing," lacking in visual strength. Critics of SF film have also been quick to dismiss it.

There is no doubt that *DB* is a low-budget film, with its share of hokum; yet it has a maturity and competence, as well as a powerful central idea, which makes it stand out among the run of SF/horror films of the 1950s.

Dr. Patrick Cory and his wife Janice are returning to their home in Green Valley with a monkey to be used in Pat's experiments. Janice is worried about the animal. "Are you going to make friends with this one too?" Pat asks. There is a note of both concern and foreboding in the question.

Arriving home, Cory finds his friend, Dr. Frank Schratt, drunk as usual. But Pat needs Frank's help, and, with plenty of coffee and a shower, he manages to get him on his feet.

Cory (Lew Ayres), Schratt (Gene Evans) and Janice Cory (Nancy Davis) look on anxiously as an experiment with a monkey brain proceeds.

Donovan's children Tom (Michael Colgan) and Chloe (Lisa K. Howard) ask Cory (Lew Ayres) if their father had any last words, but he can't help them.

Pat plans to remove the monkey's brain in an attempt to keep it alive outside the body. Janice tries to argue him out of the operation, but Pat points out his research with animals could save human lives one day, and Janice relents.

The operation is successful. The monkey's brain is kept alive in a tank of nutrient solution and maintained electrically.

While Frank naps and Pat watches the brain, Janice gets a phone call from Tuttle, a local Ranger. There has been a plane crash, and Tuttle is trying to find Schratt, who is employed by the county to deal with such emergencies. With Schratt unavailable, Tuttle asks Cory to come to the wreck. Pat refuses at first, but when Janice points out that a human life is at stake, Pat realizes his duty.

At the wreck, Pat finds the only survivor will never live to reach a hospital. Tuttle suggests they take him to Cory's home.

As Cory prepares to operate, Tuttle tells him the man is millionaire W. H. Donovan, but Pat is unimpressed. Assisted by a now-recovered Frank, Pat operates on Donovan, but is unable to save him.

Cory suddenly gets an idea. Attaching the electrodes of an oscilloscope to Donovan's temples, he finds the dead man's brain is still active.

Without a second thought, Cory prepares to remove the dead man's brain. Janice and Frank try to talk him out of it—it's illegal to operate on a corpse —but Pat is adamant. Shortly after, Cory has his second success of the day. Donovan's brain is alive and well and living in a tank in Cory's lab.

Cory becomes fascinated with the brain, barely stopping to eat or sleep. Frank finally persuades him to come to town with him. Hospital officials are after Frank for negligence in the Donovan case, and he wants Pat to speak for him.

At the hospital Pat meets Donovan's grown children. They ask if Donovan had any last words. Pat can't help them. Pat also meets a shifty photographer named Yocum who wants pictures of the place where Donovan died. Yocum has seen Donovan's body in the morgue and is curious about the stitches in the corpse's head. "There was a plane crash," says Cory.

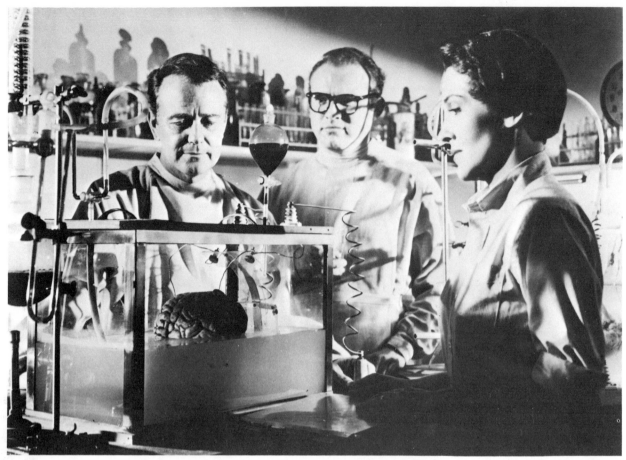

Dr. Patrick Cory (Lew Ayres) examines his second triumph, the living brain of Warren Donovan. Dr. Frank Schratt (Gene Evans) and Janice Cory look on apprehensively.

"He had extensive injuries."

Afraid to arouse Yocum's suspicions, Cory takes him to his house. Yocum notices the brain and manages to sneak a picture of it before he leaves.

The brain actually begins to grow. The oscilloscope shows definite patterns in the brain's output, but Cory is unable to figure out their meaning, and he is rapidly becoming obsessed with the problem.

Cory finally hits on the idea of contacting the brain by telepathy. He asks Jan to go to town and dig up as much information on Donovan as she can.

Pat begins to construct a mental image of Donovan. He is described as having a "lined, granitelike face and piercing eyes." Nephritis had left him with a limp, and he walked with his right hand on his side, soothing his aching kidney.

Donovan was a self-made man—cold, possessive, and merciless. The government had been trying to collect back taxes from him for years. The picture of Donovan which emerges is one of a cruel, vicious individual. But Pat doesn't seem to notice.

Late that night, as Pat observes the brain, its electrical output increases, and Pat goes into a trance. Taking a pencil from the desk, the normally right-handed Cory writes something with his *left* hand, then collapses.

The next morning, Jan and Frank find Pat asleep at his desk. In front of him is a note that says "Get to N. Fuller." The signature is "W. H. Donovan." Cory realizes he's made mental contact with Donovan's brain.

Cory begins to "imitate" Donovan's mannerisms whenever the brain is active, reverting to his normal self when the brain is dormant. Slowly, it takes complete possession of him while Frank and Janice watch helplessly.

The brain sends Pat to the city on a mysterious mission. By the time he checks into Donovan's favorite hotel, Cory's features have hardened, and he is limping, hand on his side, in the manner of the late Mr. Donovan. Pat's normally affable nature and kindness have been replaced by an unfeeling selfishness.

Cory runs into Yocum, who notes the doctor's odd behavior and follows him to a bank, where he watches Cory write a check with his left hand. The check is drawn on the account of a mysterious "Roger Hinds" for $27,000. As Cory leaves the bank, the manager phones the Treasury Department.

Next, Cory forces his way into the office of Nathaniel Fuller, a lawyer, ordering Fuller to arrange a meeting for him with Donovan's "Washington Connection." Fuller refuses, but Cory persuades him when he mentions "certain checks" in his possession bearing Fuller's endorsement.

Back at the hotel, Cory is visited by two Treasury agents. They are curious about the $27,000, suspecting it has some connection with Donovan's delinquent taxes. Cory refuses to help them, and they leave him with a warning.

Yocum appears. He has put two and two together and wants money to keep quiet about the brain. Reluctantly, Cory pays him.

Cory charters a plane to Green Valley. As he walks in the door, the brain releases him, and he collapses into a chair. A few minutes later, $8,000 worth of equipment he purchased to automatically care for the brain arrives at the house. Cory hastens to install it.

That night, worried that the brain is becoming too powerful, Frank tries to cut its electricity at the fuse box. The brain detects his actions and sends Cory after him. Janice manages to pull him off Frank before Cory strangles him, and Cory makes Frank promise not to interfere again.

Cory flies back to the city the next day to meet Fuller and the "connection," whom he calls "Mr. Adviser." Cory is now a bizarre replica of Donovan, right down to the clothes he wears and the cigars he smokes.

Cory demands that the Adviser continue his efforts to quash the tax case against Donovan. When the man refuses, Cory says he has evidence that can ruin him as well as Fuller.

After they leave, the brain releases Cory. Gasping, he tries to phone Janice, but the circuits are busy. Pat tape records a message to her, saying he may not be able to break free of the brain again. He outlines a plan of which we hear only the beginning.

With Donovan in control again, Cory leaves the hotel in a cab, a Treasury agent in pursuit. The cab-driver refuses to lose the pursuer and pulls over. Cory suddenly gets out and steps right into the path of an oncoming truck.

Jan arrives at the hospital to see Pat. He is unconscious, but his injuries are minor. When he awakens, free of the brain for a time, Pat tells her about the recording he's made, and asks her to reduce the current to the brain when she gets home. Suddenly, Donovan takes over again and orders Jan away.

Instead of leaving, however, Jan phones Frank and relays Pat's instructions. Frank tries to turn down the power, the brain uses its mental powers to stop him.

Yocum shows up at the hospital demanding more money. Cory suggests he go to the lab for more pictures of the brain. When Yocum arrives, Frank leaves him in the lab. A few minutes later, Yocum gets into his car and drives off a cliff—another victim of the brain's power.

Cory leaves the hospital. At Fuller's office he orders the lawyer to have a permanent vault constructed to house Donovan's "remains."

Returning to Green Valley, Donovan decides Frank and Janice must die. Meanwhile, Janice has listened to Pat's tape, and she and Frank have followed his instructions. However, Frank persuades her that they must act immediately. She is to keep Cory/Donovan outside while he attempts to destroy the brain.

A thunderstorm is brewing as Cory/Donovan arrives. Jan suggests they take a walk. Realizing this will give him a chance to get rid of her, he agrees. Suddenly dropping all pretense, Janice pleads with Pat to break free, but "Donovan" attacks her. In the lab Frank fires a pistol at the brain. Outside, Cory collapses in Jan's arms, apparently free of the brain.

But the brain has merely turned its attention to Frank, forcing him to shoot himself. As Janice helps Pat back to the house, the characteristic Donovan limp returns. The storm continues to build.

When they reach the lab, Janice realizes what has happened. "Donovan" forces her to look at the brain, which begins to take over her mind as a prelude to killing her.

Suddenly, a lightning bolt from the storm strikes the lightning rod on the roof. The surge of power, hooked into the brain's electrical system, according to Pat's plan, overloads the equipment and sets the brain afire, destroying it.

A few days later Pat is getting ready to go the city for an investigation of the Donovan affair. Whether he will go to prison is unresolved. Frank, who has recovered from his wound, is going along to testify in Pat's behalf.

Pat promises Janice that if he gets out of this mess, he'll settle for the life of a plain country doctor. No, she tells him, he's a scientist and always will be. Grateful for her faith in him, Cory leaves to face the consequences of his actions.

DB first appeared not in a science fiction magazine, but in the mystery magazine *Black Mask*, in 1942. In 1943 Knopf brought the novel out in hardcover. The *New York Times* praised the novel, saying "Any reader who will check his skepticism at the title page will be certain to finish it in one sitting."

This may be something of an overstatement, since the writing in *DB* is somewhat stiff and occasionally melodramatic. Yet there are moments in the novel that are handled extremely well, as when Siodmak describes Cory's sensations of being cut off from the world while trapped in his own body by Donovan.

Although the 1953 version of *DB* is closer to Siodmak's novel than any of the others, changes were made for the film. The novel is told in the form of a first-person journal by Cory. Cory himself is not quite as sympathetic a character in the book as Lew Ayres is in the film. Yet as Cory becomes more and more a victim of Donovan, sympathy for him increases.

Cory is also estranged from Janice in the novel, but their relationship improves as Cory realizes his mistakes. The Dr. Schratt of the novel is an older man than in the film, and it's Schratt who sacrifices himself to destroy the brain. Other changes were made to make some of the novel's more tangled plot elements manageable for the screen.

Siodmak did write a script for the film and had a contract to direct it as well. His script, however, was rejected and the contract terminated by the production company. Siodmak has never seen any of the films of *DB*, finding it hard to reconcile the many changes in them with his own vision of the novel.

Curt Siodmak is a prolific author, with several SF novels to his credit: *Skyport* (1959), *Hauser's Memory* (1968), *The Third Ear* (1971), and *City in the Sky* (1974). *Hauser's Memory*, though not a sequel, has connections with *DB*, and was made into a TV movie with David McCallum in 1970. (For information on Siodmak's film career, see the chapter on *The Magnetic Monster*.)

Felix Feist's direction of *DB* lacks many of the flourishes that distinguish some of the famous SF films of the fifties, such as *The Day the Earth Stood Still* or *Invasion of the Body Snatchers*, but the film is no less successful for that. The direction is plain but effective, with Feist's primary concern being to tell the story. *DB* is carefully put together, measured in its pace, and unhysterical in its treatment of its characters and theme. If sheer competence is any measure of a film, *DB* certainly deserves high marks.

This isn't to say Feist didn't take advantage of the tricks of the director's trade. Cory's lab, for example, is always dimly lit, reinforcing the darker aspects of the experiment going on in it, as well as masking the incomplete realism of the rubber "brain."

Lew Ayres, who isn't very tall, was made to seem taller and more dominating by shooting several scenes from the viewpoints of characters sitting down, so he appears to tower over them.

The scene in which the brain contacts Cory for the first time was shot on a slant, giving the moment a surrealistic effect. Feist also made sure we never get a look at Donovan either in a picture or in Cory's lab, making Ayres's performance stronger and emphasizing the idea of the brain as a malevolent, disembodied intelligence.

The last fifteen minutes or so of the film are extremely well orchestrated. Rapid intercutting between the storm, Janice and Cory outside, and Frank in the lab, builds up a powerful tension. When the supposedly dead brain forces Frank to shoot himself, we immediately cut back to Janice helping "Pat" to the house—and slowly the Donovan limp returns, unnoticed by Janice. The effect is chilling.

Janice enters the lab and realizes what's happened. "Cory" shuts the door, and the camera swiftly zooms in on his steely features. Suddenly, Donovan seems to dominate the whole screen.

As Donovan grabs Janice and forces her to look at the brain, the camera zooms in on the brain, establishing the link between the intelligence in Cory's body and the one in the tank, as well as conveying the sense of dominance again.

The tension is increased by even quicker cutting between Janice and "Cory," the brain, the mad activity of the oscilloscope, and the storm cut,—and broken finally by the lightning bolt striking the house, sending the brain up in flames. The whole sequence is a tribute to the skills of Feist and his editor, Herbert L. Strock.

Feist doubled as screenwriter for *DB*, working from an adaptation by Hugh Brooke. The screenplay is remarkably restrained, given the possibilities for lurid exploitation inherent in the idea of a brain kept alive in a tank. Later films inspired by *DB* would degenerate into such cheap shockers as *They Saved Hitler's Brain*, *The Incredible Two-Headed Transplant*, and similar gruesome efforts.

With an occasional lapse, the dialogue in *DB* is pleasantly mature for a "B" film of the fifties. Within those limitations, Feist's characters also transcend SF film stereotypes. They have a warmth and humanity generally absent in the cardboard heroes and heroines who inhabit many SF movies.

One noticeable part of this is the sexual interplay between Cory and his wife. When Janice complains that Pat's experiments aren't going to "warm her cold feet on the long winter nights," the sexual reference is unmistakable. Moreover, unlike some SF film heroes, Pat responds to the complaint, though things don't quite work out the way he plans. This small but definite violation of the sexual taboo in most SF films helps convince us that these are real people with a problem and not actors walking through a script.

Felix Feist directed more than twenty feature films in his career. None of them can be singled out as particularly distinguished, yet reviews over the years suggest his films were the work of a craftsman who knew his trade well.

Born in New York in 1906, Feist came to Hollywood in 1928 and began his directing career with short subjects. He directed several "Pete Smith" comedy shorts and a number of entries in MGM's "Crime Does Not Pay" series.

Feist's only other feature-length work in SF was the early catastrophe movie *Deluge* (1933). He directed one episode of *The Outer Limits*, ("The Probe"), and several episodes of *Voyage to the Bottom of the Sea*. Feist also served as producer of the TV series *Peyton Place*. He died in 1965.

Several other members of the *DB* production crew are worth mentioning. Producer Tom Gries worked in Hollywood as a director, producer, and writer from 1946 to his death in 1977. His western, *Will Penny* (1968), is considered an exceptional example of the genre by some critics. Gries also directed two of the better TV movies, *QB VII* (1974) and *Helter-Skelter* (1976).

Film editor Herbert L. Strock also worked on another SF film mentioned in this book, *The Magnetic Monster*, and would later direct two low-budget, horror-film parodies, *I Was a Teenage Frankenstein* (1957) and *How to Make a Monster* (1958).

Cinematographer Joseph Biroc has had a long and distinguished career in films, as has designer Boris Leven, who would later garner an Oscar for his work on *West Side Story* (1961).

It cannot be said too often that good science fiction is about the interaction of science and people. *DB* is an especially good example of an SF film which emphasizes the effects of science on its people. There are no spaceships or giant creatures in *DB*, and special effects are at a minimum. So at the core of *DB* is the actors' ability to convey the essence of the story.

Lew Ayres is immensely appealing as Patrick Cory. Cory isn't the mad scientist of so many "B" movies. Certainly, he is driven in his attempt to grasp the workings of the human mind, but that drive seems dedicated to a genuine desire to help humanity. Cory lacks the hysteria that has marked the scientist in films since Colin Clive portrayed Dr. Frankenstein.

What makes Ayres's performance even more re-markable is his transition from the warm, selfless Patrick Cory to the moral monstrosity of Warren Donovan. Ayres's ability to convey Donovan's personality through the stiffening of his features, the hard edge in his voice, and the movement of his body is a *tour de force* rivaling Spencer Tracy's portrayal in the 1941 version of *Dr. Jekyll and Mr. Hyde*. Ayres's role may have been even more difficult, since he often makes the transition from Cory to Donovan (or vice versa) in one scene, with hardly a pause between one sentence and the next. His performance as Donovan is especially interesting, since Ayres rarely, if ever, got to play a villainous role.

Lew Ayres was born in Minneapolis, Minnesota, in 1908. While studying medicine at the University of Arizona he was spotted and given a small role in *The Sophomore* (1928). A year later he played opposite Greta Garbo in *The Kiss*, then signed to play the young soldier in *All Quiet on the Western Front* (1930).

Ayres's boyish features hampered his transition to more adult roles for a time. His career took off again in 1938 when he starred in *Young Dr. Kildare*. Ayres

At Donovan's direction, Cory removes $27,000 from the account of the mysterious "Roger Hinds."

made eight more of the "Kildare" movies, becoming a movie idol in the process.

A man of strong religious and moral beliefs, Ayres's stand as a conscientious objector during World War II didn't endear him to the studios, though he served overseas as an assistant chaplain and medical corpsman. He did not work in pictures again until 1946. In 1948 he appeared with Jane Wyman in *Johnny Belinda*, and resumed his career.

Ayres dropped out of films again in 1955 to make a documentary on Eastern religions, *Altars of the East*. He returned to movies in 1962, playing the Vice-President in *Advise and Consent*.

Since his last comeback, Ayres has appeared in several films with elements of SF or fantasy: *The Man* (1972), *Battle for the Planet of the Apes* (1973), and *Damien—Omen II* (1978).

Ayres has also appeared in a number of TV films with SF/fantasy themes, including, *The People Trap* (1966, from a story by SF writer Robert Sheckley), *Earth II* (1971), *She Waits* (1972), *The Stranger* (1973), *The Questor Tapes* (1974), *Battlestar Galactica* (1978), and *Salem's Lot* (1979).

Nancy Davis complements Ayres's performance fairly well, though she sometimes seems a little too good to be true. On the other hand, she and Ayres make a warmly-convincing couple, who rapidly gain the audience's sympathies. The role itself stands out, since it portrays a loving, competent woman who remains unhysterical throughout the film.

Davis's career as a leading lady was brief. She appeared in such films as *The Next Voice You Hear* (1950), *It's a Big Country* (1953), and *Hellcats of the Navy* (1959) with Ronald Reagan, whom she'd married in 1952. Davis eventually retired from films.

DB gave Gene Evans one of his rare chances to play a good guy. Evans has been playing tough guys and heavies in films since 1947. His role in *DB* provides not only a necessary male counterpoint to Ayres, but some comedy relief as well. Evans's only other SF film—and one in which he actually got to play the hero—is *The Giant Behemoth* (a.k.a. *Behemoth, The Sea Monster*, 1959). He also had the adult lead in the TV series *My Friend Flicka*, and appeared more recently in a short-lived series called *Spencer's Pilots*. (For a note about some of the other actors in *DB* see the Appendix.)

DB isn't a film that dwells heavily on its scientific content, but the proper "hints" necessary to provide the scientific foundation are there. The correct use of the term "alpha" and "beta" waves to describe varying states of brain activity as seen on the oscilloscope suggest Cory and the others know what they're talking about.

There are other indications that Feist did his homework for *DB*. When Cory operates on Donovan, using adrenalin injected into the heart and open heart massage, he reveals a familiarity with medical techniques still fairly new for the time.

Schratt's comments on tissue preservation and Cory's on the chemical nature of thought also indicate an attempt to provide a scientific basis for the film. Also, when Cory thinks of contacting the brain by telepathy, he mentions the experiments at Duke University where scientists are still exploring the possibilities of extrasensory perception and related phenomena.

These things provide the background that makes us believe the action in *DB* is possible. Unfortunately, there are some unlikely elements as well.

The growth of the brain and its pulsations as nutrient fluid flows through it are both possible, but the latter is a bit overdone. The brain also glows at times, but we can put this, as well as the heavy pulsations, down to the needs of the visual medium to show some action in so static an object as a brain.

One unusual flaw is the repeated references to the device that shows the brain's activity as an "oscillograph." An oscillograph is properly a device which records vibrations on paper; the device that shows them on a screen is an oscillo*scope*. The error isn't a major one, but it sticks out in a film which appears to have been generally well researched.

Some critics have complained that *DB* is just another anti-scientific 1950s horror film, dressed up with scientific trappings. This, of course, depends on your personal definition of SF. Author Theodore Sturgeon defines a good SF story as one "built around human beings, with a human problem, and a human solution, which would not have happened at all without its scientific content." This definition certainly fits *DB*.

DB embraces at least two common SF themes. First, there is the theme of "possession" (for a discussion of this theme, see the chapters on *Invasion of the Body Snatchers* and *Village of the Damned*). Second, and more clearly, there is the "Frankenstein" theme, in which the creation attacks its creator, and we are left with the moral that "there are some things man was not meant to know." (For a discussion of this theme, see the chapter on *Colossus*.)

The fact that *DB* touches on the Frankenstein theme is at least partially responsible for its labeling as anti-scientific. But *DB* is essentially a cautionary tale, and such stories are as much a part of SF as those which extol the virtues of science and technology. As suggested elsewhere in this book (see the *Colossus* chapter), there is probably nothing man was not meant to know—but there are many things he should have the wisdom not to inflict on himself.

Critics often argue that the religious elements in *DB* make it anti-scientific. Frank calls the experiment "unnatural" and "unholy," to which Pat replies, "If it is, we'll let a higher power decide when it should end."

In a way this sets the stage for the providential storm which destroys the brain at the right moment. But this no more indicates an anti-scientific attitude than the ending of H. G. Wells's *The War of the*

Worlds, where the invaders are defeated by bacteria —"the humblest things," says Wells, "that God, in His wisdom, has put upon this earth."

Like so much SF, *DB* is concerned with human folly. Cory's removal of Donovan's brain is not so much evil as it is ill-considered. The central issue is not that Cory's experiment is illegal or "unholy," but that he rushes into it without considering the consequences. When opportunity knocks on Cory's door in the form of the dying Warren Donovan, he opens it without pausing first to ask, "Who's there?" Of course, if fate had delivered a dying Einstein instead of a Donovan, the results might have been quite different.

While *DB* may reflect some of the uncertainty about science of the postwar period, it clearly lacks the blatantly hysterical attitude toward science of many of its contemporaries. It remains one of the few films of the period untouched by nuclear paranoia.

DB is not antiscientific; nor is it "just a horror film." Such criticisms often reflect the prejudices of the critic rather than an objective consideration of the film in relation to the rest of SF. *DB* does imply a concern about the consequences of scientific endeavor, but such a concern is far from alien to the goals of science fiction.

It is Cory's plan which finally destroys the brain. The storm *is* providential, but the point is perhaps a symbolic one. Nature itself is unable to destroy the brain, nor can human effort, as in Schratt's attempt to shoot it. But when the scientist works with nature, when he harnesses its power, all things are possible.

Cory is ready to give up his research at the end of *DB*, but Janice persuades him of his place in science. Unlike so many scientists in SF films, Cory will be back, and with him will come a better understanding of how science can serve humanity.

DB reflects its era to some degree, but unlike many of the films in this book, it also transcends it. The fact that there have been three versions—one each in the forties, fifties, and sixties—attests to that.

When the novel appeared in 1942, tissue preservation was still a fairly new and exciting idea. The famous experiments with the "chicken heart" kept alive by artificial means were mentioned in reviews of the novel.

The continued popularity of *DB* may lie in its underlying concept of human immortality. The idea of an immortal brain divorced from a single body, yet

Under Donovan's influence, Cory orders himself a new wardrobe. Notice Yocum on the right at the window.

able to inhabit any body at will, is highly attractive in some ways. In Siodmak's novel, Cory even envisions a future in which all life is conducted by immortal brains controlling separate living bodies.

There is also a certain attraction in the character of Donovan himself. The "monster" of *DB* is no scaly dinosaur or bug-eyed alien, but a human being with very human desires. The brain in the tank may be somewhat gruesome, but the real horror we see is practiced by something in human form.

Donovan is a self-made man who fought his way up from poverty to wealth. He is a commanding figure whose power derives from his toughness and single-mindedness. In many ways he resembles someone like Howard Hughes, whose strength and independence remain fascinating despite our knowledge of his strange and often questionable ways.

The attraction we sometimes feel for such morally ambiguous figures is central to *DB*. The brain is usually thought of as the seat of reason, while emotions come from the heart. The division, of course, is incorrect; emotions also originate in the brain.

The brain of Warren Donovan is no symbol of reason, but a distillation of the darker feelings buried in the mind of Patrick Cory. On one side is Cory— the rational humanitarian who puts the good of others above his own—on the other is Donovan, an insane creature who demands instant gratification and allows nothing to stand in his way. It's no accident that Cory is right-handed, while Donovan uses the opposite, and symbolically "sinister," left hand.

Cory's desire for knowledge overcomes his reason, leading him to perform an experiment without regard for the consequences. In doing so, he makes himself vulnerable to the darker side of human nature represented by Donovan's brain.

Seen this way, *DB* becomes a Jekyll and Hyde confrontation between the Good and Evil in all of us. We are repelled by Donovan's ambition and cruelty, and at the same time secretly attracted by his power and success. Cory's fight to free himself from Donovan's influence symbolizes our own fight to control the little bit of Warren Donovan in each of us.

Donovan's Brain is a tight, suspenseful little film with a strong central performance by Lew Ayres, and direction which chooses solid craftsmanship over cinematic pyrotechnics. Most important, it reminds us, once again, that science can produce horrors as well as wonders, depending on how it's used—but that the worst horrors we must confront are the ones within ourselves.

THE MAGNETIC MONSTER

A United Artists release of an "A-Men" Production. Running time: 76 minutes. Black and White. Opened at the Globe Theater in New York City on May 13, 1953.

PRODUCTION CREDITS

DIRECTOR . . . . *Curt Siodmak*
PRODUCER. . . . . *Ivan Tors*
SCREENPLAY . . . . *Curt Siodmak & Ivan Tors*
PRODUCTION DESIGN. . . . . *George Van Marten*
CINEMATOGRAPHER . . . . *Charles Van Enger*
FILM EDITOR . . . . *Herbert L. Strock*
SPECIAL EFFECTS. . . . . *Jack Glass*
MUSIC . . . . *Blaine Sanford*

CAST

DR. JEFFREY STEWART . . . . *Richard Carlson*
DR. DAN FORBES. . . . . *King Donovan*
CONNIE STEWART. . . . . *Jean Byron*
DR. ALLARD . . . . *Harry Ellerbe*
DR. BENTON. . . . . *Leo Britt*
DR. DENKER. . . . . *Leonard Mudie*
SIMON . . . . *Byron Foulger*
DR. SERNY . . . . *Michael Fox*
CHIEF WATSON. . . . . *John Zarimba*
COLONEL WILLIS. . . . . *Frank Gerstle*
CAPTAIN DYER . . . . *John Vosper*

Strother Martin and Kathleen Freeman appear in bit parts.

The Magnetic Monster was destined, perhaps, to be largely ignored by fans of science fiction film. If the film is mentioned at all today it is usually to point out its use of stock shots from the 1934 German production of *Gold,* or to inform us that the movie was a pilot for an unsold TV series. That the film should be so obscure seems strange, since critical reaction to it was generally favorable.

The *New York Times* called *Magnetic Monster* (hereafter referred to as *MM*) a "bristling and suspenseful entertainment," although it also said the film "strains credulity" and had an "aura of improbability." *Newsweek* said it was "a modest but exciting example of science fiction," and *Time* described it as "a crackling mixture of science and fiction."

Richard Hodgens, in his essay "A Short Tragical History of the Science Fiction Film," said that "... of all the earthly monsters, only *The Magnetic Monster* .... displayed much originality and consistency." The fan magazine *Castle of Frankenstein* referred to the film as "a good, inventive little atomic thriller."

Only Carlos Clarens, in his *Illustrated History of the Horror Film,* commented negatively on *MM,* saying that "examples of this type [of film] are few and unpopular, relying.... on endless expository dialogue; and nuclear reactors and atomic piles are rather undramatic in the long run." Considering the largely positive critical response, *MM's* obscurity appears puzzling, but the explanation is actually simple.

The year 1953 was the year of *The War of the Worlds, The Beast from Twenty Thousand Fathoms, It Came From Outer Space,* and a host of other SF and fantasy films. In the face of George Pal's startling production values, the incredible special effects of a fledgling Ray Harryhausen, a prehistoric monster, and 3-D, what chance did a low-budget, black-and-white film without complex special effects or weird creatures really have?

In a decade crammed with SF and fantasy movies, it's not at all surprising that one film should get lost. Yet while *MM* has been overshadowed by so many films of the period, it has as much to offer us as any of them—its excitement and suspense resulting not from technical effects or gimmicks, but from its simplicity, intelligent script, and a unique response to the concerns of the 1950s.

Doctors Jeffrey Stewart and Dan Forbes of the Office of Scientific Investigation are called to a hardware store where all metal objects have been mysteriously magnetized. A Geiger counter detects abnormally high radiation in the store. Stewart and Forbes trace the radiation to a laboratory above the store, where they find a man dead of radiation poisoning. Putting things together, they suspect someone has been experimenting with a new element, though no trace of the substance remains.

Realizing the danger from the new element's magnetic and radioactive properties, Stewart suggests to Dr. Allard, his superior, that broadcasts be made to the public requesting information about unusual magnetic or electrical disturbances. Finally, after a

Confronting the deadly radiation of the "magnetic monster," Stewart (Richard Carlson) and Forbes (King Donovan) wear protective suits.

barrage of crackpot calls, a cabdriver at the airport reports his engine is "frozen." The driver describes his last passenger—a nervous man with a heavy briefcase.

Using the Geiger counter, Stewart and Forbes follow a radioactive trail to an insurance machine, where they learn the mystery man is a well-known physicist named Denker. They track him to his flight and find him dying of radiation poisoning. With his last breath he warns Stewart that the new element, which he calls "serranium," must be "fed," but Stewart doesn't understand. The element is removed to a laboratory for study. Believing his job finished, Stewart returns home to his wife.

The next day Stewart learns that the lab studying the element has been destroyed. From evidence in the debris the scientists determine the element had *imploded*, drawing energy from its surroundings, destroying the lab with its powerful magnetism. More incredibly, the element has doubled its size, creating matter from the energy absorbed.

The element is transferred to a special chamber where tests can be conducted and results fed to the O.S.I.'s computer, the M.A.N.I.A.C. (Mechanical Analytical Integrating Analog Computer). Meanwhile, Forbes and Stewart, watching over the element, notice the magnetic level is rising. Realizing they are seconds away from another implosion, Stewart hits on the idea of bombarding the element with electricity to satisfy its hunger for energy. Stewart and Forbes watch in amazement as energy becomes matter before their eyes, the element humming weirdly as it "feeds." Satiated, the "monster" becomes dormant again.

The M.A.N.I.A.C. predicts an implosion will occur every eleven hours, with the element doubling its size—and hunger for energy—each time. Stewart arranges for the entire city to be blacked out and the energy diverted to the monster in time to prevent the next implosion.

Stewart explains to the authorities that at the element's current growth rate its hunger for energy will soon outstrip the Earth's capacity to satisfy it. But long before the element saps the Earth's resources, it will acquire enough mass to shift the planet from its orbit, destroying the world.

Stewart suggests they try to "choke" the element by overfeeding it. The Canadian government operates a "Deltatron" in Nova Scotia, capable of producing more electricity than any other generating plant on Earth. The element is flown to Nova Scotia aboard a jet constructed of anti-magnetic materials, while Stewart follows in another plane, racing to reach the Deltatron before the eleven hours are up.

The Deltatron is buried beneath the ocean floor, a massive, electrically-operated armored door blocking off the machine from the tunnel leading to the surface in case of accident. Stewart meets Dr. Benton, who has devoted his life to the Deltatron project. Dr. Benton senses Stewart's plan may endanger his project,

but he is under orders to obey Stewart.

With the element in position, Stewart evacuates the area and prepares to bombard the element. Benton realizes Stewart plans to push the Deltatron beyond its tested limit and tries to stop him, but Stewart forces him from the control room. Mad with fear his project will be destroyed, Benton jams open the armored door to force Stewart to stop, since the open door threatens the workers should the machine explode. Stewart sets the machine to its highest output and labors frantically to free the door and escape in time himself. At the last moment he succeeds, but Benton is trapped inside.

The Deltatron sends over 900,000,000 volts of electricity coursing into the monster. The element goes wild with magnetic power, as all manner of steel objects fly through the air and stick to the outside door. Finally, the machine explodes, ripping a hole in the ocean floor.

As the blast subsides, Forbes joins Stewart outside the door. Both of them hear the sinister humming of the monster feeding on the liberated energy. Stewart tugs uselessly at the metal objects frozen to the door. Believing they've failed, Forbes and Stewart turn away in despair. Suddenly, the humming ceases and the metal objects fall away with a clang. Stewart picks up a tool and presses it tentatively to the door. It slides away. The element is dead; the world is safe.

The main plot of *MM* is subtly reinforced by a subplot concerning Stewart's pregnant wife, Connie. While the scenes between the two are occasionally silly, they fit the conventions of most "B" movies of the 1950s. The byplay between the couple provides some necessary humor that contrasts nicely with the film's general seriousness.

Stewart, the totally competent physicist, is completely at a loss to deal with his wife's pregnancy. Connie remains coolly amused by her husband's encouraging her to "get fat" so that she and the child will be healthy. Despite the occasional silliness, there is a genuine tenderness in the Stewarts' relationship. This, plus Stewart's repeated concern over the future of his unborn child, supplies a personal motivation for his battle with the "monster."

Stylistically, *MM* is fairly straightforward, but much of the film's strength derives from this. A voice-over narration by Carlson lends a semi-documentary tone to the movie, emphasizing the cold reality of the events. Yet the film is extremely well paced, starting with the summons to the hardware store and proceeding briskly to the climax at the Deltatron. There is no sense of the kind of frenzied rush that characterizes many SF films, for better or worse, such as *War of the Worlds* or *When Worlds Collide*.

The sense of the monster's menace is carefully underplayed. Indeed, we see the element infrequently, largely because there is little to see other than a dull metal cylinder. Yet the dangerous presence of the thing is felt at all times.

MM is one of those rare SF films that doesn't depend on special effects for its success. The few used are not complex: The magnetic effects of the element and some momentary shots of the monster "feeding," energy being drawn into what appears to be a kind of "mouth," are about all we see in the way of effects, and though these are competently done, they are not the focus of the movie.

Editing, however, plays an important role in *MM*. The use of what appear to be stock shots of the city being blacked out and a jet refueling in midair are skillfully integrated into the film. The most significant achievement, of course, lies in the combination of scenes from *Gold* with scenes of Carlson operating the Deltatron. The crosscutting between Carlson at the controls and the weirdly angled shots of giant tubes and arcs sparking with artificial lightning, accompanied by a crescendo of electrical noises, is responsible for the rising tension of the final scenes.

Acting in *MM* is consistent with, if not above, the standards for "B" films—sometimes melodramatic, but never less than competent. Richard Carlson, of course, established himself as a star of SF and horror films in the forties and fifties. He appeared in such films as *Hold That Ghost* (with Abbott and Costello, 1941), *It Came from Outer Space* (1953), *The Creature from the Black Lagoon* (1954), *Riders to the Stars* (which he also directed, 1954), and a variety of others. (For a list of his films, see the Appendix.)

Carlson didn't start out to be a star of fantasy films. His career began on the stage, including the starring role in the Chicago stage production of *Mr. Roberts*. His early screen credits include roles in *The Young in Heart* (1938) and *The Little Foxes* (1941). Carlson rarely took the lead in the many "straight" films in which he appeared, perhaps explaining why he gravitated to SF and horror roles where he could, but he admirably handled "backup" positions in many, such as *King Solomon's Mines* (with Stewart Granger, 1950), *Seminole* (with Rock Hudson, 1953), and *The Last Command* (with Sterling Hayden, 1955). TV watchers may remember him best from *I Led Three Lives*.

Carlson always brought a restrained intensity to his roles. He could appear cool on the surface while letting the audience know there was often something burning beneath. As the hero of so many SF and horror films, he displayed both a sense of competence and an intense human concern that often fought with each other for dominance. In *MM*, however, these two elements are carefully balanced in the character of Jeffrey Stewart, making the character enormously appealing in the context of this particular film.

Although Carlson dominates *MM*, he is ably supported by King Donovan—who would later perform a similar function for Kevin McCarthy in *Invasion of the Body Snatchers*—as Dan Forbes, Carlson's associate.

Stewart (Richard Carlson) and a group of military men and scientists studying the dangerous new element.

Dr. Benton (Leo Britt) realizes that his life's work, the Deltatron, is about to be destroyed.

Jean Byron, a perennial heroine of "B" adventure films, brings some earnestness to her role of Connie Stewart, providing the spark that makes Carlson's interest in defeating the monster more personal.

The rest of the cast is serviceable, consisting mainly of veteran actors of the period. In addition, the late character actor, Strother Martin, appears in a bit part, and Kathleen Freeman, who specialized in playing the slightly bemused secretary or housekeeper in many films and TV shows, appears as the O.S.I.'s secretary. But *MM* remains Carlson's film. It is his presence, as the dedicated, yet human, scientist which binds the film together.

One of the elements that makes *MM* stand out among many of the lesser SF films of the fifties is its painstaking attention to scientific detail. The language and paraphernalia of science appear throughout the movie.

Stewart and Forbes make careful use of the Geiger counter and photographic film badges to detect radiation, explaining their function clearly to the uninformed. When the element is found, a blind man's cane is used to keep the radioactive material at a distance, and all those exposed to the element are carefully checked for contamination. The element is removed by men in radiation-proof suits, loaded in a lead "pig," and transported in a lead-lined truck. All this is shown in detail, sharply underlining the film's efforts at scientific accuracy.

MM also probably marks one of the first screen appearances of the computer, ironically called, in this case, the M.A.N.I.A.C. Certainly, the stock shots of the miles of equipment and hordes of personnel needed for an early computer are amusing by today's standards, but the machine is shown as an integral part of solving the scientist's problem.

Another machine, the Deltatron, is the device that ultimately conquers the monster. This concern with the instruments and methods of science is unusual in the typical SF film. Only a few other movies, such as *Destination Moon* (1950), *The Conquest of Space* (1955), and *2001: A Space Odyssey* (1968), have paid such careful attention to science and technology, and it should be noted that these three films dealt with space travel.

This isn't to say that *MM* is perfect in its attempts at scientific accuracy. It is unclear, for example, how Denker creates the new element, although there are vague references to alpha ray bombardment. Nor is it clear what the "Delta" in Deltatron stands for, or what the machine is actually supposed to do.

But such tactics in SF movies, or in written science fiction are not unusual. Tossing in a few scientific-sounding terms to reinforce the plot or provide a jumping-off point is a standard technique. In the 1920s or 1930s the word "radioactive," for example, was used by science fiction writers to cover a variety of situations simply because so little was known about the properties of radioactivity.

Today the term may be "tachyon" or "black hole," but it provides the same scientific foundation for the writer or filmmaker. In any case, compared to the scientific implausibilities of giant ants, sleeping dinosaurs, and shrinking men, the few oversights of *MM* are distinctly minor.

It isn't really surprising that *MM* succeeds as well as it does, considering the writing-directing-producing team of Curt Siodmak and Ivan Tors. According to Siodmak, Tors came to him with ten minutes of stock footage from *Gold* which fitted a screenplay Siodmak was already working on. Together, Tors and Siodmak fashioned the script to fit the scenes from *Gold*, and formed the "A-Men" production company with director Andrew Marton and Richard Carlson. Shooting on *MM* took only a few days at the old Goldwyn studios in Hollywood, and the whole production was brought in for a meager but well-used $105,000.

Curt Siodmak was born in Germany in 1902 and began his long association with fantasy films as an extra in Fritz Lang's *Metropolis* (1926). Siodmak and his brother Robert were both active in the German cinema of the thirties (Robert Siodmak would also distinguish himself as a director in the U.S., especially in the area of *film noir*), but it appears Siodmak's first real work with SF was his collaboration on the script for *F.P. 1 Antwortet Nicht* (*Floating Platform 1 Does Not Reply*, 1933). Two years later he supplied the script adaptation for the British *Transatlantic Tunnel*, an English version of the earlier German film *Der Tunnel* (1933).

Arriving in Hollywood in 1937, Siodmak's first writing effort seems to have been *Her Jungle Love* (1938) with Ray Milland and Dorothy Lamour. From here his writing appears to have turned exclusively to fantasy, with *The Invisible Man Returns, The Invisible Woman, The Ape,* and *Black Friday* (all 1940).

In 1941 Siodmak produced the script for *The Wolf Man*, adding that character to the horror rolls forever and bringing stardom to Lon Chaney, Jr. Nineteen forty-three brought *Son of Dracula* (directed by brother Robert and much underrated), *I Walked with a Zombie* (directed by horror film expert Jacques Tourneur), and *Frankenstein Meets the Wolf Man*. In

the fifties Siodmak turned back to scripts of a more science fictional nature, including *Riders to the Stars* (1954) and *Earth vs. the Flying Saucers* (1956).

Siodmak turned to directing in 1951 with the dubiously titled *Bride of the Gorilla*, and has since directed widely in films and TV. He has also written several SF novels, including *Donovan's Brain,*, which has been made into a movie three times. (For more on Siodmak's writing career, see the chapter on *Donovan's Brain*. For a list of his films, see the Appendix.)

It would be foolish to classify Siodmak as one of the great writers or directors. His work has certainly varied over the years, as suggested by such titles as *Creature with the Atom Brain* and *Love Slaves of the Amazon*, though the titles often belie the content of the films.

Part of this variation may be due to the limitations imposed on Siodmak by the horror/SF field. When allowed to work with intelligent material and reasonable producers, his output has been excellent. Certainly, his long connection with fantasy films, directors, and actors—as well as an obvious enthusiasm for the fantastic as a film and literary form—prepared him for the solid effort that emerged as *MM*.

Ivan Tors, though not the SF devotee Siodmak is, brought a strong dramatic background as well as a clear interest in fantasy and the offbeat in general to *MM*. Born in Hungary in 1916, Tors started his career as a playwright in his native country, but turned his talents to writing and producing motion pictures when he came to Hollywood in 1941. His first script credits seem to have been *Song of Love* (1947) and *That Forsyte Woman* (1949), based on part of Galsworthy's *Forsyte Saga*.

Tors first venture as writer-producer occurred in 1952 with *Storm Over Europe*. His other early SF films include *Riders to the Stars* and *Gog* (both 1954). Tors also produced TV's *Science Fiction Theater* (1956), which, if never spectacular, tried diligently to present scientific speculation in a sensible manner. The underrated *Man and the Challenge* (1959) was another Tors series exploring the fringes of SF. More conventionally, yet still with an eye to the unusual, Tors produced such shows as *Sea Hunt, Ripcord, The Aquanauts,* and *Primus*.

Eventually, Tors began to concentrate on animal actors rather than humans, producing such films as *Clarence, the Cross-eyed Lion, Zebra in the Kitchen,* and the TV series *Flipper, Gentle Ben, Daktari,* and similar efforts. But he maintained his interest in SF, at least marginally, in *Around the World Under the Sea* (1965) and the TV movie *The Aquarians* (1970). Tors's concern for the peculiar, for the exploration of new worlds, whether outer space, the ocean depths, or even the animal world, characterizes him as the kind of artist well-qualified to deal with the new worlds imagined in science fiction.

Like so many science fiction films of the fifties,

Dr. Jeffrey Stewart prepares to destroy the element "serranium" by pushing the Deltatron to its limit.

MM reflected strongly on the consequences of a new force that had been unleashed upon the world— atomic energy. It may be difficult for those who have grown up in the atomic age to grasp the feelings aroused by the atomic bomb at the end of World War II.

The incredibly destructive energies of the A-bomb had reduced Hiroshima and Nagasaki to rubble instantly, and the unseen hand of its accompanying radiation would reach out for weeks, months, even years afterward, to sicken and kill in horrifying new ways. The bomb was mysterious and apocalyptic. It was barely known what the products of such inconceivable forces might be, nor, in the midst of a very Cold War, when those forces might be loosed again.

The fears and uncertainties of the atomic age were manifested sharply, if somewhat heavily, in the science fiction and horror movies of the fifties. The mysterious and unknown consequences of atomic energy appeared on the screen as the now-familiar invasions from outer space, strange forces that could grow or shrink us, giant insects, resurrected dinosaurs, and a host of other post-atomic horrors.

Such menaces are largely symbolic of the power-

ful and intimidating forces unleashed by the splitting of the atom. They have little basis in reality, but the plain metallic cylinder of *MM* presents a more realistic danger.

While the origin and properties of the element "serranium" strain our belief to some degree, there is enough plausibility in the concept to allow an easier suspension of disbelief in the magnetic monster than in its more gigantic or physically horrifying cousins. Because it is a direct product of the nuclear age, the magnetic monster is perhaps even more terrifying than those other symbols of atomic anxiety.

Cold, implacable, and utterly mindless, the magnetic "monster" differs from the giant insects and ageless creatures released from arctic ice in that it is not a victim of the atomic era, but its offspring. It is the most realistic representation of the fears that colored the science fiction movies of the fifties.

Even beyond this symbol of nuclear-age fear, Siodmak and Tors created a symbol for the start of an era when our use of science and technology was about to overwhelm every phase of our existence and begin to drain our energy resources at an ever-increasing rate. As both a symbol of the atomic era and technological need gone wild, *MM* takes on even greater signifi-

The pilot of the plane carrying Dr. Denker (Leonard Mudie) uses a blind man's cane to keep the briefcase containing the deadly element at a safe distance.

cance today.

Unlike many of its contemporaries, *MM* is not an anti-scientific film. The SF movies of the fifties were often hysterical in their treatment of science and its relation to humanity. After all, it was apparently science that had released the atomic bomb on us. In case after case it is the scientist—mad or otherwise—who is responsible for the menace, by design or accident, or simply through that infernal meddling that produced the bomb in the first place. Nor is there much faith expressed in science's ability to deal with problems. Usually, the army or some other nonscientific authority must be called in, though the scientist may cooperate.

But this antiscientific feeling goes even further. The dominant feeling emerging from many of these films is panic. There is no faith in *anyone's* ability to cope with the dangers released by science. Humanity is pictured as helpless, hysterical, and essentially stupid.

In *The War of the Worlds*, for example, the overwhelming impression we're left with is one of a terrified, selfish humanity fleeing from unstoppable invaders. In the end, it's not man who defeats the invaders but nature. This is a legitimate theme, as H. G. Wells conceived it but combined with the religious elements in George Pal's production, the image remaining is one of a panicked and useless humanity.

The Beast from Twenty Thousand Fathoms establishes the cliché in which the authorities, scientific or otherwise, deny until the last moment overwhelming evidence that the menace exists. Even the superior *It Came from Outer Space* portrays human beings as stubborn and foolish. Again and again, humanity is presented as ignorant, cowardly, or morally incapable of coping with its problems.

Whether or not this is an accurate picture of humanity is irrelevant; the point is that such a view is essentially in opposition to the attitude of science. The scientific attitude suggests that humanity can solve *any* problem with reason and intelligence. Again, the truth of this is beside the point. What is important is the presence of this anti-scientific attitude in so many SF films. Though much of it is traceable to the powerful anxieties of the atomic age, it goes beyond that to humanity's almost instinctive fear of what is new or unknown, to its lack of faith in its own ability to cope. It is a human trait not difficult to understand.

Science fiction film *should* deal with human frailties, with fear of the unknown and the abuse of science. But so much SF film, compared to written science fiction , deals with people negatively that when a film appears with a more hopeful or complicated attitude, it stands out sharply from the rest.

MM is such a film. There are no giant horrors in *MM*—merely a plain metallic cylinder, made more horrible by its seeming dullness, its unthinking deadliness. There are no panicky mobs or stupidly disbelieving authorities, merely scientists grappling with a problem unleashed by science which must be defeated by that same science. And those in authority are quick to grasp the problem and provide the assistance to deal with it. There is a calm to *MM*, a scientific methodicalness balancing the suspense of the plot and the briskness of the narrative. *MM* implies a faith in science and humanity that clearly separates it from the run-of-the-mill SF thrillers of the fifties.

Yet *MM* isn't uncritical of science. Denker, the physicist responsible for the element, tells Stewart he has realized the impossibility of being a "lone wolf" in scientific research. It is Denker, working alone in blind allegiance to science, who creates the element without considering the consequences for humanity. Later in the film, Dr. Benton displays a similar attitude toward the Deltatron. Benton sees the machine itself as the end product of his research, and his actions are bent on protecting the machine, the symbol of his scientific ideal, rather than humanity. Like Denker, he becomes a victim of his devotion to pure science, dying in its service.

Stewart, however, is an advocate of science as a tool in the service of humanity. His choice of profession, as a scientific detective for the O.S.I., emphasizes his vision of science as a method of understanding and solving human problems. To Stewart, the Deltatron is an instrument which can be used to save humanity, and if it is destroyed in the process, the end result is well worth the loss.

Stewart's position is clarified further by his attitude toward Connie and their unborn child. At the end of the film, with the element destroyed, he remarks to Connie on the difference between Denker's creation and what they have conceived together. One, conceived without love, is a monster; the other, conceived in love, is a child.

This is far from the sweeping antiscientific paranoia of many SF films. Rather it is an indictment of science divorced from human needs and concerns. It is pure, inhuman science, in the misguided personage of Denker, that creates the monster. It is science tempered with human concern, as personified by Stewart, that finds the means to destroy the element.

At the beginning of *MM* Stewart mentions that because of their constant dealings with atomic energy, the agents of the O.S.I. are nicknamed "A-Men" commenting that this sounds "a little like a prayer." We might consider that a prayer in a religious sense, but in the film's context, and recalling that the production company was called "A-Men Productions," we might speculate that the prayer is more for an awareness that science and human values must never be separated—and that together they have the potential to solve any problem.

It is largely this view of science as an instrument for evil *and* good that sets *The Magnetic Monster* apart from its contemporaries. Its attention to scientific detail and accuracy, its economy of style and execution, its strong performances, but most of all its intelligence, reflection, and anticipation of the consequences of science and technology make it a striking contribution to the field of science fiction film. Compared to a variety of SF films before and after its production, it was a small effort, but over the years its message should have grown larger to us.

INVADERS FROM MARS

A 20th Century-Fox Release. Running Time: 78 minutes. Cinecolor. Opened in New York City at the Palace Theater, May 29, 1953.

PRODUCTION CREDITS

PRODUCER. . . . . *Edward L. Alperson*
DIRECTOR/DESIGNER. . . . . *William Cameron Menzies*
ORIGINAL STORY. . . . . *John Tucker Battle*
SCREENPLAY. . . . . *Richard Blake, John T. Battle, W. C. Menzies*
CINEMATOGRAPHER. . . . . *John F. Seitz*
ART DIRECTOR. . . . . *Boris Leven*
MAKEUP. . . . . *Gene Hibbs, Anatole Robbins*
SPECIAL EFFECTS. . . . . *Jack Cosgrove*
EDITOR. . . . . *Arthur Roberts*
SOUND. . . . . *Earl Crane*
MUSIC. . . . . *Raoul Kraushaar*
ASSOCIATE PRODUCER. . . . . *Edward L. Alperson Jr.*
ASSISTANT DIRECTOR. . . . . *Ben Chapman*
ASSISTANT DIRECTOR (ADDITIONAL SEQUENCES). . . . . *Wesley Barry*
WARDROBE. . . . . *Norma*
COLOR CONSULTANT. . . . . *Clifford D. Shank*

CAST

DAVID MACLEAN. . . . . *Jimmy Hunt*
DR. PATRICIA BLAKE. . . . . *Helena Carter*
DR. STUART KELSTON. . . . . *Arthur Franz*
COLONEL FIELDING. . . . . *Morris Ankrum*
GEORGE MACLEAN. . . . . *Leif Erickson*
MARY MACLEAN. . . . . *Hilary Brooke*
SERGEANT RINALDI. . . . . *Max Wagner*
CAPTAIN ROTH. . . . . *Milburn Stone*
SERGEANT FINLEY. . . . . *Walter Sande*
KATHY WILSON. . . . . *Janine Perreau*
MR. TURNER. . . . . *John Eldredge*
DR. WILSON. . . . . *Robert Shayne*
MARTIAN LEADER. . . . . *Luce Potter*
MUTANTS. . . . . *Lock Martin, Max Palmer*

It's only in recent years that fans of science fiction film have begun to recognize the virtues of *Invaders from Mars*. Ever since its release, critics and fans alike have hotly debated whether the film is simply one of the cheapest, most lurid attempts to cash in on the SF boom of the fifties—or some kind of minor masterpiece.

Invaders from Mars (hereafter referred to as *IFM*) was barely noticed by critics of the time. The *New York Times* dismissed it as a "funnybook, full of impossible action and childish imaginings... designed to meet the demands of today's space-struck youngsters." *Films in Review* called it "much inferior to *The War of the Worlds*."

The National Parent-Teacher gave *IFM* a resounding "No" for viewing by children and rated it "poor" for teenagers and adults. Only *Variety*, its eye ever on the box office, had anything good to say for the film, calling it "a suspenseful story... charged with exploitable values."

It wasn't until 1970 that John Baxter, in *Science Fiction in the Cinema*, took the position that *IFM*, despite its many flaws, was "a remarkable exercise in SF cinema." Made in only a few weeks on a shoestring budget, butchered both before and after its release, *IFM* has a disturbing, dreamlike quality that makes it almost impossible to forget.

IFM opens with a narration (the voice belongs to Arthur Franz) against a moving background of stars and planets:

The Heavens—once an object of superstition, awe, and fear. Now, a vast region for growing knowledge. The distance of Venus, the atmosphere of Mars, the size of Jupiter, and the speed of Mercury—all this, and more, we know.

But their greatest mystery the Heavens have kept secret. What sort of life, if any, inhabits these other planets? Human life, like our own—or life extremely lower on the scale, or dangerously higher?

Seeking the answer to this timeless question—forever seeking—is the preoccupation of scientists everywhere. Scientists famous and scientists unknown. Scientists in great universities and in modest homes.

Scientists of all ages ...

The scene dissolves into the bedroom of twelve-year-old David MacLean, where the alarm clock is ringing—though it's only 4:00 A.M. David tries to muffle the noise, but the alarm awakens his parents, George and Mary.

When Mr. MacLean enters David's room, he finds the boy at his telescope, observing "Orion at its zenith," an event that won't occur again for another six years. MacLean excitedly joins David at the 'scope, until Mrs. MacLean comes in and sends them both back to bed.

David is awakened shortly after by what looks like a storm accompanied by a strange light in the sky.

From his window David sees a flying saucer disappear into the sand hill behind his home. David tells his father about the ship, but Mr. MacLean suggests he's been dreaming and sends him back to bed, promising to take a look in the morning.

But MacLean becomes curious and gets up anyway. As an engineer at a nearby plant where secret work is being done, he's required to report anything strange. Still in robe and slippers, MacLean walks up the path to the sand hill—and disappears into it.

In the morning, Mrs. MacLean finds her husband missing and calls the police. Two officers are sent to investigate, but while searching the sand hill, they too are sucked down into it.

Back at the house, David comes for breakfast and questions his father's absence. Mrs. MacLean tries to explain—when MacLean suddenly reappears, looking oddly stiff and menacing to David.

David senses something is wrong and spots a small x-shaped scar on the back of his father's neck. But when David questions him about it, MacLean strikes him.

The two policemen show up, also acting strangely. They agree with MacLean that it's best the whole incident be forgotten.

Shortly after, David watches as one of the neighborhood children, Kathy Wilson, is sucked down into the hill. David rushes in to tell his mother, but is intercepted by Mr. MacLean, who sends him away with a warning not to spread "stories." With David gone, MacLean leads his wife ominously up the path to the sand hill.

David tries to tell Mrs. Wilson about Kathy, but the child appears suddenly, wearing the same blank expression as Mr. MacLean and the two policemen.

David apologizes for scaring Mrs. Wilson, but as he leaves he sees smoke pouring from the Wilson cellar. Someone has used gasoline to set fire to the house. Mrs. Wilson asks Kathy if she's been in the cellar, but the child denies it with an oddly disquieting smile on her face.

David phones his friend, Dr. Stuart Kelston, an astronomer at the nearby observatory, but Kelston is out. The boy searches desperately for someone who'll believe him. At the police station, he demands to see the Chief.

But when David starts to tell his story, the Chief recognizes him and reaches for the phone to call Mr. MacLean, allowing David to see the scar on the man's neck. David tries to run, but is caught and locked in a cell while the Chief goes looking for Mr. MacLean.

Sensing the boy's fear, the desk sergeant decides to ask a local physician, Dr. Patricia Blake, to see David. David agrees to tell Pat his story, but only after checking the back of her neck.

Puzzled by David's tale, Pat calls Kelston, who tells her David isn't the type of boy to imagine things.

The MacLeans show up to take David away, but Pat refuses to release him, claiming he may have polio. Stymied, the MacLeans leave, warning David again

David, Stu, and Pat in
the observatory.

not to "tell stories."

Pat takes David to the observatory, where he repeats his story for Kelston. Kelston phones General Mayberry, head of the secret project at nearby Coral Bluffs, but is unable to reach him. David and Kelston speculate the saucer may come from Mars, which is then at its closest to Earth, and Kelston advances several theories about life on Mars.

Using the observatory telescope, Kelston shows David and Pat the secret project under construction at Coral Bluffs—an atomic-powered rocket. He theorizes that the Martians may have assumed the rocket is a weapon designed to be used against them, and decided to strike against Earth first.

Next, Kelston focuses on the pit adjacent to the sand hill. Kelston and David watch, horrified, as Mr. MacLean pushes General Mayberry into the pit. Kelston immediately calls Colonel Fielding, the second-in-command at Coral Bluffs, and explains what

they've seen. Fielding contacts the Pentagon and gets authority to send troops into the area.

After hearing David's story, Fielding and the others set out to investigate. They find Kathy Wilson has died of a cerebral hemorrhage—an unlikely cause of death in a child—and Pat goes off to examine the body at the hospital.

From the roof of his house David shows Fielding the spot of the disappearances. Kelston speculates the Martians may have some kind of ray enabling them to bore through the ground. Sergeant Rinaldi, Fielding's aide, sneaks away to the hill with a rifle, and, as Fielding watches, Rinaldi is sucked into the ground. Enraged, Fielding orders the area surrounded by troops.

Pat returns with a small electronic device taken from Kathy Wilson's brain. The device not only allows the Martians to control anyone in whom it's been implanted, but upon a signal from the Martians, it explodes, causing instant death.

Meanwhile, the two policemen attempt to sabotage the rocket. MPs catch the saboteurs, but the two men are killed by the implants in their brains.

At Coral Bluffs, Dr. Wilson, the man who designed the rocket, is working late. The MacLeans try to kill Wilson, but fail and are captured by soldiers. For some reason their implants fail to explode, and David's parents are rushed to a hospital where the implants can be removed.

Back at the sand hill, troops blast their way into a tunnel with blistered walls glowing with a strange, iridescent green light. But the Martians have used their heat ray to escape, sealing the tunnel behind them. Using a crystal from Kathy Wilson's implant, army technicians devise a directional locator to track the saucer down.

Pat takes David aside to explain about his parents. Suddenly, they are sucked underground and captured by Martian "Mutants"—giant synthetic humanoids created by the Martians to serve them.

Pat and David are taken to the saucer and brought before the Martian Leader—a tentacled, vaguely humanoid creature in a glass globe. Sergeant Rinaldi, under Martian control, acts as interrogator for the Martian Leader.

When Pat is unable to reveal the army's plans, she is seized by the Mutants and placed face down on a table. From above her, the machine which implants the control devices begins to whir, its needlelike point descending steadily toward the back of her neck, as David is dragged away by the zombielike Rinaldi.

On the surface, the directional locator finally discovers the saucer's hiding place. Accompanied by Kelston, Fielding leads a squad into the tunnels. The soldiers fight their way into the ship, rescuing Pat just in time. Kelston helps Pat to the surface while the Martian Leader escapes with its Mutants to another part of the ship.

Fielding sets a time bomb in the ship and goes looking for David and Rinaldi in the surrounding tunnels, where the rest of his men are battling the Mutants. Using their heat ray, the Mutants seal Fielding and his men in the tunnels while the time bomb ticks away, every second bringing them all closer to destruction.

An explosion knocks Rinaldi unconscious, and the soldiers rescue David. David uses a Martian heat ray to melt an escape route for the soldiers. Emerging from the tunnel, David and the others flee down the hill. The saucer begins to melt its way through the sand hill, but is destroyed in a stunning explosion before it can take off.

The scene dissolves back to David's bedroom, where he lies tossing in his bed. Awakening suddenly, David rushes to his parents' room and finds them unchanged. The whole adventure has been a nightmare, and David's parents send him back to bed.

But, shortly after, the sound of a storm and a strange light in the sky wake David again. He looks out his window to see the saucer landing. The nightmare is beginning again. Or is it?

IFM appears to have been a deliberate effort aimed at beating George Pal's more expensive *War of the Worlds* into theaters. Independent producer Edward L. Alperson was surely aware of the success of Pal's previous SF films, *Destination Moon* (1950) and *When Worlds Collide* (1951), and noted the growing interest in SF in the early fifties:

Forgetting that almost every studio has at least one science fiction story on its agenda, one need only check the growing popularity of the science fiction magazines to ascertain the ever increasing demand for this type of reading. Ten years ago there were fourteen such magazines. Today there are fifty-two. Circulation of such literature is skyrocketing.

Embarrassingly, Alperson's statement is almost the exact duplicate of one issued by Howard Hawks at the time *The Thing* was released.

Alperson commissioned screenwriter John Tucker Battle to create a story of global invasion. Limitations on time and money, however, forced Alperson to call in Richard Blake to rewrite Battle's screenplay, reducing its scope from an invasion of the entire Earth to one confined to a small town. Battle eventually had his name removed from the credits. *IFM* did beat *War of the Worlds* into release by six months, and the film did fairly well at the box office.

Many sources indicate *IFM* was shot in 3-D, but neither the film's advertising nor its reviews support this. There may have been plans to use the 3-D process, and many of the film's shots suggest it, but once again a shortage of money forced a change in plans.

Much of the controversy over *IFM* stems from the many cuts, additions, and alterations made before and after its release. Just before shooting began director William Cameron Menzies somehow lost all his pre-production sketches, resulting in a movie too short to release.

Menzies was forced to add stock footage of army maneuvers, and to use the same shots over and over to save money. Even the most casual viewer can spot the scenes of Mutants running back and forth in the tunnels, with the negative merely reversed to suggest they're running in a different direction.

Other changes were made after the film's release. It was thought European audiences wouldn't accept the film's "dream" ending (some versions say it was too frightening), so additional footage was shot showing the saucer exploding and David being put to bed by Pat and Stu. More scenes at the observatory were added, enabling the characters to discuss further the existence of flying saucers and life on Mars.

After that, it's hard to tell what happened. While *IFM* was reasonably successful, it was quickly sold to TV and other outlets, resulting in further cuts. Because of the film's poor reputation, little effort was made to preserve it. Producer Alperson eventually went bankrupt, and 20th Century-Fox lost the rights to the movie.

Over the years audiences have seen widely different versions of *IFM*, so two people discussing the film often feel as if they've seen different movies. It was only in 1976 that an independent producer tracked down and restored a print of *IFM*, putting together what's now accepted as a definitive version of the film (see note in Appendix).

Considering the many flaws in *IFM*, the low-budget production values, and the many cuts, it may be hard to understand why the film leaves such a strong impression on audiences. The answer lies in the implications behind its screenplay and in the superb visual imaginings of William Cameron Menzies.

Unlike many SF films of the fifties, *IFM* seems drawn from the pulp fiction conventions which dominated at least one kind of science fiction from the 1920s on. Invasions from space, stalwart heroes, beautiful heroines, heat rays, and bug-eyed aliens were part of SF's stock-in-trade during the genre's adolescence.

For many people it was just this brand of wild adventure that made SF attractive. As pure escape fiction, this kind of SF presented a world where values were simplified—a world of Earthmen and Aliens, Us and Them, Good and Evil—in much the same way the Western did. But even at its most juvenile, SF tended to stretch the imagination merely by the act of speculating about life on other worlds, the future, or the magic of science.

By the 1950s this kind of SF had largely taken a back seat to more mature efforts to consider the impact of science on humanity. Yet this wilder, adventure-oriented SF is still a part of the field. Its simplicity of ideas, combined with its ability to stimulate the imagination, makes it easily accessible to people who are unfamiliar with science fiction, especially children. The success of *Star Wars* and similar films bears this out. *IFM* is very much a part of this pulp fiction tradition.

Moreover, *IFM* is deliberately oriented towards children, particularly young boys. David MacLean's "dream" is a wish-fulfillment of every child's fantasies of self-importance. In his dream David is the respected friend of a doctor, a famous astronomer, and a military man. *He* is the one who recognizes a menace invisible to the adults around him. *He* is the one who rescues the troops with a Martian heat ray that only *he* can operate. To put it simply, *he* is the hero.

But *IFM* appeals not only to children's fantasies but to their nightmares as well. Like a bad dream, the film is confused, illogical, and hard to follow. Much of it makes no sense.

David's father, for example, talks about strange "rumors" at the plant where he works, but what these are or where they come from is never explained. Dr. Kelston describes the exact nature of Martian civilization, although he has no knowledge of it. He also manages to tilt the observatory telescope at an impossible angle to see the sand pit. Dr. Wilson, a physicist, is seen working in a laboratory with chemicals. David

David uses a Martian heat ray to melt an escape tunnel.

Dr. Wilson (Robert Shayne) in his laboratory. Notice the stylized chemical apparatus and the long corridor behind Wilson.

is the only one who can operate the heat ray, though there's no reason why he should know better than anyone else how to do it.

Much of this may have been unintentional, but the overall effect is to create the environment of a dream. We *know* none of this makes sense, and it is precisely that fact which makes the film so affecting. Somehow we have stepped into someone else's nightmare, and there is no way to wake up.

Yet *IFM*'s nightmare goes even deeper than this. In 1956 Don Siegel's *Invasion of the Body Snatchers* would probe the nightmares of adults, touching on their childhood fears. But *IFM* focuses on the nightmare of being a child caught in an adult world which often doesn't make sense from one moment to the next, and in which no one seems to understand what the child understands. It's no accident in *IFM* that David is the only one who can spot the changes in the people enslaved by the Martians, changes which are obvious to the audience, but which no adult in the film even suspects.

Nowhere is this childhood nightmare clearer than in David's relationship to his parents. At first, the MacLeans are warm, understanding people. When George MacLean finds his son out of bed at 4:00 A.M. his reaction is to join him at the telescope rather than punish him, and Mrs. MacLean seems more amused than annoyed by David's behavior. The MacLeans are really every child's fantasy of perfect parents.

But suddenly the MacLeans change. Mr. MacLean turns into an unfeeling monster who strikes his son

without reason. Mrs. MacLean becomes a cold-hearted creature who wants only to control her son. *IFM* gives us a child's perception of the parent-child relationship—an exaggerated view in which parents are kind and loving one moment and in the next, for no apparent reason, cruel and hateful.

IFM offers the child a convenient explanation for such changes. It's not that the child has misbehaved, or that parents might have problems of their own, but that some outside force—in this case, Martians—has interfered to cause the change. To a child this is the most reasonable way of explaining why Mommy and Daddy no longer seem to love him.

David MacLean finds himself trapped in the situation of all children, knowing the "truth" about the world, but unable to convince anyone around him. His friends, his neighbors, the police, are all indifferent or hostile toward him. David's predicament powerfully symbolizes the basic fear and loneliness of every child, and touches the child that still lives in every adult.

IFM also has a special appeal for science fiction fans. The film has a strong sense of wonder at its core. The opening narration, with its emphasis on "seeking . . . forever seeking," glorifies the role of the scientist, and then brings that glorification down to the child's level, stressing that seeking the answer to timeless questions is the responsibility of "scientists of all ages." To the typical SF fan, who's championed the importance of science from childhood on, such an appeal is hard to ignore.

INVADERS FROM MARS

David MacLean rushes into the Police Station. Notice the high, blank walls and the tall, narrow doorway.

But the appeal to the SF fan goes even further. Mrs. MacLean—while under Martian control, of course—complains that her son has been reading "those trashy science fiction magazines" and is "completely out of control." To typical SF fans, who spent their youth defending their choice of reading material from parents and friends, Mrs. MacLean's words create an instant identification with David. No other SF film makes such a deliberate attempt to capture the sympathies of the science fiction fan.

The "dream" ending of *IFM* also plays an important part in the overall impact of the film. When David awakens from his nightmare, we're relieved, convinced that what we've seen is in no sense real, not even as film, but just a dream on film. When David sees the saucer land again, however, we become disoriented. Was David's dream a portent of things to come? Is he still dreaming? And what of our own nightmares, *IFM* asks us finally—how real are they?

Since directing *Things to Come* (1936), William Cameron Menzies had largely confined himself to production design, working on *Gone With the Wind* (1939), *The Thief of Bagdad* (1940), *For Whom the Bell Tolls* (1943), and others. But Menzies kept his hand in as a director in the period between *Things to Come* (see that chapter) and *IFM*, though none of his films from this period are memorable.

Of interest are *Duel in the Sun* (1946), on which Menzies shared uncredited directorial duties with King Vidor and several others, and *The Whip Hand* (1951), a low-budget melodrama involving Nazis and germ warfare. Menzies directed one more film after *IFM*, a brooding horror story shot in 3-D, called *The Maze* (1953). (For a list of Menzies's films as director, see the Appendix.)

Faced with a low budget and other preproduction problems, Menzies knew the key to *IFM* lay not in realism but in creating the visual equivalent of a nightmare. Assisted by Art Director Boris Leven and Cinematographer John Seitz, Menzies succeeded in giving *IFM* a bizarre, surrealistic look.

It's not hard to tell that *IFM* was filmed totally indoors. Almost everything, excluding stock footage, looks like a set, but this only contributes to the film's sense of unreality. The sand hill, with its sloping path to nowhere, twisted rail fence, and barren trees, is one of the film's strongest examples of how set design works to create a threatening, uneasy mood in *IFM*.

Menzies's interiors are also important in conveying the dreamlike quality of *IFM*. Dr. Wilson's lab appears to be huge, though the feeling of size is largely due to the manipulation of perspective. Unlike any real laboratory, the walls are blank, without shelves or cabinets. The only equipment we see is stylized chemical apparatus, although Wilson is a physicist.

For the outside of Kelston's observatory Menzies used stock footage of the installation at Mt. Palomar, California, but the inside doesn't match up with the realistic exterior. The interior is bare, with high, blank walls, a few pieces of furniture, and the telescope sticking out of the wall.

Perhaps most striking is the police station set. Everything here is out of proportion. The walls are again blank and white, the hallway apparently endless. Doors are huge and surrounded by thick black lines. The front desk towers over David. Menzies enhanced the feeling of size by shooting up from David's point of view as he stands before the desk. Later Menzies restores some normality to the scene when Pat talks to the desk sergeant by shooting down over his shoulder. The contrast emphasizes that this is David's nightmare.

IFM's sets recall the starkness and exaggeration of German Expressionism, representing the confused images of David's dream. Everything is filtered through that dream—a child's distorted idea of an observatory, a police station, and a laboratory.

The iridescent Martian tunnels with their blistered walls is another image from *IFM* hard to forget. According to some sources, inflated rubber prophylactics were used to create some of the bubbles on the walls. This is unfortunate, since in some scenes the actors brush against the "bubbles," disturbing the illusion, yet somehow the movement unintentionally adds to the feeling of unreality.

The interior of the Martian ship is also striking. Like the film's other interiors, the inside of the ship is huge and empty, with only a few pieces of Martian apparatus visible. The walls are translucent, so action on the other side of them is seen in eerie silhouette. John Seitz's unusual camera angles combine with the set to produce a distinctly alien effect.

Menzies used many tight shots of his actors' faces, cutting in on them suddenly. That *IFM* was supposed to be shot in 3-D may explain this partially. But Menzies's close shots also give the adults an exaggerated sense of power, as in the case of the Police Chief, where a rapid close-up of his stiff, emotionless face immediately warns us that the Chief is one of *them*.

For Mr. and Mrs. MacLean the close-ups initially establish their warmth. After their enslavement by the Martians, similar close-ups reveal the terrible change in them. What were once pleasant, open faces are now hard and menacing, so much so that it's difficult to believe these are the same people.

The close-ups of the humans also foreshadow those of the Martian Leader, its alien face betraying as little emotion as the humans it has enslaved. In fact, the image of David before the huge desk at the police station begging for attention parallels the later one of him standing before the Martian Leader. The similarity of images suggests some kind of connection between authority figures like parents, policemen—and Martian invaders.

Color also plays a part in Menzies's nightmare vision. The whole color scheme of *IFM* is garish, almost lurid, with heavy emphasis on reds, blacks, whites, and greens. Colors also have symbolic functions. Before their enslavement the MacLeans are both seen in white. After their capture they appear in nothing but black, and when Pat becomes David's ally, she too wears white.

The symbolism of color goes beyond the obvious associations of good and evil. White traditionally represents sexual purity. It may be significant that in David's nightmare Mrs. MacLean changes from white to black and turns against her son after Mr. MacLean takes her up the hill.

Nor does it seem accidental that in David's adolescent fantasy an attractive young woman in white—punctuated by a red handkerchief worn over her breast—takes on the role of surrogate mother, the red

Looking down into the central chamber of the Martian saucer.

symbolically asserting she isn't *totally* pure.

When David and Pat stand before the Martian Leader, we're discreetly shown that Pat's dress is ripped, revealing one bare shoulder. Moments later Pat is placed face down on a table in a semitrance, while the ominously phallic point of the control device machine descends toward her.

If there's one image from *IFM* which stays with audiences, it's certainly this last one. The sexual symbolism in David's "dream" is hard to ignore. *IFM* is heavy with dark, disturbing symbols from the unconscious mind. The whole movie seems calculated to reach us at the deepest levels of our consciousness.

IFM moves quickly. The film is short anyway, and except for the tiresome military footage, Menzies keeps it going at breakneck speed. Toward the end events occur so fast it's often hard to tell what's going on. It's also near the end that Menzies was forced to reuse footage. Whether deliberate or not, the confusion of events and the repeated scenes contribute strongly to the feeling that *IFM* really is a nightmare.

Raoul Kraushaar's music is also part of *IFM*'s nightmare. Kraushaar's score mainly reflects the action, but at various points he uses an atonal, a *capella* chorus of voices that rises and falls in intensity. It's not entirely clear what this music represents, since sometimes the characters appear to hear it and at other times not. But this too is part of the "logic" of a dream.

The music is most often heard when someone is sucked into the sand hill, but it also shows up during the opening narration, combined with more conventional music. At the film's climax Kraushaar counterpoints the heavy, strident sounds of his conventional score with the weird, atonal voices, heightening the tension.

Whenever it's heard in *IFM*, the dissonant chorus creates an especially unnerving sensation, like fingernails scraping across a blackboard, as well as communicating a distinctly unearthly feeling. Fifteen years later Stanley Kubrick's *2001: A Space Odyssey* would use a much larger atonal chorus to convey a similar sense of unearthliness.

The special effects in *IFM* are not extraordinary. The flying saucer is seen only in the first few minutes, remaining underground for the rest of the film. The sand whirlpool which sucks people into the hill was designed by Menzies himself. It consisted of a piece of stretched canvas with a layer of sand on top. A slit in the canvas allowed the sand to be sucked down by a vacuum hose. To show the hole closing again, the film was merely reversed.

The most fascinating figure in *IFM* is the Martian Leader. There is a quick, unsettling intelligence in the Leader's eyes that's difficult to forget. In a film where things are not always convincing, the Martian Leader comes across as disturbingly real.

Menzies used a female midget, Luce Potter, to play

Kelston (Arthur Franz), Pat (Helena Carter), and Colonel Fielding (Morris Ankrum) inside the Martian saucer.

the role of the Martian Leader. Potter's face was first covered with an iridescent green makeup, and her head covered by a huge, artificial cranium. Potter then stood on a raised platform with her head inserted into the globe apparatus, including the Martian's three-limbed tentacles.

The Leader's two Mutant slaves were played by seven-foot, six-inch Lock Martin (Gort in *The Day the Earth Stood Still*) and eight-foot, six-inch former circus performer Max Palmer. Because of their size, Martin and Palmer weren't able to stand the physical strain involved in some of the scenes, so normal-sized actors were substituted for the Mutants, with midgets replacing the other actors to sustain the illusion of the Mutants' giant size.

Martin and Palmer make imposing figures as the Mutants. Unfortunately, the other Mutants are of varying shapes and sizes—one is short and chubby—and not nearly as convincing.

Despite its limited budget and many flaws, Menzies and his crew created a thoroughly disturbing visual experience in *IFM*. For every weakness in the film, there is a counterbalancing strength that makes *IFM* a truly memorable and imaginative film.

William Cameron Menzies was more interested in the potential of film than in the potential of actors, so the performances in *IFM* are subsidiary to the visual elements. Yet all the acting in the film is at least competent.

Jimmy Hunt is perhaps not quite as smooth as we might like. But his performance as David MacLean carries an undeniable vulnerability necessary for the audience, and especially children, to identify with him.

Hunt's film career began in 1949. Most of his films were forgettable, with the exception of *Cheaper by the Dozen* (1950), with Clifton Webb and Myrna Loy, and its sequel, *Bells on Their Toes* (1952). *IFM* is probably his most memorable performance in a career which ended in 1954 with *She Couldn't Say No*.

Helena Carter was born in New York City in 1926 and began her career as a model. She made her film debut in 1947 in *Time out of Mind* and appeared to be a rising star until dropping out of films soon after *IFM* (see Appendix).

Billed ludicrously for *IFM* as "The Atomic Beauty," Carter brought a warmth and understanding to her role as Dr. Pat Blake that was important in making her an acceptable substitute for David's mother in his "dream." On the other hand, there's no denying Carter's underlying sexuality and the role it plays in David's fantasy.

Along with a handful of others, Arthur Franz is one of the few actors immediately recognized for his association with SF films. Franz never achieved prominence outside "B" movies, though he played supporting roles in all kinds of films. In second features, however, Franz was a popular hero, conveying a certain intelligence as well as strength, as he does in *IFM*.

Colonel Fielding is attacked by a Mutant.

Franz was born in Perth Amboy, New Jersey, in 1920. He made many appearances on the Broadway stage, his last in 1947 in the play *Command Decision*. His first film appearance seems to have been in *Jungle Patrol* (1948). Later films include *Sands of Iwo Jima* (1949), *The Caine Mutiny* (1954), *The Eddie Cantor Story* (1954), and *The Young Lions* (1958).

Franz's association with SF/horror films began in 1951 with *Flight to Mars* and *Abbott and Costello Meet the Invisible Man*. He also appeared in *Back from the Dead* (1957), *The Flame Barrier* (1958), *Monster on the Campus* (1958), and *The Atomic Submarine* (1959). (For a list of Franz's films, see the Appendix.)

Franz also starred (along with Marshall Thompson, another occasional star of SF films) in an obscure TV series called *World of Giants*, about the adventures of a tiny secret agent and his partner. Franz has also guest-starred on such other SF TV shows as *Men*

Publicity photo of David MacLean (Jimmy Hunt) with Martian Mutant, holding heat-ray weapon

GREAT SCIENCE FICTION FILMS

Into Space, Voyage to the Bottom of the Sea, and *The Invaders.*

Another familiar face from *IFM* is Morris Ankrum (Colonel Fielding). Ankrum was actually a former professor of economics, born in 1897, who began a film career in 1936 with a series of Hopalong Cassidy movies. Ankrum took a variety of roles in low-budget pictures. Toward the end of his career, he began appearing in many SF and horror films, often as a military man. His SF films include *Rocketship X-M* (1951), *Earth Vs. The Flying Saucers* (1956), and *Kronos* (1957). Ankrum died in 1964. (For a list of his SF/horror films, see the Appendix.)

Leif Erickson (George MacLean) has been in Hollywood since 1935, with roles mostly as tough guys and villains in such films as *Sorry, Wrong Number* (1948), *On the Waterfront* (1954), and *Mirage* (1965). Erickson achieved some prominence with his starring role in the TV western, *High Chaparral.*

Hilary Brooke (Mary MacLean) appeared in dozens of second features from 1937 on. She's probably best known for her unlikely role of Lou Costello's girlfriend in the fifties' Abbott and Costello TV show.

Milburn Stone (Captain Roth) has been in films since the 1930s. Stone's good looks made him a notable hero of serials and other action pictures. He later became known for his portrayal of "Doc Adams" in the long-running TV show, *Gunsmoke.*

Robert Shayne (Dr. Wilson) was another all-purpose actor who drifted into SF and horror films. His role in *IFM* is small, but he was to become better known for his continuing role as "Inspector Henderson" on the *Superman* TV show.

Invaders from Mars may be unique among SF films. The film is obviously low-budget and full of flaws and improbabilities. It has no particularly strong performances, nor does it express any strong feelings about science, society, or life in general.

Yet *Invaders from Mars* has a powerful effect on moviegoers. It owes its strength to the striking visual images created by William Cameron Menzies, and their reflection of the secret hopes, fears, and desires in all of us. In the history of science fiction film, *Invaders from Mars* will not be remembered for any special message it carries, but because it speaks to us in the language of our dreams and nightmares.

THE WAR OF THE WORLDS

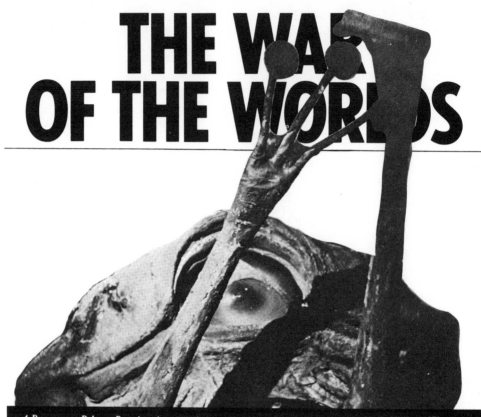

A Paramount Release. Running time: 85 minutes (8050 feet). Based on the novel by H. G. Wells. A Western Electric Recording. Commentary by Cedric Hardwicke.

PRODUCTION CREDITS

PRODUCER	*George Pal*
DIRECTOR	*Byron Haskin*
SCREENPLAY	*Barre Lyndon.*
ASSOCIATE PRODUCER	*Frank Freeman, Jr.*
DIRECTOR OF PHOTOGRAPHY	*George Barnes, A.S.C.*
ART DIRECTION	*Hal Pereira and Albert Nozaki*
EDITOR	*Everett Douglas, A.C.E.*
TECHNICOLOR CONSULTANT	*Monroe W. Burbank*
ASSISTANT DIRECTOR	*Michael D. Moore*
COSTUMES	*Edith Head*
SET DECORATION	*Sam Comer and Emile Kuri*
MAKEUP SUPERVISION	*Wally Westmore*
MUSIC	*Leith Stevens*
SOUND RECORDING	*Harry Lindgren and Gene Garvin*
SPECIAL PHOTOGRAPHIC EFFECTS	*Gordon Jennings, A.S.C., Paul Lerpae, A.S.C., Wallace Kelly A.S.C., Ivyl Burks, Jan Domela, and Irmin Roberts, A.S.C.*
ASTRONOMICAL ART	*Chesley Bonestell*
MARTIAN COSTUME AND MAKEUP	*Charles Gemora*
HAIR STYLIST	*Nellie Manley*
PROCESS PHOTOGRAPHY	*Farcoit Edouart, A.S.C.*
MINIATURE CONSTRUCTION	*Marcel Delgado*
SPECIAL EFFECTS	*Walter Hoffman*
PROPERTIES	*Gordon Cole*
STUNT COORDINATORS	*Dale Van Sickel, David Sharpe, and Fred Graham*

CAST

CLAYTON FORRESTER	*Gene Barry*
SYLVIA VAN BUREN	*Ann Robinson*

The War of the Worlds (hereafter referred to as *War*), which had been a Paramount property since 1925, became one of the first alien invasion films of the fifties. Filmed in magnificent three-strip technicolor, the $2,000,000 film proved that "a special effect is as big a star as any in the world," as George Pal later said of the success of *Star Wars*.

While Pal's film version lacks the depth and resonance of H. G. Wells's novel, it is a stunning success in purely visual terms, with its menacing Martian machines gliding relentlessly across the screen, scattering mankind before them and leaving total destruction and death in their wake.

When Paramount licensed *War* for video cassette sales in 1980, it quickly climbed into the ranks of the top twenty-selling tapes, its appeal undiminished nearly thirty years after its release.

War was generally well received by the critics when it premiered in New York on August 13, 1953 (it had a Hollywood-only premiere on February 20, 1953). The *New York Times* said: "*The War of the Worlds* is, for all of its improbabilities, an imaginatively conceived, professionally turned adventure which makes excellent use of technicolor, special effects by a crew of experts, and impressively drawn backgrounds. . . . Gene Barry, as the scientist, and the cast behave naturally, considering the circumstances."

Moira Walsh, writing in *America,* called the film a ". . . surprisingly pertinent and undated science-fiction account of an invasion from Mars. . . . Its technicolored 'special effects' (by the late Gordon Jennings) are superlative and its scientific explanations are lucid and convincing. By comparison, its handling of earthly matters, such as mass panic, boy-meets-girl (yes, even here!) and a well-intentioned but rather sappy affirmation of religious faith, is rather flat and small in conception."

The titles appear after a brief prologue (read by Paul Frees) detailing the ever greater destructive power of modern weapons. A narration, read by Sir Cedric Hardwicke, describes the Martians' need for a new world and precipitates a two-and-a-half minute "grand tour" of the solar system, ending with our green and inviting Earth.

The residents of Linda Rosa, a small California town, see a meteor fall to Earth, skidding in sideways and starting a number of small brush fires. Word of the fallen meteor is sent to three Pacific Tech scientists fishing in the area. Dr. Clayton Forrester, one of the scientists, decides to take a look.

Meanwhile, at the impact site, a gully, the townspeople gather to stare at the still-hot meteor and discuss the economic benefits it could bring Linda Rosa through increased tourism.

Forrester, a nuclear physicist, arrives at the site, where he meets Sylvia Van Buren, niece of Pastor Matthew Collins, the local minister, and a lecturer in Library Science at USC. When Forrester's Geiger counter starts clicking, indicating the meteor is radioactive, he decides to stay until the meteor cools.

While Forrester, Sylvia, and the rest of the town attend a square dance that night, three locals are deputized to stand guard near the meteor while it cools. They're about to leave when they hear a strange sound—the top of the meteor is unscrewing! A long-necked, cobra-headed probe emerges from the opening. Eager to make "first contact," the locals, waving a white flag ("Everybody understands when you have the white flag, you wanna be friends," says one), slowly approach the ominous-looking cobra head. Their words of welcome turn to screams as the cobra head turns and drops toward them, a strange pinging sound preceding the release of a heat ray that incinerates them.

At the dance, the lights and phones go out, and all the clocks and wristwatches become magnetized; a compass points toward the meteor site. Forrester, the sheriff, and a deputy rush there to discover fires, downed power lines, and the charred bodies of the three men. As they survey the scene in horror, they spot the cobra neck turning toward them, the warning pinging increasing in intensity. The deputy tries to flee in the police car, leaving Forrester and the sheriff behind, but he's destroyed by a blast from the Martian heat ray. Forrester and the sheriff escape on

foot and call in the military.

Quickly mobilized, the Army rushes vehicles full of troops to the gully harboring the Martian machine. As the troops continue digging in, an Air Force plane drops flares. The flares reveal a manta ray-shaped Martian machine, now free of its protective meteor casing. The machine fires its heat ray, destroying a radio truck, and everyone dives for cover. Still more troops and tanks are called up to encircle the Martian nest with a ring of steel. Colonel Heffner arrives to take charge of the operation. Sylvia, there with her uncle Matthew, serves donuts and coffee to the weary soldiers. Soon Colonel Heffner is joined by General Mann, who notes the Martians' position and reveals the machines are magnetically linked in groups of three.

After a long and tension-filled night, the troops

Forrester (Gene Barry) and others from the church venture out to find all the Martian machines have crashed. Here, a dying Martian feebly reaches out from a hatch in its machine.

wait for something to happen. A Martian machine rises from the gully and surveys the scene. In the command bunker, Pastor Collins argues for peaceful communication with the Martians, theorizing they must be closer to the Creator than man, since they are technologically more advanced. Slipping undetected from the bunker, he walks toward the trio of approaching machines, a Bible in his hand, reciting the twenty-third Psalm. The cobra neck of the lead machine swivels and drops menacingly toward him, then blasts him with its heat ray.

Shocked at the minister's incineration, the troops open fire. The gully around the machines is devastated by the firepower of the soldiers, but the machines themselves are unharmed, protected by translucent blisters. Using their heat rays and "skeleton" rays (so called for their effect), the machines vaporize the soldiers and their ineffectual weapons. The headquarters bunker is hit by a heat ray, turning one soldier into a human torch. Colonel Heffner orders everybody out, but is himself caught in a skeleton ray and disintegrated.

Forrester and Sylvia escape in his small airplane while jets streak toward the Martian machines. Flying low to avoid the jets, Forrester nearly collides with a Martian machine and crashes near an abandoned farmhouse. Later, rested and recovered from the crash, Forrester and Sylvia cook breakfast in the farmhouse. Sylvia tells him of a time when she, a child and lost, took refuge in a church and "prayed for the one who loved me most to find me." She was found by her uncle Matthew.

A new meteor smashes into the farmhouse, collapsing it and knocking Forrester unconscious for several hours. After he awakens, a Martian machine hovers outside, looking for life.

As Forrester and Sylvia prowl around, one of the machines lowers an electronic TV-eye on a flexible cable. Entering through a window like some great snake, the eye investigates the room the two frightened humans are hiding in. Finding nothing, the eye closes up protectively and withdraws, but another one appears after Sylvia catches a fleeting glimpse of a Martian outside. Alerted to the presence of the Martian scanner by Sylvia's scream, Forrester severs the eye from its cable with an axe.

Suddenly, a Martian lays his suckered hand on Sylvia's shoulder. Forrester throws a length of pipe at the creature—after first shining his flashlight on it—and it runs off shrieking in pain.

Calming the hysterical Sylvia, Forrester realizes there is no time for romance. Taking the severed probe with them and a sample of the Martian's blood, they escape from the farmhouse moments before the Martians destroy it.

The rout of mankind is shown through scenes detailing the Martians' destruction of Earth's greatest cities. Man seems helpless before the superior weaponry of the Martians.

At his command post, General Mann reveals the Martian battle strategy of linking up in threes and cutting through the countryside like scythes. Meanwhile, Forrester arrives at Pacific Tech with the electronic eye he severed and the blood sample from the wounded Martian. The Martian eye has three segments, each with its own pupil and each a different color: red, blue, and green. Hooking up the scanner to an "epidiascope" reveals how the Martians see us.

Since ordinary weapons are useless, an atomic bomb, carried by the "flying wing," will be dropped on the Martian position outside Los Angeles. A radio man records the scene on tape outside the bunker nearest the Martian advance, his words meant for the future—if there is any.

The Martians generate their protective blisters as the bomb is dropped. The onlookers, including Forrester and Sylvia, peer through goggles at the radioactive cloud, searching for signs of life. Suddenly, the Martian machines glide unscathed from the cloud. Man has thrown the best of his military arsenal at them to no effect. Their inexorable advance continues. Los Angeles is next.

At Pacific Tech, Forrester advocates a biological approach to defeating the Martians, since "we can't beat their machines." But the Martians are approaching the city, and an evacuation is ordered. Unable to continue their research in the city, the Pacific Tech scientists flee in a school bus driven by Sylvia. Forrester stays behind to retrieve some instruments, planning to drive out in a pickup truck. But he encounters looters desperate to escape, who beat him and throw him from the truck. Left behind, his truck gone, Forrester runs through the empty streets. He finds the truck, overturned and stripped, but the only sign of Sylvia's school bus is its destination sign lying in the street.

The Martian machines glide malevolently down the nearly empty streets of Los Angeles, their heat rays blowing up buildings, water towers, and even the Los Angeles City Hall. Explosions and flames all around him, Forrester runs from church to church looking for Sylvia. Forrester finds several Pacific Tech scientists who left on her bus, but she is not with them.

Finally, in the third church he visits, Forrester finds her. The situation seems hopeless, and they embrace amid the impending destruction of the church. Suddenly, the Martian machines slow and crash to the street. As Forrester and Sylvia go outside to investigate, they see a hatch on one of the machines open. A suckered hand emerges and flexes feebly before it stops moving. The Martians are dead, killed by our bacteria.

Sir Cedric Hardwicke's narration thanks God, saying, "And thus, after science fails man in its supreme test, it is the littlest things that God in his wisdom had put upon the Earth that save mankind."

In 1895, the twenty-nine-year-old H. G. Wells moved to a house in Woking. There, working diligently on the dining room table, Wells wrote many of his best-known short stories and three novels: *The Wheels of Chance* (a cycling romance), *The Invisible Man,* and *The War of the Worlds.* Wells, like many Englishmen of his day, had succumbed to the joys of the safety bicycle, and he began to keep accounts of his cycling adventures and the sights he saw while pedaling around Woking.

Wells's brother Frank suggested he write a work detailing an interplanetary invasion. Intrigued by the suggestion, Wells began to work out the plot. In his autobiography Wells wrote how he "wheeled about the district marking down suitable places and people for destruction." And, in a letter to Elizabeth Healey, he wrote: "I'm doing the dearest little serial for Pearson's new magazine, in which I completely wreck and sack Woking—killing my neighbors in painful and eccentric ways—then proceed via Kingston and Richmond to London, which I sack, electing South Kensington for feats of peculiar atrocity."

The novel was well received when it appeared in 1898. Sir Richard Gregory's review in the February 10th issue of *Nature* was typical of the novel's critical success: ". . . *The War of the Worlds* is even better than either of these contributions [*The Time Machine* and *The Island of Doctor Moreau*] to scientific romance, and there are parts of it which are more stimulating to thought than anything that the author has yet written."

The feeling of impending apocalypse that colors all of Wells's early works, the "scientific romances," is present in *War* and is the result of several factors in Wells's background. For one, Wells, who was often in poor health, feared he would die young. Further, his early religious training continued to affect his outlook, suggesting to him that Man, the imperfect animal, might fall from his lofty place in the scheme of things. Finally, Wells was influenced by scientific theorists who argued that the law of entropy would lead to a cooling of the sun and the ending of all life on Earth and the other planets of the solar system.

War fits comfortably into the "end of the world" tradition that has been the source of so much religious imagery. Wells was to use several variations on the end of the world theme in his works: *In the Days of the Comet* (a collision between a heavenly body and the Earth), *The World Set Free* (a massive explosion), and *The Shape of Things to Come* (the descent to Earth of Angels to establish the Kingdom of God).

Wells's *War* also followed the appearance, during the final third of the nineteenth century, of a multitude of novels and works detailing the successful invasion of England, including the first, Sir George Chesney's *The Battle of Dorking* (1871), Sir William Butler's *The Invasion of England* (1882), William Le Quex's *The Great War in England in 1897* (1894), and F. N. Maude's *The New Battle of Dorking* (1900).

These works were the expression of a prevalent mood known as *Fin de siecle,* or "end of the century, age, world." *Fin de siecle* results most often when art and behavior undergo transformations, and the old and familiar forms disappear or are replaced by new forms which seem strange or even bizarre. The nineteenth century had been full of momentous change and overpowering events. There was a longing for a new beginning, a new century in which to rebuild the social and intellectual order that fast-moving events had pushed to the brink of collapse.

Later historians were amazed when, Sir George Chesney's book in hand, they were able to find all the geographical landmarks in and around Dorking he mentioned in his fictionalized account.

Here again, Wells followed Chesney's example. He, too, made references to actual places devastated by the Martian invasion—the result of his cycling excursions. Real names like Winchester, Berkshire, Surrey, and Middlesex add to the almost documentarylike flavor of *War.*

Wells's *War* was perhaps the first book to show mankind on the run, fleeing before a merciless enemy. While such scenes are all too familiar to twentieth-century man, used to newsreels showing refugees from countless wars, they were startlingly fresh and powerful in 1898:

> For the main road was a boiling stream of people, a torrent of human beings rushing forward, one pressing on another. A great bank of dust, white and luminous in the blaze of the sun, made everything within 20 feet of the ground grey and indistinct and was perpetually renewed by the hurrying feet of a dense crowd of horses and men and women on foot, and by the wheels of vehicles of every description.
>
> So much as they could see of the road Londonward between the houses to the right was a tumultuous stream of dirty, hurrying people . . . the black heads, the crowded forms, grew into distinctness as they rushed toward the corner, hurried past, and merged their individuality again in a receding multitude that was swallowed up at last in a cloud of dust.

Wells was responsible for other firsts in *War,* most notably the first real *alien* in literature, as opposed to a giant man in Voltaire's *Micromegas.* Here is Wells's description of Man's first encounter with a truly extraterrestrial life form:

> A big greyish rounded bulk, the size, perhaps, of a bear, was rising slowly and painfully out of the cylinder. As it bulged up and caught the light, it glistened like wet leather.
>
> . . . There was a mouth under the eyes, the lipless brim of which quivered and panted, and dropped saliva. The whole creature heaved and pulsated convulsively.
>
> . . . The peculiar V-shaped mouth with its pointed upper lip, the absence of brow ridges, the absence of a chin beneath the wedge-like lower lip, the incessant quivering of this mouth, the Gorgon groups of tentacles. . . . There was something fungoid in the oily brown skin, something in the clumsy deliberation of the tedious movements unspeakably nasty. . . . I was overcome with disgust and dread.

A trio of Martian war machines advance slowly as they move out of the gully into the face of intense firepower directed at them. The wires supporting the lead machines are clearly visible in this shot.

Wells's vile Martians drink human blood, or, rather, inject it into their veins. While this practice disgusts Wells's narrator, he is quick to point out that "I think that we should remember how repulsive our carnivorous habits would seem to an intelligent rabbit."

This is perhaps Wells's greatest contribution in *War*: the turning of the tables, the looking at things from fresh perspectives, especially our treatment of "lower" life forms, including the colored races enslaved or destroyed by the white man's superior technology (see the chapter on *The Day the Earth Stood Still* for more about this). As Wells's narrator says, after hiding from the Martians as a frightened rat might hide from men, "Surely if we have learned nothing else, this war has taught us pity—pity for those witless souls that suffer our domination."

George Pal was born in Cegled, Hungary, a small town about thirty-five miles from Budapest, on February 1, 1908, the son of entertainers with a traveling theater troupe. Raised by his grandparents, Pal did not follow in his parents' theatrical footsteps, deciding instead to become an architect. In 1925 he was accepted into the Budapest Academy of Art, where, in addition to his architectural studies, he took painting, anatomy, and other fine arts classes. He also slipped into a nearby medical school's lectures on anatomy occasionally by donning a white smock and pretending to be a student. Pal made extra money by sketching muscles and bones for the medical students, which they turned in as their own work.

Architectural students were required to learn either carpentry or bricklaying, so Pal decided to become a carpenter, a craft which would help him immensely when he created his puppetoons.

Architect Pal graduated in 1928, just in time to join the swelling ranks of the unemployed in Hungary. But his knowledge of anatomy and his drawing skills got him a job as an apprentice animator at Budapest's Hunnia Film Studio. The job enabled Pal to marry his childhood sweetheart, Zsoka Grandjean.

Pal found that his salary, while enough for him, was insufficient for a newly married man, so he looked around for another, better-paying job. In 1931 he and his wife went to Berlin, where he found work as an animator at the huge UFA studio. Within two months he was put in charge of the studio's cartoon department.

By 1933 Pal found himself under scrutiny by the Gestapo, so he moved to Prague, Czechoslovakia, and set up his own cartoon studio, designing his own portable stop-motion camera when he discovered there wasn't a single animation camera in the country.

Hoping to find success making animated commercials, Pal moved again, this time to Paris, where he made cartoons for Philips Radio of Holland. Philips Radio liked his work so much they convinced Pal to pack his suitcases again and move to Holland, where he opened his first studio in a garage and his second in a butcher shop. Here, Pal and his American associate, Dave Bader, hit upon calling his "color cartoons in three-dimensions" *puppetoons,* a word created by combining puppet and cartoons.

By 1939 war was imminent, and, after several tries, Pal was finally granted a visa to emigrate to the United States, his fifth country in eight years. When Pal reached New York, Barney Balaban of Paramount Pictures saw one of the young Hungarian's puppetoons at a party and offered him a contract to produce a series of animated shorts to be released under the name "Madcap Models."

Forrester (Gene Barry), flanked by Dr. Pryor on the left (Robert Cornthwaite) and Sylvia (Ann Robinson) on the right, shows the scientists at Pacific Tech the head of the electronic TV probe he severed in the farmhouse.

George Pal, left, with Sir Cedric Hardwicke, who narrated the film, at a recording session. Pal thought it appropriate that an English voice speak Wells's words.

Within a year George Pal Productions of Hollywood, California, was producing puppetoons for Paramount. Between 1941 and 1947 Pal made over forty puppetoons for the studio, receiving six Academy Award nominations along the way. The Academy voted him a special Oscar for his unique animation techniques in 1943.

After producing two educational shorts in 1948 and 1949 for Shell Oil, Pal got the financial backing he'd been seeking from Eagle-Lion Films to produce his first feature, *The Great Rupert*, starring Jimmy Durante, in 1949. Rupert was a trained squirrel (really just another animated figurine) who finds a cache of money in an old house filled with destitute vaudevillians and gives it to his friend Mr. Amendola (Durante). The film got good reviews as a family picture and made money. Pal and his director on *Rupert*, Irving Pichel, were now ready for their next joint effort—*Destination Moon*. (See the *DM* chapter.)

Pal's project after *Destination Moon* was *When Worlds Collide*. With its successful launching, Pal began looking for another script and was excited to discover that Paramount owned the rights to H. G. Wells's classic *The War of the Worlds*.

A.

B.

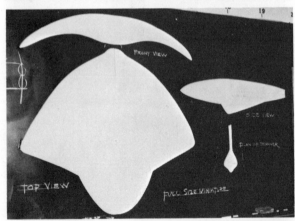

C.

D.

Cecil B. DeMille bought the film rights to *War* in 1925. In 1926 the *New York Times* reported Paramount's decision to make the film. "Arzen Doscerepy, famous German technical expert who has been producing in Berlin," said the *Times*, "has spent two years perfecting devices and mechanisms which will make Wells's Martians walk and spray death around the world."

Hollywood pioneer Jesse Lasky, who'd gained control of Paramount, offered the Wells property to famed Russian director Sergei Eisenstein *(The Battleship Potemkin)* in 1930. But, although a script was prepared, Eisenstein backed out in favor of *Que Viva Mexico* (1931), a film never completed. Later *War* was almost made a number of times, but never got past the writing of the script.

Pal, assured that Paramount owned the rights to the novel in perpetuity, called his good friend DeMille. DeMille quickly told him he was no longer interested in making the film himself and would be delighted to help Pal in any way he could.

Pal started moving ahead on the project and hired Barré Lyndon to write a new script. Lyndon, born in London in 1896, was a former journalist, novelist, and playwright who'd moved to New York from England in 1938. By 1940 he was writing movies for MGM, and in 1943 wrote *The Lodger* for 20th Century-Fox.

Pal and his director, Byron Haskin, asked Lyndon to update the story and set it in the United States. With all the talk of flying saucers, *War* was especially timely, and a California-based film would be much cheaper to shoot than a London period film.

After finding the perfect small town in the Chino hills, Linda Rosa, Lyndon began working on his first draft. At Pal's urging, Lyndon replaced his original lead, Major Bradley, with Dr. Clayton Forrester, a nuclear physicist from Pacific Tech.

Pal wanted Forrester to become separated from his wife and child and spend his time searching for them. But Don Hartman, vice-president in charge of production and the man responsible for the Crosby/ Hope "Road" pictures, said a married hero wouldn't be acceptable to the audience. Instead, he ordered Pal to give Forrester a "love interest." Reluctantly, Pal had Lyndon write in the character of Sylvia Van Buren, as well as reducing the violence in Lyndon's first draft.

When Hartman saw Lyndon's script dated June 7, 1951, he told Pal it was a "piece of crap" and threw it into a wastebasket. But associate producer Frank Freeman, Jr. defended the film to his father and president of Paramount, Y. Frank Freeman, as did Cecil B. DeMille, without whose support the film might never have been made. The elder Freeman told Pal to make the film any way he wanted, and work went ahead.

Pal began casting the picture during the summer of 1951, looking for the right actor for the Clayton Forrester role. He considered Lee Marvin, but instead went with an unknown, a young Broadway actor

Paramount had just put under contract, Gene Barry. While waiting for shooting on *War* to begin, Barry made *The Atomic City* (1952).

Twenty-four-year-old Ann Robinson, a native Californian who'd had a bit part in George Stevens's *A Place in the Sun* (1951), was signed to play Sylvia Van Buren.

In December 1951 a second-unit film crew left for ten days of location shooting near Florence, Arizona, about forty-five miles southwest of Phoenix. Byron Haskin and another crew were sent thirty-five miles northwest of Los Angeles to film the evacuation of the threatened city. In the hilly terrain surrounding the Simi Valley, Haskin shot the scenes of onlookers watching the atomic bomb explosion that fails to stop the Martian machines.

The Arizona National Guard played the part of the Army troops, and the scenes of them in their tanks, armored vehicles, and personnel carriers roaring up, jumping out, and setting up in battle positions were totally realistic in comparison with many stock-footage-filled films.

The gully where the first meteor lands took shape on Stage 18. Albert Nozaki recalled that his stage

A.

B.

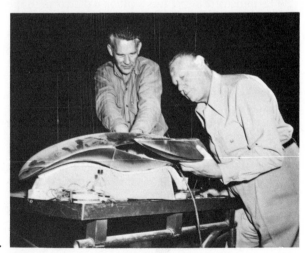

D.

C.

Page 98.
(A) Gordon Jennings, standing, watches the effects crew prepare a Martian machine for filming.
(B) Producer George Pal and director of photography George Barnes look over the script.
(C) Preliminary sketches of the full-size Martian machine model on a studio blackboard.
(D) A plaster shop employee at Paramount works on the mold which will be used in the making of Martian machines.

Page 99
(A) George Pal, promotion manager Kenneth DeLand, and director Al Nozaki study a production sketch.
(B) Lee Vasque, now head of Paramount's prop shop, works on the mechanism which operated the cobra neck and head.
(C) Effects man Chester Pate (left) and special effects chief Gordon Jennings, work on a Martian machine.
(D) Art director Al Nozaki with an early model of the Martian machines. Nozaki is drawing continuity sketches for the production.

THE WAR OF THE WORLDS

setting on 18 was basic and designed to be as economical as possible; the production's budget couldn't afford many sound stages.

Meanwhile, Haskin's crew filmed portions of the evacuation from Los Angeles on an unopened segment of the Hollywood Freeway. For the scenes of Forrester searching frantically for Sylvia, Pal got the Los Angeles Police Department to rope off part of Hill Street early one Sunday morning. The police kept the streets clear for the film company while cameras covered Gene Barry's movements through streets dressed by the prop department.

Shooting the principal photography took about a month, and was finished in mid-February 1952. Haskin had only been shooting for several days when a lawyer from the legal department ran onto the stage shouting that filming had to stop. The lawyer explained that Paramount owned only the *silent* rights to Wells's book. But Wells's son Frank was completely sympathetic and got the movie company out of hot water by selling them the "talkie" rights for an additional $7,000.

Stage 18 was cleared for four miniature sets with sky backings, the most elaborate of which was the Los Angeles street destroyed by the marauding Martian machines. A backlot street was matched with 4- by 5-inch Ektachrome still shots of Bunker Hill in Los Angeles, and rephotographed on technicolor film. A matte of the sky and background, done as an 8- by 10-inch blowup and then reduced to 35 mm film frame size, was matched with the flame effects, Martian machines, and then with the live action.

The miniature street was built on a platform so the high-speed cameras could not only shoot from street level but also get as close to the miniature buildings as necessary. Filming at approximately four times normal speed requires intense light levels, so the set was bathed in light.

For the effects of the A-bomb blast, eighty-one-year-old powder expert Walter Hoffman placed a mixture of colored explosive powders atop an airtight metal drum filled with explosive gas on Stage 7. Set off by an electrical charge, the resulting explosion reached a height of seventy-five feet and produced a perfect mushroom cloud for the high-speed cameras filming the miniholocaust.

Al Nozaki, a Japanese-American, made hundreds of sketches to storyboard the script shot-by-shot. Hired by Paramount in 1934 to work on Cecil B. DeMille's *The Crusades*, apprentice draftsman Nozaki spent a year in an internment camp in California before he was released to spend World War II working as an industrial designer in Chicago. Hans Drieir, head of Paramount's art department, rehired him in 1945.

According to George Pal, Lyndon's first script retained the Martian war machines' tripod legs. But Pal soon realized that they "just didn't look right." And, for a low-budget production, the tripods would have cost too much to construct and operate realistically. That's when the idea of basing the machines on a

manta ray resting on three beams of pulsating electronic energy occurred to Nozaki.

Nozaki put his design for the machines on paper and had the prop man build a small design model fifteen inches across. Three forty-two inch models were molded in clay and refined down to Nozaki's specifications. Copper was formed over a wooden armature for the operating models, and each had various mechanisms, lights, and gears to operate the cobra head inside. They were destroyed after the filming.

The Martian machines were scaled one-inch to one-foot. Each machine had a rotating cobra neck which emitted the heat ray and wing-tip skeleton rays, but only one machine had the TV scanner probe, and only the main machine could lower its neck as it does when it cinders Pastor Collins.

The machines were individually attached to fifteen hair-fine wires connected to a control trolley on an overhead track. Some of the wires carried electricity to operate the interior mechanisms, while others bore the machines' weight.

The triple-lensed scanner used for close-ups was made of thick plastic with hexagonal holes cut in it. Behind this, special effects chief Gordon Jennings placed rotating light shutters which gave off an eerie flickering effect.

For the scene in which the machines rise from the gully and are fired upon by the troops, over two hundred individual explosive charges were placed on piano wires, buried in the ground, or thrown onto the miniature sets by the effects crew. Three lucite domes, the Martians' protective blisters, were filmed against the miniature set while the explosions were triggered. The saucer models, which would have been destroyed by the explosions, were matted in later.

Following Nozaki's design, Gordon Jennings and his special effects crew constructed the machines to project a million volts of static electricity down three wires attached to the floor of the set. A high-velocity blower was used from behind to force sparks down the electrical "legs." Pal finally decided that the effect, while spectacular, was just too dangerous. It could easily have electrocuted a crew member or set the stage on fire.

The machines' heat rays, which emerged from the cobra head, were burning welding wire. As the wire melted, a blowtorch set up behind blew the wire out, and the result was superimposed over the neck of the machines.

The disintegration of Colonel Heffner by one of the skeleton rays took 144 individual mattes to reduce him to nothingness. In the same sequence a soldier is struck by a heat ray and staggers about the command bunker in flames. The stuntman was "Mushy" Callahan. As actor Les Tremayne (General Mann) recalled, Callahan was wrapped in a blanket to extinguish the flames, but the blanket actually funneled the fire up around his face, and he was badly burned before Tremayne and others rushed in to put out the fire.

For the destruction of the Los Angeles City Hall,

A Martian machine blasts a water tower with its heat ray in Los Angeles. The heat ray was burning welding wire superimposed over the cobra head.

powder man Walter Hoffman placed explosive charges inside the eight-foot-tall miniature, and its explosive destruction was filmed by high-speed cameras.

The unearthly sounds of the Martian machines were produced by amplifying the sounds from three electric guitars played backward. The Martian's scream when Forrester strikes it with the pipe was produced by scraping dry ice across a microphone and mixing it with a woman's scream played backward.

The Martian itself had to be convincing, but there was very little money for anything too elaborate. After Nozaki had come up with a design, he gave it to actor and makeup man Charles Gemora. From papier-mâché, latex rubber, rubber tubing, and lobster-red paint over a wooden frame, Gemora fashioned the Martian. With himself inside, Gemora could make the three fingers of the Martian's hand move. With pulsating veins and operational gills in its front, the Martian was weirdly alien-looking. Unable to walk when inside his Martian construct, Gemora was pulled about the set on a dolly which he knelt on. Extremely fragile, the Martian lasted through its few scenes before falling apart.

Pal hoped initially to film the final third of *War* in 3-D. When the Earthmen put on their protective goggles, prior to the dropping of the atomic bomb, Pal wanted the audience to put on their 3-D glasses. But Paramount, not incorrectly, believed 3-D was nothing more than a passing fad and vetoed the idea. Perhaps if *War* and other films that would have benefited

from the addition of 3-D had used the discarded process, audiences would not have thought it such a gimmick.

Low-budget or not, *War of the Worlds* still cost nearly $2,000,000 to produce, and approximately $1,300,000 was spent on the special effects. Gordon Jennings, who died shortly after the film's release in 1953, received an Academy Award posthumously for his work on *War*.

War contained the most extensive and spectacular special effects of any science fiction film since *Things to Come* in 1936, and shared the decade's honors with *Forbidden Planet* and *This Island Earth*.

War places special significance on the number three (perhaps coincidentally), as *2001* would fifteen years later. The meteors fall in groups of three, there are three Pacific Tech scientists in the vicinity, three deputized townspeople stand guard over the meteor, the Martian machines move in groups of three, the Martians have three eyes and three "fingers," and Forrester visits three churches before finding Sylvia in the third.

Pal and Haskin decided early on to have the Martians always in the east and moving toward Los Angeles in the west (screen right to screen left). Little remarked upon, this composition theory gives *War* an almost subliminal emphasis.

One of the film's first shots, in Linda Rosa, shows the meteor fireball falling from upper screen right diagonally across the screen to lower screen left, exactly bisecting the steeple of a church and providing a subtle clue to the source of the Martians' eventual destruction. A man is shown on a ladder, ready change a movie theater's marquee (the film is Cecil B. DeMille's Paramount production, *Samson and Delilah* —the story of a man with a weakness that destroys him, but not before he destroys his surroundings, as do the Martians.

General Mann, after the failure of the A-bomb, turns and faces left for a moment, a posture of defeat, then turns back to the right, toward the invaders, and vows to "fight them every inch of the way."

The occurrence of things in threes and the right-to-left emphasis gives *War* a subconscious correctness and sense of unstoppable advance that helps one become caught up in its relentless pace.

Apart from its superior special effects and manipulative use of screen composition, *War* is not a very complex film. Byron Haskin's direction, it can be argued, was shaped by Al Nozaki's hundreds of storyboard sketches. But, within the confines of following so detailed a visual blueprint, Haskin's direction is solid and clean. He keeps the action moving at a brisk pace, never allowing it to falter.

The earliest sound pictures, called, appropriately enough, "talkies," lost the art of movement. Tied down to inefficient microphones and huge, sound-proofed cameras (see *Singin' in the Rain* for a comedic look at this problem), the early talkies set back the art of making *movies* for years until improvements in technology gave back to films their lost freedom.

Under Haskin's sure hand, *War* moved. His greatest weakness, if the blame can be placed on him, is his direction of the actors. When asked about his two leads, Haskin said, perhaps unfairly, that Ann Robinson was a nice girl and very willing, but not much of an actress. As for Gene Barry, Haskin said, "Jesus, he was terrible! He has since developed into quite an actor, but at that time he couldn't get out of his own way!" (See the chapter on *Robinson Crusoe on Mars* for more about Haskin.)

Though Haskin is perhaps too harsh in his judgments about his two leads, he did get excellent performances from Les Tremayne as General Mann and Lewis Martin as Pastor Collins. And, as the three deputized townspeople who become the Martians' first victims, Bill Phipps, Jack Krushchen, and Paul Birch handled their roles nicely.

Gene Barry, born Eugene Klass in 1921, was put under contract by Paramount in 1952 after a successful series of roles on Broadway. *War*, which was to be his first film, actually became his third, since its late start of shooting allowed Barry to appear in *The Atomic City* and *Those Redheads from Seattle* (1952).

War was his only science fiction film until he appeared in John Mantley's thoughtful *The 27th Day* in 1957. Always a reliable and steady-working actor, Barry is best known for three television series: *Bat Masterson* (1959–61), *Burke's Law* (1963–65), and *The Name of the Game* (1968–70).

Ann Robinson, who played Sylvia Van Buren, was born in 1928. Although she'd had small parts in several films prior to *War*, she had to go through the ordeal of auditioning in Paramount's infamous "fishbowl"—a glass-encased stage which prevented the actors and actresses from seeing or hearing those scrutinizing them.

Robinson married Mexican matador Jaime Bravo in 1957, but got a divorce in 1967 and never tried acting again. She was a guest at the twenty-fifth anniversary celebration for *War* at Hollywood's Holly Cinema in 1977.

Les Tremayne, who played General Mann, was a star of radio drama in the 1940s. Pal chose Tremayne for his authoritative presence and impressive "radio voice." Tremayne has appeared in many films and spoke the narration at the beginning of *Forbidden Planet*.

Sir Cedric Hardwicke, who spoke the narration, was suggested by Cecil B. DeMille when Pal asked DeMille if he would narrate. Pal later observed that it was unintentionally appropriate that an Englishman narrated a picture based on a book written by H. G. Wells. (For more on the cast, see the Appendix.)

George Pal died of a heart attack at his Beverly Hills home on May 2, 1980. He was seventy-two. At the time he died, he was working on another film, *Voyage of the Berg*. He won eight Oscars for his films and was considered a genius in special effects.

Pal will perhaps be remembered more for other films, such as *Destination Moon*, *The Time Machine*, and *Tom Thumb*. But *The War of the Worlds* inspired many young filmmakers and made possible many of the special-effects-laden films being produced today. Dismissed by many as "lightweight," both *War* and George Pal will continue to grow in stature as long as the wonder of special effects continues to hold audiences spellbound in darkness.

Although produced at a time of hysteria over Communism and the fear of invasion from the skies (see the chapters on *Day* and *The Thing*), *War* has more to do with the genius of H. G. Wells and George Pal than either of those Cold War influences. Its technicolor and effects remain stunning and its low-budget inventiveness is a tribute to the men who made it. This is one *War* no one wants to forget.

THEM!

A Warner Bros. Production, 1954. Running time: 94 minutes (9,260 feet). Black and White.

PRODUCTION CREDITS

PRODUCER.. *David Weisbart*
DIRECTOR... *Gordon Douglas*
SCREENPLAY... *Ted Sherdeman*
ADAPTATION... *Russell Hughes*
STORY.. *George Worthing Yates*
PHOTOGRAPHY.. *Sid Hickox, A.S.C.*
ART DIRECTOR.. *Stanley Fleischer*
EDITOR.. *Thomas Reilly, A.C.E.*
SOUND... *Francis J. Scheid*
MUSIC... *Bronislau Kaper*
ORCHESTRATIONS.. *Robert Franklyn*
MUSICAL DIRECTION... *Ray Heindorf*
SET DECORATOR.. *G. W. Bernsten*
WARDROBE.. *Moss Mabry*
POWDER and EFFECTS... *Ralph Ayres*
PROP CONSTRUCTION... *Dick Smith*
MAKEUP.. *Gordon Bau*
ASSISTANT DIRECTOR... *Russ Sanders*

CAST

SERGEANT BEN PETERSON... *James Whitmore*
DR. HAROLD MEDFORD.. *Edmund Gwenn*
DR. PATRICIA MEDFORD.. *Joan Weldon*
ROBERT GRAHAM... *James Arness*
BRIGADIER GENERAL O'BRIEN... *Onslow Stevens*
MAJOR KIBBEE... *Sean McClory*
ED BLACKBURN.. *Chris Drake*
LITTLE GIRL... *Sandy Descher*
MRS. LODGE... *Mary Ann Hokanson*
CAPTAIN OF TROOPERS.. *Don Shelton*
CROTTY.. *Fess Parker*
JENSEN.. *Olin Howlin*
AMBULANCE ATTENDANT.. *William Schallert*
SERGEANT... *Leonard Nimoy*
WATCHMAN.. *Dub Taylor*

Them! opened at the Paramount Theater in New York on June 15, 1954, and was an immediate success with both the ticket-buying public and the critics. Oddly enough, Warner Bros. first tried to sell the screenplay to another studio. Then, after deciding to make the picture, Warners slashed its budget only days before the production was to begin. Despite Warner Bros.' lack of faith in the picture, *Them!* was the studio's top-grossing film of 1954.

Today *Them!* is remembered fondly as "that picture with the big ants," and as one of the earliest films about monsters unleashed by the radiation of the first atomic bomb tests. Although the fifties were to see a flood of giant insects, dinosaurs, birds, octopuses, Gila monsters, and more, *Them!* is unique for its blend of mystery, horror, convincing background, documentary-like approach, and excellent performances.

In *Commonweal,* Philip T. Hartung wrote that "*Them!* moves forward with suspense, from the opening scene ... right up to the finale."

The *New York Times* said: "Perhaps it is the film's unadorned and seemingly factual approach which is its top attribute. *Them!* is taut science-fiction."

The Catholic World called *Them!* "a really frightening trick film in which all the scientific lah-de-dah sounds uncomfortably convincing.... I don't know whether I'd recommend it to anyone but adults with strong stomachs. *Them!* certainly isn't for softies."

Moira Walsh, writing in *America,* said that the premise of *Them!* "furnishes the basis for the best science-fiction film since *The Thing.* Its cast goes about the fearsome task of destroying the ants in absorbingly detailed semi-documentary manhunt (ant-hunt) style."

Newsweek summed it all up when it called *Them!* "a right little fright of a picture."

Two New Mexico state troopers, Sergeant Ben Peterson and Officer Ed Blackburn, find a little girl wandering in the desert, clutching her broken doll, and obviously in a state of shock. After picking her up, the troopers check out an abandoned trailer just a few miles up the road and, leaving the little girl in the car, they investigate. The trailer's side has been pulled out, not pushed in, and the interior destroyed. No money has been taken, and Peterson finds a recently fired revolver. Strangest of all, scattered among the rubble are sugar cubes.

Peterson finds a piece of plastic and a scrap of cloth in a cubbyhole under a bunk, and Blackburn takes him to an odd-shaped print in the sand that neither can identify. Back at the car, Peterson finds the piece fits a gap in the forehead of the little girl's doll and the scraps of cloth match her bathrobe, suggesting she hid under the bunk.

As an ambulance prepares to take the little girl away, a strange sound comes from the desert. Unseen by Peterson or the ambulance attendant, she sits up in wide-eye fear, but slowly sinks back as the sound subsides. The attendant nervously attributes the

sound to the freakish desert wind.

Peterson and Blackburn stop off at Gramps Johnson's general store to see if he can tell them anything, but it's been wrecked like the trailer. The radio is still playing and there's coffee on the stove, but no sign of Gramps. Peterson finds Gramps's .30-.30 rifle bent into a V-shape and then finds Gramps's body lying in the cellar, bloodied and torn. Like the trailer, the walls have been pulled out, money left untouched, and sugar scattered about.

Leaving Blackburn behind to wait for the experts still at the trailer, Peterson goes back to town. Blackburn hears the eerie sound from the desert and goes outside to investigate. He steps offscreen, then fires his gun and screams in agony.

Back at headquarters, the investigation is stymied, and Peterson feels guilty about Blackburn's presumed death. Peterson's superior briefly considers that a homicidal maniac is responsible, but remembers that Gramps got off four rounds with his rifle and Blackburn was a crack shot.

Since the little girl's father was an FBI man, agent Robert Graham is called in to join the case. Graham arrives in time to hear the coroner's report on Gramps Johnson. Every bone in his body was broken and he was filled with "enough formic acid to kill twenty men."

Patricia Medford (Joan Weldon) is menaced by a sentry ant after she wanders off alone near the trailer site.

Doctor Harold Medford of the Department of Agriculture arrives in response to the cast of the strange print found at the trailer. Medford is accompanied by his daughter Pat, also an entomologist.

The elder Medford asks where the first A-bomb was tested and is told it was exploded at the nearby White Sands missile range nine years ago. Medford tells Pat that genetically nine years would allow enough time for mutations. Graham resents the two doctors' reluctance to tell him what's going on, but they insist they must be sure before making any definite statements.

Peterson, Graham, and the two doctors visit the little girl, who is still in shock and unable to speak. But when Medford places a glass of formic acid under her nose, she blinks and screams, "Them! Them!"

Medford insists they visit the desert site where the odd print was found, and, when Graham protests that it's getting late, the doctor enigmatically replies, "Later than you think."

At the trailer site the scientists make several observations, and Pat mysteriously notes that "without other food, *they'd* turn carnivorous." Pat defends her father to Graham, who is growing impatient with the two doctors' secrecy. Meanwhile, Medford finds a new print and exclaims, "It's gigantic!" and warns of panic if his assumptions prove correct.

Wandering off alone, Pat hears the mysterious sound, and is suddenly confronted by a giant ant. Graham and Peterson come to her rescue, and, at Medford's suggestion, fire their guns at its antenna. Peterson kills the giant insect with a burst from a submachine gun.

The doctors surmise the ant is a mutation caused by lingering radiation from the first atomic bomb. The ominous sound is the ants communicating with each other.

Flying over the A-bomb test area in a helicopter with General O'Brien, Medford and Peterson search for the ants' nest. Pat and Graham are in a second 'copter with Major Kibbee. Suddenly, Pat spots the opening to the nest. Several ants appear at the rim holding human bones, which roll down to join a pile of skulls and other rubble, including Ed Blackburn's belt and holster.

Medford tells the General the nest cannot be bombed at night because the ants would be outside foraging. They'll cover the nest with burning phosphorus during the hottest part of the day to keep the ants inside while cyanide gas canisters are thrown in.

Peterson and Graham prepare to enter the nest, but Graham resists Pat's coming with them. He gives in reluctantly when she points out they must have an expert along. Wearing gas masks that make them look insectlike themselves, they climb down into the nest where the gas appears to have done its job.

Suddenly, a wall collapses revealing several very-much-alive ants, which the men incinerate with flame throwers. Going on, they find the queen's chamber, containing her giant eggs. It's an eerie sight, made

more so by the misting cyanide gas.

Pat tells them they're too late; the eggs that contained the young queens and their mates are empty. Peterson and Graham burn the eggs that are left, but two queens have already flown away to start new nests. The danger is immense, since, as Medford later explains, a single queen can lay thousands of eggs. Because the giant ants could fly anywhere, Medford and the others go to Washington to alert the government to the danger.

In Washington, Medford shows a film describing the awesome powers of ants to a meeting of shocked officials. Medford warns them Man will be extinct within a year if the escaped queens are allowed to propagate.

News media are monitored for reports of missing persons, flying saucers, strange noises or odors, unsolved murders, suicides, thefts of sweets, and "unnatural things alive or dead."

Graham, Pat, and Kibbee investigate a report that a Texan named Alan Crotty says his plane was forced down by flying saucers shaped like ants. Crotty, who's being held in a mental ward, begs them to believe him. Crotty reports seeing one big saucer being chased by two smaller ones, all headed west. After assuring Crotty he's not crazy, Graham tells the doctor Washington will inform him when Crotty is "well" and can be released.

Months pass, and a nest hatches aboard a freighter at sea, killing all but two crewmen before the ship is sunk by naval gunfire. Investigation reveals the ship spent several days in a Mexican port with an open hatch cover, allowing the ants to get aboard.

Graham and Peterson investigate the theft of forty tons of sugar from a Los Angeles railroad yard. Suspected of the theft, the watchman says that if he were going to steal something, it wouldn't be sugar. "Is sugar a rare cargo? Is there a black market for it? Did you ever hear of a fence for hot sugar?"

A Mrs. Lodge identifies the body of her husband, found with an arm torn off after leaving early that day on a pleasure trip with their two sons. Now the boys are missing.

Acting on a tip, Peterson and Graham interview Jensen, a drunk in an alcoholic ward. Jensen tells them he's seen little airplanes and big ants outside his window. Realizing that Jensen has been there for five months and is no longer likely to be hallucinating, Peterson and Graham look out the window at the dry channels of the Los Angeles riverbed.

Graham and Peterson find a model airplane that belongs to the Lodge children near a storm drain opening—and an ant print. The boys may be inside and alive, but there are over 7,000 miles of storm drains under the city.

Martial law is declared as troops rush to take up positions near the storm drain openings. Peterson, Graham, and Kibbee lead troops into the storm drains in jeeps. They must find the nest and make sure no new queens have hatched and escaped before they

Robert Graham (James Arness), Dr. Howard Medford (Edmund Gwenn), and Ben Peterson (James Whitmore).

can destroy it.

Inside, Peterson hears a noise. Climbing through a pipe to an unfinished drain, Peterson spots the kids, alive but threatened by several ants. Peterson uses his flame thrower on the ants. As he's helping the kids up to the pipe, another ant appears and encircles his waist with its mandibles. Graham and the troops arrive and kill the ant, but Peterson dies after being assured he's saved the boys.

The troops start using explosives against the ants. Medford stops them, explaining they can't risk closing the tunnels before the nest is examined. Weakened by the explosions, the tunnel collapses behind Graham, and he finds himself facing the ants alone. Fortunately, the troops break through in time to prevent his sharing Peterson's fate.

Locating the egg chamber, Medford and the others find the young winged queens ready for flight. Medford gives the order, and the ants are burned.

A worried Graham asks, "If these monsters got started as a result of the first atomic bomb in 1945, what about all the others that have been exploded since then?"

Medford replies, "When man entered the atomic age, he opened a door to a new world. What we'll eventually find in that new world nobody can predict."

In 1953, George Worthing Yates sent a treatment for a screenplay entitled *Them!* to Warner Bros. The studio's story editor, Findlay McDermid, routinely circulated the treatment to all the Warners producers.

A new producer on the lot, Ted Sherdeman, intrigued by the treatment, asked McDermid to buy *Them!* and hire Yates to write the screenplay. Yates's contract called for him to turn in a finished script in ten weeks.

Yates was later to write *It Came from Beneath the Sea* and other successful science fiction and horror films. But his screenplay for *Them!*, his first, displayed no knowledge of the limitations and realities of filmmaking, and would have cost many millions of dollars to produce. Discouraged by what Yates was turning in, Sherdeman tried to have his contract paid off after five weeks and someone else assigned to the script. But Jack L. Warner, the tight-fisted studio head, wanted full value for his money, and Yates was allowed to finish the script. When Yates turned in his screenplay, it contained ants, but bore little resemblance to his original treatment. Sherdeman tossed the screenplay into the nearest wastebasket and started over.

McDermid advised Sherdeman to allow a writer under contract to Warners, Russell Hughes, to try his hand at turning the treatment into a filmable screenplay. Hughes plotted an outline which added the little girl wandering in the desert, and which at the end found the last surviving queen at bay in an amusement park. But after completing only a few pages of the actual script, Russell Hughes died unexpectedly.

Sherdeman took over the writing of the script and, following Hughes's outline, wrote the screenplay exactly as the late writer had envisioned it, except for the ending. Since renting an amusement park for even one day would be expensive (and would be too similar to the ending of Warner Bros.'s previous year's production of *The Beast from 20,000 Fathoms*), Sherdeman changed the film's ending from the park to the storm drains of Los Angeles, ultimately making the final scenes far more claustrophobic and chilling.

The mother-with-endangered-children aspect of Sherdeman's script may be hokey, but it adds urgency and drama to the search for the queen's nest by putting the threat into specific, understandable terms —two little boys are in danger!

Outside the studio one day, Jack L. Warner's assistant Steve Trilling saw some ants crawling on the ground and turned to Sherdeman and asked the producer if they were what he really wanted to make a film about. When Sherdeman said yes, Trilling muttered an expletive and walked away.

Rather than giving up, Sherdeman invited Trilling and Warner to see a film two young men had made in Arizona of ants, tarantulas, and other insects by slowing their movements with a special spray. Warner and Trilling arrived about thirty minutes late for the screening, plopped down to watch the film, and walked out in disgust after seeing only about a minute's worth of footage.

Sherdeman apologized to the two young men and suggested they take their footage to the Walt Disney studio. They did, and their film became *The Living Desert* and won an Academy Award for Best Short Subject of 1953.

To convince Trilling to make *Them!*, Sherdeman asked Lawrence Meggs of the studio's art department to construct a model of a harvester ant from photographs. Meggs fashioned a three-foot black ant which could move its head, antennae, and mandibles. Meggs even built the ant its own carrying case.

Sherdeman plopped the case on Trilling's desk and told him to look inside. The executive was so impressed by Meggs's articulated model ant that he ordered a film test of it that day. Sherdeman, who had

The discovery of the nest.

the ant constructed to sell Trilling on going ahead with *Them!*, hadn't intended the model to be used for test shots.

Despite Sherdeman's protests that the model was not what he would use in the movie, Trilling had it filmed tipping over several small railroad cars. The result was amateurish, but, to Sherdeman's surprise, Trilling indicated he'd like to place *Them!* back on the production schedule.

Sherdeman then learned through his agent that the studio had put the property up for sale and that 20th Century-Fox had offered Warner Bros. $25,000 for it. Dismayed but not surprised, Sherdeman began planning the production of Alfred Hitchcock's *Dial M for Murder* when Walter McCuhan, one of Warner Bros.'s top executives, decided to take a look at Sherdeman's script and see what Fox was so willing to pay good money for. McCuhan liked the story and decided Warner Bros. would make it after all, with Sherdeman as producer. The studio assigned Gordon Douglas the director's job.

Gordon Douglas, born in 1909, began as a child actor in films at the Paramount Astoria studio on Long Island before going to work for Hal Roach. Eventually, Douglas became an assistant director and gagman on the *Our Gang* shorts. At twenty-two he directed his first *Our Gang* and won an Oscar. He made twenty-four *Our Gang* shorts before directing his first feature, *General Spanky*. Douglas directed a Laurel and Hardy feature, *Saps at Sea*, in 1940.

Douglas left the Roach studios for RKO and the opportunity to direct more features. After a succession of B films, Douglas directed *The Black Arrow*, the first of what he called "clack-clack pictures," because of the armor and sword fights.

Sherdeman's screenplay does not introduce the ants until twenty-five minutes into the film, heightening the anticipation, and director Douglas wisely shows the ants as little as possible to ensure that each time we see them they remain terrifying.

Gordon Douglas, though enjoying a lengthy and successful career, has rarely risen above the level of a competent craftsman. His experience and professionalism show in *Them!*, but he is not considered a director of the first rank. (For a fuller listing of his films, see the Appendix.)

With Douglas set to direct, Sherdeman hired veteran character actor Edmund Gwenn to play Dr. Medford. Jack L. Warner, convinced that at seventy-eight Gwenn was too old for the part, replaced Sherdeman as producer with David Weisbart. Courageously, considering how he got the producer's assignment, Weisbart agreed with Sherdeman's selection of Gwenn, and the actor was signed.

Although Sherdeman's original hope of using 3-D was vetoed, Weisbart's budget provided for shooting the film in color and on location in California's Mojave Desert.

The art department built two "star" ants, only one of which was a full mock-up. The second ant, only

Ben Peterson, Pat Medford, and Bob Graham explore the ants' nest.

GREAT SCIENCE FICTION FILMS

Ben Peterson (James Whitmore), Bob Graham (James Arness), and Pat Medford (Joan Weldon) examine the queen's chamber in the nest they found in the desert. Amid the bodies of dead ants can be seen the egg cases at the left.

three-fourths complete, was mounted on a camera crane with a full crew of technicians behind it to operate the gears and levers that made the antennae go up and down. As director Douglas later recalled, the crew that operated the mock-up were "pulling wires, stepping on each other, getting in each other's way. That would have made a good comedy."

Warners technician Dick Smith (not the famed makeup artist) built a number of ants to be used when large numbers of the insects were needed but didn't have to move. These immobile ants' heads and antennae moved and bobbed in the breeze created by wind machines.

Designed for color, the ants had greenish-purple skins and iridescent eyes that seemed to change color from moment to moment. But several days before location filming in the Mohave Desert was to begin, the budget was slashed to under a million dollars. And, as Douglas recalled, "Some genius decided to shoot it in black and white."

After several days of shooting, Douglas asked the cutter how the star ant looked on film—was it "honest"? The cutter shrugged, replying, "Well, as honest as a twelve-foot ant can be."

If the full-size ants have any shortcomings, it's that they move too slowly, although it may be argued that it's their larger size that has slowed them down. The

full-size ants have advantages, too. The scene in which an ant crashes into the radio room on board the ship is truly terrifying, and Peterson's death between the mandibles of the ant in the drains is made even more brutal by a long shot showing him dangling helplessly in its jaws.

The desert sequences were shot twenty-five miles from the nearest town, so the film crew, which required a bulldozer and a helicopter, got around in jeeps. An old Army weapons carrier was converted into a sound truck, and the camera car was also modified to handle the rough desert terrain.

Real sand, because of its granular composition and weight, doesn't blow cinematically, so the crew ordered large quantities of "movie" sand from Hollywood.

After Gramps Johnson's general store was stocked with produce and canned goods by the property department, the crew gleefully smashed everything with sledge hammers and axes to make the set look as if the ants had destroyed it. Gordon Douglas and James Whitmore joined in the fun, smashing and chopping away until they were exhausted.

Attention to detail is apparent in all the sets. Most have ceilings, which lend an air of believability. They're also filled with ashtrays, file drawers, and

THEM!   **109**

The ant menacing Pat Medford (Joan Welson) is one of the two "star" ants. This mock-up, only three-quarters complete, was attached to a camera crane and operated by a full crew

beat-up furniture—people *work* there, they're real rooms. The police headquarters are properly messy and paper-strewn; the walls are adorned with no-nonsense official photographs of unsmiling administrative higher-ups. A wall-mounted fan silently reminds the viewer that this is the New Mexico desert.

The success of *Them!* spawned a number of imitators—films featuring either giant creatures or beasts that had been enlarged or produced by the lingering radiation of the atomic and hydrogen bomb tests. *Them!* was the first of the atomic mutation pictures, but it was not the first of the giant monster films.

That honor goes to First National Pictures's 1925 silent, *The Lost World*, which electrified moviegoers with a Brontosaurus on the rampage in London. The special effects, which seemed almost magical to reviewers of the day, were created by stop-motion animation genius Willis O'Brien. O'Brien also stop-motion animated *King Kong* (1933) and *Mighty Joe Young* (1949).

O'Brien's assistant on *Mighty Joe Young*, Ray Harryhausen, created the ficticious "Rhedosaurus" in 1953's *The Beast from Twenty Thousand Fathoms. Beast* preceded *Them!*'s release by a year, but although the dinosaur's blood was radioactive, the atomic bomb was responsible only for its release from entombment in Arctic ice, not for its creation or its size.

Interestingly, a 1953 George Pal/Byron Haskin film, *The Naked Jungle*, featured "a monster forty miles square"—the ravenous and aggressive *maripunta*, or army ants.

In 1955 Ray Harryhausen created a giant, fivearmed octopus for *It Came From Beneath the Sea*. Atomic bomb tests killed off its food, forcing it to the surface, where it menaced Kenneth Tobey and San Francisco's Golden Gate Bridge (monsters have an affinity for famous landmarks).

Tarantula (1955) was followed by a plague of mantises, locusts, and other creepy-crawlies. For the rest of the fifties and sixties movie screens were filled with giants. (For a fuller listing, see the Appendix.)

The plain scientific truth is, however, that the ants of *Them!* and many of the other giant creatures that came from beneath the sea or out of the ice to menace Mankind could not exist. It's against the law—the square-cube law. Gravity would close their breathing holes, or so weigh them down they could not move, even if their bones (or exoskeletons) could support their mass. The size of the blue whale, 95-feet long and weighing 150 tons, the largest animal on earth, is possible only because it lives in the buoyant salt water of the oceans.

Them!'s irascible Dr. Medford is made immediately recognizable as an absentminded professor when, after a question about his identity has to be repeated, responds, "Yes, yes, yes, no need to shout." Medford needs to be reminded by Peterson to put on his goggles, and then the trooper has to adjust them for the fumble-fingered doctor.

On the helicopter Medford resists saying "over" when using the radio, and when Peterson signs off for him by saying "over and out," he grumps, "Oh, now you're happy!" and blows his lips in disgust.

Sherdeman recognized that humor relieves the tension a horror film builds up and which it cannot sustain without wearing out the audience. When Pat points out that the walls of the nest are lined with saliva, Peterson says, "Spit's all that's holding me together, too."

In the alcoholic ward the chronically drunk Jensen chants, "Make me a sergeant and give me the booze," over and over, prompting the frazzled bum in the next bed to protest, "Please, my *nerves.*"

Gordon Douglas's choice of shots is effective and economical, and his use of close-ups is sparing but timely. After the first ant is killed, close-ups reveal the shock the characters feel.

Douglas gets good performances from the whole cast, including those in supporting roles. Fess Parker's one scene as the Texan who sees "flying saucers shaped like ants" so impressed Walt Disney that he hired the lanky actor to play Davy Crockett for his television series.

James Whitmore, born in 1921, played Ben Peterson. Considered a stocky Spencer Tracy look-a-like, Whitmore was an easy choice for producer Weisbart. His Peterson is quiet, competent, and totally believable. Whitmore's timing in his scenes with Gwenn is perfect, and his steady presence is one of the film's stronger assets.

Whitmore's first film was *Undercover Man* (1949), and his other films include: *The Asphalt Jungle* (1950), *Battle Cry* (1955), *Black Like Me* (1964), *Planet of the Apes* (1968), and *Give Em Hell Harry* (1975). He was the star of a 1960–61 TV series, *The Law and Mr. Jones.*

James Arness, born James Aurness in 1923, plays Bob Graham. At six feet, six inches, Arness towered over the rest of the cast. His impatient FBI man provides the film's modest love interest, and his scenes with Pat Medford reveal warmth under that bluff exterior. The male bond between Graham and Peterson is shown through the small, knowing looks and raised eyebrows (at scientific jargon) that pass between them.

Arness served in the Army and worked in real estate before making his film debut in *The Farmer's Daughter* in 1949. That same year he appeared in *Battleground*, and in 1950 was in *Wagonmaster* and *Two Lost Worlds.* His other films include: *The Thing* (1951), in which he played the alien, *Big Jim McLain* (1952), *Horizons West* (1952), *Island in the Sky* (1953), *Hondo* (1955), and *The First Traveling Saleslady* (1956).

Many of Arness's films were with John Wayne, and when Wayne was offered the part of the marshal in a Western television series and turned it down, he suggested Arness be hired instead.

Wayne introduced the first episode of Arness's series, *Gunsmoke. Gunsmoke* was on television from 1955 to 1973 and made Arness a major star. In 1978 he returned to television as Zeb Macahan in *How the West Was Won,* later retitled *The Macahans.*

Edmund Gwenn was born in 1875 and died in 1959. He started on the English stage, but became a film star when he moved to Hollywood in his middle age. In his later years he was mostly cast in comedy roles, although he played a villain in Hitchcock's *Foreign Correspondent* (1940). His first sound film role was in *How He Lied to Her Husband* (1931). His other films include: *Anthony Adverse* (1936), *Pride and Prejudice* (1940), *Lassie Come Home* (1943), *Between Two Worlds* (1944), *Miracle on 34th Street* (Academy Award, 1946), *Mr. 880* (1950), and *The Trouble with Harry* (1955).

Gwenn portrays Medford as the typical absent-minded professor, but his character is not all comic blunder and bluster. Gwenn captures him as often detached, musing, or deliberative, a man with weighty matters on his mind.

Them! was singer Joan Weldon's sixth picture. Weldon's Dr. Patricia Medford is tough and hard-nosed. She coolly tells Peterson and Graham to "burn them, burn everything" when she sees the young queens have already fled the nest. Her characterization is subdued, intelligent, and, except for one scene, she is not a "screamer" in need of a masculine shoulder to rest her head on.

Leonard Nimoy, Mr. Spock of TV's *Star Trek,* has a bit part as the sergeant in the room where reports are monitored for clues to the whereabouts of the missing queens. (For more about the actors and their other films, see the Appendix.)

Them! is one of the better, if not the best, of the giant monster films and the first to use atomic radiation as the rationale for its oversize creatures. It benefited from a taut, well-written script with an above average share of humor and characterization.

Today *Them!* is still seen and appreciated, and its half-mystery, half-trackdown approach to its material is as fresh as it was in 1954.

There is one strongly ironic moment in *Them!* As the two state troopers search Gramps Johnson's store, destroyed by the giant ants that are the result of man's unlocking the secrets of atomic energy, a voice on the radio notes that many diseases have effectively been wiped out.

Them! suggests that the results of scientific inquiry can be a mixed blessing—even as science eliminates one menace to man, it may be unleashing another.

THIS ISLAND EARTH

A Universal-International Release, 1954. Based on the novel by Raymond F. Jones. Running time: 87 minutes (7,830 feet). Technicolor.

PRODUCTION CREDITS

PRODUCER . . . . *William Alland*
DIRECTOR . . . . *Joseph Newman*
SCREENPLAY . . . . *Franklin Coen and Edward G. O'Callaghan*
ART DIRECTION . . . . *Alexander Golitzen, Richard H. Riedel*
CINEMATOGRAPHY . . . . *Clifford Stine*
SPECIAL EFFECTS CINEMATOGRAPHY . . . . *Clifford Stine, Stanley Horsley*
SPECIAL EFFECTS . . . . *Charles Baker*
MUTANT DESIGN . . . . *Millicent Patrick*
MUTANT CONSTRUCTION . . . . *Jack Kevan, Chris Mueller, and Robert Hickman*
EDITOR . . . . *Virgil Vogel*
MUSIC . . . . *Herman Stein*
MUSICAL DIRECTOR . . . . *Joseph Gershenson*

CAST

EXETER . . . . *Jeff Morrow*
RUTH ADAMS . . . . *Faith Domergue*
CAL MEACHAM . . . . *Rex Reason*
STEVE CARLSON . . . . *Russell Johnson*
BRACK . . . . *Lance Fuller*
JOE WILSON . . . . *Robert Nichols*
THE MONITOR . . . . *Douglas Spencer*
DR. ENGELBORGER . . . . *Karl Lindt*
THE MUTANT . . . . *Eddie Parker*
with Regis Barton and Bart Roberts

In Washington, D.C., Dr. Cal Meacham, at the conclusion of a scientific conference, poses with a Lockheed F-80 Shooting Star jet while he takes a few questions from reporters. He tells them only that he's working on the industrial application of atomic energy. Returning to Ryberg Electronics' private airfield, Meacham loses control of the jet, which plunges toward earth. Suddenly, the plane is enveloped by a mysterious green glow, which takes over the controls and lands the jet safely.

Cal's assistant, Joe Wilson, shows him a new condenser that has arrived from their regular supply company. The tiny condenser "beads" can handle thousands of volts of electricity, and a diamond drill can't even scratch the surface. A new package, from "Electronics Service—Unit 16," arrives. It contains a metal-paper catalog. The catalog is for a full line of "Interociter" parts.

When a call to the supply company reveals they know nothing of the new condensers or the catalog, Cal orders the parts necessary to construct an Interociter. Cal and Joe begin the task of assembling the parts when they arrive. When they're done, a voice speaks from the Interociter, telling them how to activate it. They follow the voice's instructions, and a man with a high-domed head and white hair materializes on the screen and introduces himself as Exeter. Exeter tells Cal that assembling the Interociter was a test and that he can now join a special research team. A plane will be sent to the airport the next morning for Cal.

As a demonstration of the Interociter's power, Exeter destroys the catalog with rays of energy from the corners of the triangular screen. On a hunch, Cal pulls the power connection from the wall, and the Interociter explodes, leaving behind just a melted puddle of metal.

Against Joe's warnings, Cal shows up to meet the plane. It lands in heavy fog without anyone at the controls. With Cal aboard, the windowless plane takes off. As Cal sleeps, the plane flies on, eventually landing at a remote airstrip in Georgia. Here he's met by Dr. Ruth Adams, an old flame. But Ruth is strangely standoffish and evasive about knowing him. Puzzled, Cal follows her to a mansion, known as "the Club," which turns out to be a research facility housing half a dozen top scientists.

Cal meets Exeter, who invites him into his office. Ruth tries to get a word with another scientist, Dr. Steve Carlson, but they're interrupted, so she joins Cal and Exeter. Exeter tells Cal that they are all scientists working for peace, and that Ruth is working along similar lines as he. Exeter reveals an Interociter located behind a wall and on it shows Cal his new laboratory, which contains its own Interociter. Suddenly, a message from another unit comes in, and Exeter hastily escorts the two scientists out. Once they're gone, Exeter takes the incoming message from someone we can hear but not see. Exeter questions and tries to resist the methods this higher authority is

forcing him to take.

After dinner Ruth and Steve Carlson show Cal around. At the first opportunity Cal takes them aside and asks what Exeter is up to—all the scientists, he has observed, are experts in atomic energy. They finally agree he can be trusted. They tell him that a device they call the "sun lamp" can rob a person of his free will and that they were fearful Exeter's assistant, Brack, may have used it on him as it had been used on the other scientists there except for Dr. Engelborger.

Arguing over the use of the mind device, Exeter and Brack use an Interociter to spy on the three humans as they speak in Cal's new lab. Assuming that lead would shield them from prying, the three continue to speak until Neutron the cat, sensing the vibrations of the spy ray, hisses. Immediately, Cal changes the subject.

In a demonstration for Cal's sake Exeter uses the rays of Cal's Interociter to burn a hole through a sheet of lead, effectively warning Cal that nothing, including conversations behind lead, is impervious to its powers. Having demonstrated the machine's capabilities, Exeter asks Cal not to have any more secret meetings with his colleagues. Ignoring Exeter's order, the three scientists meet again. Carlson tells Cal that an entire hillside has been hollowed out and the opening covered by canvas. They assume something quite large is hidden inside.

Exeter again speaks with the unseen voice—this time revealed to be his planet's leader, the Monitor. The Monitor tells him that the Earth scientists are needed on their planet of Metaluna and that they can complete their work there.

Meanwhile, Cal, Ruth, and Carlson have decided to escape. Brack, using an Interociter, sees them fleeing in a car and tries to stop them by shooting bolts of energy at the car. Carlson tells them he'll stop the car and they'll all run for cover. After Ruth and Cal jump out, however, he goes on and draws Brack's fire. A direct hit blows the car to pieces, and Dr. Engelborger is also vaporized by one of the shafts of energy.

Cal and Ruth make their way to the landing strip and take off in a small plane. As they become airborne, the hilltop research center explodes, killing all inside. The aliens' saucer, hidden in the hillside, emerges and overflies the small plane, pulling it inside by means of a green beam of energy. With Cal and Ruth tucked away inside, the saucer quickly pulls away from Earth.

In a spacious control center, Exeter greets them and tries to apologize for what has happened to them. He reveals that they are headed for Metaluna, a planet far beyond our solar system. As they pass through a "thermal barrier," flames streaming from the saucer's body, Exeter tells them they must be made ready to withstand Metaluna's greater atmospheric pressure. Cal and Ruth grip magnetized handles while glass tubes are lowered over them and the inside filled with gas (Cal jokes that he feels like a new toothbrush).

Sensitive to the Interociter's prying rays, Neutron the cat acts as the three scientists' warning system as they look at a drawing Steve Carlson (Russell Johnson) on the left, has prepared. Both Cal (Rex Reason) in the center, and Ruth (Faith Domergue) on the right, agree something funny is going on at the research facility.

Inside the tubes Cal's and Ruth's bodies become transparent, revealing their circulatory and skeletal systems.

The process complete, they rejoin Exeter as they approach Metaluna. The viewscreen reveals two flaming meteors heading toward the saucer, which are destroyed by defensive rays. Exeter tells them that the meteors are aimed and directed by another alien race, the Zahgons, whose planet was once a comet, and who are now at war with the Metalunans.

The saucer passes through a layer of ionized molecules, which serve as the Metalunan defense against the meteors. The Metalunan surface is a wasteland, barren of vegetation and full of craters from the meteors. Beneath this lifeless surface, however, the people of Metaluna now live. The saucer enters a crater opening, descends to the lower level, and docks. As Exeter takes them to see Metaluna's leader, the Monitor, by means of a small car inside a transparent tube, meteors can constantly be heard and seen impacting and exploding.

The supreme head of Metaluna, the Monitor, greets them. He explains that his race hopes to relocate on Earth. After Cal tells him that "our true size is the size of our God," the Monitor orders Exeter to take them to the "thought transference chamber." Once outside, Cal and Ruth try to escape, only to be stopped by a mutant guard—a sort of humanoid insect with a bulging and exposed brain. Exeter tries to explain that no harm will come to them but Cal slugs him. A direct hit on the building kills the mutant. Cal

and Ruth make their way back to the shuttle car. The Monitor, too, was killed by the collapse of the building and lies buried in the rubble. Exeter catches up with them and offers to help. Cal and Ruth have little choice but to accept.

A wounded mutant is guarding the saucer and grapples with Exeter, seizing his side with his pincer-like claws until Cal clubs the creature down.

The three board the saucer, unaware that the mutant has managed to crawl inside too. As the ionization layer fails, the saucer lifts off and successfully escapes from the planet. On the viewscreen they see Metaluna turned into a radioactive sun.

Exeter orders Cal and Ruth into the pressurization tubes, then enters one himself. They are about to be released from the tubes when the tottering mutant appears in the control room, bleeding from the falling pressure. Slowly, Ruth's tube begins to rise as the mutant lurches toward her. The creature chases her, managing to grab her briefly before collapsing and dissolving into nothingness.

Exeter tells Cal and Ruth they can return to Earth by means of the small plane on which they set off on their journey. The two scientists leave him reluctantly, aware that the saucer has depleted its stores of energy. Their plane drops clear of the saucer, and, as they watch in horror, the saucer burns up in the atmosphere and plunges into the ocean. Exeter, the noblest Metalunan, has died, joining his lost race.

This Island Earth (hereafter referred to as *TIE*) was

based on a novel by Raymond F. Jones (not to be confused with D.F. Jones of *Colossus* fame), published in 1952 by Shasta Publishers of Chicago. The novel was woven together from three separate "Cal Meacham novelettes" originally published in *Thrilling Wonder Stories*.

Thrilling Wonder Stories was the creation of Hugo Gernsback, the man who began magazine SF with *Amazing Stories* in April 1926. Gernsback lost control of *Amazing* in 1929 because of financial complications. He rebounded in June 1929 with *Science Wonder Stories*, adding a companion magazine, *Air Wonder Stories*, in July 1929. The two magazines were combined in June 1930 to produce *Wonder Stories*. This time Gernsback had circulation problems, and the magazine folded in March 1936.

Phoenix-like, Gernsback rose from the ashes again with the August 1936 introduction of *Thrilling Wonder Stories*. Its editor was Mort Weisinger, a member of the first real SF fan club, the Scienceers of New York City. *TWS* remained on the newsstands until January 1955, the date of its last issue.

Jones' first novelette was "The Alien Machine," published in *TWS* in June 1949. "The Alien Machine" (which was the Interociter) introduced Cal Meacham and followed his attempts to discover who sent him the parts to construct the strange machine he builds in his lab at Ryberg Electronics. The novelette ends

with Cal airborne in a pilotless plane for an uncertain destination.

The second novelette, "The Shroud of Secrecy," appeared in the December 1949 issue of *TWS* and carried the story forward to the point where Cal and Ruth Adams learn that something is wrong at the research center of the "Peace Engineers."

"The Greater Conflict," which appeared in *TWS* in February 1950, begins with Cal and Ruth on board the saucer bound for Metaluna, and ends with the destruction of the planet by the Zahgons.

The second installment of the series, "The Shroud of Secrecy," offers several opportunities to compare Jones's original concepts to the script by screenwriters Coen and O'Callaghan.

The similarities and differences are worth noting. For one thing, Cal lands just north of Phoenix, Arizona, not in a remote area of Georgia. The scientists, Ruth for one, are free to live away from the facility, which certainly would mute the suspicions of the local population.

Before he leaves Ryberg, Cal speaks on the Interociter with Dr. Warner, the (human) head of operations. Cal learns from Warner that the real boss is Mr. Jorgasnovara, known simply as "The Engineer." Warner also tells him that the "Peace Engineers," as they're called, are not interested in "pure science"— science for the sake of discovery. They want only to

Exeter's flying saucer overtakes the small plane containing the escaping Cal and Ruth.

benefit mankind in peaceful ways.

Warner says: "I told you that we are an organization of engineers and scientists who believe that the world could better utilize the productions of science if scientists themselves placed some restrictions on the use of their talents. Among us are those who have been sickened by the use that has been made . . . of our research. . . . We are on strike against such destructive uses. We propose to withhold and control the product of our research from here on."

Cal is seduced by the new lab and marvelous equipment at his command, and he asks few questions. He soon discovers that the Interociter, whose production he is to oversee, is "a superb communication device, surpassing common radio principles in a thousand ways." It can also be blanked out or destroyed—as Cal's was by Dr. Warner—if tampered with or used for "propaganda."

Over five hundred Peace Engineers are employed in sophisticated research at the facility, and one of them, Ole Swenberg, is an old college pal of Cal's. Swenberg and Ruth explain that everything is a big front—but for what, they don't know.

Cal throws himself into his work to the exclusion of everything else. Six months pass. He learns from Ruth that Ole was sedated and taken away because of a breakdown during which he heard the Engineer "thinking." Cal wonders if a "mental device" was responsible for what Ole heard.

Finally, Cal meets Jorgasnovara. The Engineer is sixtyish, big, totally bald, and possessed of a domed cranium. Jorgasnovara explains that the organization has been around since the 1700s, withholding technology until the average man was ready to receive it.

Cal discovers that over six hundred of the Interociters he's produced were shipped out secretly at night. Cal rewires his Interociter, searching for other uses for it. He accidentally picks up Jorgasnovara reporting to another planet by direct mental contact. Looking for answers, Cal and Ruth see a saucer being loaded with Interociters and watch in wonder as it lifts off straight up, traveling so fast they can't follow it with their eyes.

Many of the differences between Jones' novel and the film are due to the nature of film itself and to budgetary limitations. The movie has only half a dozen scientists working for the research center versus over five hundred in the novel—although Exeter tells Cal "Unit 16" is only one of many such units around the world. And Cal spends only a few days at the film's center as opposed to over six months in the novel.

As Exeter (Jeff Morrow) looks on, Cal (Rex Reason) and Ruth (Faith Domergue) are prepared for the pressure equalization necessary for them to withstand the atmosphere of Metaluna—the planet Exeter is taking them to in his flying saucer.

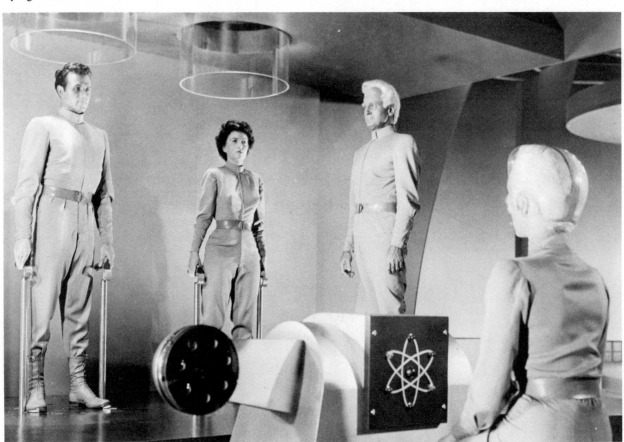

Exeter's saucer skims across the ravaged surface of Metaluna. A Zabgon fightercraft is visible at the top of the picture, and a Metalunan structure can be seen through the opening in the planet's crust at the bottom center. The Metalunan surface is actually a 110-foot miniature set, and the saucer an 18-pound model.

Exeter has assumed most of Dr. Warner's functions in the film, with Brack absorbing the rest. Cal's old friend in the novel, Ole Swenberg, is replaced in the film by Dr. Steve Carlson. And, fortunately, Jorgasnovara's name was changed to Exeter for the film.

Jones' novel presents many arguments for the elimination of war, exploring intellectual concepts no movie can encompass. The film does, however, retain the general tone of the novel's intelligence which elevates it above a mere space adventure film.

By the mid-fifties, Universal-International Pictures had been successful with low-budget SF and horror movies filmed in black and white and requiring few special effects. Growing leery of being typed as a producer of nothing but B-movies, Universal began to search for a property they could turn into a prestige A-film to compete with the major studios.

While U-I searched for the right script, an independent film company called Sabre Productions bought the film rights to Jones' novel. Sabre hired Edward G. O'Callaghan, a veteran Hollywood screenwriter who'd written many of the Charlie Chan mysteries, to write the screenplay.

When Sabre executives saw the finished script, which focused mainly on the interplanetary war, they sought backing from a larger studio. Clearly, *TIE* was going to be an expensive movie to produce. Sabre's dilemma was the opening Universal-International had been looking for. In 1954, U-I bought *This Island Earth* from Sabre.

Universal-International selected one of its staff producers, William Alland, to oversee the production of *TIE*. Alland, born in 1916, was originally an actor with Orson Welles's famed Mercury Theater acting company (responsible for radio's 1938 Halloween "panic broadcast" of the *War of the Worlds*). Alland played Thompson, the inquiring reporter, in Welles's 1941 film classic, *Citizen Kane*, and was also the narrator of the film's "News on the March" newsreel. Later, he left acting to become a producer and an investment broker.

Alland was the producer for many of cult director Jack Arnold's films, including the "Gill man" series that began with *The Creature from the Black Lagoon*. Among Alland's SF films are: *It Came from Outer Space* (1953, 3-D), the above-mentioned *Creature* (1954, 3-D), *Revenge of the Creature* (1955), *Tarantula* (1955), *The Creature Walks Among Us* (1956), and *The Space Children* (1958).

Alland's director for *TIE*, rumored to have been selected by Sabre, not by Universal, was a solid if unspectacular craftsman named Joseph (M.) Newman. Newman's career in films dates back to 1931, although he didn't direct his first feature, *Jungle Patrol*, until 1948. *TIE* was to be Newman's only SF film.

The final third of *TIE*, with the saucer's flight to the besieged planet of Metaluna, is a favorite of SF

A matte painting combined with live action (showing the actors stepping from a transport tube terminal in the left center) creates the impressive Metalunan landscape which exists beneath the war-torn surface of the planet.

film special effects afficionados. With *War of the Worlds, Forbidden Planet,* and *2001,* the Metalunan sequences of *TIE* certainly contained some of the most ambitious, expensive, and effective SFX (as filmmakers call them) ever attempted in a science fiction film.

Stanley Horsley, special effects director for U-I, had a veteran effects crew eager to work on a prestige production. Charlie Baker was assigned all the film's mechanical effects, while makeup men Jack Keven, Chris Mueller, and Robert Hickman began planning *TIE*'s mutant monster—a studio addition to Jones' novel.

Cinematographer Clifford Stine, who had worked on *King Kong* (the original, not the laughable remake), integrated the live action shots of the actors with the effects shots.

Exeter's flying saucer was made of aluminum and weighed eighteen pounds. To show the saucer in space, the model was filmed in front of a background of a thousand stars—an enlarged color photo taken by an observatory. For the takeoff from Earth, Horsley mounted a camera on a dolly, which was pulled back from a five-foot globe representing the Earth (which, like most pre-space-age models, looked nothing like the big blue marble later photographed by the astronauts) to provide the view seen from the departing saucer. A motor turned the globe while the camera shot through a slightly smeared glass to simulate Earth's atmospheric halo.

Horsley's crew created Metaluna's atmospheric shield, ionized by atomic energy, by filming red and green lights flashing against a 22 X 115 foot background painted with red and green streaks.

Faced with visualizing interplanetary warfare for *TIE,* Horsley and his crew sought advice from Mount Wilson astronomers (advisors to many SF films of the 1950s), looked at all the films of atomic explosions they could get their hands on, and examined futuristic aircraft designs.

In *TIE,* as the saucer approaches Metaluna, the passengers can see Zahgon fighter craft attacking the planet by directing flaming meteors toward the surface. The "meteors" were made of plaster reinforced by jute, and filled with magnesium and chlorate of potash. These little bombs slid down blackened piano wires and blew up when rip wires set off their small explosive charges. At the same instant the meteors struck the ground, electrical charges set off tiny containers of gasoline at the point of impact, producing realistic explosions.

The Metalunan surface was a 110-foot miniature set, above which the effects crew manipulated the diving Zahgon fighters by means of blackened wires connected to overhead rigging. The crew also flew the saucer across the miniature landscape with the same overhead "flying rig."

The Metalunan SFX sequences took twenty-six days to shoot, while assembling and integrating the footage took another fifteen weeks. In all, the SFX cost Universal-International over $100,000 of the approximately $800,000 budget for sixteen minutes of screen time.

Jack Keven, Chris Mueller, and Robert Hickman, responsible for designing the mutant, produced a design that cost approximately $20,000. U-I had wanted a "monster" in the film as a sure-fire box office draw. Much of the prerelease publicity focused on the mutant and its cost of "$25,000," making it "the costliest monster ever created for a motion picture." Keven and Mueller had both worked on U-I's *The Creature from the Black Lagoon*.

The makeup Jeff Morrow wore as Exeter wasn't uncomfortable, but the actor had to be at the studio every day at 6:00 A.M. to be ready to shoot at eight.

Among the matte paintings *TIE* used was one showing the research facility atop a hill; a second showing the inside of the saucer's bay as Cal and Ruth are led from their airplane; and a third showing parts of the Metalunan surface, including the tall landing towers connected by the transport tubes.

The live-action sequences were shot in an intensive four-week period, including Saturday shooting. Although director Newman's earthbound dramatic sequences were fine, producer Alland felt that his Metalunan scenes were less than they could be. Consequently, Alland asked his favorite director, Jack Arnold, to reshoot the Metalunan sequences on redesigned sets. Arnold, however, received no screen credit for his salvage mission.

Herman Stein wrote the music score for *TIE*.

Stein's soundtrack is dramatic and vigorous, effectively underlining and supporting the action on the screen. Since the studio later returned to producing its monster quickies, Stein's muscular score was soon turning up in many of them.

The science in *TIE* is, for the most part, plausible. Certainly, the film uses technical terms (nuclear decay factors, etc.) accurately and well, dropping them unobtrusively into the dialogue. And when Cal, Ruth, and Steve want to have a private conversation, shielded from prying atomic rays, they use a lead panel and control board as barriers. But, as they discover when the cat senses them, the lead is easily penetrated by Exeter's neutrino rays.

It seems both ironic and unlikely that the film's wonder machine, the Interociter, must be plugged into an ordinary wall outlet. (There's also very little logic behind Cal's sudden decision to pull the plug from the wall, destroying the Interociter.) Despite the fact that it looks just like an overgrown television set, the Interociter is a fascinating SF concept: an interplanetary communications device capable of catching and controlling a falling jet or destroying a fleeing automobile.

There is one huge plot hole in *TIE:* Cal is saved by a mysterious green ray, receives a metal-paper catalog, sees a stranger on the unknown machine he builds, takes a ride on a pilotless airplane, and is greeted by two extremely unusual-looking men who can speak any language—and never once does he con-

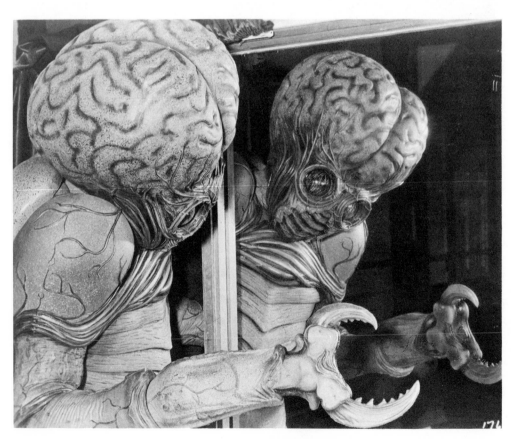

A behind-the-scenes close-up of TIE's $20,000 mutant creation. Designed by Millicent Patick and constructed by Jack Kevan, Chris Mueller, and Robert Hickman, the mutant was TIE's obligatory monster.

THIS ISLAND EARTH

THIS ISLAND EARTH

THE SUPREME EXCITEMENT OF OUR TIME!

IN COLOR BY TECHNICOLOR

2½ YEARS IN THE MAKING!

STARRING
JEFF MORROW · FAITH DOMERGUE · REX REASON with LANCE FULLER · RUSSELL JOHNSON
DIRECTED BY JOSEPH NEWMAN · SCREENPLAY BY FRANKLIN COEN AND EDWARD G. O'CALLAGHAN · PRODUCED BY WILLIAM ALLAND

An example of an advertising "6 sheet" for TIE. The artist managed to get just about everything visually exciting from the film onto one poster.

sider something unusual is afoot!

Another curious twist in the story line has Brack trying to destroy the fleeing humans (succeeding with Steve Carlson and Dr. Engelborger) immediately after the Monitor has ordered that the human scientists be moved to Metaluna.

TIE begins well as a scientific mystery and is very pro-science, giving credit to the achievements of the mind and seeing technology as an answer to some of our problems. And certainly its special effects and color photography are outstanding. If the film has a problem, it is probably the lack of an easily definable theme. *TIE is* anti-war, but the message is quickly diluted—especially when the final third of the film is given over to a spectacular interplanetary war (although Exeter does point out to Cal and Ruth how war has ravaged and destroyed his planet, subtly arguing its costs).

But *TIE* has another message, too—that the human mind cannot create under duress. As Exeter tells the Monitor, the thought transformer is morally repugnant to the humans and stifles their creativity. Only a free and willing mind can find answers.

Director Joseph Newman can take much of the credit for the generally excellent acting. Exeter is almost as much a result of Newman's firm directorial hand as he is of Morrow's skillful acting.

Newman also gets a sincere performance from Robert Nichols as Cal's skeptical assistant, Joe Wilson. One of the film's strongest moments comes after Joe has seen Cal take off in the empty plane. Nichols's Joe Wilson stares forlornly into the fog, trying to follow the plane as its droning engines carry it away. Newman holds on Nichols for a brief yet interminable period of time. Finally, Nichols drops his eyes, trudging off, reluctantly aware that he may have seen his friend and co-worker off to his death.

Newman's touch is discernible in other ways. As Cal and Ruth leave the dying Exeter, he lifts one hand slightly and waves a weak yet touching farewell to his human friends.

For the pivotal role of Exeter, producer Alland chose Jeff Morrow. Morrow's Exeter is sane and sympathetic, despite having to follow unpleasant orders, which he resists doing. That Morrow wins the viewer over so completely attests to the warmth and sincerity he brings to the characterization. Morrow told one interviewer that in the original script Exeter was more of the standard, two-dimensional heavy. He suggested playing Exeter as a tragic hero, and his changes were written into the script. All this made Exeter, along with Klaatu, one of SF film's more civilized aliens and a rarity in the paranoid fifties.

Jeff Morrow, born in 1913, began his acting career on the Broadway stage, but soon gravitated to roles on television and in films. His first part in Hollywood was in the biblical epic, *The Robe* (1953), the first Cinemascope production. *TIE* was Morrow's first SF film role and the one that many consider his best.

In 1956, Morrow teamed again with his *TIE* co-star, Rex Reason, in *The Creature Walks Among Us*—a William Alland/Jack Arnold film. Among his other SF movies were the laughable *The Giant Claw* (1957) and *Kronos* (1957), a much underrated film.

Morrow has worked frequently in television, his roles divided equally between heavies and more sympathetic characters. He was a regular in two television series: *Union Pacific* in 1958, and *The New Temperatures Rising Show* in 1973-74.

Between acting jobs, Morrow is a commercial illustrator, who has done magazine illustrations and technical drawings such as organization charts and flow charts.

Faith Domergue, born in 1925, who played Dr. Ruth Adams, was, according to *The Filmgoer's Companion*, "launched in 1950 with a publicity campaign which misfired." Her first film role came in *Vendetta* (1950). *TIE* was an early SF film, although she soon rarely appeared in any but SF and horror roles. Both she and *TIE* co-star Jeff Morrow appeared in *Legacy of Blood* (1971), about which Morrow has said, "We don't talk about that in polite society."

Domergue's Ruth Adams is a darkly-beautiful woman who combines thoughtfulness and *maturity* (something lost with the emerging dominance of the teen-oriented SF/horror films of the late fifties).

Domergue is believable as a scientist in an era of fewer opportunities for women in science, but the more conventional aspects of the script won't let her get away from the stereotyped "screaming, helpless *girl*" of the monster movies. This otherwise sensible scientist goes to pieces whenever anything vaguely frightening happens, shrieking loudly, and falling into the nearest pair of brawny arms ("Oh, Cal!").

Rex Reason was Alland's choice to play Dr. Cal Meacham, the solid and dependable hero—with a deep bass voice and strong arms to fall into. Reason, born in 1928, was at one point known as Bart Roberts (his brother is actor Rhodes Reason). His dark good looks and impressive physique made him the perfect leading man type for the 1950s. Reason's films, unfortunately, were rarely anything but routine studio "products." *Storm Over Tibet* (1952) was his first movie, followed by a number of other forgettables until *TIE* in 1955. He appeared in television's *The Roaring Twenties* from 1960 until 1962.

Reason's Cal Meacham, too, brought a measure of sincerity to an otherwise shallow role. Reason today is active in real estate.

Russell Johnson, who played Dr. Steve Carlson, was also in Alland's productions of *It Came from Outer Space* and *The Space Children*. A familiar film face, Johnson appeared on TV shows like *The Twilight Zone*, and was Marshal Gib Scott in *Black Saddle*, a western starring Peter Breck. But Johnson is best remembered as Roy Hinkley—"the Professor"—in the comedy series *Gilligan's Island* (1964-67).

Two featured players, Robert Nichols (Joe Wilson) and Douglas Spencer (The Monitor) both appeared in 1951's *The Thing*. (See the Appendix).

Had *TIE* been more successful, it might have spawned a number of big-budget imitators and SF film today would be far richer. But the simple fact is, *TIE* was not a rousing success despite its marvelous effects, and SF movies remained largely in the hands of the B-movie studios. Even Universal-International reverted to churning out its dependable and cheap black and white monster movies after *TIE* failed to soar at the box office.

TIE is remembered for many things: for its unusual flying saucer, shaped like a drop of water; for the Interociter, a truly science-fictional communications device and weapon; for the beauty and complexity of its interplanetary war on Metaluna; the weirdly effective "mutant"—its obligatory monster; but most often for Jeff Morrow's Exeter, willing to disobey his superiors to save the lives of his human friends. Exeter is one of SF filmdom's greatest aliens, a kindred spirit.

As Jeff Morrow said of his role: Exeter "gave people a feeling of hope." People could now look at the skies and see more than invaders and "Things"—they could see friends.

FORBIDDEN PLANET

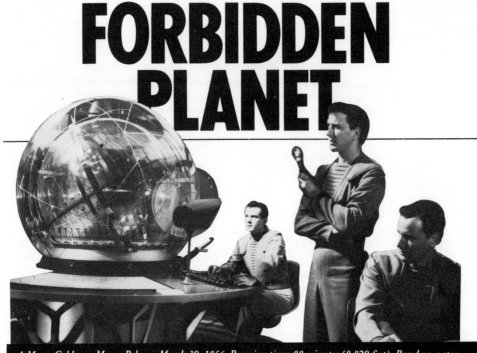

A Metro-Goldywn-Mayer Release: March 30, 1956. Running time: 98 minutes (8,820 feet). Based on a story by Irving Block and Allen Adler. In Eastmancolor and Cinemascope.

PRODUCTION CREDITS

PRODUCER	*Nicholas Nayfack*
DIRECTOR	*Fred McLeod Wilcox*
SCREENPLAY	*Cyril Hume*
ART DIRECTORS	*Cedric Gibbons and Arthur Lonergan*
SET DECORATORS	*Edwin B. Willis and Hugh Hunt*
DIRECTOR OF PHOTOGRAPHY	*George Folsey, A.S.C.*
ASSISTANT DIRECTOR	*George Rhein*
SPECIAL EFFECTS	*A. Arnold Gillespie, Warren Newcomb, Irving G. Reis, and Joshua Meador through the courtesy of Walt Disney Productions*
ELECTRONIC TONALITIES	*Louis and Bebe Barron*
EDITOR	*Ferris Webster, A.C.E.*
COLOR CONSULTANT	*Charles K. Hagedon*
HAIR STYLES	*Sydney Guilaroff*
MAKEUP	*William Tuttle*
ANNE FRANCIS'S COSTUMES	*Helen Rose*
MEN'S COSTUMES	*Walter Plunkett*

CAST

DOCTOR MORBIUS	*Walter Pidgeon*
ALTAIRA	*Anne Francis*
COMMANDER ADAMS	*Leslie Nielsen*
LIEUTENANT "DOC" OSTROW	*Warren Stevens*
LIEUTENANT FARMAN	*Jack Kelly*
CHIEF QUINN	*Richard Anderson*
COOK	*Earl Holliman*
BOSUN	*George Wallace*
GREY	*Bob Dix*
YOUNGERFORD	*Jimmy Thompson*
STRONG	*James Drury*
RANDALL	*Harry Harvey, Jr.*
LINDSTROM	*Roger McGee*
MORAN	*Peter Miller*
NICHOLS	*Morgan Jones*
SILVERS	*Richard Grant*

and introducing Robby the Robot

Forbidden Planet is perhaps the only SF film whose love story is an integral element of the plot. It is because *Forbidden Planet*'s plot is so complex and intellectually challenging that our summary of it is necessarily long.

Forbidden Planet opens with a shot of a saucer, United Planets Cruiser C-57D, in deep space. A brief narration (the voice is actor Les Tremayne's) informs us that the ship, more than a year in space, is on a mission to the great main sequence star Altair.

This dissolves into a shot of the saucer's interior, where Commander J. J. Adams and Astrogator Lieutenant Jerry Farman are preparing to decelerate the ship. The saucer emerges from hyperspace close to Altair and moves toward the outer planets, creating a spectacular eclipse as it passes Altair I.

No sign of life is apparent on Altair IV as the ship plunges toward it until a radio transmission is received from the surface. It is Dr. Morbius of the Bellerophon expedition, the colonizing party Adams has come in search of, warning him not to land. Adams explains his rescue mission, but Morbius stubbornly continues to warn the ship away. Adams ignores the warning and demands landing coordinates.

The saucer is met by a robot, who explains his name is "Robby," and that he has come to take them to Morbius. Accompanied by Lieutenant Farman and his ship's surgeon, Dr. Ostrow, Adams warily allows the robot to drive them to Morbius's home.

Morbius greets them stiffly, and over lunch tries to convince the Earthmen he is both comfortable and safe. To prove this, he demonstrates Robby's built-in lab—capable of synthesizing any material—Robby's devotion to him, and the robot's harmlessness by ordering it to shoot Adams "right between the eyes." Adams faces the robot bravely, but Robby is powerless: killing rational beings is against his directives, and he remains frozen until Morbius cancels the order. Morbius also demonstrates the steel shutters Robby built around the house for protection, although Morbius says he's never needed them.

As for the other members of the Bellerophon expedition, Morbius tells the officers that every one of them was killed, literally torn apart, in the first year of the expedition by some mysterious Force. Adams, meanwhile, grows more and more suspicious at the strangeness of the Doctor's story.

The four men are suddenly joined by a beautiful young woman. Morbius is displeased at her appearance and introduces her as his daughter Altaira. The Bellerophon records show no married couples, but Morbius explains he was married on the voyage, his wife dying later of natural causes. Sensing an opportunity, Farman moves to capitalize on the situation.

Adams and Ostrow express concern for Altaira's well-being: is she never lonely? In response, Altaira calls her "friends"—two deer and a tiger.

Having assured his visitors that he neither needs nor wants their help, Morbius tries to persuade Adams to return to Earth at once. Adams, still suspicious, says he'll have to contact Earth for orders.

Adams figures he will have to remove the ship's energy core for the brute power required to make contact, but shielding that much energy presents a problem. Anxious to see the Earthmen go, Morbius orders Robby to supply the needed shielding.

Robby arrives at the saucer the next day with the shielding, accompanied by Altaira. Farman manages to get her alone, but the two are interrupted by Adams. Altaira innocently informs him she and Farman were merely getting "a little healthy stimulation from hugging and kissing." Flustered, Adams tries to explain his anger, especially his objections to Altaira's short, clinging dress, but his words make no sense to her. Hurt by his inexplicable anger, she runs off.

Meanwhile, the ship's Cook takes Robby aside to ask if the robot knows where he can get some of the "real stuff"—and produces a bottle of bourbon. Robby grabs the bottle, emptying it into his built-in lab, and after a quick analysis shows it to contain "simple alcohol molecules with traces of fusel oil," offers to run off sixty gallons of the potent brew.

That night, while two crewmen stand guard, the ship is entered by an unseen presence, and vital communications gear is destroyed. Adams is furious at the destruction and at the intrusion into *his* domain. He orders his electronics chief, Quinn, to repair the damage, and sets off with Ostrow to Morbius's home for an explanation.

Robby tells them Morbius is in his study and is not to be disturbed. While Ostrow waits for Morbius, Adams sees Altaira swimming. She invites him to join her, but he begs off, explaining he has no bathing suit. "What's a bathing suit?" Altaira asks naively. Adams quickly turns his back.

Altaira emerges from the water and puts on a long dress she has asked Robby to make for her, inspired by Adams's protests about her short skirts. Suddenly aware of their feelings toward each other, they kiss. Without warning, Altaira's pet tiger appears and attacks them, forcing Adams to disintegrate it. Altaira is mystified by this attack from one of her "friends."

Rejoining Ostrow, Adams enters the study to find Morbius is not there. When Morbius enters through a hidden doorway and finds them hovering over his desk top, he realizes he must tell them about his great discovery—the Krell.

Altair IV, Morbius explains, was once the home of a mighty race called the Krell, a people millions of years more advanced technologically and morally than mankind. They explored Earth millions of years ago, bringing back the tiger and other animals to their own world. On the verge of some great breakthrough, the Krell were destroyed in a single night. A child by their standards, Morbius has devoted his life to recovering their lost knowledge for mankind. He plays for the two officers strangely haunting music recorded by Krell musicians over a half million years ago.

Adams, Ostrow, and Morbius in the shuttle-car taking them to see the wonders of the Krell.

Taking them on a tour of the Krell wonders, Morbius suggests that Adams try his blaster on one of the Krell steel doors—which is totally unaffected.

Beyond the door is one of many Krell laboratories. Morbius shows them what he calls a "plastic educator," an I.Q. measuring device and a plaything for visualizing images. Morbius demonstrates it by producing an image of Altaira. Both Ostrow and Adams take the I.Q. test and register poorly. Morbius tells them that when he first made an image he was badly injured, but his I.Q. was permanently doubled.

Pointing around the lab, Morbius shows the two men a series of gauges, each registering ten times the previous one—"the number ten raised almost to the power of infinity." The function of the gauges remains a mystery.

A shuttle car takes them to the heart of one of the Krell ventilation systems—called a cube by Morbius because it extends 20 miles in every direction, 7,800 levels in each cube, and a total of 400 such cubes sunk into the bowels of Altair IV. The ventilation shafts service a vast, self-repairing machine, powered by the energy of the planet's core, whose purpose is unknown.

It is night on the surface. At the saucer, Farman tests the disintegrator fence protecting the ship. The Cook asks Farman to allow him to go outside the fence. Dubiously, Farman agrees.

The Cook finds Robby and 480 pints of the promised bourbon. As the Cook samples the liquor, Robby turns as if hearing something. When the Cook asks if something is coming this way, Robby says, "No sir, nothing coming *this* way."

The fence around the ship sputters and shorts, then stops, but there's nothing to be seen. Giant footprints appear in the soft desert soil, and the stairs to the ship buckle as if under some massive weight. There is silence, then a piercing scream of terror and agony.

Meanwhile, in Morbius's study, Adams and Ostrow argue with the Doctor about the importance of his find and the need to share the Krell knowledge with Earth. A call from the saucer interrupts them: Chief Quinn has been killed, his body "plastered all over the communications room." Adams and Ostrow rush out while Morbius sits stunned, knowing the mysterious Force has struck again.

In the morning, Ostrow shows Adams a cast made from one of the footprints; it is the foot of "some impossible tree sloth . . . a nightmare anywhere in the galaxy."

The Cook faces discipline for his drunkenness, but provides an alibi for his drinking companion "Robert." Adams tells Ostrow that one of them must get into the Krell lab soon to take the brain boost as Morbius did.

The atmosphere at the ship that night is tense. Suddenly, the radar detects something huge approaching. The fence sputters, and as the crew fire their blasters at the target, a horrible two-legged creature is outlined in the beams, roaring wildly.

Two crewmen are seized by the creature and dashed to the ground. Farman rushes forward, firing his electron rifle, but the thing tosses him aside like a broken doll.

In the Krell lab Morbius dozes fitfully, the gauges behind him flickering madly. Altaira screams, waking him. She describes a terrible dream with something hideous stalking through it. As Morbius comforts her, the gauges fall back to normal.

At the ship the monster has abruptly disappeared. Adams tells his men their weapons stopped it, but neither he nor Ostrow believes it. Now it is even more imperative that one of them take the brain boost.

At the house, Robby refuses to let them in, neutralizing their weapons. Altaira appears and, countering her father's orders, admits them.

While Adams tries to convince Altaira she is in danger, Ostrow slips into the Krell lab. By the time Adams realizes Doc's gone, it's too late. Ostrow has taken the brain boost and is near death. But before he dies he tries to tell Adams what he has learned, gasping about "true creation," "civilization without instrumentality," and "monsters from the Id."

Morbius enters and seeing only Adams and Altaira says, "How romantic." Then he sees Doc's body and calls him a fool. Upset by his callousness, Altaira tells him she's leaving with Adams. While she goes to collect her things, Adams has Morbius tell him about the "Id." Morbius explains it is an obsolete term describing the "elementary basis of the subconscious mind." Slowly, Adams begins to grasp Ostrow's last words.

Robby tells them that something is approaching the house. The thing is invisible, but its progress is marked by the trees it uproots as it approaches. Morbius closes the protective shutters, but the thing begins to force its way in.

Morbius asks Robby to kill it, but the robot cannot. It knows what Adams has guessed: The thing outside is a projection of Morbius's own mind, fed by the power of the giant Krell machine. The Krell forgot the urges of the subconscious mind, Adams tells Morbius, and in one night their unleashed Id monsters destroyed their perfect civilization.

The three of them flee to the Krell lab, where Adams scrambles the combination to the door so that the thing can't reach into Morbius's mind for it. Grappling with Adams, Morbius still refuses to accept his explanation, but Adams tells him "we're all monsters in our own subconscious minds." That's why we have laws and religion—to protect us from the "mindless primitive within." Morbius finally begins to understand.

The Krell door turns red hot as the machine feeds the monster unlimited power. Adams draws his gun, but cannot bring himself to kill the tormented Morbius. Altaira pleads with her father, and Morbius rushes to the door, shouting, "I deny you! I give you up!" What happens next is unclear—all that is certain is that Morbius somehow confronts his evil self and turns it away; we see only the horrified and disgusted reactions of Altaira and Adams.

Morbius collapses as Adams and Altaira rush to his side. He instructs Adams to activate controls that will destroy the planet in twenty-four hours. With that, Morbius dies—finally at peace.

Far out in space, with Robby at the controls of the saucer, Adams and Altaira watch as Altair IV explodes in a great fireball. One day, Adams tells her, when mankind has worked its way up to the heights of the Krell, her father's name will shine once again, "like a beacon in the galaxy."

Few people would disagree that *Forbidden Planet* is one of the best science fiction movies ever, sharing top honors with a handful of other SF films, most notably *The Day the Earth Stood Still, The Invasion of the Body Snatchers,* and *2001: A Space Odyssey.*

Forbidden Planet was shot entirely on Hollywood sound stages by accomplished technicians working for filmdom's premier studio, Metro-Goldwyn-Mayer. *Forbidden Planet* was Metro's first SF film and the first major widescreen science fiction movie ever.

Not until MGM released Stanley Kubrick's $9.5 million epic, *2001: A Space Odyssey,* was there a serious challenge to *Forbidden Planet*'s place as the most expensive, ambitious, and visually arresting science fiction film ever made. (*Variety*'s review of *2001* observed that it lacked "the humanity of *Forbidden Planet.*")

Forbidden Planet embodies qualities of excellence that are rare in mainstream films and rarer still among science fiction films. It offers a logical and plausible story, enhanced by good acting and imaginative special effects. It is this integration of plot and special effects that makes *Forbidden Planet* unique among SF films.

World War II was responsible for a growth in the popularity of SF in the late forties and early fifties. The war had seen the development of the German V-1 and V-2 rockets, the jet airplane, and the American doomsday weapon, the atomic bomb. These advances had shown that "that Buck Rogers stuff" could be—should be—taken seriously. Suddenly, hidebound and inflexible chemistry and physics professors were no longer mocking the idea of "outer space" or enumerating reasons why the human body couldn't survive the stresses of reaching escape velocity in a rocket.

After World War II the science fiction genre was being rediscovered by the magazine publishing world, and a new boom in magazine SF began, a boom that crested in the early 1950s and began to diminish by 1956–57.

A great deal of trash was published, in accordance with SF writer Theodore Sturgeon's Law (which admits that 90 percent of SF is crap, but also that 90 percent of *everything* is crap), but magazines devoted to quality SF began to appear among the garbage. In 1949, *The Magazine of Fantasy & Science Fiction,* edited by the talented duo of Anthony Boucher and J. Francis McComas, went on sale for the first time. It was followed in 1950 by *Galaxy Science Fiction,* edited by the brilliant if quirky Horace L. Gold. These two magazines were the major additions to the field, and their excellence challenged the primacy of the long-established giant, *Astounding Science Fiction,* edited

Allied Artists had released *Atomic Submarine* and Campbell, Jr.

New magazines and reissues of old magazines (during the war a lack of paper had forced many "pulps" out of business) began to appear monthly; at one point there were at least thirty-five science fiction magazines on the stands or in the works. That was too many for the marketplace to support. Most died; a few lasted.

It was this surge of interest in SF in the late forties and early fifties that bore a floodtide of science fiction scripts into the offices of Hollywood producers and studio heads. Both *Rocketship X-M* and *Destination Moon* were released in 1950, and were followed in 1951 by the sober and thoughtful *The Day the Earth Stood Still*.

One of the men who had worked on *Rocketship X-M* was artist Irving Block. He and his partner, Jack Rabin, had been responsible for the low-budgeted film's special effects, although they were not quite as low budget as *Atomic Submarine*'s, where Block's arm had a starring role as the eye creature.

While working as a special effects technician, Block, like so many aspiring writers in Hollywood, was also working on treatments and screenplays he hoped to sell to the studios. (He later contributed the story to 1957's *Kronos*.)

Television writer Allen Adler sought out Block and suggested a writing partnership. By early spring, 1954, Adler had contributed to the treatment that they were working on its science fictional aspects, and Block had added the characters and situations of his favorite play, Shakespeare's *The Tempest*.

Most critics and reviewers point out *Forbidden Planet*'s similarity to *The Tempest*, observing that the island in the play is visited by outsiders and that Dr. Morbius is Prospero, with Altaira as Miranda, Robby as Ariel, and the Id Monster as Caliban. But film scholar Joseph Milicia, in his introduction to the Gregg Press reissue of the novelization, finds the similarities trivial and says: "The crucial difference is that Prospero remains in control and, despite a certain arrogance, remains wise to himself. In no way is he as self-deluding as Morbius, or at the mercy of the powers he has learned. . . . He is never in real danger of losing control to Caliban, unlike the case of Morbius and his monster. In short, he is not a failure."

There was a great revival of interest in Freudian psychology in the fifties, an interest reflected in current novels and films like *The Cobweb* and *Spellbound*. Irving Block capitalized on this interest to create a "Monster from the Id."

From the beginning Block wanted to get away from the typical BEM, or bug-eyed monster, then rampant on the covers of SF magazines. As Block explained, "The idea of a bug-eyed monster is a pretty childish illusion, but there are real monsters and demons that exist within us that we know nothing about. We're capable of doing the most horrendous things and we're often shocked at this truism."

since the late thirties by the larger-than-life John W. were the kings of the science fiction B-picture; they seemed to be the logical studio for Adler and Block to approach with their story, entitled "Fatal Planet." When Adler and Block's agent learned they hoped to sell their treatment to Allied Artists, he persuaded them to try MGM first.

Metro-Goldwyn-Mayer had the reputation of being resistant to science fiction films, but the two writers figured they could always give Allied Artists a try if MGM's bosses turned a cold shoulder to their idea.

They pitched their treatment to producer Nicholas Nayfack in his Culver City office. Nayfack had been in pictures since the mid-thirties, serving in the Navy in World War II and returning to Hollywood as a producer when the war ended. It didn't hurt him at MGM that one of his uncles was Nicholas Schenck, the founder of Loew's, Inc., MGM's parent company. Nayfack died in 1958, after the release of *The Invisible Boy*, which returned Robby the robot to the screen.

Block acted out the story after Nayfack declined to read it, pantomiming the invisible monster's rampages by stalking about the room and then stopping to breathe heavily, giving the monster menace and suggesting its presence through sound. Nayfack realized that an invisible monster could be inexpensive to film and yet still scary. He agreed to approach studio head Dore Schary with *Fatal Planet*.

Schary bought the idea. As he told an interviewer, "I liked the idea of the Id force and its effect on Morbius. It was an imaginative concept, and I felt it was the type of idea that could transcend the average space adventure story—the type of picture that was then being mass produced by everyone else."

Once Schary committed MGM to the project, the film underwent a name change, from *Fatal Planet* to *Forbidden Planet*, and Nayfack, assigned the role of producer by Schary, brought in Cyril Hume to write the screenplay.

Irving Block, his painter's skills still intact, was retained by MGM to provide a series of sketches that would give the studio designers and technicians an idea of how the picture would look. Once the script was completed, however, Mentor Heubnor became the film's production illustrator, providing color paintings of scenes like the saucer's landing.

In January 1956, when the release of the movie was still three months away, Farrar, Straus, and Cudahy published a hardcover novelization of the screenplay, written by W. J. Stuart (according to copyright records, a pseudonym for Philip McDonald, but who McDonald is remains a mystery).

The novelization (hereafter simply called the novel) is interesting for several reasons, not the least of which is that it presents ideas and plot developments in the original screenplay not seen in the film. Stuart's book is also richer in characterization and explains things more fully than does the streamlined film.

In the novel, the story is presented in the first person by three of the main characters. Doc Ostrow and Commander Adams are the voices for all the chapters but one; the chapter dealing with the Krell wonders is told from Morbius's point of view, which allows the reader to enter fully into the sick and anguished mind of Morbius and to be shown the marvels of the Krell by the man who knows them best.

It's difficult to compare films and books, given their obvious structural differences. Still, movies are limited as to what they can do when placed beside the unlimited resources of the novelist—who can call up in the reader's imagination great fleets of battle cruisers engaged in furious combat in space, and yet probe intimately into the minds and thoughts of his characters while following them over hundreds of pages. And there's no budget worry for the novelist.

Given this basic advantage of the novel, it's only natural that Commander Adams, Doc Ostrow, Morbius, and even Jerry Farman speculate and just plain *think* more in the novel than they do in the movie.

Doc Ostrow is a much more rounded character in the novel than he is in the movie; Warren Stevens is a fine actor and a reassuring presence in the film, but he has few good lines. An older man, Ostrow was clearly chosen by novelist Stuart to show the day-to-day routine of life on board a starship. As a newcomer to the rigors and wonders of life in space, Ostrow is lectured about the working of the QG Drive and how to prepare for the ship's wrenching deceleration from light speed. His ignorance and wonder are shared by the reader.

Robby is a less developed and less comedic presence in the novel and often sounds like a central casting Indian: "I am monitored to react to word Robby," "Yes, word Robby is contraction," and "Here is material."

The myth of the Unicorn is explained in both the screenplay and novel while references to it in the movie have been cut out, notably conversations in the garden between Morbius, Doc Ostrow, and Commander Adams. In the first conversation Doc says "The old Unicorn routine, maybe" to explain Alta's control of a wild animal—the tiger—and Morbius shoots him a knowing look. Later that evening, when Ostrow and Adams are alone, strolling outside the ship, Adams asks Doc to tell him what that Unicorn business was all about.

Doc tells him that the myth is that only a young *virgin* can ever capture a Unicorn, the bewitched beast approaching her as she sits quietly and finally laying his single-horned head in her lap (the massive horn, of course, symbolizes the male penis). "Maiden" was used in the screenplay, and "virgin" in the novel. *That* word hadn't assaulted moviegoers' virgin ears until 1953 when Otto Preminger's *The Moon Is Blue* caused a furor over its use and the film's lighthearted attitude toward sex.

In both film and novel, Morbius and Altaira have

a rather special relationship, an understandable one given the circumstances, which implies a certain sexual tension. Morbius is the only man in her world while Altaira is the only woman in his. The Id monster, then, is not the only Freudian concept to be made concrete in the movie; there is also the subconscious sexual longing of a father for his daughter and she for him.

When Morbius shows Adams and Ostrow how the "plastic educator" in the Krell lab works, he chooses to materialize an image of his daughter—a projection of his mind—wearing one of her skimpiest miniskirts. That he "sees" her like this is revealing; that she dresses like this all the time doesn't refute the point. After all, she dresses for Morbius's eyes only.

In the novel Doc Ostrow relates how Adams and Altaira wander off together and consummate their love. Their love-making happens "offstage" as does the tiger attack; the reader is only told about both incidents. Here, the tiger's attack is more sexual, more openly Freudian, because the tiger and all of Altaira's "friends" were created by Morbius and not brought back from Earth as the movie has it. Thus, betrayed sexually by his daughter, his love object, Morbius sends his mind's creation, the tiger, out to seek vengence, an act similar to his summoning up the Id monster to kill the crewmen.

Doc performs an autopsy on the body of a titi monkey Adams has accidentally killed and tells him "the titi didn't have the works for living. Inside, it was a biologist's nightmare. A heart and only two main arteries. No stomach . . . and everything padded, filled up with a mass of cross-weaved fibrous tissue no more use than a stuffing of cotton."

Doc Ostrow also uses the plastic educator's brain boost several times in the novel, not just once as in the film. He leaves a notebook for Adams, and it mentions "The animals. Altaira's animals, which—so far as she can remember—weren't here when she was 'a very little girl,' but then 'just came.' They were experiments by Morbius. Experiments which served the secondary purpose of providing companionship and interest for his daughter."

As Doc notes, the little titi monkey he dissected "*couldn't* have lived. But it did. It lived by the power of Morbius's mind. Which had made it in the outward image of his thought, his memory."

The novel's explanation of the Earth animals is better than the movie's, and they complement Morbius's other mental projection, the Id monster. The fact that they are the creations of Morbius's mind explains why they haven't undergone an adaptive evolutionary process in the hundreds of thousands of years they've been on Altair IV.

Commander Adams is more of a thinker in the novel, and he develops a reasonable theory for the loss of the Bellerophon expedition and Morbius's possession of technologically advanced devices, especially the sophisticated Robby—a remarkable creation for a philologist, a specialist in languages. Adams believes that Altairians *do* exist today and that Morbius, for unknown reasons, is acting as their agent. Doc doesn't agree with Adams's theory and is always jesting about "the Force" (shades of *Star Wars*!) Morbius speaks of.

The movie Morbius dismisses any similarity between himself and the mad scientists of "the taped thrillers," and Walter Pidgeon's portrayal adds credence to that point. In the novel, however, Morbius is more like the traditional mad scientist: he is patronizing, egocentric, and impatient. Hovering on the brink of a breakdown, Morbius does collapse briefly after showing the Krell cube to Adams and Ostrow, his strain and exhaustion the result of his pushing back to his "mid-mind"—to be forgotten and lost to his conscious mind—the knowledge that he's the planet's monster, the evil Force. This is the major difference between the Morbius of the movie and the Morbius of the novel: In the book Morbius *knows* he is the Id monster—he has conveniently *willed* himself to forget it; in the movie he knows it in his dreams only and, as he says, "What man can remember his own dreams?"

Forbidden Planet was filmed entirely on soundstages and under artificial light (apart from the miniatures). The studio broke with tradition and didn't choose to take the easy, cheap way out by simply "dressing" (adding props to) a stretch of California desert with supposedly alien-looking plants and vegetation and hoping this suggested another planet. Instead, the burden of producing an "other worldly" look on the sound stages fell on MGM's art and scenic departments.

Since the mid-thirties, an Irishman named Cedric Gibbons, who designed the "Oscar," had been head of MGM's art department, imprinting his style on every film the studio made, even though he rarely touched pen or brush himself. He assembled a crew of talented men who gave substance to that "rich, unmistakable Metro look" film historians rave about.

Always the lushest, richest-looking, and most "American" of the major studios (other studios' productions copied European film-making styles), MGM was able to impart a "wonderful extravagance" to each production, given Gibbons's vision and absolute power over his department.

Forbidden Planet's special effects wizard, A. Arnold (Buddy) Gillespie, was one of Gibbons's top men. Buddy Gillespie came to Hollywood in 1922 and soon landed a job in Cecil B. De Mille's Paramount art department for eight months. Working twelve to fourteen hours a day, seven days a week, at what he called "the De Mille Academy," Gillespie told his disapproving mother "they don't charge tuition, and they're even paying me $25 a week."

Gillespie became a draftsman for a more reasonable $65 a week when he moved over to the Goldwyn Studio, which later became part of MGM. That mollified his mother.

After spending nineteen months in Italy working on the original *Ben Hur*, Gillespie returned to Hollywood in 1924 and was made an art director under Cedric Gibbons, a position he held until 1936.

In 1936, as a consequence of Gillespie's outstanding work on *Ben-Hur* and *San Francisco*, Gibbons asked him to work in the special effects department.

Forbidden Planet's director of photography, George Folsey, had been at MGM since 1932. His work for the studio included *Meet Me in St. Louis* (1944), *Adam's Rib* (1949), and *Seven Brides for Seven Brothers* (1954). In 1922 Folsey shot his first SF film, a black-and-white 3-D thriller for Biograph Studios in New York entitled *The Man from Mars*.

Because of *Forbidden Planet*'s B-picture budget, Schary and Nayfack routinely selected a B-picture director, Fred McLeod Wilcox, to direct. Wilcox had initially been a publicity man at MGM, then an assistant to director King Vidor, and finally he got a chance to become a director by entering through the back door—directing screen tests. Wilcox made nine films for MGM before *Forbidden Planet*, none of them especially memorable, including his first picture, *Lassie Come Home*, released in 1943. *Forbidden Planet* was his last film for MGM.

Cedric Gibbons's handpicked and highly skilled crew rose to the challenges presented by *Forbidden Planet*. They responded by building complex, futuristic sets and by providing the production with a number of immense, proper perspective cycloramas. Cycloramas are simply large painted backdrops, often done on canvas. The studio had been using color cycloramas for years because Gibbons had had success with them during the filming of *The Wizard of Oz*.

Three saucer miniatures, ranging in size from twenty inches to eighty-eight inches, were built for *Forbidden Planet* at a cost of approximately $20,000. These detailed, aero-dynamically designed models contribute to the film's overall effect from the moment the first one is seen.

The opening shots of United Planets Cruiser C-57D in space were filmed by suspending the twenty-inch and forty-four-inch saucer miniatures from music wire and positioning them against a star field backdrop on MGM's Stage 14. Since the saucer models were stationary, the camera itself provided all the relative movement by either tracking in toward the models or panning past them. With a larger budget and twenty years of development time to aid him, John Dykstra employed a much more sophisticated computer-assisted camera tracking system for *Star Wars*.

Photographer George Folsey found shooting in the saucer's control room set to be a difficult task because of light reflecting off the bright metal and plastics. Folsey was almost stumped by the reflections off the large plexiglass globe in the middle of the bridge's navigation center. His solution was to painstakingly reposition all the set's lamps and mask out the areas that presented the most difficulties.

It was a large and complex set. As Folsey noted, "A

As night approaches on Altair IV, the crew of the saucer looks anxiously toward the force-field fence. The lower portion of the saucer was a mock-up and the top half was never built—it was matted in for long shots. The two stairways were operational.

crew of nineteen men worked a month to install the twenty-seven miles of electrical wiring used in the control cabin. . . . In order to be able to successfully control the extensive illumination for this one set alone, a set-lighting switchboard was set up and manned by a score of electricians."

The sleek saucer's approach and landing on the pastel-colored desert surface of Altair IV was shot outdoors with miniatures on MGM's Lot 3. It is on this big "standing set" lot that the St. Louis street from the musical *Meet Me in St. Louis* stood among other silent small town and big city streets, an aging reminder of the times when the studios were factories churning out hundreds of features a year.

Filming miniatures is a time-consuming chore. Because of differing model sizes, lighting needs, and the film stock chosen, miniatures can be shot at either high or slow film speeds. Since *Forbidden Planet's* miniatures were shot at high speed, the camera was locked down tightly to prevent any movement as the film sped through it. Projected at normal sound speed, ninety feet per minute, the jerky and awkward movements of the models were not apparent.

High-speed filming requires huge amounts of light; the set must be bathed in light. As Gillespie said, "There's no electrician like the sun," so the brilliant California sun provided this intense illumination.

A lattice of track hung over the 300 X 75-foot cyclorama backing, so that the saucer models could be maneuvered into landing from a small control car above the set. The height of the 75-foot high backing, plus the lattice atop the set, provided further incentive to shoot outdoors.

The "landing" was accomplished by manipulating the forty-four-inch model over the miniature Altairian desert, and then the larger eighty-eight-inch saucer model was substituted for the final approach and touchdown. A brief cutback to the interior of the control room masked the switch from the smaller to the larger model. Blasts of compressed air from the floor of the set simulated the saucer's landing ray disturbing the sand of the desert.

Once United Planets Cruiser C-57D had landed, a full-scale saucer mock-up and exterior set were required and were built on Stage 15. Instead of a complete mock-up, just enough of the saucer was built—a sixty-foot wedge of the lower hemisphere, with fully operational stairways—to suggest the whole ship.

The 350 X 40-foot cyclorama that surrounded this set was a masterpiece of movie illusion. The rocks and boulders seemed to retreat into the horizon, and the set was dressed with fake rocks to blur the distinction between it and the painting.

Artist's sketch of the
"Monster from the Id."

Morbius's "House of Tomorrow," as his home was called by the studio, was to be built on Stage 30. Irving Block, screenwriter Cyril Hume, and art director Arthur Lonergan all wanted something that *could* conceivably have been designed by Frank Lloyd Wright while still suggesting a future home. Producer Nayfack opted for a desert setting with lots of lush vegetation and a swimming pool so that Anne Francis, a former model, would have both an excuse and an opportunity to expose her charms. Ironically, Altaira's swimming scene is part of the "mushy stuff" MGM cut for the movie's subsequent rerelease as a kiddy matinee feature.

Set decorator Hugh Hunt recalled that the budget was too tight to allow for the set to be dressed with brand new furnishings, so he made do by commandeering a glasstop table from art department chief Cedric Gibbons's home, and by putting new seats and back on chairs used in earlier MGM productions.

Hunt's actions were typical of the way those involved in the production of *Forbidden Planet* schemed to make an A picture on what was initially a B-picture budget. Lonergan and Gillespie designed the picture the way they thought it ought to be designed, the budget be damned. Gibbons suspected as much, but deliberately chose not to find out. As it turned out, the sets required the floor space of four of MGM's largest soundstages, took nearly two months to construct, and cost nearly a million dollars.

Around the exterior set of Morbius's home was the production's second largest cyclorama, 168 feet long by 28 feet high. A smaller cyclorama was behind the road by which Robby originally brings the Earthmen to Morbius.

One of the highlights of the scene in the Krell laboratory is Morbius's creation of a 3-D image of his daughter within the plastic educator. This was accomplished by creating a tiny cloud of aluminum dust particles above the plate, then superimposing discharging electrical arcs and a spinning figurine over the cloud. Footage of Anne Francis in her miniskirt.

According to photographer George Folsey, the laboratory set "required 50,000 feet of wiring, 2,500 feet of neon tubing, and 1,200 square yards of plexiglass in its construction. To achieve precise lighting on this set during shooting, a staff of fifteen electricians handled 110 separate switches on a giant control panel."

In *American Cinematographer*, Folsey describes a scene in the Krell laboratory which ran for nearly ten minutes and more than six pages of dialogue. He recalls that "in one single unbroken take more than 1,300 words were spoken while our camera, mounted on a mobile crane, made sixteen different moves on cue, short-cutting the necessity of having to make an equal number of separate setups." Viewing the movie today reveals no such long take. What probably happened, after all that effort to film it in one take, was that the scene was edited a bit, tightened and trimmed, and its carefully-conceived continuity shattered.

Buddy Gillespie filmed the Krell furnace and Electronic room miniatures on Stage 14. The word miniatures can seem a misnomer when a miniature as large as the "Krell ventilation shaft" is used. This thirty-foot-long "miniature" was constructed on its side (to give the impression the camera is looking *down*) with a painting at the end to extend the view into infinity. It is across this shaft, as seen from far above, that Morbius, Ostrow, and Adams walk as monstrously large globes discharging electrical arcs rise and fall.

Gillespie shot the miniature shaft by mounting a camera on tracks. For the figures walking across the span, the matte element was shot from a moving company's warehouse roof, the camera looking down on midgets in place of the actors. Matte artist Matthew Yuricich (he also worked on the *Star Trek* movie), an assistant in Warren Newcombe's matte department, convinced Newcombe the tiny moving figures would go unseen unless attention was drawn to them. Newcombe allowed Yuricich to paint a pulsating light pattern on the span across the shaft so the minuscule human figures would be detected walking across, looking like tiny dots.

In all, *Forbidden Planet* required five matte paintings. Two were of the saucer; one was a long shot of Morbius's home, used when Adams, Ostrow, and Farman first arrive via Robby's jeep; one was a long shot of the graveyard where the bodies of the members of the Bellerophon expedition are buried; and one was the poorly done Krell Cube.

The weakest special effects shot in the movie is probably the matte showing the "Krell Cube," which got its name from Hume's screenplay when Morbius tells the officers that it is "a single machine, a cube twenty miles on each side."

For the scene, a four-foot-square matte painting was lit from behind, with flashing lights added later. The whole thing looks fake and cartoonish; it is an inferior shot that stands out because of the excellence of the other effects.

Until the Id monster was made visible by Joshua Meador during its attack on the ship, it had to be given substance through "special lighting, shadowing, and the use of color," according to George Folsey. He described shooting the night attack on the saucer, noting that "much of the desired effect was achieved by putting colored filters over the arcs." For the scene where the monster passes by the guards and enters the saucer, Folsey achieved the effect of the monster's approach by "changing the lighting in a predetermined pattern, using venetian-type shutters over each arc. Onlookers ... felt the invisible visitor pass in front of the camera, so realistic was this lighting effect."

For the climactic scene in which the Id monster melts the door to the Krell lab, Gillespie had a technician rig a miniature doorway that could accept two doors. The first door was steel and was replaced when it was red hot by a paper-thin sheet of lead covered by a special coating which mimicked the Krell steel first turning white hot and then crumbling into glowing coals.

Joshua Lawrence Meador, who died in 1965, was responsible for creating the animated effects in *Forbidden Planet*. Long a top animator in Walt Disney's fabulous animation shop, Meador was given the job of producing the film's effects when MGM executive Harper Goff contacted the Disney studio and requested their best animator.

Among the scenes requiring animated effects was one in which Robby tosses a piece of fruit into the household disintegrator beam. Without Meador's animation, the audience would have seen the fruit simply hit the far side of the disintegrator chamber and fall to the floor.

Other examples of Meador's work include:
—Robby short-circuiting twice, first when Morbius orders him to shoot Commander Adams, and then when he is ordered by Morbius to destroy the Id monster as it breaks into the house.
—Robby firing Adams's blaster and disintegrating a fruit tree *(Althaea Frutex)* in the terrace.
—Adams, at Morbius's urging, trying his blaster on a door made of Krell steel.
—The arcs of electricity, twisting sinuously around each other, released by one of the giant globes rising in the Krell ventilation shaft.
—Adams's disintegration of the leaping tiger as it attacks Alta.
—The streams of electron volts from the ship's main batteries and the crewmen's guns during the Id monster attack.

Certainly, Meador's biggest contribution involved the Id monster's night attack on the saucer. Animating the scene was difficult at first because no consensus could be reached on what the "Monster from the Id" should look like. Irving Block originally conceived the Id monster as some sort of massive, sluglike bulk—Morbius's darkest imaginings made flesh and bone. Nayfack, however, wasn't satisfied with this concept and had both art director Arthur Lonergan and production illustrator Mentor Huebner provide their own versions of Morbius's nighmarish other self. Huebner's vision was of a "bloated, horrible insect, like something you've never seen before."

Meador finally went outside both the Disney and MGM organizations and hired freelance animator Ken Hultgren, correctly guessing that everyone else was too close to the problem and hoping Hultgren could provide a totally new concept. Hultgren conceived the massive head atop the two legs that was finally accepted. While MGM insiders joked that it was a reworking of the MGM trademark, Leo the Lion, a close inspection reveals that the Monster from the Id looks like the person from whose mind it sprang—Morbius. Indeed, the creature even has a small goatee to match the one worn by Walter Pidgeon.

For reasons unknown, the Id monster was never made visible at the film's climax, although the screenplay called for it. Perhaps Nayfack believed the Id monster's appearance was illogical, since there was no way to explain it—or perhaps the Disney studio's new production of *Sleeping Beauty* limited Meador's services.

CLOSE SHOT (PROCESS)—MORBIUS WITH HIS BACK TOWARD THE CAMERA, AND THE MONSTER TOWERING OVER HIM AS THEY FACE EACH OTHER AT LAST.

Simply the briefest flash of the thing as it stands now fully visible in all its hair and horror—the dull pig eyes, the small drooping ears, the vampire snout, the gaping jaws of nightmare. Then, as it sweeps Morbius into its embrace, sinks its claws—

TWO SHOT—ADAMS AND ALTA

forgetting even each other as they stare up insanely o.s. All at once, the bellowings gurgle off into silence. As Alta cries out, darts forward, PAN to Morbius slumping on the floor. He is dying, but physically unmarked—and the monster is gone for good.

In all, the work of Meador and his crew took them six months to complete. Perhaps that's the simplest reason the Id monster wasn't visualized at the end: MGM decided it couldn't afford to spend any more money on Meador's costly effects.

Robby is one of the best robots ever to appear in a science fiction film. A bulky yet graceful cross between a long-suffering manservant and a genial genie, Robby is godfather to all the lovable movie robots to follow him.

In Cyril Hume's screenplay Robby "has no face—only a complicated arrangement of electronic gadgets which crackle and light up at unexpected moments. In spite of his disproportioned arms and legs, he only very roughly suggests the human shape. His hands are tools, and various spare parts (one of these actually a metal hand) are neatly clipped to his body, back and front. He is able to rotate the upper part of his dome, and so seems to 'face' the person addressing him. A small radar antenna [comes] up out of Robby's dome and slowly [rotates]."

The prop shop made changes in Hume's suggested design, doing away with most of the tools clipped to Robby and replacing his tool-hands with a simple design having three rubber digits, or "fingers."

Writing about his career for an American Museum of Modern Art exhibition honoring "The Hollywood Art Director," Buddy Gillespie said: "One of my best creations was Robby, the robot in *Forbidden Planet*. Up to that time robots in science fiction films looked like men in starched aluminum suits. I thought of an old pot-bellied stove like the ones they used to have in grocery stores. So Robby was really the outgrowth of my fondness for pot-bellied stoves. He was the first robot with a sense of humor."

Production illustrator Mentor Huebner was given Gillespie's rough sketches by art director Lonergan. Huebner rejected Gillespie's design for Robby's legs for a "jointed ball configuration" of his own.

Two short actors, Frankie Carpenter and Frankie Darro, alternated playing Robby. The voice box of the robot was constructed so the men could look out and see where they were going. When Robby spoke, a "voice activator" made his neon voice tubes flash on and off. The operator spoke the dialogue, but Robby's distinctive voice was dubbed in later by Marvin Miller (of TV's *The Millionaire*).

George Folsey marveled at the skill and hard work that went into Robby. He observed that "it took two months to successfully install the 2,600 feet of electrical wiring that made Robby independent and self-operating." Robby, however, wasn't really all that self-operating. To control the six electric motors which activated the six rocker arms in Robby's dome, clicking and clacking whenever he spoke, a heavy electrical cable snaked from his left heel to a remote control panel operated by effects man Jack McMasters. For those scenes in which the cable would be visible, Robby could operate briefly from internal batteries which had a short life.

Robby's body was made of one-eighth-inch plastic, and his head dome was a clear plastic made by Kodak.

Helen Rose, who had worked on an earlier Nayfack production, *The Scarlet Coat*, designed the costumes Ann Francis wore as Altaira. With the exception of one long dress—the one Robby designs for Alta when she's trying to please Adams after he's criticized the way she dresses—all of Rose's creations were the forerunners of the miniskirt.

Walter Plunkett, costume designer for *Gone With the Wind, Singin' In the Rain*, and other MGM classics, created the men's outfits. Among the costume designs discarded were helmets and radiation armor for the scene in which the crew unships the core, and "tropical" uniforms which featured shorts instead of trousers. The tropical outfit was to be worn by Leslie Nielsen when he found Alta swimming. The screenplay originally called for him to join Altaira by jumping in—clothes and all. Since this was a highly unlikely act for the stern if mellowing J. J. Adams to perform, it was cut from the screenplay before it was filmed.

Walter Plunkett felt that he didn't do his best work on *Forbidden Planet* because the studio "didn't want anything too extreme or exaggerated."

Plunkett also believed that Anne Francis's Altaira "ended up looking like a Rockette instead of something of the future," and concluded by admitting, "Very frankly, it's one of my least favorite pictures."

On the whole, *Forbidden Planet* can be given high marks for its attempts to be scientifically accurate. The saucer, as explained in the narration at the beginning, is able to surpass the speed of light because of the discovery of [Quanto-Gravitetic] hyperdrive. As

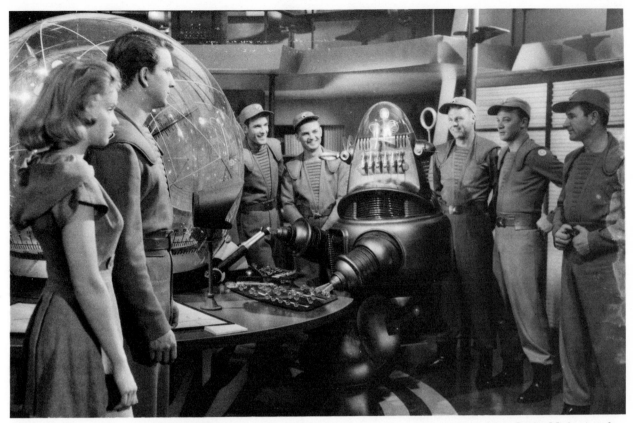

After Altair IV has been destroyed, Robby takes over the saucer's controls as Commander Adams (Leslie Nielsen) and Altaira (Ann Francis) and the crew look on (including James Best, next to the plexiglass globe, and George Wallace, at the far right). The shot is retouched to make it appear that Robby is seated—something the robot could not do.

the saucer emerges from hyperspace, it is still traveling at .3896 of light speed, or roughly 2.6 million mph.

Altair I passes between the saucer and the "main sequence" star Altair, creating an astronomically correct eclipse, the corona of the sun flaring brightly.

Deceleration (D-C) of the saucer's great speed is shown to be a step process, and one that physically drains the crew.

Altair IV is 4.7 percent richer in oxygen than Earth, with only .897 percent of Earth's gravity. All this makes Altair IV a comfortable planet to visit: a 150-pound crewman would weigh only 134.5 pounds and have oxygen-rich, pollution-free air to breathe.

Robby follows Isaac Asimov's three laws of robotics, although Asimov is not credited. One of the laws is that a robot cannot harm a rational being or allow him to be harmed through inaction. When Morbius orders Robby to kill the attacking Id monster, Robby recognizes the thing as really a projection of Morbius and, hence, a rational being. Faced with the dilemma presented by Morbius's direct order and his inhibitions, Robby sputters and becomes inoperative. This confirmation that the Id monster and Morbius are the same shows how carefully the filmmakers tied everything together.

Long used by dog trainers, but new to the movie public in 1956, was Alta's high-pitched animal whistle.

Two pioneers in electronic music, Louis and Bebe Barron, were hired by Dore Schary in October 1955 to compose the score for *Forbidden Planet*. They traveled west to Hollywood to meet the staff of MGM's music department, most of whom were impressed by the compositions the Barrons played for them. With everyone enthusiastic about the possibilities for a unique score, the Barrons went back to their Greenwich Village studio and put together the soundtrack. They received $25,000 for a twenty-five-minute score, which they finished in January 1956. For the next six weeks they oversaw the soundtrack's integration with film editor Ferris Webster's rough cut.

The Krell music that Morbius plays for Adams and Ostrow, with its strange and haunting shadings of sound, was in reality the "electronic tonalities" of the Barrons—its weirdly dissonant notes following the men down a Krell corridor.

So that there would be no trouble with the powerful Musicians Union, studio head Schary changed their screen credit from "electronic music by . . ." to "electronic tonalities by Louis and Bebe Barron." Louis Barron recalls today, "it was lawsuit proof!"

The score for *Forbidden Planet* represents a breakthrough in music for the screen. SF film and music would not be so thoroughly integrated until *2001*, more than ten years later, and would not be as eerie and essential to the film until *A Clockwork Orange*, also by Stanley Kubrick, almost fifteen years later.

The music establishes the atmosphere of the movie from the very beginning, announcing that this will be no ordinary motion picture. The Barron's "electronic tonalities" were not only music, but sound effects as well, providing an ominous aural backdrop to some scenes and totally dominating others—as in the roaring bass tones of the Id monster's attack on the saucer. The only mystery is why the Barrons didn't do more film soundtracks.

The role of Dr. Morbius went to Walter Pidgeon (1897–), a Canadian import who has been working in Hollywood since appearing in *Mannequin* in 1925. Pidgeon was *Forbidden Planet*'s only name player, and he received top billing. His Dr. Morbius seems almost too cool to contain the passions and longings of a "mindless primitive," but his smug superiority captures the essence of the not-so-good Doctor perfectly. Pidgeon allows the viewer to guess at the human being hidden beneath the man of science's logical and cold exterior, the human being who's slowly let himself be dominated by his thirst for knowledge until he has no compassion left for others. Clad in his gun-metal-blue suit, Pidgeon's Morbius is straight, correct, and unfeeling—on the surface.

Publicity photo of Leslie Nielsen as Commander J. J. Adams.

Walter Pidgeon's more than a hundred movies include *Dark Command* (1940), *How Green Was My Valley* (1941), *Mrs. Miniver* (1942), *Advise and Consent* (1962), and one of Irwin Allen's glossy SF movies, *Voyage to the Bottom of the Sea* (1961).

Anne Francis (1932–) appeared in her first film, *Summer Holiday* (1948), when she was just sixteen. Not very well known before *Forbidden Planet*, she had nonetheless appeared in several major motion pictures, among them *Bad Day at Black Rock* (1954) and *The Blackboard Jungle* (1955).

She was an efficient and curvaceous female detective with a male sidekick in her 1964 television series *Honey West*.

A beautiful young woman of twenty-three at the time she made *Forbidden Planet*, Miss Francis was the only female in an otherwise all-male cast and might have been expected to do nothing more than breathe deeply, look adoringly at first her father and then Adams, and scream when and if the script required it. That she contributed more is a tribute to her acting skills.

Leslie Nielsen's (1925–) role as Commander J. J. Adams has him barking orders and disciplining his crew most of the time, but he invests the role with more good humor and depth than one might expect. Nielsen, Stevens, and Pidgeon play well together, Nielsen holding his own with the older, more experienced actors. Nielsen's love for Altaira as Adams allows him to soften the Commander's tough-talking, traditional military man stance, imbuing Adams with very human feelings.

Leslie Nielsen was a Canadian leading man before getting into American pictures with *The Vagabond King* (1955). In 1956 he appeared in another Nicholas Nayfack production in addition to *Forbidden Planet*, a social drama entitled *Ransom*.

Nielsen never made it as a top star in motion pictures. After appearing with Debbie Reynolds in *Tammy and the Bachelor* (1957), his starring roles declined, and by 1972 he was playing yet another of the type of roles he seemed destined to act—the captain of the ill-fated luxury liner S. S. *Poseidon* in *The Poseidon Adventure*.

On television Nielsen's star shone more brightly, and he has played a wide variety of roles, his strong visage and white hair giving him the authority to portray tough yet gentle men. Between 1959 and 1961 he appeared in eight episodes of (*Walt Disney Presents*) "The Swamp Fox," later starring in *The New Breed* and a single-season series, in 1972, *The Bold Ones*.

Warren Stevens's (1919–) Doc Ostrow is solid, loyal, intelligent, and clearly a *good* human being. It is a modest role, with Stevens's Ostrow always in the shadow of Adams and Morbius, yet Stevens never melts into the background. He is, perhaps, the forerunner to *Star Trek*'s ship's doctor—a medical man yet a human being with all-too-real human emotions.

Warren Stevens has worked as much as any actor in Hollywood, appearing in countless movie and TV productions. His film career began with *The Frogmen* (1951), although his face is familiar to most people because of his many television roles.

Stevens's TV series have included *77th Bengal Lancers* (1956) and *The Richard Boone Show* (1964). His guest appearances on TV have been numerous and include shows like *Star Trek* ("By Any Other Name") and *The Twilight Zone* ("Dead Man's Shoes").

Jack Kelly's (1927–) Jerry Farman is a typical Jack Kelly character: brash and aggressive, a bit of a wolf, but loyal and courageous underneath his veneer of smooth Irish charm.

Kelly will always be Bart Maverick to millions of TV viewers, though it was a role he played for only a few years on *Maverick* (1957–61), ABC's successful western spoof. He also appeared in the Warner Bros. series *King's Row*.

With his matinee idol looks, Kelly found it hard to be taken seriously as an actor—much like his *Maverick* costar, James Garner. Kelly's first film was *Where Danger Lives* (1951), and his two best films were released the same year, 1956: *Forbidden Planet* and Audie Murphy's autobiographical *To Hell and Back*.

As the Cook in *Forbidden Planet*, Earl Holliman (1928–) stands out for his "Ah shucks" performance and for his adroit timing when playing straight man for Robby. Like many actors, he has favorite roles and films, as well as those he'd just as soon forget. Not *too* surprisingly, Holliman would rather not discuss his Cook's role in *FP* because he's convinced his later work as an actor is superior.

Holliman is another fine character actor who worked steadily but found few roles as a leading man until starring in a successful TV series, *Hotel de Paree* (1961). Though his character in the series, Sundance, brought him fame, he had been a film actor since *Destination Gobi* in 1953. His best motion pictures were early in his career: *The Bridges at Toko-Ri* and *Broken Lance*, both 1954, and *Forbidden Planet* in 1956.

Besides *Hotel de Paree*, his TV series have included *The Wide Country* (1962) and *Police Woman* (1974–78).

Holliman appeared in *The Twilight Zone's* first episode, "Third from the Sun," about an astronaut who returns to Earth to find everyone gone. (For more information on the cast, see the Appendix.)

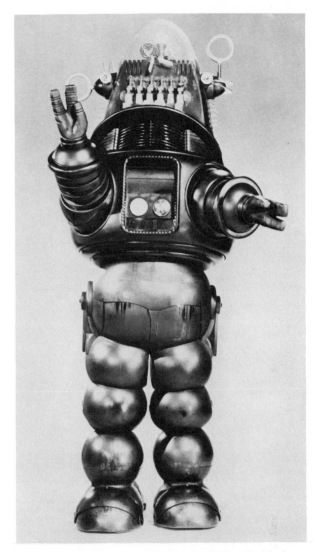

A studio publicity shot of Robby the Robot. Robby was one of the screen's best robots—certainly the most likeable until the robots of *Star Wars* came along.

An SF film classic, *Forbidden Planet's* studio-created magic still dazzles and entertains us twenty-five years after its release, and its name continues to shine "like a beacon in the galaxy."

INVASION OF THE BODY SNATCHERS

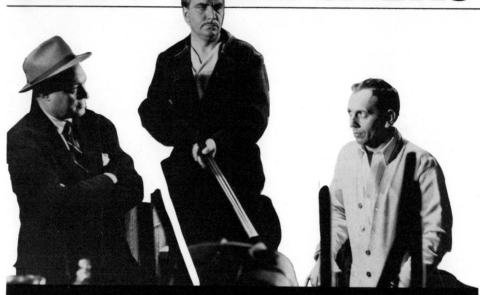

An Allied Artists Production. Running Time: 80 minutes. Black and White. Superscope (35mm). Based on the novel The Body Snatchers *by Jack Finney. Preproduction title:* Sleep No More; *Shooting Title:* They Came from Another World. *Opened May 1, 1956.*

PRODUCTION CREDITS

PRODUCER	Walter Wanger
DIRECTOR	Don Siegel
SCREENPLAY	Daniel Mainwaring
CINEMATOGRAPHER	Ellsworth Fredericks
ART DIRECTOR	Edward Haworth
SPECIAL EFFECTS	Milt Rice
FILM EDITOR	Robert S. Eisen
MUSIC	Carmen Dragon
ASSISTANT DIRECTORS	Richard Mayberry, Bill Beaudine
MAKEUP	Emile LaVigne
SOUND	Ralph Butler, Del Harris

CAST

DR. MILES BENNELL	Kevin McCarthy
BECKY DRISCOLL	Dana Wynter
DR. DAN KAUFMAN	Larry Gates
JACK BELICEC	King Donovan
THEODORA BELICEC	Carolyn Jones
NICK GRIVETT (POLICE CHIEF)	Ralph Dumke
SALLY (MILES'S NURSE)	Jean Willes
WILMA LENTZ	Virginia Christine
IRA LENTZ	Tom Fadden
GRANDMA GRIMALDI	Beatrice Maude
JIMMY GRIMALDI	Bobby Clark
CHARLIE BUCKHOLTZ (GAS MAN)	Sam Peckinpah
DR. HILL	Whit Bissell
DR. HARVEY BASSETT	Richard Deacon
MAC (GAS STATION ATTENDANT)	Dabs Greer

"I've seen how people have allowed their humanity to drain away. Only it happened slowly instead of all at once. They didn't seem to mind. All of us—a little bit—we harden our hearts, grow callous. Only when we have to fight to stay human do we realize how precious it is."

Those words form the cornerstone of one of the most remarkable SF films of the 1950s. In 1956, Allied Artists, eager to cash in on the SF/horror boom of the period, released a film with as silly-sounding a title as one might hope *never* to expect. They didn't know then that *Invasion of the Body Snatchers* would become a film which even today cuts to the heart of the question of what it means to be a human being.

Invasion of the Body Snatchers (hereafter referred to as *IBS*) was such a small entry on the 1950s bill of SF movies that so far as can be ascertained it was never even reviewed by any major periodical of the time. This isn't too surprising; in a period when SF films generally received little notice, another AA programmer with such an incredibly lurid title probably made even the staunchest critic roll up his eyes in a kind of horror having nothing to do with scary movies.

But in retrospect critics have recognized *IBS* as a classic. Georges Sadoul, author of *A Dictionary of Films,* calls it "one of the subtlest films of the genre . . ." and "one of the most passionate and involving." Leslie Halliwell, in *The Filmgoer's Companion,* refers to it as "the most subtle film in the science fiction cycle." And in *Science Fiction in the Cinema* John Baxter describes the film as having "a fiery relevance that makes it durable even today." *IBS* is unquestionably a film that leaves an indelible mark on the human consciousness.

IBS begins with Dr. Hill of the State Mental Hospital being rushed to the emergency room in a police car. Hill has been summoned by his colleague, Dr. Bassett, to examine a man who is apparently psychotic. As they enter Bassett's office, we see a man being restrained by two police officers, pleading madly for someone to listen to him.

Hill offers to listen, but when the man hears Hill is a psychiatrist, he becomes wild again, insisting he is *not* crazy. Calming him, Hill asks the patient, Dr. Miles Bennell, to tell his story.

It all began, Miles says, when an urgent message from his nurse, Sally, summoned him from the medical convention he'd been attending to his hometown of Santa Mira in Marin County, California. Sally meets Miles at the railroad station, explaining how his office has been besieged by patients demanding to see him.

As they drive toward town, a small boy, Jimmy Grimaldi, suddenly plunges out into the road—nearly being struck by the car. Miles speaks to Jimmy's mother, who claims the boy simply doesn't want to go to school. Miles pays little attention to the incident.

Strangely, only a few of Miles's patients appear for their appointments. He is about to leave when Becky Driscoll, an old flame, comes in. Becky, who has been living in England with her husband, is now back in Santa Mira.

Becky tells Miles that her cousin Wilma is suffering from the strange delusion that her Uncle Ira is an imposter. Miles agrees to talk to Wilma, and as he walks Becky to her father's store, discovers that, like himself, Becky is recently divorced. As she leaves him, Miles realizes he is still interested in her.

That afternoon Miles is visited by Jimmy Grimaldi and his grandmother. The hysterical boy insists his mother is *not* his mother. Miles prescribes tranquilizers and suggests the boy stay with his grandmother for awhile.

Curious at the similarity between this case and that of Becky's cousin, Miles stops off to see Wilma, but fails to convince her that her uncle is really her uncle.

Miles takes Becky to dinner at a local restaurant. In the parking lot they meet Dan Kaufman, the town's only psychiatrist. Kaufman tells them there is an epidemic of cases resembling Jimmy's and Wilma's, but he is unable to account for them.

Miles and Becky find themselves the restaurant's only customers. But before they even sit down, Miles gets a call from his friend Jack Belicec, asking him to come over right away.

When Miles and Becky arrive, Jack shows them a body lying on his billiard table. There is no sign of injury, and this is clearly not a corpse. The body seems unfinished, like "the first impression stamped on a coin." And it has no fingerprints.

As Jack fixes drinks, his wife Teddy asks Miles how tall he thinks the body is and how much it weighs. "Five feet, ten inches, 140 pounds," Miles guesses. "Jack's five feet, ten inches and weighs 140 pounds," she replies—and Jack drops the bottle he's holding, cutting his hand. Miles suggests Jack and Teddy keep an eye on the body and phone him immediately if anything happens.

Miles takes Becky home, and she invites him in. Just as he is about to kiss her, a shadow appears on the basement stairs—it is only Becky's father. Miles says a hurried goodnight.

At the Belicecs' Jack dozes at the bar. Teddy casually glances at the body, only to see it is now identical to Jack, right down to the cut on his hand—and its eyes are open! She screams, waking Jack, and the two of them flee to Miles's house.

Miles calms them and calls Dan Kaufman. Jack suddenly asks Miles if he thinks Becky is all right. Overcome by a premonition, Miles races out of the house, still in robe and pajamas, and drives to Becky's. Cautiously letting himself in through a basement window, Miles searches around in the darkness, discovering a "double" for Becky hidden in a bin. Frightened, Miles spirits the real Becky away to his house.

Miles tells his story to a skeptical Kaufman. They return to Jack's. But the body is gone. Kaufman suggests there is a mystery, but only a "normal" one—a murdered man with his fingerprints burned off by

Becky's Cousin Wilma explains to Miles that Uncle Ira is *not* Uncle Ira. From left to right: Kevin McCarthy, Dana Wynter, Virginia Christine.

acid. They go on to Becky's and find nothing there either. Kaufman thinks Miles is another victim of Santa Mira's mass delusion.

Suddenly, Becky's father appears with a shotgun. Hearing prowlers, he has called the police. Nick Grivett, the Police Chief, sticks his head through a window, demanding to know what's going on. Kaufman explains, and Nick tells them a corpse with its fingerprints removed has been found in a burning haystack outside town. Miles and Jack leave, still puzzled by the night's events.

Next morning at Miles's house, things seem more relaxed as Becky cooks breakfast and she and Miles talk a little more about their relationship. Miles hears a noise from the basement. Tensing, he asks who it is, and Charlie Buckholtz, the gas man, appears. Miles chalks up his nervousness to lack of sleep.

On his way to the office Miles meets Wilma, who apologizes for her odd behavior. Jimmy Grimaldi and his mother show up at the office, apparently normal.

When Miles returns home that night, he finds Jack, Teddy, and Becky getting ready for a barbecue. Miles enters his greenhouse to get some lighter fluid and hears a strange popping noise. Looking under the table, Miles sees giant seed pods bursting open, a milky fluid bubbling out. Weird forms, like the body at Jack's, are growing from them—only these are growing into duplicates of himself, Becky, Jack, and Teddy. Miles yells frantically for Jack.

These pods, they realize, are the source of Santa

Mira's "delusion." They speculate that the change must take place when the person is asleep, as it did at Jack's, the original disintegrating when the duplication is complete. Miles realizes that the people around him—Wilma, Jimmy, the Police Chief, Dan Kaufman—have all been "taken over" by the pods.

Miles phones the FBI and the state capital, but the lines are either "dead" or "busy." He tries to send the women out of danger with Jack, but Becky refuses to go. Jack and Teddy depart to get help.

Miles and Becky try the phone several more times and get no response. Finally realizing they are cut off from the outside world, Miles and Becky drive to Sally's house, hoping to find sanctuary there.

On the way Miles stops at a gas station, praying the pay phone is still uncontrolled. He glances over to see the attendant closing his trunk. Miles dashes back to the car and drives away. Stopping up the road, he opens the trunk and finds two pods! Frantically, he sets them afire with a road flare.

At Sally's, he creeps up to a window, only to see Sally and several others calmly discussing the pods. A hand darts out for him. It's Nick, the Police Chief. Miles slugs him and flees.

The whole police force is after them now. Miles and Becky hide in his office, barely missing discovery. They must not sleep, so Miles dispenses stimulants, while they wait desperately for Jack to bring help.

Next morning they see from Miles's window that the town is unusually busy for 7:00 A.M. Police meet the bus, arresting all strangers. Suddenly, people begin to converge on the town square as trucks arrive —loaded with seed pods.

Miles and Becky watch in horror as the pods are divided among people with relatives and friends in other towns. The invasion is spreading.

Just then, Miles hears Jack's voice in the hall. But Jack is now a pod, and, accompanied by Dan Kaufman, supervises the placing of two fresh pods in Miles's waiting room.

Kaufman explains how the pods drifted to Earth from space, taking root in a field. He tries to convince Miles and Becky of the benefits they bring—a world without love, desire, ambition, faith—a peaceful, untroubled, emotionless world. Miles and Becky reject Kaufman's sterile vision of the future. But they are trapped. Jack and Dan adjourn to the waiting room to watch the pods grow, leaving Miles and Becky alone, knowing they must eventually sleep.

Desperate, Miles formulates a plan. Sneaking up behind Jack and Dan, he injects them with a sedative. The hall door springs open, and Miles is attacked by the Police Chief. Becky stabs him in the neck with another hypodermic.

Miles and Becky walk slowly to the street, trying to imitate the emotionless character of the other "people." But when a truck nearly runs down a dog, Becky screams, and the game is up.

Now the whole town is after them. They escape into the hills, taking refuge in an old mine. They hear singing, and, hoping against hope, Miles leaves the exhausted Becky to see if this is a sign there are other real people left. It turns out to be only a radio on one of the trucks being loaded with pods harvested in the greenhouses of the valley.

Miles returns to the mine and tries to force Becky to go on. He starts to carry her, but falls in a puddle at the mine entrance. He kisses her—and knows suddenly that *this is not Becky*. She has gone to sleep. Now she is one of *them*, and she screams for her new brethren, calling them down on Miles.

Miles runs for the highway, the townspeople in pursuit. But when he gets there, they let him go, confident no one will believe his story. Sure enough, as Miles begs the passing drivers for help, he is ignored and insulted. Climbing on the back of a truck, he is horrified to see it loaded with pods. He drops off, screaming for the drivers to listen to him. *"You're next!"* he shouts. But the cars speed past him blindly.

The scene dissolves into Miles telling his story to Dr. Hill. Hill and Bassett move away, leaving a distraught and hopeless Miles weeping.

"Will psychiatry help?" Bassett asks Hill.

"If all this is a nightmare—yes," Hill replies.

"Of course it's a nightmare," Bassett says disdainfully. "The man's as mad as a March Hare."

But as Hill and Bassett leave the office, another doctor is bringing in the victim of a wreck. Bassett asks about the case, and the doctor explains about the collision of a truck and a bus, and how they had to dig the truck driver out from under a pile of "great big seed pods."

"Where was the truck coming from?" Hill asks.

"Santa Mira," says the doctor.

Hill leaps into action, calling the FBI. The film fades out as Miles gives thanks that someone has finally believed him. The fight is not over yet.

The theme of the human being taken over or replaced by some kind of alien life form is an old one in literature. In mythology, it recalls the concept of demonic possession. The theme has appeared in many forms in the history of SF—as both good and evil—in such works as "Who Goes There" (1938) by John W. Campbell, *Needle* (1949) by Hal Clement, and "The Father-Thing" (1954) by Philip K. Dick, as well as many others. Perhaps the best known SF novel on the theme is Robert A. Heinlein's *The Puppet Masters* (1951).

Jack Finney's original novel, titled simply *The Body Snatchers*, is probably the only serious novel-length rival to *The Puppet Masters* as definitive treatment of the "possession" theme in SF. Although Heinlein's novel has overshadowed Finney's, *The Body Snatchers* was generally well received by SF reviewers.

P. Schuyler Miller, writing in *Astounding*, called the novel a "well-done variant of the theme [Heinlein] used in *The Puppet Masters*," although he felt the novel was weakened by a "not entirely convincing denouement." Groff Conklin, in *Galaxy*, said, "There is absolutely nothing wrong with this novel except that it has been done again and again and again," but he did praise Finney's writing and treatment of the theme. Anthony Boucher, then editor of *The Magazine of Fantasy and Science Fiction*, also praised the novel, with one reservation: "A . . . number of inconsistencies and inaccuracies prevent wholehearted acceptance of the book as [SF], but Mr. Finney is, as always, intensely readable and unpredictably ingenious."

The theme of possession, accompanied by loss of emotion, has also been a favorite of filmmakers. Films that deal with the idea include *Invaders from Mars* (1953), *It Came from Outer Space* (1953), *It Conquered the World* (1956), *Enemy from Space* (*Quatermass II*, 1957), and *I Married a Monster from Outer Space* (1958), and many others. The TV series *The Invaders* was also built largely around the possession theme.

The script of *IBS* follows Jack Finney's novel closely. Even a good bit of the dialogue, such as Miles's comment about it "not being so easy to go crazy even nowadays" and Dan Kaufman's speech on the nature of the human mind, come straight from the book.

But there are differences between film and novel. Finney's book lacks the "frame" that opens and closes the film (more about this later), although the novel is told in the first person. Becky Driscoll is recently divorced in both versions, but in the book she hasn't been living in England—the device used to cover Dana Wynter's British accent. The Belicecs are not caught by the pods in the novel, though the psychiatrist Kaufman—*M*anny in the book and *D*anny in the film—is.

The novel also explains more about the pods themselves through the character of a science professor named Budlong who does not appear in the film. The book makes clear that when a pod takes over a human identity, the original person turns into a kind of "gray fluff," with the pod disintegrating into the same substance should the transformation not be complete.

Finney dwells heavily on the theme of dehumanization in the novel, citing examples such as the impersonality of the telephone company, the degeneration of Santa Mira as a town, the insensitivity of government, and Miles's own fear of emotional involvement with Becky.

More importantly, the book presents the pods as even more inimical to human life than the film does. In a scene similar to one in the film, Miles peers through Sally's window at a group of pods as they imitate the speech and mannerisms of human beings, mocking them, making vicious fun of the common decencies of human relationships. In this scene the pods appear not just inhuman, but anti-human as well. It is one of the novel's most striking scenes.

The false Kaufman also explains to Miles that the pod duplicates are unstable; they will dissolve within five years. But since the pods plan to take over the whole Earth, they will eventually leave it devoid of *any* life, and then move on to other worlds to work their destruction. At the end of the universe, it's suggested, there will be nothing left but pods. The idea has a chilling effect in a manner totally unlike that of the film.

One incident in the film that doesn't appear in the book came from director Don Siegel. Siegel recalled an incident from his youth in which a dog was run over by a car while he watched, powerless to save it. This formed the basis for the scene where Becky reveals she and Miles are not pods by screaming, showing emotion, when a dog is almost hit by a truck.

The most significant differences between novel and film are in the endings. In the novel Becky is not a victim of the pods and the invaders are defeated, not by any conventional means, but by the sheer stubborn refusal of Miles, Becky, and others to submit to them. Sensing they can never overcome the human spirit, the pods leave Earth for a more easily conquered world. Finney's novel ends with the duplicates slowly dying off, and Santa Mira returning to its old, vital self.

In many ways the film of *IBS* is a lot tighter than Finney's book. Yet the film lacks the thoughtfulness and philosophical perspective that the more leisurely novel provides. The novel is as tense as the film, but the techniques used to produce that tension are different, reflecting the differences in the potential of two different media. Finney's novel and the film complement each other, and one shouldn't be ignored because of the existence of the other.

Jack Finney is the pen name of Walter Braeden Finney, a journalist and author, born in Milwaukee, Wisconsin, in 1911. Finney's first story wasn't published until he was thirty-five, but throughout the fifties his work appeared in many of the slick magazines such as *Collier's* and *The Saturday Evening Post*. Many of his stories were later reprinted in *The Magazine of Fantasy and Science Fiction*.

Collier's published a good deal of SF in the early fifties. In 1951, for example, they serialized John Wyndham's *The Day of the Triffids*. *The Body Snatchers* appeared in *Collier's* beginning December 10, 1954. A year later it appeared in an expanded form as a Dell "First Edition" paperback, with many subsequent printings since then. In 1976, the Gregg Press published a facsimile edition of the novel in hardcover, with a critical introduction by Richard Gid Powers.

Finney denies being an SF writer, describing his work as "fantasy" fiction. Finney has written extensively outside the SF genre, but much of his work contains some element of the fantastic. His short story collections, *The Third Level* (1956) and *I Love Galesburg in the Spring* (1963), and his novels, *The Woodrow Wilson Dime* (1968), *Marion's Wall* (1973), *The Night People* (1977), and *Time and Again* (1970)— perhaps his masterpiece—all use SF or fantasy to some degree.

Finney's denial probably springs from a misunderstanding of the breadth of the definition of SF current today, associating it with the purely "nuts and bolts" approach of earlier years. Or it may simply reflect a desire not to be labeled as a genre writer, in the same way that authors Kurt Vonnegut and Harlan Ellison reject the SF label.

Critics of both the book and film have pointed to the supposed absence of scientific content in both, suggesting *IBS* is not SF, but a horror story with science fictional trimmings. This too implies a narrow view of science fiction. Heinlein's *The Puppet Masters* has as little scientific "fact" in it as Finney's book, but the importance of such works has little to do with the issue of scientific content.

Finney appears to have liked the film version of his book, with some reservations—particularly about the ending. Finney's work consistently embraces a belief in the strength of the human spirit. He may have felt the darker implications of the film's ending were contrary to his faith in humanity's ability to triumph over a dehumanizing menace. The message of both the film and the novel are the same, but Finney's position is ultimately more positive.

The magazine version of *The Body Snatchers* was brought to the attention of Allied Artists and director Don Siegel by veteran producer Walter Wanger. Both Wanger and AA were aware of the box office success of the SF/horror films of the postwar period. AA was eager to cash in on the trend in the manner of its other low-budget films. But Wanger, it seems, was prepared to bring a little more to *IBS* than AA expected.

Wanger had been in films since 1921, working with such directors as John Ford, Alfred Hitchcock, and Fritz Lang. His career finally came to a halt during the filming of *Cleopatra* (1963) when the film went far over budget.

Wanger had worked with Siegel on *Riot in Cell Block 11* (1954), and knew Siegel's abilities would be perfectly suited to the nightmarish qualities of Finney's novel. Some versions say that at this point Wanger turned the idea over to Siegel, who brought in screenwriter Daniel Mainwaring, art director Edward Haworth, and star Kevin McCarthy. Other sources say it was Wanger who selected McCarthy and Dana Wynter. Later reflections by Siegel, however, indicate Wanger made many useful suggestions throughout the filming, and many decisions may have been made jointly.

The shooting title for *IBS* was originally *They Came from Another World.* Siegel favored the title *Sleep No More,* a provocative choice referring to the danger faced by the protagonists in falling asleep, and to Hamlet's soliloquy—and perhaps with the thought in mind that after seeing the picture, the audience might have trouble sleeping as well.

AA, however, opted for a more marketable title,

adding "Invasion of" to Finney's "The Body Snatchers." The studio promoted the film in the same lurid manner used for other SF/horror films of the period, unaware it had something a little more subtle in *IBS.*

Like most low-budget films, *IBS* was made quickly, with only ten days of rehearsal and nineteen of shooting. Siegel used many ordinary Hollywood streets for locations, adding to the sense of reality that makes the film's terror so convincing. For the scenes on the main streets of Santa Mira, Siegel took the cameras to the town of Sierra Madre, near Pasadena. Again, it's the town's ordinariness and the use of townspeople rather than actors that contribute to the film's overall effectiveness.

Aware of the almost automatic dependence on special effects in SF movies, Siegel went out of his way to avoid them. He wanted a film with very little violence and no monsters, a film in which the combination of mood, theme, and action would provide the suspense. From a budget of about $250,000, only about $15,000 was spent on special effects. The only major effects for the film involved the creation of the pods and the scenes in which they burst, expelling the duplicates. The effect was achieved by a combination of rubber duplicates of the actors surrounded by soap bubbles, which seemed to disappear as the scene was

Jack Belicec (King Donovan), Theodora Belicec (Carolyn Jones, background), Miles (Kevin McCarthy), and Becky (Dana Wynter) examine the "body" that is slowly beginning to resemble Jack.

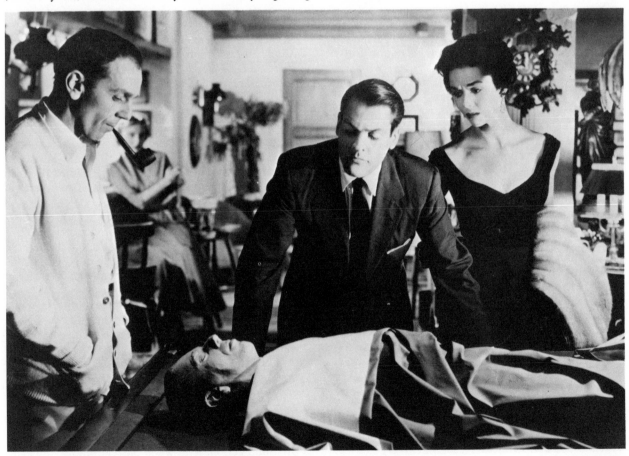

Miles discovers Becky's "double" in the basement.

filmed at a higher than normal speed.

Siegel considers *IBS* his favorite film—not necessarily his best—but the one closest to his heart, simply because it is "about" something, a claim Siegel himself admits can't always be made about his films. But it was Siegel, along with Walter Wanger, who embraced the idea that people, including many of their studio superiors, were emotionless pods.

Don Siegel was born in Chicago in 1912. His family moved around a lot, and Siegel wound up getting his college education at Cambridge in England. Around 1930, Siegel worked his way back to the U.S., eventually getting an interview with Hal Wallis at Warner Bros., who put him to work in the studio film library, mostly carrying film cans.

Siegel worked his way up in the editing department at Warners (he worked for Byron Haskin some of the time), eventually becoming head of the montage department and a second unit director. Siegel's montages appear in such films as *Yankee Doodle Dandy* and *Casablanca*.

Much of Siegel's time at Warners was spent shooting whole scenes for directors who were too busy— or lazy—to do it themselves. Siegel claims that in this way he may have shot more footage than any director on the Warner lot.

In 1945 Siegel directed a short for Warners, *A Star in the Night*. The following year he did another short, *Hitler Lives*. Both of them won Academy Awards. With an Oscar-winning director on their hands, Warners had to do something, so Siegel was given *The*

Verdict (1946), with Peter Lorre and Sidney Greenstreet, to direct, launching his career as a feature film director.

Siegel says he is uninterested in science fiction, and *IBS* is his only SF film. He did direct two episodes of *The Twilight Zone* "Uncle Simon" and "The Self-Improvement of Salvatore Ross"—for TV. In the early sixties Siegel did other TV work, directing pilots for the series *Convoy*, *Destry*, and *Jesse James*, as well as serving as producer on the last.

But Siegel has stuck mostly to films, and although over the years he has directed all kinds, he is best known for movies that depict the conflict between strong individuals and various kinds of mindless authority. Although these individuals are often outcasts from society, they have a code and a morality of their own. Unlike the emotionless establishment they must fight, they have feelings.

In recent years this theme and the stark, tense style that characterizes Siegel's work, have crystallized in such films as *Madigan* (1968), *Dirty Harry* (1971), *Escape from Alcatraz* (1979), and many others. While neither the theme nor the style originated for Siegel in *IBS*, the film embodies both in their purest forms. (For a listing of Siegel's films, see the Appendix.)

The style of *IBS* has sometimes been called documentary, perhaps because the camera work is so plain, employing few of the complicated techniques Siegel must have learned during his time at Warners. But his simple, direct use of the camera adds to the realism of the surroundings, which contrast so powerfully with the film's action. And when Siegel does use the camera unusually, the contrast with the more typically filmed shots only heightens the effect.

Siegel uses low shots to particularly good advantage, as in the film's beginning, when we see Jimmy Grimaldi running toward us, almost over us, fleeing from the thing that is his mother. Similarly, when Miles surprises "Jack" and "Danny," stabbing them in the back with hypos, they burst through the doors of the waiting room to come flying out almost on top of us. Later, when Miles and Becky hide in a ditch in the mine tunnel, Siegel shoots the scene from their viewpoint, looking up between some boards, as the townspeople trample over them, for a chillingly coffinlike, claustrophobic effect.

This claustrophobia is repeated throughout the film by Siegel's use of light and shadow on dark stairways, narrow streets, and cramped cellars. One scene of particular interest occurs when Miles and Becky hide in a closet in his office. They crouch beneath a screen window while a pod searches for them. When it leaves, Siegel takes the camera outside again, as Miles and Becky peer through the screen, looking like caged animals.

Some of the most remarkable direction comes at the film's end, when Becky and Miles flee from the pods (it's here that the distinction between the work of director and screenwriter often blurs).

Siegel uses repetition here to hit the audience hard. Early in the film, when the menace is still vague, Miles jokingly kisses Becky to see if it is still "her." Later, when he kisses her after she has fallen asleep, the sequence is paralleled when he realizes this is definitely *not* her. When Miles rises, the camera focused on his face, livid with fear, the effect is devastating.

Now Miles flees down the road—the same road Jimmy Grimaldi fled down earlier—while Miles tell us, "So I ran, I ran; I ran as little Jimmy Grimaldi had run the other day," bringing us full circle to the film's beginning, keying in on childhood fears we have forgotten existed.

At the film's climax there is the scene on the highway as the disheveled Miles cries desperately for help, like a man lost in a nightmare—until with stunning force the camera zeroes in on him shouting his warning directly to the audiences that we, *we*, are the next victims.

There are many small touches that contribute to the effectiveness of *IBS:* the shot of the body on Jack's pool table, seen from behind with the body in the foreground, dominating the characters in front of it; the sudden bleating of a cuckoo clock or ringing of a telephone; the hand that reaches out from off screen to grab Miles as he looks in Sally's window. These things and many more combine to generate the incredible tension of the film, a tension which can still affect audiences no matter how often they see the film.

But *IBS* has its flaws too. The explanation of Dana Wynter's British accent—that she's been living in England—is rather contrived. And Miles plunging out into the night in pajamas, robe, and slippers, and driving to Becky's to rescue her, leaving his car in the middle of the road, often elicits laughter from audiences.

Perhaps the film's greatest error of logic involves Becky's transformation into a pod. It's been implied earlier in the film that when the pods grow into duplicates, the real bodies disintegrate. Yet there is no pod around when Miles leaves Becky in the mine, nor would one have time to grow. Becky's transformation therefore defies all the careful explanation that has gone before.

Some critics have tried to provide a rational explanation for this logical gap, but it has to be acknowledged as an error, pure and simple, which the filmmakers appear not to have noticed.

Yet, unintentional as they might be, these flaws actually add something to the film. *IBS* has the quality of a nightmare, a sense of running in place and getting nowhere, of opening your mouth to scream and hearing no sound come out. The flaws in the film somehow contribute to this sense of nightmare.

Dana Wynter's accent makes her seem something of an "alien" to Santa Mira from the start, and is especially unsettling after her transformation. Miles's late-night rescue in his pajamas, coupled with the sexual overtones of "stealing" Becky from her home, has a dreamlike quality to it. In nightmares, such things occur regularly, despite their defiance of reason or propriety.

Becky's change into a pod *is* totally illogical. But isn't that what *IBS* is really about? That nothing is really what it seems, that no logic can prevail in a world where the people we think we know intimately turn out to be strangers bent on our destruction? As in *King Kong*, where critics note that models of the giant ape varied in size from scene to scene, contributing to the film's unreality, so do the flaws in *IBS* contribute to its being the ultimate nightmare.

Some sources credit Sam Peckinpah with providing part of the script for *IBS*. According to Siegel, this is false. Peckinpah, who would become a director of some note years later, was Siegel's assistant on the film, and while he may have made some important suggestions, he had no hand in the actual script.

Credit for the screenplay belongs to Daniel Mainwaring. Mainwaring appears to have had only one other screen credit prior to *IBS*. *The Phenix City Story* (1955) is another minor film critics have praised over the years. In fact, the story of one man's fight to save a town from political corruption is sometimes compared to Miles Bennell's fight to save Santa Mira from the pods.

Despite the fact that much of the script is drawn directly from Finney's novel, Mainwaring did contribute (again considering the collaboration of writer and director) a good deal to the film, tightening and clarifying Finney's narrative for the screen. Miles's speech, quoted at the beginning of this chapter, which so succinctly sums up the movie's theme, is from Mainwaring's script.

Both Mainwaring and Siegel wanted more humor in the film. Their idea was to show people reacting to the idea of pods taking over one's identity as naturally as possible, sensing most people would treat the whole thing as a joke—at least at first.

But Allied Artists (some sources say Walter Wanger) was afraid audiences wouldn't accept too much humor in a horror film, and a large part of it was cut. The humor remaining in the script is unusual for a 1950s film. Becky, for example, after listening to one of Miles's attempts to charm her, remarks, "Is this some of your bedside manner, Doctor?" "No," Miles replies. "That comes later."

Audiences usually laugh at this exchange, simply because it's so risqué for a fifties SF/horror film. But it's the kind of exchange that separates the characters in *IBS* from the stereotyped figures of other SF films of the era.

These are not soldiers or scientists fighting a battle, but real people, with real concerns, like love and marriage, facing a situation they are hardly prepared for. Miles, for instance, is subtly drawn as a man genuinely guilty about his failed marriage and uncertain about getting involved again, an element that underscores the film's theme of people's insensitivity to one another.

Mainwaring worked with Siegel again on *Baby Face Nelson* (1957) and *The Gun Runners* (1958). But the rest of his films have largely been programmers of varying quality, such as *Cole Younger, Gunfighter* (1958) and *The Woman Who Wouldn't Die* (1965). His only other SF credit appears to be *Space Master X-7* (1958), written with George Worthing Yates, who worked on *It Came from Beneath the Sea* and *Earth Vs. the Flying Saucers*.

Perhaps the greatest controversy surrounding *IBS* concerns the "frame" that begins and ends the movie. The original script called for the movie to begin with Miles returning to Santa Mira, rather than with him telling his story to Dr. Hill. It would have ended with Miles on the highway, shouting his warning to the world. The pessimistic ending was intended to leave the audience shocked and uneasy, driving home the filmmakers' feelings about the world growing more podlike every day.

Miles (Kevin McCarthy) uses a flare to burn the pod that a gas station attendant, a pod person, placed in the trunk of his car.

Miles and Becky flee down the main street of Santa Mira, pursued by the townspeople.

According to Mainwaring, the film was previewed to several "bad" audiences who didn't seem to understand it. Nervous about their investment, the studio asked for the frame to help clarify the picture. Mainwaring persuaded Siegel to shoot the frame and add the voice-over narration so the studio wouldn't bring in another crew to do it, completely mangling the film's original intent.

Another version has it that there were three previews without the frame. Audiences laughed at the film at first, but became more engrossed as it went on. The studio, afraid the laughter meant the audience wasn't scared, demanded the frame, and Walter Wanger convinced Siegel to do it himself. A third version says Siegel made the decision on his own.

Actually, who made the decision is unimportant. The question is whether the frame ultimately helps or hurts the movie. Siegel doesn't like it because he feels it reveals too much and weakens the film's impact. Many critics agree, and the film is often shown today with the frame cut, though McCarthy's narration must puzzle some audiences.

The problem of studio interference in the making of a film is a thorny one. As creative control of a film drifts from the hands of filmmakers to studio executives interested only in box office success, the quality and originality of the film almost inevitably decline. Today in Hollywood, where filmmaking is even more of a multimillion-dollar business than it used to be, the interference in films by people uninterested in the creative side of the business leaves critics and filmgoers outraged every time a promising idea is ruined by obvious studio interference.

This wasn't always the case, however. In the great days of MGM, for example, executives like Arthur Freed and Dore Schary often contributed to the success of their studio's films. The frame surrounding *IBS* may represent one of the rare cases when a studio —with the participation of an experienced producer like Walter Wanger—"deviated" into wisdom.

It isn't easy to do, but when *IBS* is imagined without the framing sequences, it is possible to understand the confusion of the first audiences. Fading out on Miles's shouted warning might easily have inspired a

The climax of the film, Dr. Miles Bennell's pleas for help fall on the deaf ears of passing motorists.

collective "huh?" from relatively unsophisticated fifties SF/horror audiences. Even when the film was remade in 1978, it was structured differently, so the pessimistic ending made more sense.

The more optimistic, but not conclusive, ending of *IBS* added by the frame is certainly more in line with Finney's original intention (though filmmakers and critics are prone to ignore such things), and with the generally optimistic tone of much science fiction. And for the first-time viewer, the frame adds the question of whether Miles's story *is* true—or simply the ravings of a hopeless paranoid.

The frame eases us into the film's mounting tension more smoothly, as what first appears to be a madman's story becomes horrifyingly true. We identify with Miles's frustration at not being believed, and at the end, when it seems he is headed for an asylum, the discovery of the proof he needs always brings a cheer of relief from audiences.

Whether you prefer the film with or without the frame is a matter of personal choice, but its function in *IBS* is too often dismissed by critics who, rightly, have an ax to grind with studios who interfere with filmmakers. But *IBS* deserves to be judged objec-

tively on its own merits in the form in which it was finally released.

From the beginning, Siegel and Wanger knew they wanted *IBS* to be about people, and this required a careful choice of actors.

IBS is unquestionably Kevin McCarthy's movie, and his performance in the film is incomparable. He is totally convincing at the film's beginning and end, when the idea that he might be mad is still in our minds, and throughout the film he runs the gamut of emotions from tenderness to stark fear.

McCarthy is especially effective in conveying this last emotion. The expression on his face when he finds Becky's double in the cellar, when he discovers the pods in the greenhouse, and when he realizes Becky has been taken over, is at the core of the film's ability to provoke terror in us.

McCarthy, who was born in Seattle, Washington, began his stage career in 1938. His film debut came in 1951 as Biff in the film version of *Death of a Salesman*. Since then McCarthy has worked steadily in films and TV in a variety of starring and character roles.

Curiously, McCarthy has never appeared in another SF film—aside from his brief guest appearance in the remake of *IBS*—but he has done extensive work in the fantasy field in TV, appearing in such early shows as *Lights Out* and *Inner Sanctum*. In 1959 McCarthy was in a *Sunday Showcase* production called "Murder and the Android" by Alfred Bester, which appears to have been based on Bester's famous story "Fondly Fahrenheit."

McCarthy guest-starred in an episode of *The Invaders*, titled "The Watchers," with a story not unlike that of *IBS*. In "Long Live Walter Jameson," an episode of *The Twilight Zone*, McCarthy played an immortal man. In 1972 he had a role in a PBS production of Kurt Vonnegut's *Between Time and Timbuktu*. McCarthy also appeared in a 1967 pilot for a show about the supernatural called *Ghostbreaker*, and was a star of an instantly forgettable non-SF series, *The Survivors*, which most people instantly forgot.

If there's such a thing as an "actor's actor," Kevin McCarthy is certainly one. No matter what the role, McCarthy has always brought a high degree of professionalism and believability to his work.

Despite the gnawing memory of her accent, Dana Wynter is also effective in *IBS*. While she has less to do than McCarthy, she convincingly portrays a real person suddenly confronted with the unthinkable. Wynter is especially successful in the moment of her transformation into a pod, when all the humanity she's built up in the film's first three quarters is suddenly replaced by an eerily convincing alienness.

Wynter's film career began in Britain with the film *White Corridors* (1951). She has avoided SF since *IBS*, appearing in such films as *Shake Hands with the Devil* (1959), *Sink the Bismarck* (1960), and *The List of Adrian Messenger* (1963). Wynter was one of the stars of a short-lived TV series called *The Man Who Never Was*, and has made numerous guest appearances on other TV shows.

King Donovan, who played Jack Belicec (not Velicheck, as some sources have it), was a perennial figure in B-films. Carolyn Jones, who played his wife Teddy, would have a reasonably successful career in films, as well as appearing as Morticia in the TV series *The Addams Family*.

Whit Bissell, who appears as Dr. Hill, is a longtime character actor in films, playing anything from bartenders to U.S. senators. SF/horror fans may recognize him from *I Was a Teenage Frankenstein* (1958), *The Time Machine* (1960), and TV's *Time Tunnel*, as well as many, many others.

Richard Deacon, the film's disdainful Dr. Bassett, specialized in such snobbish roles in films and TV for years. His longest run was on the old *Dick Van Dyke Show*. His role in *IBS*, though small, is significant in that it contrasts with his colleague, Dr. Hill. Bassett is totally unsympathetic to Miles's story, dismissing the man as mad. He is the film's clearest example of a pod who isn't a pod—just a human who acts like one.

Sam Peckinpah, Siegel's assistant on the film, also took on the minor role of Charlie Buckholtz, the gas man. The casting of Larry Gates as the psychiatrist, Dan Kaufman, is interesting since Gates usually played the fatherly, nice guy role in films. He appears so wise and concerned throughout the film that the revelation he is a pod is especially shocking.

The remainder of the players in *IBS* are so ordinary they appear anything but sinister. Yet this is the quality that drives home the film's theme that everyone is capable of insensitivity to the needs of others—that anyone may be a pod.

IBS works on many levels. It is a nightmare—particularly a child's nightmare—in which nothing is what it appears to be. The paralleling of Jimmy Grimaldi's flight from his mother with Miles's later flight from Becky stirs childhood nightmares of loss of love and abandonment.

IBS also hints at dark, hidden things within the mind. Certainly from an objective, outside view the film is a paranoid fantasy, obsessed with the question of what is real and what is a delusion.

Miles must tell his story to a psychiatrist, and it's to a psychiatrist he turns when unable to cope with the events around him. Before we know the truth about Santa Mira, the possibility of a town gone mad is almost convincing, considering Kaufman's theory that the town's problem is caused by "worry about what's going on in the world" and Miles's comment that "Even these days it isn't as easy to go crazy as you might think." For a moment we find ourselves ruefully disagreeing with him.

Before we know Kaufman is a pod, his explanations seem sensible. In the light of cold reason, the idea of mysterious doubles suddenly appearing in a town seems mad. When Kaufman says, "The human mind is a strange and wonderful thing. I'm not sure it'll ever be able to figure itself out—everything else, maybe, from the atom to the universe—everything except itself," it seems remarkably reasonable, especially when we recall the story is being told by a man who may be mad. But Kaufman's (and our) attempts to rationalize the situation through scientific psychology prove false. We can't always trust our reason or our science over our feelings. And that's part of what *IBS* is about.

IBS also reflects its era in a number of ways. The uncertainty and confusion of the postwar period is seen again in Kaufman's attributing the so-called mass neuroses to concern over the world situation and Miles's remark about going crazy "these days." The threat of invasion suggested by the cold war is clear in *IBS* as it is in other films of the time. The unemotional sameness of the pods and the way they take over resembles the uniformity of communism and the brainwashing techniques that emerged from the Korean War.

Fear of science and the atom appears in Miles's initial explanation of the pods: "So much has been discovered these past few years, anything is possible. Maybe the results of atomic radiation on plant life or animal life. Some weird alien organism—a mutation of some kind." Miles covers just about every area where science might be held responsible.

But the real key to *IBS* is in Siegel's own statement about the film, made in an interview with Stuart Kaminsky: "People are pods. Many of my associates are certainly pods. They have no feelings. They exist, breathe, sleep. To be a pod means you have no passion, no anger, the spark has left you."

Siegel's statement comes from a deep concern about the loss of individualism and human sensitivity that seemed to invade the postwar world. The death of so many people during World War II, both on and off the battlefield, seemed to dull human sensitivities to the tragedy of war.

Those deaths were also the product of a new and better technology that spilled over into the postwar era. A kind of "mass-man" was born, an imaginary "average" human distilled from the hopes, desires, and fears of many people, then homogenized by radio, TV, advertising, industry, and government. Speed and efficiency, backed by the power of technology, became society's goal. The threat of nuclear war

forced people to view the world differently. Things were no longer stable or predictable in a world where total destruction was just minutes away.

This combination of factors produced a human being better suited to coping with the pressures of the modern world. If the individual was to survive in a world growing more and more complex, he would have to restrict his feelings, or take the risk of being overcome by them.

To Jack Finney and Don Siegel the answer to psychological survival in the postwar world lay in exactly the opposite direction. In a time when forces beyond us were forcing us into a single mold, squeezing out our last drop of emotion, the answer was to assert our individuality to the fullest, express our real feelings, and embrace the human values of pride, dignity, friendship, and love more strongly. It was necessary for us to fight back against those things—things of our own design—that threatened to "dehumanize" us in a very real sense.

Invasion of the Body Snatchers, while flawed in some ways, gives the lie to some standard notions about SF

Miles, Jack, Becky, and Teddy discover the pods in the greenhouse (clockwise, from upper left: Dana Wynter, Carolyn Jones, Kevin McCarthy, and King Donovan).

GREAT SCIENCE FICTION FILMS

film. It proves it isn't necessary to spend millions of dollars on special effects to make a successful SF film. It proves that an SF film can be exciting, intelligent, and successful. And it proves that SF films don't always have to be made by people deeply involved in science fiction.

While this last may be hard to swallow for some, the key is in recognizing that a good SF film (like *any* film) demands a strong source, whether from another medium or an original script, and a passionate belief in the film by the people involved. These are the things Don Siegel, Daniel Mainwaring, Walter Wanger, Kevin McCarthy, and the rest of the cast and crew of *Invasion of the Body Snatchers* brought to the film.

In 1978, United Artists released an updating of *Invasion of the Body Snatchers*, set not in a small town this time, but in San Francisco. Don Siegel appears briefly in the film as a pod-cabdriver, as does Kevin McCarthy—still running, still trying to warn us that the pods are after us.

In a world where the generations seem unable to communicate, where government seems less and less responsive, where business appears unconcerned with the needs of people, where the media churn out endless hours of entertainment geared to the lowest common denominator, and life grows more confusing each day, the message of *Invasion of the Body Snatchers* —that we must fight back against the dehumanizing forces around us—seems even more relevant today.

Critics have complained for years about how the addition of the ambiguous frame to *Invasion of the Body Snatchers* implies that we eventually won our fight against the pods. As we look at the world around us, at each other and ourselves, the question must remain—Did we?

VILLAGE OF THE DAMNED

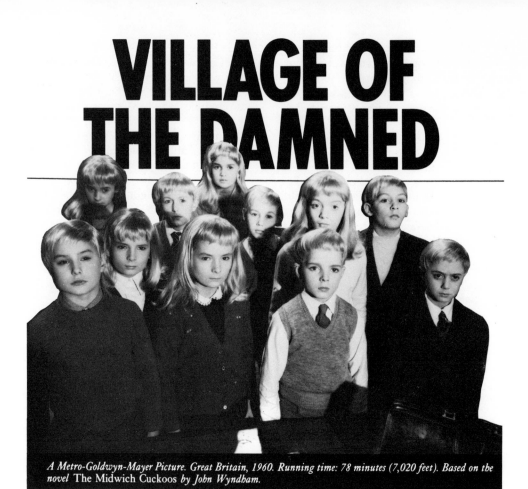

A Metro-Goldwyn-Mayer Picture. Great Britain, 1960. Running time: 78 minutes (7,020 feet). Based on the novel The Midwich Cuckoos *by John Wyndham.*

PRODUCTION CREDITS

PRODUCER.. *Ronald Kinnoch*
DIRECTOR... *Wolf Rilla*
SCREENPLAY .... *Sterling Silliphant, Wolf Rilla, & George Barclay.*
PHOTOGRAPHY.. *Geoffrey Faithful*
EDITOR .... *Gordon Hales*
ART DIRECTION .... *Ivan King*
MUSIC .... *Ron Goodwin*
PHOTOGRAPHIC EFFECTS.. *Tom Howard*
PRODUCTION MANAGER .... *Denis Johnson*
SECOND UNIT PHOTOGRAPHY... *Gerald Moss*
ASSISTANT DIRECTOR .... *David Middlemas*
SOUND... *A.W. Watkins*
HAIRSTYLES .... *Joan Johnstone*
MAKEUP .... *Eric Aylott*
WARDROBE .... *Eileen Sullivan*
SOUND RECORDIST .... *Cyril Swern*

Location scenes filmed at Letchmore Heath, England.

CAST

GORDON ZELLABY .... *George Sanders*
ANTHEA ZELLABY.. *Barbara Shelley*
MAJOR ALAN BERNARD .... *Michael Gwynne*
DAVID .... *Martin Stephens*
DR. WILLERS .... *Lawrence Naismith*
GENERAL LEIGHTON .... *John Phillips*
SIR EDGAR HARGRAVES .... *Richard Vernon*
MRS. HARRINGTON .... *Jenny Laird*
MR. HARRINGTON .... *Richard Warner*
JAMES PAWLE.. *Thomas Heathcote*

JANET PAWLE . . . . *Charlotte Mitchell*
MISS OGLE . . . . *Rosamund Greenwood*
CORONER . . . . *Alexander Archdale*
VICAR . . . . *Bernard Archard*
MRS. PLUMPTON . . . . *Susan Richards*
CONSTABLE GOBBEY . . . . *Peter Vaughan*
MILLY . . . . *Pamela Buck*
MR. SMITH . . . . *John Stuart*
NURSE . . . . *Sheila Robins*
DR. CARLISLE . . . . *Keith Pyott*
EVELYN HARRINGTON . . . . *Sarah Long*
PILOT . . . . *Tom Bowman*
LIEUTENANT . . . . *Anthony Harrison*
W.R.A.C. SECRETARY . . . . *Diane Aubrey*
SAPPER . . . . *Gerald Paris*
JUNE COWELL . . . . *Linda Bateson*
JOHN KELLY . . . . *Carlo Cura*
LESLEY SCOBLE . . . . *Mark Milebam*
ROGER MALIK . . . . *Peter Priedel*
THERESA SCOBLE . . . . *Elizabeth Munden*
PETER TAYLOR . . . . *Howard Knight*
BRIAN SMITH . . . . *Janice Howley*
PAUL NORMAN . . . . *Robert Marks*
JOHN BUSH . . . . *Billy Lawrence*

Howard Thompson, in the *New York Times,* called *The Village of the Damned* (hereafter *Village*) "One of the trimmest, most original and serenely unnerving little chillers in a long time. . . ." Writing for the *New York Herald Tribune,* Paul V. Beckley called *Village* " a delightfully shuddery film . . . Rilla directed with a canny feel for the uncanny that shows him to have a fine, wry taste for the plausible implausible."

Time called it "Fascinating. . . . Apparently assuming that a picture with only one star (George Sanders) of a second magnitude could not possibly be any good, MGM is hustling *Village* around the neighborhood circuits without even bothering to give it a Broadway send-off. It is missing a good bet. Based on a clever thriller . . . *Village* is one of the neatest little horror pictures produced since Peter Lorre went straight." *Films in Review* said it was "recommended . . . low-budgeted but intelligent . . . sci-fier."

Among the poor reviews was one by *Variety's* "Rich," which called the film "mediocre. . . . A rather tired and sick film which starts off very promisingly but soon nosedives."

Everyone in the small village of Midwich, England, unaccountably passes out one morning at the same time. Gordon Zellaby, a physicist, is talking on the phone to his brother-in-law, Major Alan Bernard, when it happens. Alarmed because Midwich seems cut off, Alan drives to the town's outskirts but learns no one can get closer without passing out. The Army, in the area on maneuvers, quickly cordons off the area and tries to penetrate closer, but gas masks are ineffective. As the village doctor, Dr. Willers, arrives on the scene, a low-flying surveillance airplane's pilot blacks out and his plane crashes.

Soon the people of Midwich begin to awaken, feeling stiff and strangely chilled. The Army immedi-

ately runs tests on the air and soil, but no trace of what put everyone to sleep can be found. Soon after, while Zellaby tends his suddenly flourishing plants, his wife Anthea tells him they're going to have a baby. He is overjoyed. But many local men, like Jim Pawle, who was away at sea for a year, are grim and upset. *Every* woman of child-bearing age, the doctor learns from the Vicar, virgin or other, is pregnant.

Anthea has a normal son who weighs just over ten pounds, as all the Children do, and possesses "unusual" eyes. Little David, as they name him, begins growing rapidly. One day Anthea tries to give the child a bottle which is too hot. Something forces her to put her hand in boiling water as David glares at her.

The Children quickly master a complex puzzle box after just one of them, David, has discovered how it works. Aloof from Midwich's other children, the six boys and six girls are always together, led by the cold and emotionless David.

Gordon and Alan attend a conference about the Children, who are not unique to England. Other such Children have been born around the world—some to Eskimos, who killed them, and some in Russia, where they were allowed to survive. The conferees wonder if the Children are aliens. Apparently the women were impregnated by means of a "radio" beam from outer space. Aware that the Children have strange, possibly destructive, powers, Alan and the other conferees discuss destroying them. Gordon defends the Children and asks for a year to study them. Reluctantly, the others go along.

While acting as the Children's teacher, Gordon discovers they can read his surface thoughts at first and later *all* his thought processes. The Children refuse to discuss life on other planets when he brings the subject up and insist upon moving into the school to live together.

Gordon Zellaby (George Sanders) talks to the Children—including his son David (Martin Stephens)—in the schoolroom in which he is teaching them. Note the subtle domelike impression created by special effects director Tom Howard's blond wigs.

When a car almost hits one of the six girls accidently, David and the others force the driver to commit suicide by driving into a wall. At the inquest, Anthea cannot remember the incident clearly.

Gordon is talking to Alan, Anthea, and the town's doctor when a phone call comes in telling Alan the Russians have used an atomic gun, capable of firing a shell 60 miles, to destroy the town where the other Children were born—a ruthless but desperate way of stopping their Children before they got too powerful.

Upset at events in the village, (the death of the car's driver is ruled an accident), angry townspeople march to the schoolhouse where David calmly faces them down and, his eyes glowing, forces the leader to set himself on fire. Outraged by what he's seen, Alan confronts David, who tells him the Children will do what they must to survive because they are the only ones left. As punishment for his outburst, Alan is mentally paralyzed for a time by the Children.

David wants his father to arrange for the Children to be dispersed across the countryside so they won't

suffer the same fate that befell the Russian Children. Gordon asks for time, aware at last that the Children are evil and something must be done to stop them before they are too powerful.

Seeing Anthea off to London, Gordon takes a time bomb to class with him. When the Children try to find out what he is thinking, he forces himself to visualize a brick wall until the bomb explodes, killing him and the Children.

From *Webster's New Collegiate Dictionary:* "Cuckoo **1.** A largely grayish brown European bird (*Cuculus Canorus*) that is a parasite given to laying its eggs in the nests of other birds which hatch them and rear the offspring."

The Village of the Damned, released in 1960, is a variation on one of the fifties' growing fears: dehumanization. The troubled decade between 1950 and 1960 had seen the brainwashing of American soldiers by the North Koreans, as well as more government intrusion into individual freedom, and the increasing use of mind-altering drugs to control or cure anti-social behavior. It was the era of the corporate nonentity *(The Man in the Gray Flannel Suit,)* cookie cutter suburbs, and the rise of manipulative mass advertising linked to new understandings of mass psychology.

The films of the fifties and early sixties reflected an awareness of these threats to humanity: *Invaders from Mars, The Invasion of the Body Snatchers, The Manchurian Candidate,* and *The Village of the Damned.*

The invasion of the body or the mind by an outside force—gods, animal spirits, devils and demons, and aliens—is an idea as old as man himself. For much of prehistory, madness was attributed to these invading entities and most cultures had rituals to drive out the unwanted cohabitors.

The twelve Children in *Village,* born in Midwich of earthly mothers, are the first wave of an invasion. Not an invasion as H. G. Wells imagined in *The War of the Worlds,* with tripodal machines overmatching our tanks and artillery, but one just as effective in conquering us. It is an invasion by a long distance "radio" beam—an invasion by remote control rape.

The Children of this unnatural union are human in outward form, but mentally they are part of an "over-mind" gestalt that places survival first—*their* survival. A "gestalt" mind is a linking of several minds to form a whole stronger than any individual mind. Theodore Sturgeon's 1953 novel *More Than Human* is about a gestalt mind consisting of six individuals, but the six are natural mutations.

In *Village,* primitive societies, such as the Eskimos', recognize the Children for what they are and kill them (and their mothers) outright. They sense that the Children represent an invasion and a loss of racial identity. On the surface they may only be reacting to blonde-haired, golden-eyed children born of Eskimo mothers, but they instinctively recognize what takes the Russians and the English longer to discover, that such children can bring no good.

When the Russians realize the mind control and telepathic powers of their Children growing stronger, they sacrifice a whole town to catch them unaware, killing the innocent along with the dangerous. It is a high, but necessary, price to pay. In contrast, Gordon Zellaby kills only the Children and himself, perhaps as a sort of penance for allowing them to grow so strong.

Children mean many things to adults. They are our hope for the future—the inheritors of our genes, our names and property, and our world. We view them with both love and dread because they are our replacements. Not yet fully civilized, children are small aliens—beings as unknown to us as the surface of Pluto—in our midst.

The child in written science fiction is often presented as cold, unfeeling, different—or monstrous. In Ray Bradbury's "The Small Assassin," the baby is "one in a billion, born aware and able to think instinctively." By placing a toy on the stairs and crying in the night, the infant kills his mother when she breaks her neck in a fall. The child kills his father by crawling to an unlit heater while he sleeps and turning on the gas. No explanation is offered for the child's homicidal attitude toward his parents other than his resentment at leaving the security of the womb.

In Bradbury's "The Veldt," a couple's son and daughter become addicted to the "nursery," an electronic playroom that visualizes whatever a child wishes to see. Wonderland and Oz gradually give way to an African veldt where the lions can be seen feeding on something in the distance. The parents, aware the children are spending too much time in the nursery, plan to turn the room off for a month or so. Taking one last look inside, they discover their children have locked them in. The lions, frighteningly real, come closer and closer until.... After the screaming is over, the lions feed on their kill and the vultures swoop lower and lower.

The children in "Mimsey Were the Borogoves" by Henry Kuttner and C. L. Moore ("Lewis Padgett") are a son and daughter who find a box full of toys from millions of years in the future. The toys teach the children new ways of thinking, alien to our Euclidean-logic universe. A child pyschologist tells the parents, "Babies of course are not human—they are animals . . . and have minds which work in terms and categories of their own. . . ."

The children having assimilated the lessons of the future toys, finally disappear into thin air, leaving their bewildered parents behind.

William Tenn's "The Malted Milk Monster" is a fat and pimply adolescent named Dorothy who imprisons an advertising man she has a crush on in her fantasy world—a child's drawing where chocolate rivers flow past lollipop trees and all wishes come true.

The three-year-old boy in Jerome Bixby's "It's a *Good* Life" has transported his small town to another dimension. Anthony doesn't like "bad" thoughts and those who anger him end up dead or worse. So everyone mumbles all the time and thinks only "good" thoughts. Perhaps things will change when Anthony grows older; in the meantime, it's a *good* life.

We have always had ambivalent feelings about children. Our view of children often mirrors our view of ourselves. At times we have looked upon children as small adults; as wild and savage creatures needing taming; as innocents untouched by the harsh realities of life; as unpaid laborers required to work long hours in our fields and factories; as a form of insurance against the terrors of old age; and, finally, as unfeeling monsters.

The child of the Middle Ages was expected to possess the piety of an adult, and he suffered the punishments of an adult if he did not. In contrast, the modern child is given his own "space," his own room and stereo, and sex education.

The child, then, is less a reality than an image each of us has formed inside his mind. And each child that we encounter is unconsciously measured against the still-living child buried deep within us. But each passing year takes the adult we have become farther away from the child we used to be. And all too soon, like the children in *Peter Pan*, we can no longer escape to Never Never Land each night.

In films the good child came first. This unspoiled darling could be seen in the Lassie, Andy Hardy, Shirley Temple, and many other film series. She was Dorothy Gale, returned to Kansas by a pair of ruby slippers and the phrase, "There's no place like home."

Things changed in the fifties. The children born during the baby boom years following World War II began to distort society, to be the cause for much change, upheaval, and concern.

With the release of *The Bad Seed* in 1956, the curly topped moppet played by Shirley Temple had metamorphosed into the emotionless murderess played by eleven-year-old Patty McCormick.

The children of *1984* (1956) gladly turned their parents in to the state for saying things against Big Brother. In 1958 *The Space Children*—the sons and daughters of scientists working at a missile facility—aligned themselves with an alien "brain" to sabotage the missile development program. It was one of the first SF films to deal with the growing alienation (no pun intended) between parents and children.

The child as monster was firmly established in 1960 when MGM released *Village*. Martin Stephens, who played David in *Village*, later turned up in 1962's *The Innocents*, again as a sinister child.

The financial and grudging critical success of *Village* inspired a sequel in 1963 called *Children of the Damned* (which some critics like more then *Village* because it raises more philosophical issues).

[These Are] The Damned, based on a novel called *The Children of the Light* by H. L. Lawrence, was released in 1963. Also inspired by *Village's* success, *The Damned* is about a group of radioactive children living in a cave under a British military base. The children are a scientist's attempt to create human beings immune to the effects of atomic radiation. Their touch is deadly, however, and two adults who try to free them (MacDonald Carey and Shirley Ann Field) are fatally contaminated in the process. (For more on children in SF/horror films, see the Appendix.)

The villagers' attitudes toward the Children reflect

Anthea Zellaby (Barbara Shelley) stands between her husband Gordon (George Sanders) on the left and her brother Alan Bernard (Michael Gwynn) on the right as they discuss the Children.

GREAT SCIENCE FICTION FILMS

Dr. Willers (Lawrence Naismith) examines Anthea's hand after she plunged it into hot water after giving her son David a bottle which was too hot. Her husband Gordon (George Sanders) comforts her.

the circumstances surrounding the pregnancies and their uncertainty about their origins.

Zellaby is pleased he's going to be a father, especially at his age, and is comically solicitous toward Anthea. Although he's saddened to learn the child may not be his, he continues to defend the Children and advance their education. A scientist, he sees the Children as a potential source of knowledge and not as a threat to the human race. It is only when David and the others nearly kill Alan that Zellaby finally realizes the danger they represent.

Anthea, despite David's mentally forcing her to put her hand in boiling water, reacts as a mother. She realizes there's something strange about her son, some missing spark of human warmth, but she continues to love him and worry about him. Only after the Children have injured or killed a number of villagers does she confess David and the others frighten her.

After the details of the ubiquitous pregnancies are known, an air of sadness and uncertainty hangs over Midwich; the villagers are confused, angry, and upset. They are indeed a village of the damned, the women impregnated by unknown fathers. Feeling cursed, the men stand around drinking in the local pub, sullen and full of anger but with nowhere to direct it except at the unborn Children. One man mutters he hopes none of them will live.

After the Children are born, one village boy gets into a fight with them and is drowned (off screen). The other youngsters quickly learn to leave the twelve Children alone.

At the inquest into the death of the villager whose car crashed into a wall after nearly striking one of the girls, the man's brother shouts, "*They* killed him!" The fear and hatred of the men of the village transforms them into a mob and they try to burn the Children out of their school—an attempt which fails when David forces the leader to set fire to himself.

The Midwich Cuckoos, by John Wyndham, was first published in 1957. "John Wyndham" was the pseudonym of John Beynon Harris, an English writer. Harris, as Wyndham, also wrote *The Day of the Triffids* (which was also filmed), *Re-Birth, Out of the Deeps,* and

Tales of Gooseflesh and Laughter.

Wyndham's novel is extremely well written. Its overall scheme and story are quite close to the film made from it, but there are a number of differences between them.

The novel is narrated in the first person by Richard Gayford, a resident of Midwich who was away at the time of the "Dayout," as the residents call the incident. Gayford doesn't appear in the film. Alan Bernard is Alan Hughes in the novel, and he is not Gordon Zellaby's brother-in-law. Instead, he becomes Zellaby's son-in-law when he marries his daughter Ferrelyn (by Zellaby's first wife). Ferrelyn gives birth to one of the alien Children while Zellaby's wife Anthea has a normal child conceived before the Dayout.

In the novel, Midwich is cut off at 10:17 P.M., not during the late morning. Area residents not affected by the Dayout report seeing fires and an "aircraft" of some sort descending into Midwich. A high flying military intelligence plane (a lower flying one crashed) takes photographs which reveal something large and circular in Midwich near the Grange. The "Grange" is a super-secret government research facility based in the otherwise ordinary Midwich.

The lifting of the Dayout reveals eleven fatalities by fires, drowning, falls, and shocks to the nervous systems of elderly residents. The circular object is gone.

The film's budget limited the number of alien Children to twelve; in the novel sixty Children are born: fifty-three to Midwich women and seven to young women workers at the Grange. All are blonde, golden-eyed, and very healthy.

The film's brevity and rapid pace cannot accommodate the many philosophical, moral, religious, scientific, and social questions the novel raises. Zellaby, an agnostic writer of "deep" books, and the Vicar have far-ranging conversations about the meaning of the Children. The Vicar wonders if perhaps the Children are a test, to see if the babies would be accepted by their host mothers.

Zellaby, after pointing out the similarities between the Children and the eggs left by mother cuckoos in other birds' nests, calls the Children changelings—the offspring of elves or other supernatural beings left to be raised by humans. He differs from the Zellaby of the movie in being suspicious of the Children from the first.

Whereas the Children in the film are led by David, Zellaby's son, the Children of the novel have only two minds between them and need no leader. All the boys possess *one* interconnected male mind and all the girls possess *one* interconnected female mind; to talk to a single girl or boy is to talk to them all. While the Children are telepathic among themselves and can coerce human beings into following their commands through mind pressure, they can't read others' thoughts.

It is not until the final pages of the novel that Wyndham reveals that other such Children have been born around the world, meeting a fate similar to that of the Eskimo and Russian Children in the film.

Because he is an old man with few years left to him, Zellaby takes it upon himself to eliminate the threat posed by the Children. He, too, uses a time bomb, although he has no need to think of a brick wall to keep them from reading his mind.

Village's relatively small budget of £ 82,000—roughly $225,000 in 1960—shows in a number of ways. Color was deemed prohibitive, although it can be argued that for a "thriller" color is both unnecessary and not nearly as effective as the shadings of black and white.

The shooting schedule was six weeks, and director Rilla found a small village suitable for shooting the exteriors just half an hour from the Boreham Wood Studio.

Photographic effects director Tom Howard made the Children's eyes glow by using a matte insert which changed them from positive to negative. Not wishing to use contact lenses, producer Ronald Kinnoch cast child actors with extremely dark eyes.

Makeup man Eric Aylott designed special blonde wigs which suggested the Children's bulging foreheads.

Stumped for an ending, Rilla was driving to the location shooting when he saw workmen demolishing an old brick house. He then devised the finale which had Zellaby thinking of a brick wall so the Children couldn't read his mind about the bomb he had brought with him.

To get the effect of the mental wall crumbling slowly, Tom Howard used a high-speed, slow-motion camera to shoot some loosely-constituted material being blown away by a fan.

Sterling Silliphant's script revealed his lack of knowledge about English village life, so director Wolf Rilla and producer Ronald Kinnoch rewrote it in a weekend.

Rilla and Kinnoch divided the script into four sections and each man took two sections to revise. When they were done, they exchanged sections and each polished what the other had written. They worked only from Silliphant's script, lacking the time to go back to Wyndham's novel. Kinnoch appears in the credits for the screenplay as "George Barclay."

Wolf Rilla, who was born in 1920, is the son of Walter Rilla, a well-known German actor who emigrated to England in the mid-thirties. *Village* was his eighth film and the one he is best known for directing. A graduate of Cambridge University, Rilla wrote scripts and became a producer for BBC radio.

Rilla's fast-paced direction doesn't allow time for doubts about the plot to creep into the viewer's mind. He is also effective in establishing quickly the low key air of menace that pervades the film. But perhaps his strongest contribution is getting excellent performances from his uniformly fine cast.

Rilla wanted the Children to appear attractive and polite, so that their behavior would be that much more frightening. Since children are normally very restless, Rilla made the child actors move very stiffly —in a controlled, unchildlike way—to suggest their alien origins and lack of human emotions.

Rilla's other films include: *Noose for a Lady* (1953), *The End of the Road* (1954), *Pacific Destiny* (1956), *Witness in the Dark* (1960), *Piccadilly Third Stop* (1960), *The World Ten Times Over* (which he also wrote, 1963) and *Secrets of a Door to Door Salesman* (1973).

A former advertising executive, Sterling Silliphant, born in 1918, has written and produced television shows as well as motion pictures, including *Naked City* and *Route 66*.

Silliphant won an Academy Award for his screenplay for *In the Heat of the Night* (1967). His other films include: *The Joe Louis Story* (1953), *Five Against the House* (coproducer, 1955), *The Slender Thread* (1956), *Damn Citizen* (1957), *Charly* (1968), and *The Killer Elite* (1975).

The cast of *Village* was headed by George Sanders (1906–1972). Born in St. Petersburg, Russia, Sanders for the most part played scoundrels, crooks, and cads (his 1960 autobiography was called *Memoirs of a Professional Cad*).

Sanders brings a quiet and intelligent dignity to the role of Gordon Zellaby. Noted for walking through his roles in films which he didn't particularly care for, Sanders shows little evidence of that inclination here. He is especially effective in the scenes played between himself and his son David (Martin Stephens), because you never sense that his Zellaby is condescending or patronizing. He genuinely respects the Children.

Sanders's first film role was in Alexander Korda's production of H. G. Wells's *The Man Who Could Work Miracles* (1936), but he did not achieve semi-stardom in America until Alfred Hitchcock's *Rebecca* was released in 1940. As *Time*'s review of *Village* makes clear, Sanders never achieved super-stardom.

Although he appeared in more than sixty movies, only a handful were science fiction or fantasy: *Man/-Miracles* (1936), *The Picture of Dorian Gray* (1944), *From the Earth to the Moon* (1958), *Village* (1960), and *Psychomania* (1972).

His 1958 TV series, *George Sanders Mystery Theatre,* lasted one season.

A sad and disillusioned man, Sanders committed suicide in 1972. (For a fuller listing of his films, see the Appendix.)

Barbara Shelley, born in 1933, who plays Anthea Zellaby, has made a career of acting in SF/horror

Gordon Zellaby (George Sanders), the teacher of the twelve Children and the father of their leader, David, prepares a time bomb which will blow them and him to pieces if he can successfully keep from thinking about its existence.

VILLAGE OF THE DAMNED

films. As the mother of the Children's leader, David, Shelley is effective and restrained, displaying first motherly love, then fear at what she's given birth to.

Her films include: *Cat Girl* (1957), *Blood of the Vampire*(1959), *Shadow of the Cat* (1962), *The Gorgon* (1964), *Dracula, Prince of Darkness* (1965), *Quatermass and the Pit (Five Million Years to Earth* 1967), and *Ghost Story* (1974).

Martin Stephens, born in 1949, played David Zellaby. Only eleven when he made *Village*, Stephens is a major reason for the film's success. His David is perfect: cold, emotionless, articulate, and self-assured. When, near the film's end, he says, "Father, I want to talk to you," it is a chilling, perfectly delivered line.

Stephens' other films include: *The Hellfire Club* (1961), *The Innocents* (1961), *Battle of the Villa Fiorita* (1965), and *The Witches* (1966).

Michael Gwynn (1916–1976) was a British stage actor who appeared occasionally in films. Gwynn played Major Alan Bernard in *Village*. His other films included *The Revenge of Frankenstein* (as the Monster, 1958).

Lawrence Naismith, born in 1908 as Lawrence Johnson, played Dr. Willers. A familiar face to American moviegoers, Naismith is a durable British character actor, often appearing in SF or fantasy films. Among his many films are: *A Night to Remember* (1958), *Jason and the Argonauts* (1963), *Camelot* (1967), *The Valley of Gwangi* (1968), *Eye of the Cat* (1969), and *The Amazing Mr. Blunden* (1972). He was a regular on the TV series *The Persuaders* (1971).

Critic Leslie Halliwell calls *Village* "Modestly made . . . cleanly presented." Much as do *The Mind of Mr. Soames* and *The Man in the White Suit* (also British made), *Village* creates its impact without resorting to ray guns, flying saucers, or extensive special effects. It is a quiet, low key, and intelligent little film that compares favorably with written SF.

By no means a masterpiece, *The Village of the Damned* remains a superior and often-overlooked contribution to the genre.

DR. STRANGELOVE OR: HOW I LEARNED TO STOP WORRYING AND LOVE THE BOMB

Great Britain, 1964. Produced by Hawk Films. Distributed by Columbia Pictures. Running time: 94 minutes (8,460 feet). Black and White. Based on the novel Red Alert *by Peter George.*

PRODUCTION CREDITS

PRODUCER/DIRECTOR .... *Stanley Kubrick*
ASSOCIATE PRODUCER .... *Victor Lyndon*
SCREENPLAY .... *Stanley Kubrick, Terry Southern, Peter George*
PHOTOGRAPHY .... *Gilbert Taylor*
EDITOR .... *Anthony Harvey*
PRODUCTION DESIGNER .... *Ken Adam*
ART DIRECTOR .... *Peter Murton*
SPECIAL EFFECTS .... *Wally Veevers*
MUSIC .... *Laurie Johnson*
AVIATION ADVISER .... *Captain John Crewdson*
SOUND .... *John Cox*

CAST

GROUP CAPTAIN LIONEL MANDRAKE
PRESIDENT MUFFLEY
DR. STRANGELOVE .... *Peter Sellers*
GENERAL "BUCK" TURGIDSON .... *George C. Scott*
GENERAL JACK D. RIPPER .... *Sterling Hayden*
COLONEL "BAT" GUANO .... *Keenan Wynn*
MAJOR T. J. "KING" KONG .... *Slim Pickens*
AMBASSADOR DE SADESKY .... *Peter Bull*
MISS SCOTT .... *Tracy Reed*
LIEUTENANT LOTHAR ZOGG, BOMBARDIER .... *James Earl Jones*
MR. STAINES .... *Jack Creley*
LIEUTENANT H. R. DIETRICH, D.S.O. .... *Frank Berry*
LIEUTENANT W. D. KIVEL, NAVIGATOR .... *Glenn Beck*
CAPTAIN G. A. "ACE" OWENS, COPILOT .... *Shane Rimmer*
LIEUTENANT B. GOLDBERG, RADIO OPERATOR .... *Paul Tamarin*
GENERAL FACEMAN .... *Gordon Tanner*
ADMIRAL RANDOLPH .... *Robert O'Neil*
FRANK .... *Roy Stephens*
L. HERDER, J. MCCARTHY, H. GALILI .... *Members/Burpelson Defense Corps.*

An opening narration tells of a Soviet "Doomsday" device.

Planes are taking off from Burpelson Air Force Base. Group Captain Mandrake, an exchange officer from the RAF, is called into base commander Jack D. Ripper's office. Ripper has ordered a condition red and is implementing Plan R—a war plan to be used when the President has been killed in a sneak attack.

Narration about the B-52s constantly in the air is followed by a cut to the inside of one: Major "King" Kong is reading *Playboy*. Kong's plane receives Wing Attack Plan R from Burpelson. Confirming the message, Kong puts on his cowboy hat and tells the crew most of the U.S. was probably wiped out.

General Buck Turgidson is in the bathroom when his bikinied secretary, Miss Scott, takes an urgent message from the Pentagon—General Ripper has sent his planes to attack Russia despite the absence of any alert on the "threat board."

At Burpelson, Ripper warns his men to be ready for a "Commie" attack and confiscates all radios. Mandrake accidently finds a radio and discovers there's no Russian attack on.

Major Kong's crew is preparing their plane for an attack on the ICBM missile complex at Laputa. The recall code prefix is set to receive on the letters OPE. When Mandrake takes the radio to Ripper, he is told there is no Russian attack—and only Ripper knows the recall code letters.

While talking about Communist conspiracies sapping our precious bodily fluids, Ripper casually uncovers a .45 automatic and tells Mandrake that the President has no choice but to opt for total war since he's sent the Wing into Russian air space.

In the War Room of the Pentagon, Turgidson is explaining how Ripper could have sent planes into Russia without the President's permission. The human element of the plan failed, obviously. A decision is made by the War Roomers to attack Burpelson with Army troops and the President and Turgidson discuss how many people might die in a nuclear exchange. Ten to twenty million Americans might be killed, Turgidson concedes, but he argues that the attack is a perfect chance to catch the Ruskies with their pants down. The President rejects his arguments and has the Russian Ambassador brought to the War Room.

Turgidson discovers the Russian Ambassador taking pictures in the War Room and wrestles with him. An outraged President Muffley tells them, "Gentlemen, you can't fight in here—this is the War Room!" After the President has difficulty finding Premier Kissoff, the ambassador gives them an unlisted number to call.

The defenders of Burpelson Air Force Base open fire on the Army troops and the battle for the base begins. Ripper and Mandrake sit silently, listening to the fighting outside.

President Muffley and Premier Kissoff have a strained conversation about "the bomb." Kissoff is drunk and slow to understand the problem. Muffley offers to help the Soviets destroy the planes and both men dispute who is "sorriest" about the attack.

Ripper tells Mandrake about water fluoridation and our precious bodily fluids. Since fluoridation is a Commie plot, Ripper drinks only rainwater and grain alcohol. Suddenly the office is raked by bullets. Ripper pulls a machine gun from his golf bag and asks Mandrake to feed him the bullet belt.

The Russian ambassador tells everyone in the War Room about the secret Doomsday machine, although Turgidson thinks it's all "Commie bull." Dr. Strangelove, an ex-Nazi scientist, slowly rolls into the light in his wheelchair. He discusses the Doomsday machine with the ambassador and confirms that such a device is indeed possible.

At Burpelson Base the attack continues, and Ripper fires back. Ripper then tells Mandrake that fluoridation is responsible for "loss of essence"—something he discovered while making love. Outside, the base's troops start surrendering. Ripper asks Mandrake about torture before going into the bathroom—where he shoots himself.

Major Kong's B-52 is nearly shot down by a missile, but survives.

Mandrake is looking at Ripper's doodlings, trying to figure out the recall code, when Colonel "Bat" Guano shoots his way into the office and arrests him.

The B-52's recall box and radio were destroyed by the missile. Three engines are out, but they continue their attack plan.

Guano, suspicious of Mandrake, allows him to try to call the President from a pay phone. Mandrake doesn't have the change, so he has Guano shoot open a Coke machine.

Mandrake was right: OPE *is* the recall code and most of the planes respond and turn back; four are reported destroyed. The celebration in the War Room is short-lived, however. Premier Kissoff is back on the phone: one plane is still on its attack route. Muffley convinces the Premier to put every interceptor in the area of Laputa, the plane's intended target.

Since they haven't enough fuel to reach Laputa, Major Kong decides they will attack a closer target. As they close in, Kong discovers that the bomb bay doors won't open. They're over the target by the time Kong repairs the doors and they open, dropping him toward the ground while he's still on one of the bombs. He rides it like a bronco—until the explosion.

Dr. Strangelove proposes moving the government underground into deep mine shafts where they'll have to remain for a hundred years. Strangelove tells the President that the leaders could be saved (struggling meanwhile with his own balky artificial right arm and hand.) There would be ten desirable women for each male, he points out. Most important, though, a "mine shaft gap" must not be allowed to develop.

Standing, Dr. Strangelove shouts in amazement,

"*Mein Fuhrer*, I can walk!"

The film ends with the Doomsday device's hydrogen bombs exploding to the tune of "We'll Meet Again"—an ironic thought.

Red Alert, by Peter Bryant, the novel on which *Dr. Strangelove* is based, was published in 1958. "Peter Bryant" was the pen name of a former Royal Air Force navigator, Peter George. It is George's knowledge of the air defenses of the U.S. that gives the novel its air of authenticity and allows him to show so convincingly how an unauthorized attack on the Soviet Union could be accomplished.

Red Alert resembles *Dr. Strangelove* in many ways —hardly surprising since the novel was the basis for the screenplay and Peter George was one of the screenwriters. There are, however, quite a few differences. The most obvious difference concerns the names of the bases and characters. Burpelson Base is Sonora Air Force Base in the novel, and the SAC general who initiates the attack is named Quinten, not Ripper. There is no RAF officer, though Major Paul Howard serves the same function in the novel as Group Captain Mandrake does in the movie.

The reasons behind Quinten's attack order are

George C. Scott (as Turgidson) and Tracy Reed (as Miss Scott) listen as director Kubrick explains how he wants them to play a scene.

more subtle than Ripper's. Quinten, plagued by brutal headaches, is suffering from an undisclosed illness which is close to killing him—and he knows it. Worried about the buildup of weapons on the part of the Soviets, he is convinced the Russian leaders will strike as soon as they are strong enough. Quinten wants SAC to strike first, and he is helped by several lucky breaks: a major Soviet ICBM base isn't operational yet, and two of the three senior base officers who know the recall code are on a hunting trip while a third is airborne with the attacking Wing itself.

The film's narration about each airborne B-52 being "two hours from its target inside Russia" is close to the novel's version. Quinten's speech to his men about defending the base is substantially the same as Ripper's, as is Quinten's message to SAC headquarters: "Sure, the orders came from me. They're on their way in, and I advise you to get the rest of SAC in after them. My boys will give you the best kind of start. And you sure as hell won't stop them now." Quinten, however, unlike Ripper, is not concerned about fluoridation or "our precious bodily fluids."

In *Red Alert*, the B-52 bomber is called the *Alabama Angel*, and the Captain's name is Clint Brown. In *Dr. Strangelove*, the plane is attacked only once, by a missile which explodes near enough to damage the radio and other communications gear but not to destroy the plane itself. The *Alabama Angel's* odyssey is more terrifying and fatal: the plane is attacked first by an experimental missile from a Russian ship in the Bering Sea, then wards off radar-guided missiles before being attacked by jet fighters which it destroys. Another fighter fires missiles which damage the plane and kill three of the crew. Finally, the *Alabama Angel* is forced to fly through a wall of heavy flak which kills two more crewmen and further damages the already-crippled aircraft.

There is no Doomsday device as such in *Red Alert*. Instead, the Russians have buried a large number of plutonium-encased hydrogen bombs in the Ural mountains which will be detonated in a last defiant gesture by the Kremlin leaders if the Soviet Union is successfully attacked; the resulting radiation will wipe out all life on Earth in ten months.

As does Mandrake in the film, Major Howard figures out the doodles on Quinten's desk and calls the President with the recall code. All the planes except for the shattered *Alabama Angel* respond.

The Russian leader (the "Marshal") demands the sacrifice of an American city if the city of Kotlass, near the target, is destroyed by the *Alabama Angel*. Reluctantly, the President agrees and Atlantic City is chosen.

The *Alabama Angel* continues its run, mortally wounded, and drops its payload, which fails to trigger correctly and explodes as an atomic blast six miles

This long shot shows the size of the elliptical table the President and his advisors use in the top-secret War Room of the Pentagon.

from Kotlass. The few remaining crew members perish when the plane is dashed into the earth by the bomb's fury.

Red Alert is gripping and suspenseful, but not especially well written, perhaps because it was Peter George's first novel. For a book which is concerned with American characters exclusively, it also suffers from a preponderance of British spellings and idiom. For instance, at one point Quinten says, "Colonel England would have smelled a rat immediately I mentioned Plan R." Still, the novel captured the fear and paranoia of the cold war and inspired Stanley Kubrick to choose it as his vehicle for a movie about the bomb.

Red Alert was written in the late fifties, a time when America seemed to be losing ground to the Communists. The Russian bear had brutally repressed the Hungarian uprising while the Western world sat back and watched, and the Soviets' scientific establishment had used its lead in missile technology to put the first man-made satellite, Sputnik, into earth orbit. (Hence, the joke at that time that "their German scientists are better than our German scientists.")

By the early sixties, the cold war had reached its high water mark: from the building of the Berlin Wall, to the CIA's poorly planned and executed Bay of Pigs invasion of Cuba, to President Kennedy's 1962 eyeball to eyeball showdown over Soviet missiles in Cuba. This "missiles of October" crisis seemed finally to sober both sides, and the tensions ebbed somewhat.

The time produced other books similar to *Red Alert*. *The Bedford Incident* dealt with an episode involving a U.S. Navy destroyer and an unknown submarine, and *Fail-Safe* could almost be called *Dr. Strangelove* without the black humor.

A question good science fiction often asks is "what if . . .?" Many science fiction films are *what if?* films. *What if* the Martians invaded our planet? (*War of the Worlds*); *what if* atomic radiation caused ants to grow 10 feet high? (*Them!*); and *what if* the person next to you isn't a person at all but a "pod"? (*Invasion of the Body Snatchers*).

Dr. Strangelove is a *what if?* film. Kubrick shows us what *could* happen *if* a SAC general ordered an attack on Russia.

After acquiring the film rights to *Red Alert*, Stanley Kubrick began writing the screenplay with Peter George and Terry Southern. Kubrick later estimated that in researching the bomb he had read nearly seventy-five books on the subject and amassed an enormous collection of articles dealing with nuclear destruction. His digging led to talks with prominent nuclear war authorities such as Herman Kahn, the author of *On Thermonuclear War* and *Thinking About the Unthinkable*. Richard Corliss, a film historian, reported that Herman Kahn "observed that Strangelove combined the popular images of himself, Wernher von Braun, and Henry Kissinger": Kahn thought about the unthinkable, von Braun made it possible,

and Kissinger provided Strangelove's German accent and inhuman theories.

Peter George worked on the first drafts of the screenplay and his participation probably insured that the film would not lose the suspense and authenticity which made *Red Alert* gripping and powerful.

From Kubrick came General Jack D. Ripper and General Buck Turgidson—the first a madman, and the second a warmonger: "I'm not saying we won't get our hair mussed," he tells the President. "But I do say no more than ten to twenty million killed, tops—depending on the breaks."

As Kubrick said in his notorious *Playboy* interview, ". . . I'm not entirely assured that somewhere in the Pentagon or the Red Army upper echelons there does not exist the real-life prototype of General Jack D. Ripper." Later he presciently added, "It's improbable but not impossible that we could someday have a psychopathic President, or a President who suffers a nervous breakdown, or an alcoholic President who, in the course of some stupefying binge, starts a war." One need only read Woodward and Bernstein's *The Final Days*, about Richard Nixon's last weeks in office, to see how close we came to *that* precipice.

Something happened to the sober and almost documentarylike film Kubrick was going to make when he began working on the screenplay. Kubrick later explained, "As I tried to build the detail for a scene I found myself tossing away what seemed to me to be very truthful insights because I was afraid the audience would laugh. After a few weeks of this, I realized that these incongruous bits of reality were closer to the truth than anything else I was able to imagine. And it was at this point I decided to treat the story as a nightmare comedy. . . . In the context of imminent world destruction, hypocrisy, misunderstanding, lechery, paranoia, ambition, euphemism, patriotism, heroism, and reasonableness can evoke a grisly laugh."

It was at this point that Terry Southern, author of *Candy*, a wildly successful retelling of *Candide* which combined humor and sex, was called in to contribute his unique skills to the Kubrick-George collaboration. Although Kubrick later downplayed Southern's contribution, Richard Corliss asserts it was substantial, citing "deviated prevert" and "purity of essence" as two of Southern's phrases which have entered our comic heritage. Corliss also credits Southern for Major Kong and Colonel Bat Guano ("I think you're some kind of deviated prevert, and I think General Ripper found out about your preversions and that you were organizing some kind of mutiny of preverts," Guano says to a startled Captain Mandrake).

Stanley Kubrick will not discuss what *Dr. Strangelove* or any of his films "mean." He wrote to the author of one article, "I would not think of quarreling with your interpretation nor offering any other, as I have found it always the best policy to allow the film to speak for itself." Later, he restated this view, say-

George C. Scott (as Buck Turgidson) and Peter Sellers (as President Muffley) rehearse a scene while director Kubrick, operating the camera, sets up the shot in the War Room.

ing, "How much would we appreciate *La Gioconda* today if Leonardo had written at the bottom of the canvas: 'This lady is smiling slightly because she has rotten teeth'—or 'because she's hiding a secret from her lover'? It would shut off the viewer's appreciation and shackle him to a 'reality' other than his own."

Much of *Dr. Strangelove* deals with the interactions between men, machines, and modern technology. It is a theme Kubrick would return to five years later in *2001*. Throughout *Dr. Strangelove* machines designed by men efficiently carry out their functions, often to the detriment of their makers. And just as often, the men in charge of machinery are presented as inferior to their "tools."

Ironically, Burpelson Base's computers tirelessly work out attack profiles and coordinate flight plans while the officer in charge, General Ripper, is quietly going crazy. And it is a machine, an overlooked transistor radio, that innocently transmits the knowledge that there is no Russian attack in progress, alerting Group Captain Mandrake to the awful truth of Ripper's madness.

The B-52s' code recall boxes do *exactly* the job they were meant to do, preventing the President from recalling the planes. The technology aboard the efficient B-52s—the radar, the detection avoidance systems, the back-up mechanisms—frustrates all efforts to stop the planes.

The ultimate machine, one closed to arguments, rational or otherwise, is the Doomsday device. Its function has been determined and programmed in, and it will carry out its programming regardless of what the humans who created it might later desire. It is mankind's ultimate Frankenstein's monster— designed to prevent nuclear war, but inexorably wreaking havoc and destruction. (For a fuller discussion of this theme, see chapter on *Colossus*.)

In order to guard against surprise nuclear attack, America's Strategic Air Command maintains a large force of B-52 bombers airborne twenty-four hours a day. Each B-52 can deliver a nuclear bombload of fifty megatons —equal to sixteen times the total explosive force of all the bombs and shells used by all the armies in World War II. Based in America, the airborne alert force is deployed from the Persian Gulf to the Arctic Ocean. But they have one geographical factor in common: they are all two hours from their targets inside Russia.

The above narration (close to a similar passage in the novel) is followed immediately by a shot revealing Major Kong looking at the centerfold of a copy of *Playboy*. This is the first time his B-52 is seen, and the rest of the crew read, eat, play cards, doze, or otherwise try to keep themselves amused during another "routine" flight. The crew, then, is put in direct contrast to the efficient machines they nominally control. They are shown as sex-obsessed, bored, and all too human.

General Buck Turgidson (George C. Scott) makes a point while around him are seated other important military and defense personnel. Behind them looms the "Big Board" of the Pentagon's top-secret War Room.

Later, Kong's crew will confound the joint attempt by SAC and the Russians to stop them by pressing on to their secondary target—doing the human, and therefore unexpected, thing.

Dr. Strangelove is filled with sexual allusions, puns, symbols, and other esoteric erotica. The blatantly obvious names of the characters follow this pattern, from General Jack D. Ripper to Colonel Bat Guano. Some scholars see less satire than sex allegory.

Dr. Strangelove begins with a dreamy aerial ballet: planes being fueled in flight (taking on essence) by means of long tubes extending down from larger, dominant craft. This graceful midair "coitus" is accompanied by a gentle instrumental rendition of *Try A Little Tenderness*.

The determinedly paranoid General Jack D. Ripper wears his infamous name well and exudes a powerful yet obviously disturbed manhood. Like his namesake, he feels threatened by the hunger of women: "Women sense my power and they seek the life essence. I do not avoid women ... but I—I do deny them my essence."

Kubrick's camera accentuates Ripper's posturing, his aggressiveness, by often filming him from low angles, a cigar clenched between his teeth. And although Freud himself said that sometimes a cigar is just a cigar, in this case it functions (with Ripper's .45 automatic pistol) as a classic phallic symbol.

Striking back at the Army troops trying to storm the base, Ripper out-machos Clint Eastwood by taking a .50-calibre machine gun in his hands and pumping out a stream of bullets.

The characters are admittedly caricatures with absurd names: Buck Turgidson, Lionel Mandrake, Ambassador de Sadesky, Bat Guano, Dimitri Kissoff, and Merkin Muffley. Buck is a common synonym for male, while turgid means swollen. And swollen with lust aptly describes George C. Scott's character: when the Pentagon reaches him, he's dallying with his secretary-cum-mistress.

Miss Scott, Turgidson's bikinied secretary, is lounging on a bed in his room when the call from the Pentagon comes. Tracy Reed's pose (she was both Miss Scott *and* the centerfold) will be duplicated later in Major Kong's *Playboy* centerfold.

Group Captain Lionel Mandrake's surname is derived from the mandrake root, a tuber which looks like a penis. Lionel is from the Greek leo, which means lion. Mandrake is an RAF officer, a British lion, and presumably sexually active.

Part of the rescue assault force, Colonel Bat Guano storms into Ripper's office and finding Mandrake there, suspects him of being a "deviated prevert." Bat guano is, of course, simply bat droppings, often used as fertilizer. At Mandrake's insistence, Guano shoots open a Coke machine to get enough change for the Group Captain to call the Pentagon, reluctantly violating the virginity of one of capitalistic America's best-known symbols.

Vaguely an eggheaded liberal in the Adlai Stevenson mold, President Merkin Muffley possesses another name throbbing with sexual connotations. "Merkin" refers to a part of clothing that emphasizes the external female sex organs, and Muffley may suggest either the same thing (the vulgar "muff") or simply an ineffectual or effeminate man.

Dr. Strangelove's German name is Dr. Merkwuerdigichliebe—a rough translation means "a strange love." It is an apt name for a man who is half man, half machine and who loves his work, preparing for total war— more than he does humanity.

Inside the B-52, Major Kong reads *Playboy* and the other crew members titillate themselves by decorating the safe where the attack plans are kept with nude pictures and centerfolds. The crew's survival kits each contain "one .45-calibre automatic; two boxes of ammunition; four days' concentrated emergency rations; one drug issue containing antibiotics, morphine, vitamin pills, pep pills; sleeping pills, tranquilizer pills; one minature combination Russian phrase book and Bible; $100 in rubles; $100 in gold; nine packs of chewing gum; one issue of prophylactics; three lipsticks; three pairs of nylon stockings." The quantity of pills and sexual enticements will allow the crew to do more than just survive. As Major Kong says, "Shoot! A fella could have a pretty good weekend in Vegas with all that stuff."

With the Wing heading for Russia, Turgidson advises the President that this is the perfect time to "catch the Ruskies with their pants down." Although Muffley disagrees, his phone call to Premier Kissoff *does* catch the Soviet leader with his pants literally down—he's cavorting drunkenly with a mistress.

When Major Kong's plane reaches its target, he's mounted atop a hydrogen bomb fixing the bomb bay doors, his legs wrapped around the cylinder. Wildy waving his ten-gallon hat, Kong takes a final orgiastic plunge (rather like his namesake's fall from the Empire State Building) to an explosive climax when the bombs are released.

Dr. Strangelove proposes that the nation's elite be saved by living in mineshafts for a hundred years, or until the radiation abates. Leering coldly, he announces (to General Turgidson's obvious glee) that a scientific breeding program providing ten sexually attractive women for each man is the way to build up the population again quickly.

Dr. Strangelove is Stanley Kubrick's film, his personal vision. Kubrick coauthored the screenplay, oversaw Ken Adam's design of the sets, chose the music, cut the final film with editor Anthony Harvey, and directed the advertising campaign. It was the first film on which Kubrick was able to exercise the kind of control a director needs if he is to commit something unique to film.

Like Kubrick's earlier films (except for *Spartacus*), *Dr. Strangelove* was shot in black and white. By using "available light," Kubrick was able to achieve the hard, gritty look of a documentary—an approach underscored by the newsreel style footage, shot with a handheld camera, of the attack on Burpelson.

Kubrick's art director on *Dr. Strangelove* was the late Ken Adam, art director for many of the James Bond films, including the first, *Dr. No* (1962). Kubrick saw his work on the low-budget *Dr. No* and asked him to design *Strangelove*. Later, he was to work with Kubrick again on the beautiful but commercially unsuccessful *Barry Lyndon* (1975).

Born in Germany, Adam was an architecture student before getting into films, a fact which becomes apparent to anyone who's seen his complex sets for *You Only Live Twice* (1967) and *Moonraker* (1979).

Because Kubrick was certain the film would fail as a black comedy unless it was as grimly realistic as possible, he made sure Adam's sets were as close to the Air Force and Pentagon originals as reasearch could make them. Adam's most impressive set was the War Room of the Pentagon. Working closely with Kubrick, Adam devised the room's semi-triangular shape, one perfectly suited to withstand the effects of a blast directly overhead. Again, Kubrick and photographer Gilbert Taylor used only available light in this cavernous set and in the B-52's interior for maximum realism.

The B-52 set was designed from hundreds of photographs Kubrick had clipped from American and British aviation magazines. An impressive mock-up, it cost over $100,000 to build. Kubrick had to resort to photos and other drawings because the Air Force refused to provide any assistance in the making of the movie, maintaining it was an inaccurate portrayal of Air Force personnel and SAC fail-safe procedures. In other words, it wasn't a flattering film like *Strategic Air Command* (1955).

Major Kong's bomber was also a ten-foot model and the flight sequences were filmed by positioning the model in front of a moving matte made up of shots taken over the Arctic.

As noted earlier, Kubrick underlines General Ripper's insanity by shooting him from below, his cigar jutting from his mouth. After ordering the base on full alert, Ripper, in a long shot that emphasizes his distance from the rest of humanity, watches as lights go out all over the base and the sirens sound. Slowly, he closes the shutters on his office windows, symbolically locking himself in as he locks the others out. It is a brief but beautifully realized sequence.

In two of his earlier films, Kubrick uses the plastic qualities of film to play with time. In *The Killing,* Kubrick "puts back the clock" as each segment of the robbery at the racetrack is played out to its climax, using a team of horses pulling the starting gate into position as the beginning of each new sequence. *Paths of Glory* shows us the World War I battle of the trenches first from the soldiers' viewpoint, in the midst of the action, and then from the viewpoint of the generals, a safe thousand yards away watching through binoculars.

Similarly, in *Dr. Strangelove,* Mandrake takes the radio he's found to Ripper to prove there's no attack going on and tells the General that the Wing will be "inside Russian radar in twenty minutes; later, in the War Room, Turgidson tells the President that the Wing will be "penetrating Russian radar inside of twenty-five minutes." Both scenes take place at virtually the same time; Kubrick is giving the filmgoer an omniscience denied him in real life.

Kubrick's attention to realistic detail can be seen in his scenes inside the B-52. Believing that authenticity pays off and that comedy, even nightmare comedy, must be grounded in reality, Kubrick had his crewmen stick closely to Air Force procedures. The B-52's crew members each perform individually assigned emergency duties when the ship is damaged by the missile's near miss. One need only recall the antics of the crewmen of the "Seaview" in *Voyage to the Bottom of the Sea,* as they lurch about the bridge while sparks fly and colored lights flash, to appreciate Kubrick's care and honesty.

The crew members themselves are a throwback to the "melting pot" soldiers of the war films of the forties and fifties, who always included among their ranks a farmboy, a juvenile delinquent, and a "dese and dose" kid from Brooklyn. Kubrick's ethnic mix includes a Texan, a black, and a Jew: a common enough mix for a war film but nearly unheard of for an SF film.

Stanley Kubrick was born in the Bronx on July 26, 1928, the son of a physician. While still attending Taft High School, Kubrick began selling photographs to *Look,* joining the magazine's staff after graduation. Photography was his main passion, but chess became a lifelong obsession with Kubrick and he's managed to work chess theory or actual games into a number of his films (Poole and HAL play a game which HAL wins in *2001*).

His interest in photography led him to filmmaking and he produced two low-budget shorts for RKO. The first, *Day of the Fight* (1950), cost the young filmmaker $3,900 and focused on middleweight boxer Walter Cartier. Kubrick was then twenty-one.

Sterling Hayden (left, as the mad General Jack D. Ripper) and Peter Sellers (center, as the RAF Group Captain Mandrake) rehearse a scene in Ripper's office at Burpelson Air Force Base while director Kubrick checks out the shot.

DR. STRANGELOVE

167

After deciding to quit his job at *Look*, Kubrick produced a second short, *Flying Padre* (1951), about a Roman Catholic priest flying around his 400-mile parish in a Piper Cub. Both shorts made a modest profit for RKO.

Kubrick's next two films were full-length features, and he says of them that they were "crucial in helping me learn my craft." For *Fear and Desire* (1953), Kubrick raised $10,000 to start production while poet and playwright Howard O. Sackler finished the screenplay. The film, which followed a group of soldiers on patrol, got good reviews and had several bookings. The final cost of the feature reached $30,000—an absurdly low figure by today's standards —despite Kubrick's serving as producer, director, photographer, and editor.

Killer's Kiss (1955), Kubrick's second feature, was shot in New York City for $75,000. It dealt with a boxer and his relationship to another man's woman. Again, Kubrick made money for his distributor, United Artists, because the movie cost so little to produce.

The first film Kubrick is truly proud of making is *The Killing* (1956). Made on a $325,000 budget and utilizing familiar Hollywood faces like Sterling Hayden, Elisha Cook, Jr., and Jay C. Flippen, *The Killing* is technically stunning. It incorporates a series of time-overlapping flashbacks to the start of the racetrack robbery, the film's centerpiece. It was filmed entirely on sets except for those scenes set at the racetrack and airport. (For brief notes on Kubrick's other early films, see the Appendix.)

Peter Sellers gives three strong performances in *Dr. Strangelove:* as President Merkin Muffley, as Group Captain Lionel Mandrake, and as the eponymous Dr. Strangelove. Sellers was now getting up to a million dollars a movie, causing Kubrick to observe, "We got three [performances] for the price of six." It might have been four for the price of six: Sellers was originally going to play the role of Major King Kong as well.

Unable to get a hold on the Texas pilot's voice or mannerisms, a weeping Sellers confessed to actress Janette Scott, whom he was seeing at the time, that "everybody expects so much, so bloody much." Although she urged him not to take on the fourth characterization, it was not until Sellers broke his ankle that Kubrick finally cast Slim Pickens in the role.

Freed of the pressure of playing Kong, Sellers was convincing as the President and Mandrake, but absolutely riveting as the wheelchair-bound Dr. Strangelove. Though he didn't win, Sellers was nominated for an Academy Award.

Sellers was almost entirely responsible for the dialogue of his three characters. As Richard Corliss observed, Group Captain Mandrake is "a very gentle exaggeration of Trevor Howard's wartime persona, which Sellers had parodied back on the Goon Show."

Colonel "Bat" Guano gets a face full of soda after shooting open a Coke machine to get change for Mandrake to call the Pentagon. Keenan Wynn played Guano.

Sellers's Mandrake is the sanest character in the film. Trying futilely to convince Ripper to recall the Wing, Mandrake drawls, "Now, Jack ... why don't you give me the recall code, Jack?" His character is moved to outrage only when Colonel Guano asks what kind of suit he's wearing. "Suit!" he exclaims, "What do you mean, suit? This happens to be an RAF uniform."

After filming *Strangelove*, Kubrick told an interviewer, "Peter has the most responsive attitude of all the actors I've worked with to the things I think are funny. He's always at his best in dealing with grotesque and horrifying ideas. I've never felt he was as funny in conventional comedy roles; his greatest gift is for the grisly, horrifying areas of humor that other actors wouldn't think playable at all."

As President Muffley, Sellers has a painfully funny phone conversation with Premier Kissoff:

"Now then, Dimitri, you know how we've always talked about the possibility of something going wrong with the Bomb ... The *Bomb*, Dimitri, the hydrogen bomb.... Well, now, what happened is that, eh, one of our base commanders, he had a sort of, well, he went a little funny in the head. You know —just a little funny. And he went and did a silly thing. Well, I'll tell you what he did. He ordered his planes to attack your country. Well, let me finish, Dimitri . . . let me finish, Dimitri. Well, listen, how do you think *I* feel about it? Can you imagine how I feel about it, Dimitri? Why do you think I'm calling you? . . . Just to say hello? Of course I like to speak to you . . . of course I like to say hello. . . ."

Finally, as Dr. Strangelove, Peter Sellers created a character of monstrous proportions, a mad scientist for the ages. As Richard Corliss put it, "Sellers transcends mimicry, or even satire. He defines madness; he embodies it."

Reminiscent of the black-gloved mad scientist of *Metropolis*, Rotwang, Strangelove is half man and half machine—with both halves in constant conflict. He must battle his mechanical arm and pull the fingers of its hand from his throat as it tries to strangle him. When he forgets where he is, he is apt to let slip a few *"Mein Fuhrers."*

There are two other performances in *Dr. Strangelove* worth noting: George C. Scott's Buck Turgidson and Sterling Hayden's Jack D. Ripper. Hayden gives credence to Ripper by the intensity with which he plays the role. He is never intentionally funny; you never see a conspiratorial wink in his eye which says "I'm letting you in on the joke." When Ripper says to Mandrake, "I can no longer sit back and allow Communist infiltration, Communist indoctrination, Communist subversion, and the international Communist conspiracy to sap and impurify all of our precious bodily fluids," you laugh, but it is an uneasy laughter.

Some critics have argued that Sellers, unable to play the part of Major Kong, should still have played a fourth role, that of Buck Turgidson. George C. Scott's interpretation seems too broad, too frenzied. Still, if his belly-whompings, eye-rolling, nostrils-flaring, gum-chewing performance is not quite right, surely some blame must be laid at the director's feet.

Kubrick filmed a sequence that called for the people in the War Room to start a custard pie throwing melee just before the end-title montage of hydrogen bomb explosions. President Muffley was to get a pie in the face during the "battle," but Kubrick decided the whole thing didn't really work at that point in the picture and cut it. Ironically, Turgidson was to cry out, "Gentlemen, our beloved President has been struck down in his prime." That line alone would have ensured that the sequence would have been cut—had not Kubrick already decided not to use it—after John F. Kennedy's assassination in Dallas.

Similarly, Slim Picken's line, "Shoot—a fella could have a pretty good weekend in Dallas with all that stuff," was "looped" so that Vegas replaced Dallas on the soundtrack.

Dr. Strangelove is a black comedy that builds tension and suspense by cutting back and forth among its three main locations: Burpelson Base, the War Room, and the B-52. As the film progresses and the level of violence and absurdity increases, there is a palpable tug of war between the comedy and the horror.

The relentless advance of the B-52 into Russian territory closes off one alternative after another; mankind, by building the Doomsday device, has left itself no escape hatches.

Audiences were unsure how to respond to *Dr. Strangelove* when it first hit the nation's theaters. Was it meant to be serious, a parody, a satire, or a black comedy about total nuclear annihilation? As one critic noted, "Just as the individual begins to laugh at the antics on the screen and forgets the seriousness of the plot, the director switches to another location. . . . Each shift from one location to another is accompanied by increasing the tempo of violence. The audience is not allowed to relax and enjoy the movie as merely a spectacle, but instead is caught in the progressive acceleration of the film."

More than fifteen years later, we are no further from the brink of total annihilation than we were at the time of *Dr. Strangelove*'s release. It is a disturbing thought, but perhaps we have indeed learned to stop worrying and love the Bomb.

ROBINSON CRUSOE ON MARS

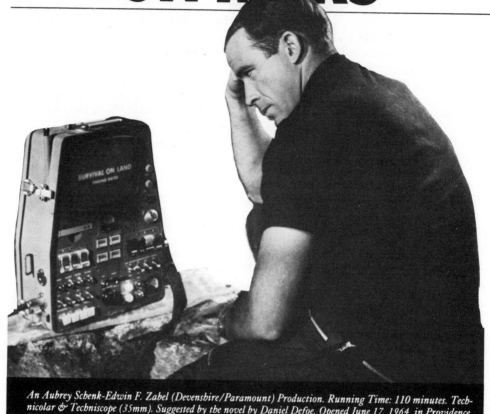

An Aubrey Schenk-Edwin F. Zabel (Devenshire/Paramount) Production. Running Time: 110 minutes. Technicolar & Techniscope (35mm). Suggested by the novel by Daniel Defoe. Opened June 17, 1964, in Providence, Rhode Island; General Release to Showcase theaters in New York City, August 1964.

PRODUCTION CREDITS

EXECUTIVE PRODUCER . . . . *Edwin F. Zabel*
PRODUCER . . . . *Aubrey Schenk*
DIRECTOR . . . . *Byron Haskin*
SCREENPLAY . . . . *Ib Melchior & John C. Higgins*
CINEMATOGRAPHER . . . . *Winton C. Hoch*
COLOR CONSULTANT . . . . *Richard Mueller*
ART DIRECTION . . . . *Hal Pereira & Arthur Lonergan*
FILM EDITOR . . . . *Terry O. Morse*
MUSIC . . . . *Nathan Van Cleave*
SOUND . . . . *Harold Lewis & John Wilkinson*
ASSISTANT DIRECTORS . . . . *Arthur Jacobson & Robert Goodstein*
MAKEUP . . . . *Wally Westmore & Bud Bashaw*
SPECIAL PHOTOGRAPHIC EFFECTS . . . . *Lawrence W. Butler (Butler-Glouner Inc.)*
PROCESS PHOTOGRAPHY . . . . *Farciot Edouart*
TECHNICAL ADVISER . . . . *Edward V. Ashburn*

CAST

COMMANDER CHRISTOPHER "KIT" DRAPER . . . . *Paul Mantee*
FRIDAY . . . . *Victor Lundin*
COLONEL DAN McREADY . . . . *Adam West*

On May 25, 1961, in his State of the Union Message, President John F. Kennedy committed the United States of America to the goal of landing a man on the moon by 1970. On February 20, 1962, John Glenn became the first American to orbit the Earth. The Gemini and Apollo Space Programs were well into the planning stages. America was on its way to the moon and there was little doubt it would get there. With a moon landing in sight, it was obvious the next step would be Mars. After that, anything seemed possible. The dynamic combination of American technology and American will power appeared unstoppable.

It was in this era of excitement about space exploration that *Robinson Crusoe on Mars* appeared. It wasn't a major film—it didn't even have an official New York "opening"—nor did it attract much attention. The *New York Times* credited Byron Haskin, "the experienced director with the enjoyable result. His Mars has a genuine look to it, and the space pilot's adventures . . . have verisimilitude. The film manages to avoid the heavy literalness of less expert fantasies by taking a calm approach."

Time called the film "a piece of science fiction based on valid speculation, a modest yet provocative attempt to imagine what might happen . . . in the next decade or so." *Newsweek*, however, gave it a stinging negative review in the form of an open letter to star Paul Mantee: "It seems . . . ungrateful of you that you don't thank your scriptwriter for finally getting you the hell out of *Robinson Crusoe on Mars*."

Over the years, however, critics have placed *Robinson Crusoe on Mars* (hereafter referred to as *RCOM*) in the category of the so-called "realistic" SF film, along with *Destination Moon, The Conquest of Space,* and others. In his introduction to *Focus on the Science Fiction Film*, William Johnson refers to *RCOM* as one of the "exercises in craftsmanship" that distinguished many of the SF films of the sixties from the monster films of the fifties. While *RCOM* is often mentioned in this way, little has been said about the film itself. Yet *RCOM* really represents the basic elements of one kind of SF, as well as the spirit of an era.

Mars Gravity Probe One, a U.S. space vehicle piloted by Colonel Dan McReady and Commander Christopher Draper, accompanied by Mona, an experimental space monkey, is exploring the outer reaches of Mars' gravitational field when a meteor forces the ship (nicknamed the *Elinor M.* after McReady's wife) to take evasive action. Avoiding the meteor, McReady and Draper (known respectively as "Mac" and "Kit") find their ship being drawn into Mars' gravity and, in trying to escape, exhaust their fuel.

Their only choice now is to abandon ship before it crashes into the planet. Since each man is in a separate capsule, Mac orders Kit to eject first, with the assurance they will meet after both have landed.

Draper's capsule blasts clear, descending to the Martian surface, but tumbles over on landing. Shaken, but unhurt, Kit emerges—just in time to duck as a fireball flashes by, scorching the capsule.

Kit samples the Martian atmosphere, but the thin air leaves him gasping, and he reactivates his life-support system. Examining his battered capsule, Kit finds much of his equipment destroyed, including his precious spare oxygen tanks.

By this time, Mac has also ejected, and Kit tries to contact him on the portable communications unit which has survived the crash. There is no response. Salvaging what he can, Kit is about to set off in search of Mac when he hears an uncanny howling. Suddenly aware he may not be alone, Kit removes a pistol from one of the packs, cautiously approaching the source of the noise, but it turns out to be only the wind whining through the wreck of his capsule.

Kit's first hardship is to spend a chilly night on the Martian desert. Next day, he has another near miss with a fireball. But in its wake he finds strange yellow rocks which burn like coal. Locating a cave, Kit decides it will make an excellent shelter against the Martian night—if he can get some of the yellow rocks burning for heat. But his matches will not ignite in the thin air. Finally, using a crystal to focus sunlight and a little oxygen from his tanks, Kit manages to get a fire started.

Kit begins a diary, using the tape recorder built into his communications unit. He is rapidly running out of food and water, but oxygen remains his biggest survival problem.

Eventually, Kit falls asleep, only to awaken gasping, his oxygen exhausted. Choking, he crawls across the cave, reaching his spare tank in time. Kit concludes that under normal waking conditions, he can breathe for about fifteen minutes before needing a "booster" from his tank. Asleep, he can go for an hour. With this in mind, he calculates he can stretch his oxygen supply, but resolves to find Mac the next day. He is sure Mac has solved the survival problems.

As he leaves next morning, Kit notices the frame of the *Elinor M.* still in orbit, the ship having achieved a balance between its acceleration and the Martian gravity. But the spacecraft is out of his reach.

Kit finally locates Mac's capsule—but his friend is dead, the victim of another landing mishap. Sadly, Kit buries Mac, giving him a final salute.

Suddenly, Kit sees what looks like a tentacle waving behind a rock. Afraid he's about to meet his first Martian, Kit aims his pistol at it. But before he can shoot, the other end of the "tentacle" appears—it is Mona!

Grateful for even this small companionship, Kit starts the trek back to his cave, but his air runs out. Nearly unconscious, he climbs back to the cave, collapsing near the still-smouldering fire, convinced he is doomed.

Sometime later, Kit awakens to find oxygen escaping from the yellow rocks. He concludes the rocks must contain their own oxygen, like solid rocket fuel.

Using a hand pump, Kit refills his tanks and devises a tin can alarm to prevent himself from sleeping past the time for a booster.

Kit's portable radar unit shows the *Elinor M.* approaching. He orders the ship to land, using the radio, but gets no response. The ship's supplies are lost to him.

Kit must still find water if he is to survive. Noticing that Mona refuses his offers of water repeatedly, and suspecting she has found a supply, Kit restricts her to the cave without water for several nights. Finally releasing her, he tracks her to an underground pool. Kit notices the monkey munching on a reedlike plant with a sausage-shaped fruit on it and finds it edible. Later, he discovers the reeds can be woven into clothing. Kit has now been on Mars for four months.

With food, water, clothing, shelter, and oxygen, Kit truly sets up housekeeping on Mars. He goes swimming at the pool and constructs a primitive bagpipe. But he is still lonely.

One night, Kit cooks the sausage plants in a stew, and the concoction makes him ill. Shortly afterward, a shadowy figure appears at the cave entrance. It is Mac. Kit is jubilant at his friend's appearance, but Mac is strangely silent. Kit pleads with him to speak —and is awakened by the oxygen alarm. He has been dreaming, the effect of the meal and his loneliness. Kit concludes that no amount of training can lick the problem of isolation.

Exploring one day, Kit finds a human skeleton with odd bracelets around its wrists. Fearful again that he is not alone, Kit removes all traces of his existence from the surface and orders the *Elinor M.* to self-destruct.

Three weeks later, a ship lands beyond the mountains. Kit assumes it's a rescue mission, but when he approaches, he finds strange ships blasting the surface with rays, clearly unaware of him. Using a portable video camera, Kit films them from hiding.

A figure appears suddenly behind Kit. Noticing the stranger wears the same bracelets as the skeleton, Kit realizes the stranger is fleeing from the mysterious ships and leads him back to the cave.

The stranger, who resembles a South American Indian, is completely uncommunicative. Kit replays the video tape, seeing more men like his visitor, as well as space suited figures carrying ray guns. At the sound of the taped ray guns, the stranger reacts fearfully. Kit concludes his visitor is an escaped slave, fleeing from his masters, who appear to be on a mining expedition.

Kit's visitor remains suspiciously silent, so Kit retires with a knife and club at hand. Later, Kit catches him refilling the sand counterweight on his oxygen alarm. Uncertain whether this is mere curiosity or a deliberate attempt on his life, Kit warns the stranger away forcefully. The stranger offers Kit one of the red pills he carries, but though Kit suspects this is what allows the other to breathe without a booster, he refuses.

Just then the enemy ships return. The stranger's bracelets clash together, enveloped by a pulsing red light. Kit rushes to the entrance as the aliens zoom away, the stranger believing their departure is Kit's doing. As the stranger silently thanks him, Kit wryly decides to name him Friday, a la *Robinson Crusoe.* Suddenly, Friday speaks, and Kit vows to teach his new companion English.

At the water pool, Kit's language lesson becomes mutual. As a meteor rumbles by overhead, Friday abruptly disappears. Kit hurries in search of him, but Friday is only playing a little alien "hide and seek."

Friday leads Kit to the ravine where they first met. Here they find the remains of more of Friday's people —killed by the aliens. Friday thanks Kit deeply for saving his life.

A meteor suddenly crashes into the surface, burying Kit in a shower of cinders. Friday digs him out and gives him an oxygen pill, saving his life in turn. Now, as Kit thanks him, they are equals and friends.

Kit begins taking Friday's oxygen pills. He learns his new friend is from a star in the constellation Orion —and that the aliens, drawn by Friday's bracelets will return. Kit vows to remove the bracelets, but as he files at them the aliens return and blast the mouth of the cave.

Kit, Friday, and Mona flee, taking shelter in an underground crevasse. Friday explains these crevasses are the legendary canals of Mars, and Kit suggests they use them to escape the aliens. But the enemy is still tracking them.

Volcanic activity forces the party back to the surface. They are in sight of the polar icecap, with the aliens right behind. Friday implores Kit to leave him and save himself, but Kit refuses. They must reach the icecap and find water. Kit also discovers Friday has been saving his oxygen pills for him.

Reaching the icecap and life-giving water, they climb into the mountains, constructing an ice shelter, using their own body heat to keep them warm.

Kit finally removes Friday's bracelets, asking how long he has worn them. "Sixty-two years," Friday answers, confessing he is seventy-eight years old.

Suddenly, a flaming meteor strikes the icecap, melting everything around them. Kit is ready to give up, but Friday urges him not to lose hope. The radar picks up a blip and Kit assumes it's the aliens—but Friday senses a difference. A human voice crackles over the radio, indicating it is an Earth ship.

Excitedly, Kit signals the ship and a capsule blasts off, descending to the Martian surface to rescue them.

Byron Haskin considers *RCOM* to be the best film he ever directed, although he was dissatisfied with the movie's title and the plans of the producer and distributor for its promotion and release. This is no small admission from the man who directed *The War of the Worlds, Treasure Island, The Power,* and many others.

RCOM isn't a fast-paced movie, but this isn't the fault of either the director or the screenwriters. The

Publicity still of Kit (Paul Mantee, right) and Friday (Victor Lundin, left).

ROBINSON CRUSOE ON MARS

Kit and Mona. Notice the food tube in Kit's hand. *(Courtesy of Ib Melchior.)*

film has little in the way of conventional adventure movie plotting. *RCOM* succeeds more in its ability to evoke a sense of wonder in the minds of its audience at the exploration of a new and different world.

Haskin achieves this by making Mars one of the film's "characters," interacting with Kit and Friday. Haskin does this right from the film's opening when the titles flash over shots of the *Elinor M.* approaching the planet, the great orb rising into view.

Haskin dwells on the Martian landscape, contrasted with the lone man, using long shot after long shot to establish an overpowering sense of desolation and loneliness. This is especially effective in the scene where Kit discovers an echo at the underground pool. As he demands the echo "talk" to him, the camera frames him against the vast, weird architecture of the cavern, a tiny figure almost lost to the viewer's eye.

The techniques of Kit's survival provide most of the film's action, and Haskin makes sure we notice them. We get many lingering shots of Kit's life-support system, portable communications unit, video

camera, oxygen alarm, the sausage plants, burning yellow rocks—even his bagpipe. In a sense, *RCOM* is an adventure in the technology of survival and, like ourselves, Haskin is interested in the mechanics of it.

But Haskin's direction isn't just concerned with things. Good SF is always the result of the interaction of things, ideas, and people, and while things and ideas may overshadow the people in *RCOM* to a degree, Haskin knows that without people there would be no story at all.

Haskin displays his awareness of this in the dream sequence. After Kit collapses, the scene is set by shots of the weirdly flickering Martian aurora that has appeared at various points in the film. Next, we see a shadow at the cave door (but wasn't the door open a moment ago, we ask?). When Mac enters, Kit's reaction, shot from an angle across the zombielike Mac, looking down at him, is eerily disorienting—reinforced by a sudden close-up of Kit's hysterical face. When Kit is awakened by the clattering of the oxygen alarm, the effect is distinctly shocking. The whole sequence emphasizes Kit's isolation, and shows Haskin's ability to manipulate the human element of the film as well as the background.

Byron Haskin was born in Portland, Oregon, in 1899 and educated at the University of California at Berkeley. Haskin began as a newspaper cartoonist, later going into advertising as an industrial film photographer. He entered commercial films as a cameraman for the Pathé and International newsreel companies. About 1920, he became an assistant director for the Selznick Company, later serving as an assistant cameraman for silent film directors Marshall Neilan, Sidney Franklin, and Raoul Walsh.

Haskin took part in the first exercise in sound films, *Don Juan* (1926). He is also credited with developing some of the technology that eventually improved the quality of sound filming.

In 1927, Haskin tried his hand at directing for Warner Bros., but left Hollywood for England in 1930, hoping to expand his career in the British film industry. He returned to Warners in 1932 as a cameraman, eventually becoming head of studio special effects. He returned to directing after twenty years with *I Walk Alone* (1947).

Haskin's association with SF began in 1953 when he directed *The War of the Worlds* for George Pal. His other SF films directed for Pal are *The Conquest of Space* (1955) and *The Power* (1968). Haskin's collaboration with Pal, and their realistic approach to SF film, have sometimes confused critics into thinking *RCOM* is a Pal production. Haskin also directed the 1958 adaptation of Jules Verne's *From the Earth to the Moon*, as well as several episodes of the TV series *Outer Limits*, including Harlan Ellison's well-known "Demon with a Glass Hand."

Other Haskin films of interest to SF and fantasy fans include *Treasure Island* (1950), which was Walt Disney's first live-action film, *Tarzan's Peril* (1951), *Captain Sinbad* (1963), and *The Naked Jungle* (1954), in which hordes of ants attack Charlton Heston's Amazon plantation with an effect more frightening than that of many horror films. (For a list of Haskin's films, see the Appendix.)

Haskin has said that much of *RCOM's* strength comes from its script. Much of the credit for this belongs to experienced screenwriter Ib Melchior. Although Melchior's SF films have been uneven in quality, his name figures prominently on the list of people who have tried to promote SF on the screen.

Melchior was born in Denmark in 1917, son of opera star Lauritz Melchior. After graduating from the University of Copenhagen, he joined a touring theatrical company, eventually making his way to the U.S. in 1938. It was also around this time that Melchior became hooked on science fiction, devouring the work of Robert Heinlein, Isaac Asimov, Theodore Sturgeon, and others. Melchior served with U.S. Intelligence during World War II, becoming active in TV and films after the war's end.

Melchior's SF credits as both writer and director are *The Angry Red Planet* (1959), *Reptilicus* (1963), and *The Time Travelers* (1964). On *Journey to the Seventh Planet* (1962), he served as writer only. Melchior also provided (with Louis M. Heyward) the English language dialogue for Mario Bava's *Planet of the Vampires* (1965, see Appendix), as well as the original story idea for *Death Race 2000* (1975).

Melchior's TV work includes scripts for the series *Men into Space* and *The Outer Limits*. Since 1973 Melchior has devoted himself to writing novels based on his experiences with U.S. Intelligence. But in 1976 the Academy of Science Fiction, Fantasy, and Horror Films saw fit to honor him with a Golden Scroll Award for his work in the SF field. (For a list of his work, see the Appendix.)

Melchior conceived the idea for *RCOM* on a visit to Death Valley, imagining it as something of an "alien" world. He wrote a long, detailed screenplay, including a map of possible locations in Death Valley. Producer Aubrey Schenk bought the idea, but when the film went into production, Melchior was already involved in directing *The Time Travelers*. Schenk hired screenwriter John C. Higgins to cut the script down to size. Higgins, a screenwriter since 1934, did the necessary editing and made other changes, including the addition of Mona, the monkey, to the script.

RCOM has sometimes been criticized because the film seems divided into two parts, almost like two different movies. The first half is a fairly simple depiction of Kit's survival on Mars, while in the second he meets Friday and escapes from the alien slavers. Critics suggest the film's second half is both unlikely and a little silly, distracting from its overall realism.

RCOM does seem to be split into two parts, but Melchior's idea had its roots in Daniel Defoe's novel, and while there was no requirement to stick to Defoe's plot, it is a story whose strength has carried it through the years. Kit's encounter with Friday and the aliens merely follows the outline of Defoe's novel with its description of Crusoe's adventures with cannibals and mutineers.

Another target for criticism has been *RCOM's* occasional religious overtones—specifically Kit's recitation of the twenty-third Psalm and his discussion of "cosmic order" with Friday. In trying to preserve the flavor of the Defoe novel, Melchior introduced some discreet religious elements into his script, but the theological dialogue was embellished slightly after the script left his hands. Even so, the religious elements are handled carefully, the concept of "cosmic order" providing a point of mutual understanding for two men of different worlds.

For the film's technical side, Haskin assembled an experienced crew. Cinematographer Winton Hoch had three Oscars for his photography, and had worked on such fantasy films as *Dr. Cyclops* (1940), *Darby O'Gill and the Little People* (1959), and *The Lost World* (1960). Hoch would later work on TV's *Time Tunnel* and *Voyage to the Bottom of the Sea*.

Hal Pereira was art director on *When Worlds Col-*

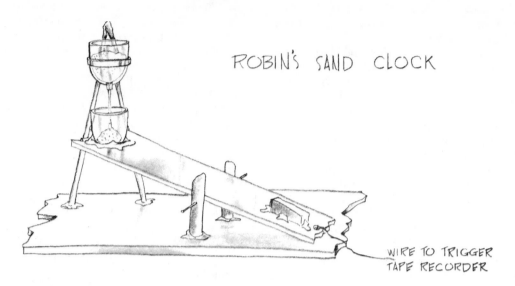

ROBIN'S SAND CLOCK

WIRE TO TRIGGER
TAPE RECORDER

ROBIN'S BOOSTER BREATHER

OXYGEN
CYLINDER

HARNESS

BREATHING
CUP

BREATHING
REGULATOR VALVE

HIGH PRESSURE
VALVE

GOOSENECK
TUBING

Original drawing of Kit's ("Robin" in the original script) sand clock. *(Courtesy of Ib Melchior and Cleo Baldon.)*

Original drawing of Kit's breathing apparatus. *(Courtesy of Ib Melchior and Cleo Baldon.)*

lide, War of the Worlds, and *The Conquest of Space,* as well as several other SF films. Arthur Lonergan had worked on *Forbidden Planet,* and the career of special effects expert Lawrence Butler went back to *Things to Come.*

While special effects are important to *RCOM,* they are not the film's focus as in, say, much of *Star Wars;* rather, they support the film's action. While many films had been shot on the floor of Death Valley before, the locations chosen for *RCOM* were largely up on the ridges, where the "alienness" of the landscape was most noticeable and where the sky could be seen. But Haskin felt the natural blue sky ruined the "alien" effect, so Butler used optical printing techniques to matte out the blue sky, substituting an orange-red one.

RCOM depends heavily on optical printing techniques, including an extensive use of matte paintings. In some cases, this is highly evident, as when the explosions from the aliens' rays occur *behind* the matte line of the mountains, rather than in the foreground. The overall effect of this, however, is not to detract from the film, but to give it a distinctive look.

The alien spaceships appear to have been animated against a painted sky with a kind of stop-motion technique, with each ship photographed in a certain position, repositioned, then photographed again. With the sequence projected at a slightly higher than normal speed, the result is a fleet of spaceships that move in a sudden, jerky manner that is unique to *RCOM.*

The alien ships, incidentally, were actually the Martian War Machines from the earlier *War of the Worlds,* with some modifications (see Appendix note). The ships' destructive rays and their accompanying noises were produced by methods similar to those used for the rays from the "cobra heads" of those same Martian Machines (see chapter on *War of the Worlds*). In addition, the spacesuits worn by the aliens were modified versions of the spacesuits from *Destination Moon.*

Reviews of *RCOM* said almost nothing about the film's performances, though *Newsweek'*s ironic review extended to lead Paul Mantee. *Time* did say that Mantee "really looks like an astronaut," but that was all. Considering that Mantee has to carry the film almost

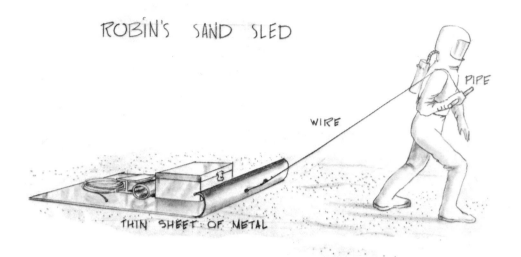

ROBIN'S SAND SLED

PIPE

WIRE

THIN SHEET OF METAL

ALIEN GUN
DESIGNED TO SHOOT EXPLOSIVE BULLETS

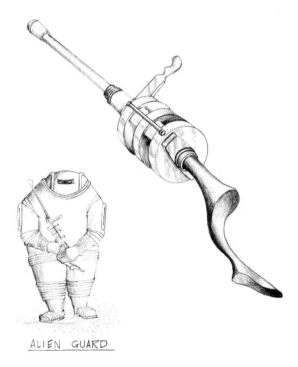

ALIEN GUARD

Original drawing of Kit's sand sled. *(Courtesy of Ib Melchior and Cleo Baldon.)*

Original drawing of alien and weapon. *(Courtesy of Ib Melchior and Cleo Baldon.)*

well. From the few moments we see them together, it's clear Mac is the senior partner in their relationship. After landing, Kit assumes Mac will have solved all the problems which have stumped him. The whole dream sequence is dominated by Kit's efforts to impress Mac with his accomplishments. *RCOM* focuses not just on Kit's survival, but on his growth towards independence and self-reliance.

Kit also grows in his relationship with Friday. At first, his suspicions toward Friday make Kit assume the role of "boss." In the sequence where Friday thanks Kit for saving him, Friday kneels before him, placing Kit's hand on his forehead. The gesture is one of slave to master.

Shortly thereafter, when Friday rescues Kit from the rain of cinders, Kit repeats Friday's gesture and his words. The gesture equalizes their relationship, and from that moment they are no longer master and slave, but friends and co-workers. Kit's growth, as interpreted by Mantee, may not be a major element in *RCOM*, but it is part of the film's effort to show the possibility of cooperation between people of different backgrounds, and it is convincingly done.

Most of Paul Mantee's other roles have been character parts, although he did take the lead in the distinctly minor spy-spoof, *A Man Called Dagger* (1967). His other films include *Blood on the Arrow* (1964), *An American Dream* (1966), *They Shoot Horses, Don't They?* (1969), *Breakout* (1975), and others. Mantee has also appeared frequently on TV.

Victor Lundin's performance as Friday is certainly competent, considering he has little more to do than look impassive and speak in Hollywood Indian fashion. Yet in the few scenes where he does get something to do, as when he thanks Kit for saving him, he

by himself, he does an exceptional job of portraying a man realistically coping with the problems of survival and loneliness—especially when we realize Mantee was fairly new to films. A certain amount of unconvincing innocence creeps into Mantee's character at times, but this seems more the result of the whole script than of the actor's performance.

Mantee must also cope with Kit's maturation in the course of the film. It's significant, perhaps, that Kit is copilot of the *Elinor M.*, with Mac outranking him as

Kit sets his sand clock.
(Courtesy of Ib Melchior.)

is genuinely effective.

Lundin's role in *RCOM* is interesting as an example of versatility, since he was more often cast as a heavy or in bit parts, as in *Island of Love* (1962) or the 1966 remake of *Beau Geste*. Lundin has also appeared on many TV shows, but his career is perhaps unfortunately summed up by his appearance as "Machine Gun Kelly" in a 1960 programmer entitled *Ma Barker's Killer Brood*.

Adam West appears only briefly in *RCOM*, so there's little that can be said about his performance. While active in both films and TV, West is best known for his role as TV's Batman.

In *RCOM*, as in much SF film, a "look" of scientific or technological accuracy is used to convince us that what we're seeing is "real." *RCOM* achieves this look by concentrating on the familiar sights and sounds of the space program in the sixties.

Great attention is paid to the paraphernalia of spaceflight. The camera dwells on the design of the *Elinor M.*, showing us her inside and outside in detail —right down to buttons, gauges, and wiring. We also get to examine Kit's spacesuit, communications unit, portable radar set, food concentrates, etc.

The film implies a thriving American space program, suggested when the astronauts communicate with a NASA space station—not to mention the existence of a manned Mars probe in the first place. Mona, aside from adding comedy relief, recalls the experimental monkeys NASA used early in the space program. The use of NASA jargon ("A-OK," "Delta Velocity," etc.) also adds to our belief in the film's authenticity. Kit's various references to his survival training and time in the isolation chamber also reinforce our belief that we're seeing a real astronaut on a mission.

The Mars of *RCOM* is fairly consistent with knowledge of the planet at that time. It was known that Mars was a dry, cold world with a thin atmosphere and a rocky surface, probably devoid of vegetation and other life. The NASA Viking probes would later find Mars even less hospitable than we imagined.

The Viking probes also revealed that the Martian sky is pink, so the film's guess of red-orange was not far off. Friday's explanation of the Martian canals as crevices in the surface caused by the settling of the planet's crust is not an unreasonable one, but the Viking probes appear to have laid the myth of the canals to rest once and for all.

The presence of water and edible plants on Mars requires a greater leap of the imagination. In 1964, however, the possibility had not been altogether ruled out, and even now the verdict is not in. *RCOM* takes some pains to suggest water might be below the surface, and that plants might grow in that water.

Kit's yellow rocks that burn with their own built-in oxygen is another one of the film's "inventions" which requires a stretch of the imagination. There's little reason to suspect such a uniquely structured compound would exist on Mars and not on Earth. But science fiction has always depended on imaginative leaps of this sort, and while they aren't always consistent with actual knowledge, they at least *appear* logical, and it's this logic which makes them ultimately convincing.

But there are areas in *RCOM* where the logic as it relates to scientific possibility becomes questionable. Like Friday, the alien slavers are from outside our solar system. If so, why have they come all this way on a mining expedition? And given the activity of our space program, why haven't they been detected?

Friday's age raises another such question. When Friday tells Kit he's seventy-eight the viewer is shocked for a moment, and this is surely meant to reinforce our idea of Friday's alienness. But since there's no evidence Kit has ever given Friday a knowledge of Earthly years, and since the length of a year depends on any planet's revolution around its sun, Friday's statement is really meaningless.

Actually, the effect of these logical gaps on the film is minor. They rarely occur to the viewer while watching the movie, and are small enough to be ignored when the film is considered overall. In another time, unanswered questions about the aliens and Friday would doubtless have inspired a sequel.

Next to trying to define science fiction, the biggest question for fans and critics is probably what SF should *do*. One view holds that SF is essentially social criticism. Another suggests SF forms the mythology of the twentieth century. A third sees it as celebrating science and technology. And there are other views as well. But SF may do all these things, singly or in combination—and more. There is no single formula.

But if *RCOM* belongs to any "school" of SF, it's to that which celebrates science, technology, and reason. More specifically, it seems to fit a pattern devised by the late John W. Campbell, Jr., as editor of the

Kit pulls his belongings across the Martian desert. *(Courtesy of Ib Melchior.)*

ROBINSON CRUSOE ON MARS

magazine *Astounding Science Fiction* (later *Analog.*)

When Campbell became editor of *Astounding* in 1938, SF was still largely devoted to exploring the wonders of science for their own sake, rather than to how scientific change affected the human condition. Writing was often heavy and stilted, and characterization practically nonexistent. Much of SF dealt with superhuman scientists racing about the galaxy saving humanity from impossibly evil bug-eyed alien monsters.

As editor of *Astounding*, Campbell demanded certain things from his writers that would change the course of SF and establish definite features for an *Astounding/Analog* story. He wanted his stories smoothly written, without the the heavy-handedness of earlier SF. Characters were no longer stereotypes, but flesh and blood people. Campbell's authors wrote about people in a variety of professions: spacemen, businessmen, wives, policemen, doctors, lawyers—even scientists.

Science and technology were carefully integrated into stories to show realistically what life in the future might be like. Scientific experiments no longer became the be-all and end-all of the SF story. The desirability of alien contact was explored, with beings from other worlds depicted sympathetically.

Astounding also specialized in something which might be called the scientific problem story. In these, characters were usually faced with some problem solvable only through a combination of scientific knowledge, reasoning, and determination. Writers

such as Robert Heinlein, Isaac Asimov, Ross Rocklynne, and others—while not limited to this kind of story—produced them regularly. These stories fostered an attitude important to that school of SF which celebrates science and technology—an attitude which says that when reason, knowledge, and determination are combined, no goal is beyond human reach.

RCOM is really this kind of *Astounding* story. Kit is separated from the stick-figure heroes of the fifties monster films by well-defined qualities of insecurity, courage, fear, kindness, prejudice, and loneliness. His astronaut training sets him apart, but it's possible for the audience, given similar circumstances, to identify with Kit and his problems.

The technology of *RCOM* is skillfully integrated into the story. The existence of the NASA space station, which implies a thriving space program, is casually introduced. Kit takes for granted the technology of his portable communications unit, radar, video camera, and other devices. Nor does he stop to question the highly advanced technology of his alien enemies. For Kit, technology is a simple fact of life.

Kit's relationship with the alien Friday is another element typical of the *Astounding* story. At first, the men of different planets are suspicious of each other. Slowly, however, as they live and work together, they grow to realize they have much in common, including an idea of universal order.

Finally, *RCOM* is a scientific problem story. The film asks the question: How does one survive on an

Spacesuited aliens and slave. *(Courtesy of Ib Melchior.)*

GREAT SCIENCE FICTION FILMS

Production crew on location in Death Valley.

ROBINSON CRUSOE ON MARS 181

alien planet? The answer is by reason, knowledge, determination—and a little luck. The film treats each problem in an almost scientifically methodical way, as Kit solves his problems of shelter, warmth, oxygen, food, water, and clothing, one by one.

But Kit must also overcome his self-doubt, loneliness, and prejudice, as well as escape from powerful enemies. It's this combination of scientific and personal adventure that makes *RCOM* seem typical of the *Astounding/Analog* story. Actually, this isn't surprising when we consider that *RCOM* is part of the cycle of "realistic" SF films that began with *Destination Moon*, scripted by Robert A. Heinlein, a writer who grew to prominence in the pages of John W. Campbell's *Astounding Science Fiction*.

This whole idea of solving problems through knowledge, reason, and determination seems representative of the era in which *RCOM* was made. It was a time when American power, backed by American technology and will power, seemed unlimited.

America's position around the world was virtually unchallenged. The cold war was a stalemate, with the U.S. slightly ahead by virtue of its victory in the Cuban missile crisis. The Russians had beaten us into space, but we had responded with a massive effort that would make their attempts in the next decade look puny. American technology was taking full advantage of what appeared to be limitless energy and resources to progress further and further.

With John Kennedy as president, there was a feeling that crossing new frontiers was almost easy. When Kennedy suggested Americans ask what they could do for their country, there was a silent belief that the answer was "anything and everything."

RCOM reflects that optimism of the early sixties—that sense of being able to overcome any obstacle if the right kind of knowledge and determination are present. Kit's survival on Mars reflects all the qualities we like to think are part of the American consciousness: intelligence, bravery, humor, resolution, the ability to grow and learn, and to accept new people and ideas.

But this optimism also has a darker side. There are no Russians mentioned in *RCOM*, no hint of a rival or cooperative space program. When Kit sets up housekeeping, he makes sure there is an American flag there to salute. In fact, Kit's "liberation" of Friday from his masters, and his initial position that he is "boss," suggests a pattern of foreign entanglement that U.S. overconfidence was already leading the country into.

This isn't to say *RCOM* has a political statement to make. The values which allow Kit to survive and build a friendship with Friday have nothing to do with politics. Like most films, *RCOM* is of its time— undertaken before a president was assassinated, released before Vietnam became a quagmire, before three astronauts died, and before the growth of pollution and the shrinking of resources told us that technological progress might demand a more careful consideration of what we wanted our future to be.

Actually, *Robinson Crusoe on Mars* is a very simple film. It uses special effects and a solid story to evoke our sense of wonder, and to make some points about friendship and human will to survive. Its simple confidence in the ability of the human mind to overcome any obstacle in its path may seem a little naive today, but we would do well never to forget it.

2001: A SPACE ODYSSEY

A Metro-Goldwyn-Mayer Release in Cinerama. Great Britain/U.S.A. Running time: 141·minutes (12,690 feet) Color, Super Panavision. Based on the story "The Sentinel" by Arthur C. Clarke.

PRODUCTION CREDITS

PRODUCER/DIRECTOR . . . . *Stanley Kubrick*
SCREENPLAY . . . . *Stanley Kubrick, Arthur C. Clarke*
SPECIAL PHOTOGRAPHIC EFFECTS
DESIGNED & DIRECTED BY . . . . *Stanley Kubrick*
SPECIAL PHOTOGRAPHIC EFFECTS SUPERVISORS . . . . *Wally Veevers, Douglas Trumbull,*
Con Pederson, & Tom Howard
PRODUCTION DESIGNED BY . . . . *Tony Masters, Harry Lange, & Ernest Archer*
FILM EDITOR . . . . *Ray Lovejoy*
WARDROBE BY . . . . *Hardy Amies*
DIRECTOR OF PHOTOGRAPHY . . . . *Geoffrey Unsworth, B.S.C.*
ADDITIONAL PHOTOGRAPHY . . . . *John Alcott*
FIRST ASSISTANT DIRECTOR . . . . *Derek Cracknell*
SPECIAL PHOTOGRAPHIC EFFECTS UNIT . . . . *Colin J. Cantwell, Bruce Logan,*
Bryan Loftus, David Osborne,
Frederick Martin, John J. Malick
CAMERA OPERATOR . . . . *Kelvin Pike*
ART DIRECTOR . . . . *John Hoesli*
SOUND EDITOR . . . . *Winston Ryder*
MAKEUP . . . . *Stuart Freeborn*
EDITORIAL ASSISTANT . . . . *David De Wilde*
SOUND SUPERVISOR . . . . *A. W. Watkins*
SOUND MIXER . . . . *H. L. Bird*
CHIEF DUBBING MIXER . . . . *J. B. Smith*
SCIENTIFIC CONSULTANT . . . . *Frederick I. Ordway III*

MUSIC: *Gayane Ballet Suite* by Aram Khachaturian, performed by the Leningrad Philharmonic Orchestra, conducted by Gennadi Rozhdestvensky; *Atmospheres* by György Ligeti, performed by the Southwest German Radio Orchestra, conducted by Ernest Bour; *Lux Aeterna* by György Ligeti, performed by the Stuttgart State Orchestra, conducted by Clytus Gottwald; *Requiem* by György Ligeti, performed by the Bavarian Radio Orchestra, conducted by Francis Travis; *The Blue Danube* by Johann Strauss, performed by the Berlin Philharmonic Orchestra, conducted by Herbert von Karajan; *Thus Spake Zarathustra* by Richard Strauss, The Berlin Philharmonic Orchestra, conducted by Karl Boehm.

CAST

DAVID BOWMAN	*Keir Dullea*
FRANK POOLE	*Gary Lockwood*
DR. HEYWOOD FLOYD	*William Sylvester*
MOONWATCHER	*Daniel Richter*
HAL 9000	*Douglas Rain (voice)*
SMYSLOV	*Leonard Rossiter*
ELENA	*Margaret Tyzack*
HALVORSEN	*Robert Beatty*
MICHAELS	*Sean Sullivan*
MISSION CONTROL	*Frank Miller*
STEWARDESS	*Penny Brahams*
STEWARDESS	*Edwina Carroll*
POOLE'S FATHER	*Alan Gifford*
"SQUIRT" FLOYD	*Vivian Kubrick*

WITH

Glenn Beck	*Mike Lovell*
Edward Bishop	*Bill Weston*
Ann Gillis	*Heather Downham*
John Ashley	*David Hines*
Jimmy Bell	*Tony Jackson*
David Charkham	*John Jordan*
Simon Davis	*Scott Mackee*
Jonathan Daw	*Laurence Marchant*
Peter Delmar	*Darryl Paes*

AND

Terry Duggan, Joe Refalo, David Fleetwood, Andy Wallace, Danny Grover, Bob Wilyman, Brian Hawley, and Richard Wood

2001 is considered by many to be the finest science fiction film ever made. And with three of the best SF films to his credit (*Dr. Strangelove, 2001,* and *A Clockwork Orange*) Stanley Kubrick can arguably be considered the best science fiction filmmaker of all time.

After premiering in Washington, D.C, on April 2, 1968, *2001* opened in New York the following day at the Capitol Theater. The New York film critics' first reviews were generally negative, and Kubrick told *Playboy* that "New York was the only really hostile city. Perhaps there is a certain element of the *lumpen literati* that is so dogmatically atheist and materialistic and earthbound that it finds the grandeur of space and the myriad mysteries of cosmic intelligence anathema." Mainly, the New York critics found the film boring, dull, slow-moving, and bereft of a discernible plot.

"... for all the beautiful models, the marvelous constructions, the sensational perspectives, the effort to equate scientific accuracy with imaginative projections, there is a gnawing lack of some genuinely human contact with the participants in the adventure," wrote Hollis Alpert in the *Saturday Review.*

Judith Crist said, writing in *New York,* "Were *2001* cut in half it would be a pithy and potent film, with an impact that might resolve the 'enigma' of its point and preclude our wondering why exactly Mr. Kubrick has brought us to outer space in the year 2001."

Science fiction author Lester del Rey summed up the feelings of many of the older SF writers in his review in *Galaxy* when he said, "This isn't a normal science fiction movie at all, you see. It's the first of the New Wave-Thing movies, with all the usual empty symbolism. ... It will probably be a box office disaster, too, and thus set major science fiction moviemaking back another ten years. It's a great pity."

Renata Adler of the *New York Times* stated that "the movie is so completely absorbed in its own problems, its use of color and space, its fanatical devotion to science fiction detail, that it is somewhere between hypnotic and immensely boring ... the uncompromising slowness of the movie makes it hard to sit through without talking."

Variety's "Robe" called the film "big, beautiful, but plodding and confusing.... The surprisingly dull prologue deals with the 'advancement of man,' centering on a group of apes (the makeup is amateurish compared to that in *Planet of the Apes*). The film is not a cinematic landmark ... it actually belongs to the technically-slick group previously dominated by George Pal and the Japanese."

But where the New York critics found fault, other critics and viewers found beauty and truth—and an exciting intellectual odyssey open to anyone willing to take the time and effort to *look* at the film.

Mike Steele, of the *Minneapolis Tribune*, wrote that "listening to audiences after the movie and reading most of the reviews only verify the opinion that we're still hung up on literary interpretation, even though we've been surrounded by various forms of this non-linear, nonsequential attitude.... I have no doubts that persons under twenty-five who grew up on television images will understand *2001*. They've seen television commercials dealing with nothing but stomachs."

William Kloman, in the *New York Times*: "I suspect that much of the critical hostility to *Space Odyssey* originated in the theater lobby during intermission. Critics (some of whom seem to dislike movies and wish they were more like books) met their friends and found that nobody was able to verbalize what the film, so far, had 'meant.'"

Kubrick himself tells this story: "At one point in the film, Dr. Floyd is asked where he's going. And he says, 'I'm going to Clavius,' which is a lunar crater. Then there are about fifteen shots of the moon following this statement, and we see Floyd going to the moon. But one critic was confused, because he thought Floyd was going to some planet named Clavius. I've asked a lot of kids, 'Do you know where this man went?' And they all replied, 'He went to the moon.' And when I asked, 'How do you know that?' they all said, 'Because we saw it.' Those who 'don't believe their eyes' are incapable of appreciating the film."

"The Dawn of Man," is set in Africa, four million years ago. We see the desert wasteland that has lain barren and sunbaked for eons, its food supplies in slow decline. Bands of man-apes, slowly starving, feed on vegetables and tubers while pigs and other animals graze unmolested beside them. Water is precious and the man-apes, perhaps the early hominids known as *Australopithecus africanus*, confront another tribe across a desert waterhole. Weaponless, the other tribe's strength lies in its numbers and they win the waterhole confrontation. Later, against the long night, full of leopards and other predators, the man-apes huddle together in fear and apprehension.

In the midst of this long march to extinction, one band of man-apes awakens to find a smooth black rectangle in their midst. Trembling with curiosity, they slowly approach it. Gingerly, they touch its surface and run their fingers over its glassy surface in awe and bewilderment.

One member of the tribe, Moonwatcher, suddenly sees the bones of a skeleton as something else—weapons. Seizing a large leg bone, Moonwatcher soon learns that it can crush the skull of a tapir—or another man-ape. The weapon, the bone, now means that the man-apes will have meat to eat, solving their food problems. Armed with his newly discovered weapon, Moonwatcher and his band force another confrontation with the tribe that controls the waterhole. Moonwatcher approaches the leader tentatively and, almost by accident, knocks him to the ground with a blow from the bone. Frenzied, Moonwatcher repeatedly smashes the fallen enemy's head with the bone.

In triumph, food and water assured now, Moonwatcher joyously throws the bone high into the air and, in one dramatically associative cut, the bone becomes a spacecraft orbiting Earth in the year 2001.

Dr. Heywood Floyd, a scientist from Earth, is aboard Pan Am's commercial shuttle craft *Orion* headed for a wheel-shaped space station majestically revolving in space. The trip is routine, so Dr. Floyd dozes. The pilot of the *Orion* matches his ship's speed and movement to the space wheel's and *Orion* slowly moves toward the space station like a giant dart moving toward its orbiting target.

Aboard the space station, Dr. Floyd is greeted by a receptionist who says, "Here you are, sir"—the first words spoken since the film's beginning, nearly thirty minutes earlier.

Like Pan Am, other American corporations have moved into space and the space station boasts its own Howard Johnson's restaurant and Orbiter Hilton for travelers. Floyd talks to his daughter "Squirt" by Picturephone, asking her what she wants for her birthday, while behind his head a glowing Earth rotates.

Floyd has a more serious conversation with a trio of Russian scientists returning to Earth from their own moon base. They are aware of unusual activity at Clavius, the U.S. base. Since a Russian ship was denied an emergency landing there and the base is under tight security, they question Floyd about rumors of an outbreak of disease. Tight-lipped and uncomfortable, Floyd can only tell them that "I'm not at liberty to discuss this." They shake hands and part.

Now aboard the ball-shaped *Aries*, which will carry him the rest of the way to Clavius, Floyd sleeps, eats, and studies the instructions on the use of a zero gravity toilet. Finally, approaching the moon, the *Aries* makes an about-face and brakes as it falls toward the landing grid. Safely down, the *Aries* hydraulically descends into the well of the airlock in solemn majesty as, all around it, tiny human beings work in glass-walled control rooms.

"Hi, everybody. Nice to be back with you," Dr. Floyd says to the attendees of a top secret briefing called to discuss what to do about "the discovery" which "may well prove to be among the most significant in the history of science." We don't learn what "the discovery" is, and the meeting quickly adjourns.

Dr. Floyd and two others, Halversen and Michaels, skim across the surface of the moon at an altitude of

A shot showing the interior of Space Station Five, the mid-point in Dr. Floyd's flight from the Earth to the moon. Behind the Russian pilots and stewardess are a Bell System Picturephone booth and a restaurant—Howard Johnson's Earthlight Room, reflecting Clarke's and Kubrick's belief that large corporations will quickly enter the space era when the opportunity comes.

several hundred feet in a moon bus on their way to Tycho crater, the site of the mysterious discovery. "That was an excellent speech you gave us Heywood," says Halversen. "Certainly was," seconds Michaels. "I'm sure it beefed up morale a helluva lot."

As weird and wonderful moonscapes pass beneath the moon bus, the men pass out sandwiches and more banalities: "Are those sandwiches ham? Chicken? They *look* like ham." "Yes, well, they're getting better at it all the time."

At TMA-1, six spacesuited scientists, including Floyd, approach the newly-discovered monolith. One of them, like the man-apes of four million years ago, touches it tentatively with a gloved hand. The others are waved in front of the monolith by a photographer. As they pose like tourists in front of the pyramids, the monolith (dug up during the long lunar night) is touched for the first time by a ray of light from the sun, which is in conjunctive orbit with the Earth. Activated by the sunlight, the monolith emits a high-pitched squeal of electro-magnetic energy directed toward Jupiter.

Eighteen months later, the 700-foot-long spacecraft *Discovery* is on its way to Jupiter. On board for the half-billion-mile journey are three scientists deep in artificially induced sleep in coffinlike hibernacula, two coolly efficient astronauts named Frank Poole and Dave Bowman, and a talking super computer called HAL 9000. Artificial gravity is maintained by the *Discovery*'s ball-shaped command module centrifuge. Poole is seen jogging around the track of the centrifuge, shadow-boxing while an indifferent Bowman eats in the background.

Bowman and Poole eat bland-looking soft food served in plastic trays while they watch an interview with themselves taped earlier by the BBC. Questioned about his relationship with the human members of the crew, HAL tells the interviewer, "I enjoy working with people."

The boredom of a long space flight is shown through scenes of Poole endlessly jogging around the centrifuge, Bowman and Poole eating, Poole receiving birthday greetings from his parents, HAL beating Poole at chess, and Bowman sketching scenes of his surroundings which he shows to the unblinking red eye lens of HAL.

HAL "senses" an imminent breakdown of the AE-35 unit in the antenna that carries their communications with Earth. Checking the unit, Poole and Bowman can find nothing wrong. On the advice of Mission Control and HAL's twin unit on Earth, the astronauts replace the unit to see if it will fail as HAL predicts. When asked for his opinion of the discrepancy, HAL says, "This sort of thing has cropped up before, and it has always been due to human error."

Suspicious of HAL, Poole and Bowman enter one of the ship's space pods to discuss confidentially what to do if HAL is malfunctioning. They are unaware that HAL is reading their lips through the pod's window.

While Poole is outside the ship, HAL disconnects the life support systems of the sleeping scientists, killing them. Hal also directs Poole's pod to sever the astronaut's airhose and send him spinning away into deep space. Quickly, Bowman jumps into a pod and sets out to rescue the fast-disappearing Poole, forgetting to wear a helmet. When Bowman finally catches up to Poole, it's clear he's dead. Bowman brings the body back to the ship.

HAL denies Bowman reentry to the *Discovery*, saying, "This mission is too important for me to allow you to jeopardize it."

Bowman positions his pod so that the door, fitted with explosive bolts, is aligned with the airlock of the *Discovery*. Taking a deep breath, Bowman blows himself into the airlock like a man shot from a cannon. With the rush of air into the vacuum of the airlock comes the welcome return of sound.

Safely back inside the *Discovery*, Bowman now moves grimly toward HAL's brain circuits, planning to disconnect all of the computer's higher reasoning functions. An audibly nervous HAL tries to dissuade him: "Look, Dave. I can see you're really upset about this. I honestly think you should sit down calmly, take a stress pill, and think things over. . . . I know everything hasn't been quite right with me. . . . I feel much better now. I really do. I've made some very poor decisions recently. I want to help you."

As he's lobotomized, HAL speaks of his creation in Urbana, Illinois, in 1992, and sings *Daisy*. Suddenly, Mission Control, in the form of Dr. Floyd, breaks in, activated by Bowman's disconnection of HAL's circuits: "Good day, gentlemen. This is a prerecorded briefing made prior to your departure, which for security reasons of the highest importance has been known on board during the mission only by your HAL 9000 computer. Now that you are in Jupiter space, and the entire crew is revived, it can be told to you. Eighteen months ago, the first evidence of intelligent life off the Earth was discovered. It was buried forty feet below the lunar surface, near the crater Tycho. Except for a single, very powerful radio emission aimed at Jupiter, the four-million-year-old black monolith has remained completely inert, its origin

and purpose still a total mystery." Those are the last words spoken in the film.

In *2001*'s final segment, "Jupiter and Beyond the Infinite," Bowman sets out in one of the pods to approach the giant planet. The monolith appears for the third time, now floating toward Jupiter's moons, which are in orbital conjunction. Bowman enters a star-gate in which time and space are warped in fantastic ways. Colors and sensations sweep over the dazed astronaut as overpowering images bombard him: the birth and death of stars, whole galaxies in exploding motion, cities of light, and dancing geometric patterns.

All this abruptly ends as Bowman finds his pod has come to rest in a bedroom suite decorated with Louis XVI period furnishings. A visibly aged Bowman looks in horror at his now wrinkled face in the bathroom mirror and, hearing a noise outside, turns to see the back of a white-haired old man, dining. The old man is Bowman, older still. This Bowman drops his wineglass and sees himself, perhaps twenty or thirty years older, dying in the room's huge bed. Slowly, the old man raises his hand and points to something at the foot of the bed—the monolith.

The old man's body is transformed into an infant, a star-child. The star-child, perhaps the next step in man's evolution, returns to stare in large-eyed wonder at the Earth:

"There before him, a glittering toy no star-child could resist, floated the Earth with all its peoples."

Arthur C. Clarke's "The Sentinel" was published in 1950. The short story recounts a 1996 lunar expedition to the Mare Crisium, the Sea of Crises. An expedition member, Wilson, sees a flash of light high above the lunar plain and goes to investigate. He finds an artificially leveled and smoothed plateau, now pitted and scarred by eons of falling meteors. In the plateau's center is "a glittering, roughly pyramidal structure, twice as high as a man, that was set in the rock like a gigantic, many-faceted jewel." At first, Wilson thinks it the relic of some long lost lunar civilization. Then he notices that the pyramid's surface is unscratched. He throws a rock and discovers that it is protected by an invisible shield. After twenty years, the Earthmen break through the barrier with atomic energy, but they cannot begin to grasp the nature of the complex alien mechanisms inside. Still, by defeating the barrier, man has stopped the beacon's signal to the stars; the aliens who left it will now know that life from the third planet has reached its moon and will return to their beacon.

In the last line of the story, Wilson says, "I do not think we will have to wait for long."

Arthur C. Clarke was in his adopted country of Ceylon (Sri Lanka) when he was reached about working with Stanley Kubrick to turn his story "The Sentinel" into a film. His telegraphed reply was simple and direct:

"INTERESTED IN WORKING WITH ENFANT
TERRIBLE STOP CONTACT MY AGENT STOP
WHAT MAKES KUBRICK THINK I'M A RECLUSE?"

Clarke and Kubrick met for the first time in
Trader Vic's, a New York City restaurant, on April
22, 1964, to discuss their collaboration. It was Kubrick's idea to develop the script by first writing a
complete novel from which they would derive a
screenplay. It was an unusual approach but Clarke
quickly agreed and in early May the two men began
to develop ideas for what Clarke jokingly referred to
as "How the Solar System Was Won."

On May 28, 1964, Clarke formally sold five stories
to Kubrick which would supplement "The Sentinel"
and provide the novel and film with a number of
adventures. The five stories were "Breaking Strain,"
"Before Eden," "Into the Comet," "Out of the Cradle,
Endlessly Orbiting . . .," and "Who's There?"

Although he would laugh at his optimism later,
Clarke's original schedule with Kubrick for the writing, rewriting, shooting, and editing of the novel and
film called for everything to be accomplished in ninety-two weeks, or nearly two years. In truth, the
project took almost four years.

It wasn't until April 1965—several months after
MGM had announced Kubrick and Clarke were
teaming on a film to be called *Journey Beyond the Stars*
—that Kubrick selected *2001: A Space Odyssey* as the
film's eventual release title.

In early script drafts, the computer that was to

With Poole (Gary Lockwood) on the bridge of Discovery's command module, Bowman (Keir Dullea) operates a pod that has just emerged from the ship's still-open pod bay. Poole's image was projected onto a glossy white card and matted in later with the shot of the Discovery and pod.

become HAL was conceived as a "female" computer called Athena who spoke with a woman's voice. Athena was the goddess of wisdom who emerged, fully formed, from the forehead of Zeus. Socrates was another name considered and dropped before the computer was finally christened HAL.

The writing sessions were long and arduous. Kubrick estimated that he and Clarke spent four hours a day, six days a week, writing the script. Kubrick, contending that it gives dialogue a more natural rhythm, dictated his first drafts into a tape recorder.

Kubrick's films prior to *2001* had all made some use of narration (see *Dr. Strangelove*) and he planned to use it in the Dawn of Man prologue, according to one 1965 script. The narration would have *explained* things rather than shown them: "The remorseless drought had lasted now for ten million years, and would not end for another million. . . . In this dry and barren land, only the small or the swift or the fierce could flourish, or even hope to exist. The man-apes . . . were on the long, pathetic road to racial extinction."

Finally, Kubrick and Clarke cut the narration—as

they did the novel's overly explicit scenes of the monolith teaching the man-apes how to use weapons and other tools by projecting onto its surface scenes of apes carrying out those activities. These scenes remained in the novel version, however.

Beginning in January 1965, Frederick I. Ordway signed on as the film's scientific and technical consultant. A Harvard-educated research scientist, Ordway was 2001's adviser for eighteen months. He strongly advised Kubrick to put back the narration that was cut from the film and to restore dialogue that made the plot more accessible—which Kubrick did not do.

In December 1967, composer Alex North was living in New York when Kubrick contacted him to score 2001. In early December, North flew to London for two days of consultation with Kubrick. Kubrick told him flatly that he might still retain several of the "temporary" tracks he'd been using for some time. North was not pleased with trying to integrate his work with that of other composers, but he agreed to do the film. North returned to London on December 25, 1967, and began working on the score on January 1.

North wrote two pieces of music for the opening sequence, but he wasn't convinced Kubrick was prepared to give up Strauss's *Thus Spake Zarathustra*, the temporary track he was using.

In all, North composed and recorded over forty minutes of music in two weeks of intensive work, and he was anxious to see the balance of the film and begin work on it. In early February, Kubrick told him that no more music was needed; breathing effects would be used in the rest of the sequences.

When North attended a special screening of 2001 in New York, there were all of the "temporary" tracks—and none of the music he'd scored for the film.

Kubrick's reluctance to give up the Richard Strauss theme, often called the World-Riddle theme, is understandable. The World Riddle opens with an ascending phrase of three notes, C-G-C, which represents Nietzche's view of the evolutionary rise of man. The three notes are integral to 2001's symbolism. These three notes serve notice that the number three is essential to the film: from the perfect alignment of the three spheres of Earth, moon, and sun at the beginning to the appearance of things in threes, or three times.

Requiem for Soprano, Mezzo-Soprano, and Two Mixed Choirs and Orchestra by György Ligeti was used by Kubrick for the first appearance of the monolith among the man-apes and for all subsequent appearances of the mysterious black artifact.

The Blue Danube by Johann Strauss was Kubrick's choice for the sequence that details Dr. Floyd's trip to the space station on the Pan Am shuttlecraft *Orion*. If *Thus Spake Zarathustra* was 2001's most dramatic —and parodied—piece of music, then surely *The Blue Danube* selection was the most controversial. *Time*'s comment was typical of those who found the waltz

music inappropriate: "As the ship arcs through the planetary void, it is an object of remarkable beauty— but . . . to convey the idea of careening motion, the soundtrack accompanying the trek plays *The Blue Danube* until the banality undoes the stunning photography." Others saw it more for what it was—just another example of Kubrick's sense of humor.

Lux Aeterna, again by György Ligeti, was used during Floyd, Halversen, and Michaels' moon bus flight to TMA-1 site.

For the endless scenes of Poole exercising, Kubrick chose the *Gayne Ballet Suite* by Khachaturian.

Bowman's psychedelic journey into the star-gate is accompanied by the Ligeti composition, *Atmospheres*.

After the first wave of bad reviews, mostly from New York critics, 2001 was taken more seriously by those who wrote about the film. Few motion pictures have provoked such an outpouring of critical and interpretive comment from film reviewers, mass media experts, and scholars. Certainly, this would not have been the case had 2001 been empty and banal as its detractors insist.

Many of the pieces published about 2001 argued its "meaning"; like any great film, 2001 has many possible interpretations, each "right." Stanley Kubrick has said, "I don't like to talk about 2001 because it's essentially a nonverbal experience. Less than half the film has dialogue. It attempts to communicate more to the subconscious and to the feelings than it does to the intellect."

While there are many ways of interpreting 2001, there are several elements which seem more important than others, concepts which Kubrick and Clarke want us to think about. The first is man's search for spiritual meaning and the promise of self-renewal, which is the basis for all religion. The second is Kubrick's concern with intelligence and the forms it might take.

Kubrick and Clarke have the alien monolith appear to the man-apes of four million years ago just as they are peering into the abyss of racial extinction. The monolith, sent by unknown and perhaps unknowable makers, is a catalyst for evolutionary change at the precise moment such a change is necessary for the apes' survival.

When the monolith appears for the second time, the bone of yesteryear has become the spacecraft of 2001 A.D. By reaching Earth's only natural satellite, the moon, man has unwittingly signaled that he is prepared for a second major evolutionary step, and 2001 presents the same chronology as does Nietzsche: from ape to man and from man to superman.

To show the necessity of a leap forward in consciousness, 2001 argues convincingly that modern man has triumphed intellectually and technologically, but has advanced little socially and psychologically from the man-apes; the human race seems as lost as it was four million years ago.

Orbiting nuclear warheads and the superpower

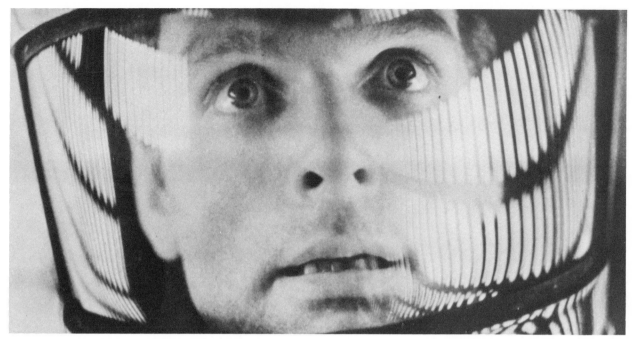

Bowman (Keir Dullea) disconnects HAL's higher reasoning circuits after the computer has killed the other members of the mission.

tensions between the Americans and Russians (reflected in Floyd's tense encounter aboard the space station) prove that man has not progressed beyond the apes' howling confrontation at the waterhole. The conflict is now in space and the bone has become a nightmarish device capable of destroying all life on Earth.

The curiosity of the man-apes, perhaps the very reason they were selected to receive the gift of expanded intelligence, has given way to the cool professionalism of Dr. Floyd and the astronauts. Mind-boggling sights, such as those glimpsed on Floyd's voyages to the space station and the moon, are taken for granted. Later, flying across the spectacular lunar surface in a moon bus, Floyd and his companions ignore the wonders outside for bland talk about whether to have a ham or chicken sandwich. Familiarity breeds contempt—or at least indifference.

HAL, the brain and central nervous system of the *Discovery*, represents machine intelligence, capable of human vices such as lying and murder, but less flexible than human intelligence. While HAL can beat Poole at chess and appears more human, and, ultimately, more interesting, than the cold, humorless astronauts, he lacks Bowman's capacity for creativity (Dave's drawings of the ship and crew) and improvisation (the astronaut's emergency reentry into the *Discovery's* airlock).

Since man has attained a plateau in his intellectual and moral growth, Bowman's final odyssey into the star-gate leads to his death and renewal as the star-child, an embryo representing the next evolution of human consciousness: the Superman.

HAL's machine intelligence is a futile direction for

consciousness to pursue. Artificial intelligence, until it can attain spiritual meaning, is a cul-de-sac. Only man is offered the opportunity for the eternal renewal of mind, body, and spirit—an evolution beyond mere intelligence.

Nietzsche in *Thus Spake Zarathustra:* "What is the ape to man? A laughing-stock, a thing of shame. And just the same shall man be to the Superman: a laughing-stock, a thing of shame."

Arthur C. Clarke: "MGM doesn't know it yet, but they've footed the bill for the first $10,500,000 religious film."

HAL's final appearance was decided at the last minute. He was originally to be mobile, like a robot, and went through several changes before Kubrick settled on a stationary machine utilizing voice and eye lenses only. HAL's name is an acronym formed by combining the first letters of the two major learning systems, *h*euristic and *al*gorithmic. (Clarke insists it was a coincidence that HAL is but one letter removed from IBM.)

Kubrick hired Douglas Rain, a Canadian actor, to speak some of the film's narration. But Kubrick grew more and more convinced that narration would intrude on what was clearly a visual experience, so he kept putting off recording Rain's lines. Finally, as the Canadian's contract was about to lapse, Kubrick asked Rain to speak a part that had already been recorded by actor Martin Balsam, with whom Kubrick was dissatisfied. The part was that of HAL. Rain later said that "I wrapped up my work in nine and one-half hours . . . I never saw the finished script and I never saw a foot of the shooting."

One critic of HAL's murderous rampage com-

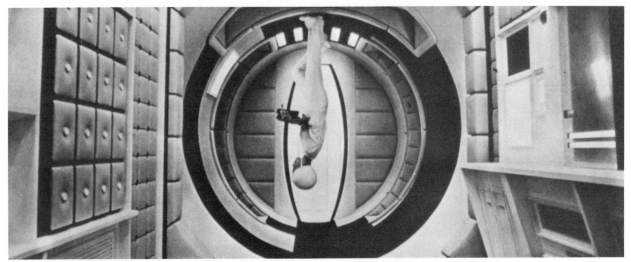

Aboard the Aries on the way to the moon base, Clavius, a stewardess, literally walks up the wall to the cockpit. Actually, the camera was fixed to the room in the foreground; the actress remained right-side-up while the room and camera rotated.

plained that it made the supercomputer all too much like the mad machines and monsters in the old "science horror" films whose actions defy analysis. The writer argued that there was no follow-through on HAL's obviously poor programming or whatever else might have caused him to malfunction so malevolently.

A case can be made that HAL's breakdown and ultimate lobotomy result from his caring too much for the mission. Material suggesting that HAL was programmed to deceive the astronauts, and that his breakdown was the result of his having to lie about the mission, was eliminated from the film. After killing Poole and the "sleeping beauties" and denying Bowman reentry to the *Discovery*, HAL declares that "this mission is too important for me to allow you to jeopardize it."

Facing the disconnection of his higher reasoning circuits, the death of his brain, HAL pleads with Bowman not to end his existence. To many, it is the most wrenching, emotionally charged scene in *2001*; it is painful to watch the step-by-step extinction of a living mind:

"Dave, stop. Stop, will you. Stop, Dave. Will you stop, Dave. I'm afraid. I'm afraid, Dave. My mind is going. I can feel it. I can feel it. My mind is going. There is no question about it. I can feel it. I can feel it. Good afternoon, gentlemen. I am a HAL 9000 computer. . . ."

Reduced to his most elemental functions, HAL sings *Daisy* for Dave, the irony lodged in the line, "I'm half crazy. . . ." (See the *Forbidden Planet* Appendix for Asimov's Three Laws of Robotics.)

2001 was filmed at the MGM studios in Boreham Wood, England, a complex made up of ten huge sound stages constructed in nondescript buildings that belie the magical happenings inside.

Shooting began on December 29, 1965, inside Shepperton's Stage H, 250 X 120 feet and, at that time, the second-largest soundstage in Europe. The first scene filmed was Dr. Floyd's visit to the TMA-1 excavation site to see the newly discovered monolith. The excavation pit was 120 feet long, 60 feet wide, and 60 feet deep. Ordinary sand was washed and dried and—it was hoped by Ordway and the other experts—given the color and feel of real moon soil. The lunar terrain (a model) surrounding the pit was not matted into the shot until a year later, requiring that the exposed film from the shot be kept safe in a locked vault until it could be matched with the model footage.

The twelve-foot-long monolith used in the scene was the largest of the production's five monoliths, a three-ton block of black lucite which was difficult to light and shoot while being terribly easy to smear if touched. Some monoliths were as small as three feet long. Originally, Kubrick and Clarke envisioned the monolith as a black tetrahedron, but that didn't look right. According to effects supervisor Con Pederson, "The tetrahedron didn't look monumental or simple or fundamental. It tended to express diminution more than impressive scale. And there would be people who would think of pyramids."

Boreham Wood was soon the hub of an intense effort, comparable to a military operation. A 3-man operations room was set up to coordinate and keep track of the activities of the 106-man production unit. This "command post" was the nerve center of *2001: A Space Odyssey*

Kubrick and his crew estimated that there would be 205 effects shots in *2001*, each requiring an average of ten major steps to complete. To keep track of all those scenes, the command post's walls were covered with charts detailing the shot history of each. According to Kubrick, "Every separate element and step was recorded on this history—information as to shooting dates, exposure, mechanical processes, special requirements, and the technicians and departments involved." Since there were so many steps involved, and many had to be reshot to achieve perfection, Kubrick estimated that "the true total is more like 16,000 separate steps."

The realistic-looking "Dawn of Man" sequences were all shot at Boreham Wood. Kubrick had had several thousand still photographs taken in southwest Africa printed as 8 X 10-inch transparencies. The projector, especially built for *2001* and directly facing the 40 X 90-foot front projection screen, emitted a very weak light source. The light that fell on the actors was not bright enough to be seen by the camera, but the screen, developed by the 3M Company, reflected the African scenes directly back at the camera at a level of intensity many times brighter than the original projected image. An unexpected bonus was the intense glow of the leopard's eyes—its retinas were as reflective as 3M's screen!

An arrangement of lenses aligned the camera on a direct angle with the screen. The projection system produced so much heat that the studio doors had to be kept closed during the shooting or the glass in the lenses would shatter on contact with the cooler outside air.

The actors playing the apes were unusually thin mimes and dancers with narrow hips—Kubrick wanted no thoughts of "men in monkey suits" to distract the viewer. Perhaps he was too successful; as Arthur C. Clarke later said ruefully, "*2001* did not win the Academy Award for makeup because the judges may not have realized the apes were actors."

The only scene in this sequence (and the movie) not filmed in a studio was Moonwatcher's smashing of the skull, which was shot in a grassy field just yards outside the studio doors while cars, buses, and trucks roared past on a busy nearby highway.

For the scenes of Dr. Floyd aboard the *Orion* on his way to the space station, a three-foot-long model was used. The *Orion* model, like all the models, was extremely detailed and the camera could get quite close without revealing that it was a model.

For the space shots, Kubrick decided that ordinary traveling mattes were inadequate and that something better was needed. The major problem was that the stars had to disappear and reappear as spacecraft or astronauts passed in front of them. Kubrick, Trumbull, and Pederson shot the foreground action first, then painted it out with black paint and photographed the result on an animation stand. Technicolor Ltd. then optically printed a master with the star background, resulting in a crisp and bright image.

As Floyd sleeps, the *Orion* approaches Space Station Five, a rotating space wheel 1,000 feet in diameter. The space station was actually an eight-foot model with air-cooled lights inside. The *Orion's* approach was accomplished by shooting a six-inch transparency on an animation stand and moving it .0025 inches per frame. The space station interior

corridor set was curved and almost 300 feet long by 40 feet high.

The designer of the Telstar communications satellite (an idea first suggested by Arthur C. Clarke), John R. Pierce of Bell Labs, helped design the Picturephone Dr. Floyd uses to call Earth. Pierce also wrote science fiction under the name J. J. Coupling.

The *Aries*, the ball-like ship which carries Dr. Floyd from the space station to the Clavius crater on the moon, was an animated cutout for the space scenes. A scene on board the *Aries* that always makes audiences gasp is the one in which a stewardess carrying food trays steps into a passageway and, using Velcro-coated shoes on a Velcro-covered floor, slowly walks up the wall and enters the cockpit area. The camera was fastened to the front of the set, which rotated 180 degrees. The actress simply walked in place just beyond the turning set. On screen, it appeared that it was the stewardess moving, not the room. (See also the *Destination Moon* chapter.)

Reaching the moon, the *Aries* lands at a domed landing pad whose eight pie-shaped panels withdraw underground. This was a miniature set ten feet in diameter and its panels were each three feet long. The bright lights ringing the landing platform were extremely bright bulbs available only from West Germany.

The airlock itself was a fifteen-foot-deep miniature set, while the *Aries* that descended into it was a two-foot-diameter model. Inside the airlock, people could be seen moving around through the windows. Each window was shot separately on 35mm film to the correct perspective and then printed onto several takes of the airlock "held" on 65mm film. The final step in this process was printing in the airlock around them on the Lin Dunn Matte Camera. This was done by blacking out the windows of the *Aries* and the airlock and shooting the scene. Then the camera was backed up to its initial sync frame and the shot repeated with the *Aries* covered by a black cloth and the interior action front-projected onto a glossy white card approximating the window area.

The *Discovery*, which critic Judith Shatoff wrote of as looking like "the vertebrae of some extinct reptile as it speeds through the space night," was supposed to be 700 feet long. In reality, it was a finely detailed model 54 feet long with a 6-foot-diameter "command module" ball. For long shots, a less detailed 15-foot-long model was employed.

For the scenes of Poole jogging in the *Discovery*'s centrifuge, the Vickers-Armstrong Engineering Group built a thirty-eight-foot-diameter, ten-foot-wide "ferris wheel" that cost $750,000. Rotating at a maximum speed of about three miles per hour, the centrifuge contained built-in bunks, desks, consoles, and "sarcophagi" for the sleeping scientists. Sixteen millimeter projectors were mounted on the outside of the centrifuge and moved with it as it turned. Everything inside, including the lights, was secured to the centrifuge structure. Super-Panavision cameras were especially refitted to perform at any angle, including upside down.

Shooting inside the centrifuge presented several problems and required two unique camera setups. One setup necessitated that the camera be mounted directly to the centrifuge, so that when the set moved in a 360-degree circle, the camera moved with it—making it seem that the camera is still while Poole jogs away from it, up the "wall," around the top, and down the other side. The second setup required that the camera be mounted on a miniature dolly so it could stay with the actor at the bottom while the whole set moved around him. The camera was positioned fifteen or twenty feet up the wall (floor), held there by a steel cable from the outside which was attached to the dolly through a slot in the center of the floor running around the entire centrifuge. The slot was concealed by rubber mats which fell back into place as soon as the cable passed them.

The scenes inside the centrifuge were lit by strip lights along the walls. Kubrick directed the centrifuge scenes from the outside by watching a TV monitor connected to a small vidicon camera positioned beside the Super-Panavision camera.

2001 has several scenes showing the *Discovery's* small workcraft, the ball-like "pods," in operation. Three of the pods in the pod bay were dummies, two of which had working doors. A separate interior-only pod was built with full instrumentation and controls.

To film the full-size pod emerging from the *Discovery's* command module, the exposure time needed was four seconds per frame; it took an hour to film the pod emerging inch by inch (so that the pod's movements would be smooth and not jerky). A thirteen-inch pod was used with the six-foot-diameter *Discovery* command module to show the pod emerging on the pod bay ramp.

For the scenes in which Bowman and Poole remove and replace the "faulty" AE-35 communications unit that HAL insists will soon fail, a full-size set was utilized. The main dish of the antenna was approximately twelve feet in diameter.

Bowman's emergency implosion into the airlock was filmed vertically to appear horizontal when projected. Since the camera was shooting up at Dullea, his body hid the wires suspending him from the ceiling. A shot of the door blowing open was filmed and combined with Dullea being lowered toward the camera, giving the impression he was being blown into the airlock and straight at the camera.

All the space walks and pod maneuvers were filmed vertically so that the bodies of the astronauts or the bulk of the pods would hide the wires suspending them from the velvet-draped ceiling of the studio.

What Kubrick and effects supervisor Trumbull called the Star-gate effect was created by the "slit-scan" process. Trumbull was playing around with a 70mm Oxberry animation stand rigged with a Polaroid camera and some artwork. One of the effects he produced was flat walls of exposed light. Kubrick saw Trumbull's experiments and told him to see what he

could develop from them. With Kubrick's blessing in hand, Trumbull then designed a special camera setup for his idea on MGM's Stage 3, which he later moved elsewhere when Stage 3 was needed for another project.

The slit-scan process is so complicated and technical that to attempt to *fully* explain it here would be impossible. Briefly, slit scanning is a form of streak photography, which is the shooting of extended time exposures on a single frame of film. Trumbull's slit-scan process optically and mechanically produces visual motion on film one frame at a time, each frame containing a complex streak exposure. When projected, these frame-by-frame streak exposures move and change, just as in animation as series of still drawings becomes moving cartoon characters.

Trumbull's camera is a normal movie camera outfitted with a stop-motion motor and the assorted selsyn motors needed to create the streak photography. The camera, which can move forward twelve to fifteen feet, shoots transparent artwork mounted on a glass plane which can move ten inches or less.

On a second, nonmoving glass plane is a small slit opening. As the camera moves toward or away from the static glass plane, its shutter open, the artwork, also moving, is scanned onto the film. As Trumbull says, "Since the artwork is traversing a distance of ten inches behind the slit, this has the effect of stretching the artwork over the twelve-foot distance."

These movements, combined with the lengthy exposure time, are equal to filming a fifteen-foot-long wall from one inch away. Since the camera moves twelve feet to the artwork's five inches, the image is optically stretched and appears to be moving very fast.

For the Star-gate effect, Trumbull had to shoot the two "walls" of light separately because of the camera angle relative to the artwork. (For a more detailed look at the slit-scan process, see Trumbull's article in the October 1969 issue of *American Cinematographer*.)

About directing, Kubrick has written that he believes it is a continuation of the writing, and that a writer-director is the "perfect dramatic instrument." The writer-director is at the core of the *auteur* theory, which holds that great films are the result of a single, unifying vision, coupled with the power to protect that vision. Of those considered to be the *auteur* of their films, most are writer-directors and, some, like Kubrick, are producer-writer-directors. Notable writer-directors include the late Alfred Hitchcock, John Cassavetes, Woody Allen, Mel Brooks, George Lucas, and John Carpenter.

While a better understanding of how films are made has led to a devaluation of the *auteur* theory, its applicability to Kubrick is obvious. Arthur C. Clarke said as much when he confessed, "I would say that *2001* reflects about ninety percent on the imagination of Kubrick, about five percent on the genius of the

Blow-up of artist's sketch for *2001* poster.

2001: A SPACE ODYSSEY

special effects people, and perhaps five percent on my contribution."

Kubrick the Director and Kubrick the Writer bring together Kubrick the Man's unique strengths: a strong visual sense and the ability to convey dramatic themes nonverbally. These could be a product of his training and work in still photography and documentary film plus his chess-player's skill at devising plots which chart the inevitability and inertia of events set in motion by human weaknesses or desires.

Kubrick realizes that most film and novel plots rarely reflect "real life." Real life is often as dramatic as fiction, if not more so, but lacks scenes, continuity, and resolutions. Movies have happy endings; real life rarely has endings of any kind, let alone happy ones. Kubrick has said a film can but obliquely reflect the truth of real life, and only by avoiding "pat conclusions and neatly tied up ideas."

Kubrick's visual sense is evident in *2001*'s spatial sophistication, with actors or spacecraft entering one side of the giant Cinerama screen and exiting on the other. Scenes are composed either symbolically (the sun, Earth, and moon in the opening shot) or dramati-

cally (the apes seeing the monolith for the first time). This strong visual narrative is what undid many of the harsher critics of the film who wanted a more literary approach to telling the "story."

Rather than finding Kubrick's elimination of all but forty-three minutes of dialogue in the film a plus, good *motion* picture making, Stanley Kauffman found it a minus—doubly so because "those forty-three minutes are pretty banal." Kauffman, who confessed hostility toward space exploration and the space program in his *New Republic* review, was so engrossed in looking for conventional storytelling, that he missed much of the visual narrative and completely misread Kubrick's deliberately satiric dialogue (satiric because it is so close to the way we actually talk).

Dr. Floyd's briefing is purposely trite and tepid, a pointed jab at the participants' inarticulateness. It is uncomfortably close to real speech, the empty, throwaway language of everyday conversation, and bears no resemblance at all to the fully formed, plot-advancing sentences put into characters' mouths by clever, word-conscious writers.

Dr. Floyd and the other scientists at the TMA-1 site on the moon. This was the first scene Kubrick shot for *2001*. The excavation with the monolith was filmed in December 1965/January 1966 on Shepperton's Stage H and the lunar landscape model was matted in a year later.

"It is, I believe, the way the people concerned would talk," Kubrick told an interviewer. In researching *Dr. Strangelove*, Kubrick discovered that think-tank researchers bantered lightly about *any* topic, from nuclear devastation to overpopulation, and refused to let themselves see the personal consequences involved. The most terrifying topics soon reached a saturation level, today called MEGO—My Eyes Glaze Over.

While the acting in *2001* has often been dismissed as lightweight, Kubrick got the most out of his top-notch cast of bread-and-butter actors.

Keir Dullea, who played David Bowman, was born in 1936 and began his film career in 1961 with *The Hoodlum Priest*. His film acting has been characterized by the air of tension and undefined menace he brings to each role. Dullea is equally proficient as the stalwart hero or the neurotic villain and many of his characters have blended both, his heroes suggesting darker depths and his villains harboring complex motivations.

While he has never been a spectacular actor, Dullea's combination of sharp-edged features and all-American good looks were what probably led

Kubrick to cast him as the cool and emotionless astronaut Bowman. Of *2001*, Dullea was quoted as saying, "I was disturbed by its ambiguity when I first saw the film. But I think it will turn out to be the *Citizen Kane* of our era."

Dullea's other films include: *David and Lisa* (1962), *The Thin Red Line* (1964), *Bunny Lake Is Missing* (1965), *The Fox* (1968), *De Sade* (1969), *Black Christmas* (1975), and *Brave New World* (1980—made for TV).

Gary Lockwood played astronaut Frank Poole. Lockwood, born John Gary Yusolfsky in 1937, also made his first film in 1961, *Splendor in the Grass*. Lockwood's "jock" appearance was perfect for Poole, endlessly jogging and shadow-boxing around the centrifuge. A solid actor, appearing more often on television than in films, Lockwood has made few memorable films apart from *2001*. He first worked for Kubrick in 1959 as an extra in *Spartacus*. As Lockwood recalls, "I got $50 a day and a hot meal."

Lockwood's other films include: *Wild in the Country* (1961), *Firecreek* (1967), and *RPM* (1970). Lockwood also starred in *Earth II* (1971—made for TV), and the second *Star Trek* pilot, "Where No Man Has Gone Before."

Lockwood's two short-lived television series were *Follow the Sun* (1961) and *The Lieutenant* (1963).

Others in the cast include William Sylvester, who played Dr. Heywood Floyd. Born in 1922, American actor Sylvester has been in British films since 1949, although he popped up as a reporter in the Hollywood-produced remake *Heaven Can Wait* (1978).

His films include: *Give Us This Day* (1950), *Gorgo* (1959), *Devil Doll* (1964), and *The Hand of Night* (1967). He appeared in a single-season television series in 1976, *Gemini Man*.

Leonard Rossiter, a British comic born in 1927, played Smyslov, one of the Russian scientists on the space station.

Margaret Tyzack, a British character actress born in 1933, played Elena, another of the Russian scientists. She also appeared in *A Clockwork Orange*.

Robert Beatty, born in Canada in 1909, has long resided in England, generally playing leading man roles and Americans. He played Halvorsen, one of Floyd's colleagues.

The Mission Control spokesman was Chief Warrant Officer Franklin W. Miller, an American Air Force traffic controller stationed in England. Although his hiring was opposed by several British actors' unions, Kubrick used him for added realism.

Stanley Kubrick's daughter Vivian played "Squirt," Floyd's daughter. Her footage was shot first, and William Sylvester responded to her answers.

Kubrick originally planned to begin *2001* with a ten-minute black and white series of interviews with experts in their fields—theology, chemistry, physics, etc.—on the possibility that life exists elsewhere in the universe. Kubrick and Clarke soon saw its inadvisability and dropped the idea, although not before the interviews were filmed and edited.

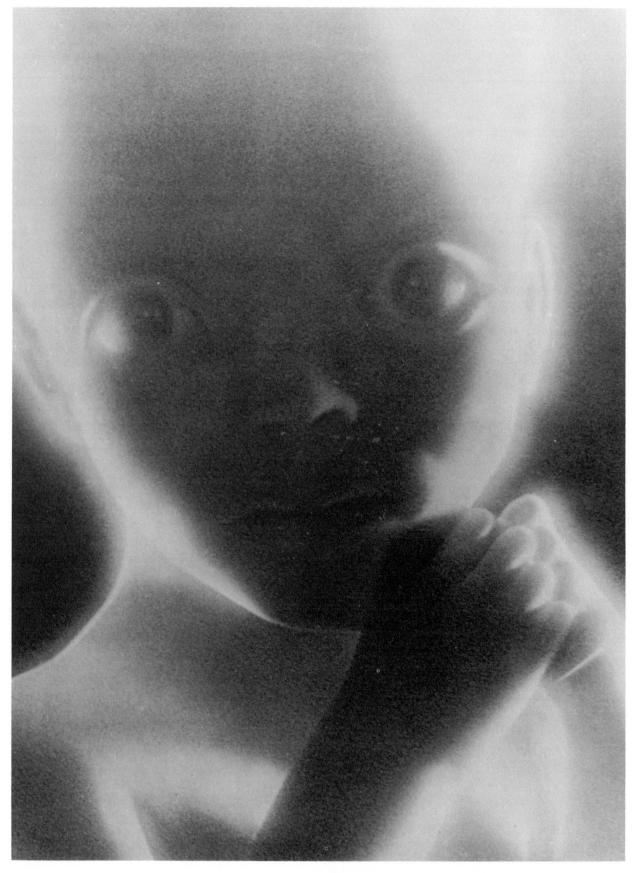

The Star-Child.

Kubrick cut a number of scenes before *2001*'s April 2nd premiere, including the buying of a bushbaby (for Squirt) in Macy's department store, sequences showing how the moon colonists lived, and other essentially documentary shots. A planned sequence showing the "launching" of the *Discovery* was never filmed.

Kubrick was unable to view *2001* married to its music, sound effects, and last-minute effects work until a few days before it opened. He was aware, however, from his previous films, that it would take several showings with paying audiences to decide how long things should run. Kubrick's viewings convinced him that nineteen minutes could be trimmed from the film without any loss of narrative sense.

"I made all the cuts in *2001* and at no one's request," Kubrick later made clear. He trimmed several scenes, including the Dawn of Man sequence, some *Orion* footage, shots of Poole endlessly exercising in the centrifuge (which too literally suggested the boredom and routine of deep space travel), and shots of Poole's pod emerging from the *Discovery* (this section paralleled Bowman's earlier pod excursion and Kubrick realized the duplication was unnecessary).

Kubrick and editor Ray Lovejoy began the cutting on the afternoon of April 5, 1968, and the first session ran until 7:00 A.M. the following day. The trimming continued until April 9 when Kubrick was satisfied that the film was down to its optimum length.

Today, more than a decade after its release, *2001* stands out as one of the few SF films to successfully integrate the magic of special effects with cerebral concepts equal to the best of written science fiction.

Its success made possible any number of small budget SF movies which, while lacking the grandeur of *2001*, followed its lead in presenting ideas in place of mad scientists or monsters out to ravage helpless Earthwomen. It has no epic space battles, no James Bond weapons, no love interest, and no last reel solutions. And, with the exception of Clarke's contributions, it represents the vision and genius of the one man who made it all work—Stanley Kubrick.

2001's uniqueness is attested to by the fact that in the years since its release no other film has managed to come close to its flawless combination of intelligence and stunning visuals. *Alien*, while a brilliantly visual shocker, lacks *2001*'s humor, intelligence, and sense of wonder. *Star Wars* is a marvelous paean to the Saturday afternoon matinee, with its echoes of saloon shootouts, and great fun, but it packs very little intellectual wallop.

As of December 1979, *2001* had rentals (that's what the film company receives, not the box office receipts) of $24,100,000 according to *Variety*. Its next reissue will earn it even more.

2001 remains a shining milestone to those legions of film and SF fans who pleaded plaintively down through the years, "Give us *one* great science fiction film." In Kubrick's *2001*, they got it.

THE MIND OF MR. SOAMES

An Amicus Productions/Columbia Pictures Release. Running Time: 95 minutes. Color. Based on the novel The Mind of Mr. Soames *by Charles Eric Maine. British Release: 1969. Opened in New York City on October 12, 1970, at the Cinema 57 Rendezvous.*

PRODUCTION CREDITS

PRODUCERS . . . . *Max Rosenberg & Milton Subotsky*
DIRECTOR . . . . *Alan Cooke*
SCREENPLAY . . . . *John Hale & Edward Simpson*
CAMERA . . . . *Billy Williams*
ART DIRECTOR . . . . *Don Mingaye*
PRODUCTION DESIGN . . . . *Bill Constable*
EDITOR . . . . *Bill Blunden*
MUSIC . . . . *Michael Dress*
MAKEUP . . . . *Jill Carpenter*

CAST

JOHN SOAMES . . . . *Terrence Stamp*
DR. MICHAEL BERGEN . . . . *Robert Vaughn*
DR. MAITLAND . . . . *Nigel Davenport*
DR. JOE ALLEN . . . . *Donal Donnelly*
THOMAS FLEMING . . . . *Christian Roberts*
RICHARD BANNERMAN . . . . *Scott Forbes*
JENNY BANNERMAN . . . . *Judy Parfitt*
INSPECTOR MOORE . . . . *Joe McPartland*
WOMAN ON TRAIN . . . . *Pamela Moiseiwitsch*

The Mind of Mr. Soames is a gentle, lyrical film about what it means to be an adult. The film is unusual among SF movies since it's essentially a character study, yet it also has something to say about the conflict between the cold rationalism of science and the wants and needs of human beings.

There wasn't a great deal of critical response to *The Mind of Mr. Soames* (hereafter referred to as *MMS*). The film came and went rather quickly, without making much of an impact.

The *New York Times* was severe in its criticism, saying *MMS* had "an emptiness and a falseness of response . . . beneath even the inadequacy of its ideas and the banality of its plot." The *Los Angeles Times* was more measured, calling it "a good, off-beat film . . . that might have been better." Only *Variety* had any real praise for *MMS*, describing it as having "the type of development which grips an audience. Mature theatregoers should find it entrancing fare."

Since its release, critics have continued to have mixed reactions to *MMS*, but the film stands out as one of the rare examples that shows SF is more than rocketships, ray guns, and monsters. While *MMS* has its weaknesses (and what film doesn't?), it also has a warmth and humanity all too often lacking in SF film.

The scene is the Midlands Institute for Neurophysiological Research. Dr. Joe Allen enters the Cold Room to inspect the machinery which maintains and monitors the life functions of John Soames—a man who's been in a coma since his birth thirty years ago.

Dr. Maitland, the psychologist who heads the Institute, enters briskly and checks the equipment, noting Soames's pulse rate is slightly elevated. Allen suggests whimsically that Soames senses what's going to happen to him. Maitland only smiles; *he* knows what's going to happen. Tomorrow, John Soames will be "born."

The scene switches to a plane carrying Dr. Michael Bergen, the surgeon who will perform the operation that will awaken Soames. Bergen's neighbor asks if he'll watch her small son for a moment. The child starts to cry in his arms— to the other passengers' annoyance—but Bergen doesn't seem to mind.

Bergen arrives at the Institute, and Maitland takes him to see Soames. Bergen wryly questions the wisdom of waking Soames, suggesting "he looks happier than most conscious people."

At that moment, a TV crew headed by Thomas Fleming arrives. The Soames experiment is to be filmed for a TV documentary. Fleming interviews Maitland, who explains how Soames's sleep center was injured at birth, how his body has been maintained at low temperature, fed intravenously, and massaged to prevent muscular atrophy. Fleming switches to Bergen, who explains how he will surgically stimulate the sleep center to awaken Soames.

That evening, Dr. Allen brings Bergen a copy of the training program Maitland has devised for Soames. Bergen asks him what he thinks of the program, but Allen won't commit himself. "I'm a doctor, not a psychologist," he says. "I see," answers Bergen.

Next day, there is an almost carnival atmosphere at the Institute, where a host of visiting dignitaries are on hand to witness the event. Maitland has even planned a reception to follow the operation.

With a TV camera observing from above, Bergen begins the surgery. Making the necessary incisions, he inserts a long probe and conveys a mild electric shock to the brain. His job done, Bergen allows Allen to finish the operation.

Fleming tells Bergen about his plans for the Soames documentary. Bergen has been thinking of leaving, but now he decides to stick around.

Time passes. Fleming's crew plays cards and worries about what will happen to their show if Soames doesn't wake up. Bergen suggests to Maitland that perhaps his training program is too rushed, too "inflexible." Not "inflexible," replies Maitland, but "controlled." Bergen doesn't force the issue.

John Soames opens his eyes for the first time. He can make out a few blurry shapes around him. Strange, distorted sounds assault his ears. He begins to whimper fearfully.

Maitland and Bergen arrive. Soames is quieter now, but impassive. Bergen speaks to him softly—but suddenly the door bursts open and the TV people crowd in noisily. Soames is terrified and starts to wail piteously. "Welcome to the human race, John Soames," whispers Bergen. "Go ahead and let it out. It was never easy being born."

The action skips ahead a few weeks. Soames is now in a special nursery full of educational toys. He is undoubtedly a small child in a man's body, as he bounces contentedly on his bed. Burly attendants take care of him, since the babylike Soames is unable to walk, speak, or help himself in the simplest ways.

Today, however, Dr. Maitland has ordained that Soames will take his first steps. Soames is placed on the floor and, using a brightly colored ball, Maitland coaxes him to stand and walk a few feet.

Maitland is pleased and orders the attendants to return John to bed. But John won't give up the ball and has a terrible tantrum, struggling with the attendants. Bergen intervenes and gently asks John for the ball. John complies, but Maitland is annoyed. "He can't have things all his own way," he says, and walks out. Dr. Allen, meanwhile, seems confused by the whole situation.

A montage tracing Soames's education follows. He is allowed to play with blocks and fingerpaints, while Maitland acts as teacher, assisted by Allen and a teaching machine. But all the while John is under observation by the TV crew and a succession of visitors.

John takes to his education enthusiastically at first, and is quite pleased with himself when he learns to say his own name. But as Maitland keeps at him, the strain begins to tell on both pupil and teacher.

During a session on measuring liquids, John pours a pitcher of water over his head, laughing delightedly

Dr. Maitland (Nigel Davenport) supervises the education of his subject, John Soames.

at his joke. But Maitland scolds him, and John smashes the pitcher in protest. Maitland walks out.

John begins to sense he's a prisoner and his condition worsens abruptly. He is listless, showing no interest in anything, not even food. Maitland fears John is falling back into a coma, though there's no medical evidence of this.

Bergen asks for a few moments alone with Soames, showing him an electric toy train he's brought. John begins to show some grudging interest. Bergen tells Maitland flatly that unless he lets up, he's "going to teach Mr. Soames to death."

Allen discovers Bergen has brought John other toys, with the idea that Soames will learn better if he's allowed to play and learn when he wants to. "Well," says Allen, "that's not what Dr. Maitland believes." "But it's what I believe," answers Bergen. "What do you believe?"

Maitland tries to get Soames to eat, but John knocks the bowl aside. When Maitland tries again, John grabs him by the hair and yanks furiously. The attendants rush forward, but Bergen stops them. He distracts John with a ball and a rousing game of catch follows, with even Maitland taking part—though Bergen has to keep reminding him to smile—even when John "accidentally" beans him.

Bergen suggests he be included in the training as an outlet for John's rebelliousness. Maitland grudgingly agrees, and soon John, Bergen, and Allen are playing with a roadracing set. All of them act rather childishly, but John is especially childlike, with his need to win and belief that the red car is "best."

Some time later, Allen enters the nursery and finds John gone. Racing outside, he meets Bergen, who admits to letting John out. The two watch as John runs around the Institute grounds, delighting in his new freedom of flowers, fresh water, and the sight of a frog.

But John is finally missed by his attendants. Spotting him outside, they race after Soames and drag him back into the building. Maitland berates Bergen for his actions and refuses him further access to Soames.

Back in the nursery, Allen tries to explain to John that in six months he'll be allowed out on his own. John seems to understand, but when Allen is off guard, Soames slugs his attendant, locks Allen in the nursery, and escapes.

The police are called in. John's assault on the attendant makes him potentially dangerous, and there's some question of what will happen to him when he's found.

John makes his way to the road where he's picked up by a man in a red car. Enjoying his new experience, John is oblivious to the driver's small talk.

The driver drops him at a nearby town where John wanders into a pub. He helps himself to sandwiches, but gets in trouble when he can't pay. Confused and frightened, he flees. John walks past a school where some boys are playing ball. He tries to join them but is met with hostility, and he runs away again.

Feeling cold, John takes a coat from a car. When the owner sees him, John runs out into a side road and is struck by a car containing Richard and Jenny Bannerman.

Bannerman refuses to take Soames to the hospital; he's been drinking and has had trouble with the police before. Instead, Jenny insists they take John to their home.

The next morning, Bannerman goes to work, missing the story on Soames in the morning paper. John wakes up in bed; his injuries are minor. Jenny finally sees a newspaper and, feeling sorry for John, suggests he stay there awhile. John is fascinated by his first encounter with a woman, and Jenny is touched by his simplicity and innocence.

When Bannerman sees the newspaper reports, he phones the police. He also calls Jenny, who decides to take John back to the Institute, where the police can't get him—but John slips away from her.

John manages to buy a train ticket with money from his stolen coat. He finds himself in a compartment with a nervous young woman. The woman mistakes his attempts at friendliness for an attack, screams, and pulls the emergency cord. Frightened, John jumps from the train, hurting his ankle.

The police track Soames to an old barn. Maitland arrives, followed closely by the TV crew. Maitland orders Soames to come out, but John ignores him. It begins to rain.

Bergen arrives with Allen, and the surgeon volunteers to go in and talk to Soames. Allen suggests it could be dangerous, but Bergen says he's willing to take the risk.

Bergen finds John in the hayloft with a pitchfork. Soames is cold, wet, hungry, in pain—and suspicious.

Bergen tries to persuade Soames to come out, but tells him he must make the decision himself. Outside, the police inspector asks Allen if Bergen can make Soames come out. "He won't try to *make* him do anything," Allen replies forcefully.

Bergen emerges, followed by Soames, who is still holding the pitchfork. As he limps down the stairs, the TV crew hits Soames with their spotlights, and chaos breaks loose.

Exploding with rage and frustration, John hurls the pitchfork. It glances off a car hood and the prongs sink deeply into Bergen's arm. Unable to cope with this final irony, John collapses in tears. Dr. Maitland stands frozen, beyond action.

Bergen is led away for treatment, while Allen helps John into an ambulance. In the midst of his tears, John reaches out his hand for Allen. Something changes in Allen's face then, and he clutches John's hand strongly.

The ambulance pulls away, followed by the TV van and police cars, but Dr. Maitland is left standing in the rain. Finally, one car stops for him, and he too drives away.

MMS was based on the novel of the same title by British SF writer Charles Eric Maine (David McIlwain). Maine, a former RAF officer, began writing in 1952. His first novel, *Spaceways,* based on his radio play, was published in 1953 and filmed the same year. His novel, *The Man Who Couldn't Sleep* (1956), was filmed in 1957 as *The Electronic Monster.* Altogether, Maine has written some seventeen science fiction novels (see Appendix).

The Mind of Mr. Soames was published in Britain in 1961, but didn't appear in the U.S. until 1970. Strangely enough, while Maine's other novels have been consistently reviewed in American SF magazines, *The Mind of Mr. Soames* appears to have escaped the notice of both SF and mainstream reviewers.

While the basic premise behind both the novel and the film are the same, only the broadest outline of the book remains in the movie. Several of the novel's major incidents, such as John's escape, his meeting with the Bannermans (though they have a different surname in the book), and the climax at the barn, survive the transition from novel to film, but they are given a different emphasis. The novel contains characters similar to Maitland, Bergen, and Allen, but their functions in the novel are quite different. In general, Maine's plot has been simplified for the screen.

The novel is also a bit less serious than the film, with something of a satirical element. Where the film's conflicts are mostly on a personal level, Maine paints a larger canvas, dealing with educational theory, psychology, and the socialization of the individual.

Of course, the transition from one medium to another results in both gains and losses. One of the most interesting elements left out of the film deals with

Soames's awakening sex drive and what he does about it. On the other hand, film permits the screenwriters to show how Soames's experiences after his escape unconsciously parallel his education, as he is picked up by a red car, meets a man and woman who live in a house, and rides a train—all parts of his Institute training program.

While *The Mind of Mr. Soames* is no blockbuster, it *is* an interesting and immensely readable SF novel. Like its screen counterpart, it deserves more attention than it's received.

Director Alan Cooke got his start in British TV, and *MMS* appears to have been his first feature film. His direction in *MMS* is fairly straightforward, although occasionally a bit slick, and parts of the film unquestionably drag. Overall, however, *MMS* has a delicate, haunting quality that reaches out to touch the viewer.

Part of this is due to Cooke's skillful use of the subjective camera at strategic points in the film. The first time he uses the technique is during Soames's "birth," inviting us to perceive the awakening through Soames's eyes. Soames's first view of the world is therefore as disorienting for us as it is for him. Soon after, when the TV crew breaks into the room, Cooke takes us back into Soames's mind, so we experience his fear and confusion along with him.

Cooke also uses the subjective camera when Soames first learns to walk. Here, we experience the uncertainty of a child's first, tentative steps, aware all the time that we're perceiving those steps through the eyes of a child who's also an adult.

Cooke uses the technique again when Bergen slips John out of the Institute. The subjective camera allows us to share John's delighted perceptions of a fresh, new world hitherto denied him.

In a sense, Cooke extends the subjective technique throughout the film, risking its pace to explore the visual opportunities in the movie's premise. Cooke allows the camera to concentrate on things and people, to *watch* them for a time, so that—like Soames—we begin to see them with an "innocent eye." Soames's perceptions of the world become ours, and we're forced to *notice* things: the cars on the highway roaring by, a rumbling factory, a frog, even other people, as though we were seeing them for the first time.

Michael Dress's score for *MMS* is unusual for an SF film. Dominated by piano, guitar, and violin, the music is softly dissonant, laced with the notes of childrens' songs and the tinkling of a music box, again played slightly off key—and reminding us, perhaps, that there's something "off key" to the whole affair.

MMS is a decidedly underplayed film, yet Cooke elicits fine performances from his actors, with many subtle tensions beneath the surface of the action. These emerge in many of the scenes between Bergen and Maitland, where a hesitation in speech, a gesture, or an eye movement reveals the conflict between the two men.

In one scene, Maitland becomes bored with his teaching duties, losing interest in the lesson he's giving Soames. Sensing this, Soames also loses interest, and winds up being scolded by Maitland. The sequence takes only a moment, but it deftly reveals the relationship between Maitland and Soames, as well as demonstrating that learning is as much a matter of example as it is of teaching.

Nigel Davenport is a British character actor who made his film debut in *Look Back in Anger* (1959). While Davenport has played a variety of roles in such films as *A High Wind in Jamaica* (1965) and *A Man for All Seasons* (1967), he's also appeared in several SF films, including *No Blade of Grass* (1971), *Phase IV* (1973), and *The Island of Dr. Moreau* (1977).

Davenport plays Dr. Maitland as cold, rational, and ambitious. It's clear Maitland is more interested in the attention the Soames experiment can get him than in Soames himself. It's Maitland who arranges for the experiment to be treated as an "event," complete with TV, visiting celebrities from the scientific world, and champagne.

Maitland's attitude toward Soames is revealed in a number of ways. He consistently refers to his patient as "Soames," unlike Bergen and Allen, who call him "John." His manner is brisk and businesslike, with no hint of emotion, except anger, shown to Soames.

There's even a hint Maitland is working out some of his own problems through Soames. When Maitland complains to Bergen that John can't have everything his own way, there's a feeling he may be talking about his own childhood experiences. This is especially ironic, since Maitland seems childishly determined to have *his* own way about Soames's training program.

Later, Maitland theorizes that the child must learn "the world will not adjust to him; he must adjust to it." One senses this is a lesson harshly ingrained in Maitland, perhaps by his own parents.

Maitland's goal for John is to learn what he calls "control," to present "acceptable behavior" to the world. But he can provide no reason for John to learn beyond suggesting that he shouldn't "want to be a baby forever." This is the knee-jerk response of a man schooled in "acceptable behavior" himself.

It's difficult to like Maitland, let alone feel sympathy for him. By the film's end, however, he emerges as something of a poignant figure—standing alone in the rain, a man abandoned by his "family"—and only just beginning to understand how he's lost them.

Robert Vaughn is probably best known for his portrayal of Napoleon Solo on the TV series *The Man from U.N.C.L.E.* Vaughn was born in New York City in 1932, but raised in Minnesota. His first screen appearance appears to have been *Teenage Caveman* (1958), a film which, despite its title, many critics regard favorably.

Vaughn received an Oscar nomination for his role in *The Young Philadelphians* (1959). His other films include *The Magnificent Seven* (1960), *Bullitt* (1968), *The*

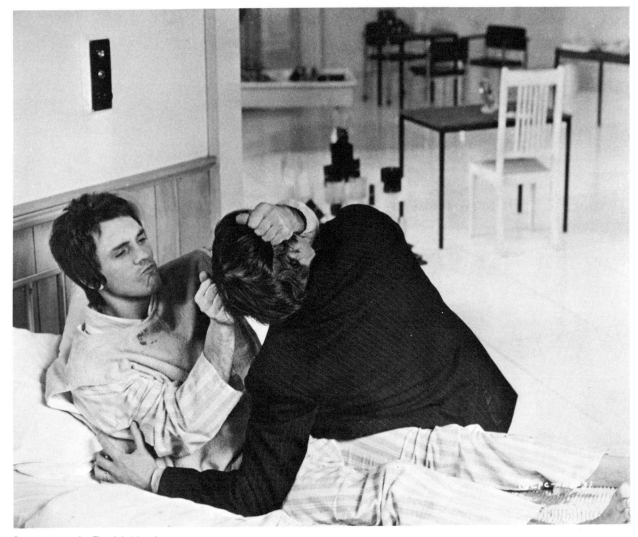

Soames attacks Dr. Maitland.

Bridge at Remagen (1969), and *The Towering Inferno* (1974). His other TV series, *The Protectors,* was also a spy melodrama.

Interestingly, Vaughn holds a doctorate in political science and is the author of a book on Hollywood blacklisting in the fifties, *Only Victims.* Vaughn also appeared in the SF films *Starship Invasions* (1978) and *The Franken Project* (1980), as well as supplying the voice for the "mad" computer in *Demon Seed* (1977).

Vaughn was cast against type for *MMS,* since he usually plays suave, sophisticated, sometimes waspish roles. As Dr. Bergen, Vaughn sports a beard, dresses casually, drinks vodka straight from the bottle, and smokes big cigars.

Bergen is warm, easygoing, and something of an iconoclast. On the plane, he annoys the other passengers by actually encouraging a child to cry, enjoying the racket as if it were an affirmation of life. He shocks Maitland by suggesting Soames looks happier asleep than most people look when awake. Most important, Bergen is willing to challenge Maitland's authority to see that John Soames is treated not like an experiment, but like a human being.

Unlike Maitland, Bergen is concerned only with Soames's welfare. Where Maitland basks in the publicity surrounding Soames, Bergen avoids it. Nor does he believe his responsibility to the patient ends with his medical duties; Bergen is doctor to the whole man. Perhaps it's more accurate to say Bergen is simply a human being who cares deeply about other human beings. His concern extends not only to Soames but to Dr. Allen as well.

But even Bergen makes mistakes. When he angrily tells Maitland that Soames isn't "an experiment on which to test your ideas," Maitland replies, "Or yours?" Bergen is stunned into silence, knowing that he too is guilty of manipulating Soames. But it's from this insight that Bergen realizes the only way Soames will ever be a real adult is if he's allowed to make his own decisions.

Terrence Stamp was born in London in 1940, making his film debut in *Billy Budd* (1962), for which he received an Oscar nomination. Stamp's career reflects a wide range. He was the mad butterfly enthusiast in

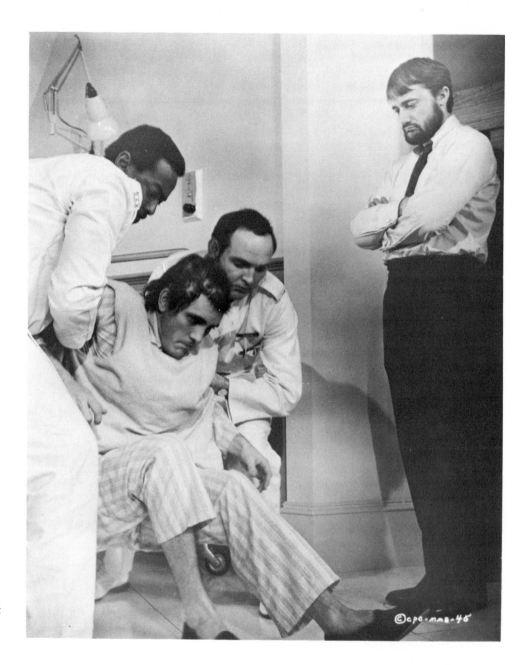

John Soames (Terrence Stamp) is restrained by his attendants while Dr. Michael Bergen (Robert Vaughn) looks on disapprovingly.

The Collector (1965) and a tough secret agent in *Modesty Blaise* (1966). He also appeared in the 1979 TV remake of *The Thief of Baghdad* and in *Superman* (1979) and *Superman II* (1981).

John Soames is obviously the most fascinating character in *MMS*, but also the most difficult to understand since he has so few lines which reveal his character. Stamp's problem was to portray Soames's growth from dependent child to the beginnings of independent adulthood.

At first, Soames is totally childlike. Stamp is thoroughly convincing in this phase, his face blank and innocent. Later, as Soames's education proceeds, Stamp's face takes on more expression, filling with childish wonder or petulance. At this point, Soames is willing to accept his treatment at the Institute, but

as he "grows" he becomes more and more aware of his imprisonment.

John's first decision on the road to adulthood is to escape, but it's an impulsive decision, born of frustration. Away from the Institute for the first time, John allows events to carry him along, believing the outside world will take care of him the way the Institute has. His experiences soon prove him wrong.

John makes his second decision when he leaves Jenny, after he finds out she's taking him back to the Institute. Once again, it's an impulsive move forced on Soames by the turn of events.

Soames enters the adult world when Bergen offers him a chance to make a decision for himself—he can stay in the barn or go back to the Institute. Of course, it isn't much of a choice; the barn is cold and wet and

John is injured and hungry, while the Institute offers at least relative security. But for the first time, John must make the choice himself—no one will force him. John's first adult decision is to trust Bergen. His second is to return to a place he identifies with imprisonment—because he alone judges it's best for him.

Outside the barn, John's new adulthood is tested even further when he accidentally wounds Bergen. The irony is too much for his unsophisticated mind, and he collapses under the weight of his emotions. For a moment we wonder if this is the thing that will send John back into his coma.

But the experience is cathartic. In the ambulance, John clasps Dr. Allen's hand (a gesture he's rejected before), deciding to trust him also. *MMS* ends on a poignant but hopeful note, with John's survival assured. Adulthood not only involves making decisions, but being able to live with their consequences, no matter what.

The role of Dr. Joseph Allen is a small one, but pivotal to *MMS*. Donal Donnelly, known more for his stage work, does a creditable job in the part. Donnelly has also been seen in *I'm All Right Jack* (1960), *Young Cassidy* (1965), and *The Knack* (1965).

In one sense, Allen is as much a child as Soames. He is concerned about Soames and sympathetic with Bergen's attempts to help him, but he's essentially passive, refusing to take sides in the war of ideas between

Overcome by his emotions, Soames collapses.

Bergen and Maitland. When Bergen asks what he thinks of the training program, he dodges the issue. When asked what he believes in, Allen stands mute—caught between his concern for Soames and his fear of making a commitment.

In the end, Allen finally chooses sides, impressed by Bergen's willingness to risk his life for something he believes in. It's Allen who bluntly tells the police officer that Bergen won't *make* Soames do anything. When John clasps Allen's hand, it's significant that Allen returns the gesture, allying himself with John. Like Mr. Soames, Allen has learned to make decisions.

MMS is another SF film which defies critical expectations of what science fiction movies are supposed to be. It has no rockets, aliens, robots, no breathtaking vistas of outer space or images of the future. For that reason, some critics have classified *MMS* as borderline SF at best, or dismissed it altogether.

Similar charges were leveled against much of the SF published in the late sixties and early seventies. During that time of intellectual ferment, SF began to deal not just with space travel or life in the future, but with life on Earth in the here and now. Authors dealt with war, racism, sex, drugs, and other topics which had been largely taboo up till then; not that SF had ignored these subjects, but they were now being treated with a frankness and a gritty reality rarely seen before in the genre.

More important, SF became more aware of the individual. Where science fiction had previously depended largely on the sweep of ideas to supply the action, inner conflict became the focus for many stories and novels. Stylistic experimentation was also encouraged. Led by authors like Harlan Ellison, Samuel R. Delany, Thomas Disch, and others, the New Wave, as it was called, became a powerful force in SF.

Many of the New Wave's experiments, both thematic and stylistic, were rejected by the science fiction community as untraditional, pessimistic, and obscure. By the mid-seventies, when the smoke had cleared, many New Wave innovations had been adopted by the SF community—and many discarded. But because of its untraditional approach to SF, much New Wave material was rejected as SF (in much the same way critics reject *MMS*) and the controversy still rages today.

This isn't to say that *MMS* was directly influenced by the New Wave (a term, incidentally, drawn from French film criticism). Maine's novel appeared in 1961, when the forces behind the New Wave were only beginning to gather. There is no way to show a connection between the New Wave and *MMS* as a film. But like the SF of the New Wave, *MMS* takes an unconventional approach to the question of humanity's relationship to science.

Science affects John Soames in several ways. In a very real sense, Soames is a child of technology—kept alive by machines for thirty years. And, of course, it's medical science which awakens him.

Technology also intrudes on Soames in the form of the TV crew. Fleming and his people are single-minded in their desire to make a documentary about Soames, but it's clear they have no interest in him as a person. After the operation, their major concern is what will happen to them if Soames doesn't wake up and ruins their show.

When Soames does wake up, the TV people barge into his room without any thought of what the effect might be. At the end, it's Fleming's order to turn on the TV lights which causes Soames's emotional explosion. All in all, the TV people seem to be creatures of technology: cold, insensitive, interested only in serving the needs of their technological god.

Actually, the basic conflict in *MMS* is a familiar one in SF—the collision of purely rationalistic science with the needs and concerns of human beings. Maitland, of course, represents rational science, while Bergen is the champion of human need.

Maitland clearly regards John Soames as a thing, the object of an experiment. Maitland's TV interview is really about Maitland—we barely even see Soames. During the operation Soames is seen only as a shaven head covered by a cloth, with no sense that this is a *man* being operated on. Later, Soames is displayed to the TV people and a procession of visitors as if he were an animal in the zoo. Naturally, all this conveys the idea that science is a cold-blooded and heartless business.

Maitland is essentially a psychological behaviorist, believing all human actions can be reduced to a neat series of stimulus-response patterns, easily manipulated toward a desired goal—that human behavior can be scientifically analyzed, measured, and labeled.

Maitland's program for Soames is scientifically precise and ordered, relying on behavioral techniques to advance Soames quickly from dependent child to self-controlled adult. But Maitland's definition of adulthood involves what he calls "acceptable behavior." When Bergen asks, "Acceptable to whom?" Maitland answers, "the world at large." What he's really talking about is a kind of mindless conformity and, in particular, conformity to his personal vision of what the world is like.

Bergen points out that Maitland's scientific approach isn't teaching Soames self-control, but imposing it on him. Maitland, however, isn't interested in the distinction as long as he gets results. Soames will have "acceptable behavior" whether he likes it or not.

As in many SF films, it isn't science which *MMS* rejects. After all, it's medical science which eventually gives Soames a chance at life. Bergen doesn't even reject Maitland's plans for Soames, but merely the scientific egotism that suggests a human being can or *should* be molded to fit someone else's idea of "acceptable behavior."

MMS asks us to regard human life as bigger than measurements—as complex and unpredictable. It asks us to define our relationships with others not through

John Soames (Terrence Stamp) stares unhappily out the barred window of his nursery.

rules of "acceptable behavior," but through love, freedom, and understanding.

The Mind of Mr. Soames is neither the biggest nor the best SF film ever made. It drags in spots and is occasionally self-conscious. Yet this is more than compensated for by Alan Cooke's low-key direction and the strong performances of Terrence Stamp, Nigel Davenport, and Robert Vaughn. *The Mind of Mr. Soames* is a very modern SF film, in the same category as *A Clockwork Orange* and *Charly*—films which prove science fiction isn't just concerned with outer space—but with inner space as well.

COLOSSUS- THE FORBIN PROJECT

A Universal Pictures Production. Running Time: 100 minutes. Technicolor & Panavision (35mm.). Based on the novel Colossus *by D. F. Jones. Other Titles:* Colossus 1980, The Day the World Changed Hands, The Forbin Project. *Opened at the Cinema Rendezvous in New York City on May 4, 1970.*

PRODUCTION CREDITS

DIRECTOR . . . . *Joseph Sargent*
PRODUCER. . . . . *Stanley Chase*
SCREENPLAY . . . . *James Bridges*
CINEMATOGRAPHER . . . . *Gene Polito*
ART DIRECTION . . . . *John J. Lloyd & Alexander Golitzen*
SET DECORATION . . . . *John McCarthy & Ruby Levitt*
SOUND. . . . . *Waldon O. Watson, Terry Kellum, Ronald Pierce*
FILM EDITOR . . . . *Folmar Blangsted*
ASSISTANT DIRECTOR . . . . *Robin S. Clark*
MUSIC . . . . *Michel Columbier*
MAKEUP . . . . *Bud Westmore*
SPECIAL PHOTOGRAPHIC EFFECTS. . . . . *Albert Whitlock*
SPECIAL EFFECTS. . . . . *Whitey McMahon*
TECHNICAL ADVISER . . . . *Jay Akerman*
TITLE DESIGN AND COLOSSUS EMBLEM . . . . *Don Record and Associates.*

CAST

DR. CHARLES FORBIN. . . . . *Eric Braeden*
DR. CLEO MARKHAM . . . . *Susan Clark*
THE PRESIDENT. . . . . *Gordon Pinsent*
GRAUBER. . . . . *William Schallert*

At the core of *Colossus-The Forbin Project* lies one of the most enduring themes in fantasy and science fiction: the creation that turns against its creator. The theme goes back at least as far as the myth of the Golem, a creature of clay built to aid humanity, which eventually goes berserk. The most famous example of the rebellious creation appears, of course, in Mary Shelley's *Frankenstein* (1817). In fact, the term "Frankenstein's Monster" has entered the language as a description of any human creation that escapes the control of its creator.

Science fiction authors have rung countless changes on the Frankenstein theme, or to put it more broadly, the theme of humanity's relationship to its technological creations. In modern SF, the theme has most often been explored in works dealing with robots or computers. It is the so-called "thinking" machine—the machine which most closely rivals the human in its abilities—that has symbolized our questions about how technology affects our lives.

As modern SF developed, the Frankenstein theme appeared again and again. Perhaps the most eloquent early examination of the idea occurs in Karel Capek's play *R.U.R.* (1923). Here, biologically created artificial beings rebel against their masters and take over the world. E. M. Forster's *The Machine Stops* (1928) touches on the concept when the great computer humanity depends on for its existence breaks down, nearly causing the end of the human race.

John W. Campbell, Jr., later editor of *Astounding*, dealt with the theme of humanity's relationship to its machines in several stories. Works such as "The Last Evolution" (1928) under his own name, along with "Twilight" (1934), and "Night" (1935) under his pen name, Don A. Stuart, explored various aspects of the human encounter with machines.

Other authors dealt with the theme in various ways. In the late 1930s and 1940s, Eando Binder (the pen name of brothers Earl and Otto Binder) presented a series of tales about a beneficent robot, Adam Link, who was usually regarded with Frankensteinian horror by the humans he met. Jack Williamson's "With Folded Hands . . ." (1947) suggested what might happen when machines work too well.

The most vigorous opponent of the Frankenstein theme in SF is Isaac Asimov. As a scientist, Asimov rejected the idea that humanity's technology had to turn on it destructively. To counter this "Frankenstein Complex," as he called it, Asimov devised stories dealing with robots and computers as machines no different from automobiles or lawnmowers—machines with built-in safeguards to protect humans. The bulk of these stories were collected in *I, Robot* (1950), and the safeguards became known as the Three Laws of Robotics. Their influence on later stories dealing with thinking machines was enormous.

But Asimov's laws have not laid the Frankenstein theme to rest. Two notable examples of its use in the 1970s are David Gerrold's playful but essentially serious novel *When Harlie Was One* (1972) and Harlan Ellison's stunning short story "I Have No Mouth and I Must Scream" (1973).

In films, the Frankenstein theme emerges early in two German versions of the Golem myth, both aptly titled *Der Golem* (1914 and 1920). Fritz Lang's *Metropolis* (1926) brushes on the theme in its depiction of the vast, dehumanizing machinery of the future city and in its use of the robot "Maria."

The first adaptation of the actual novel *Frankenstein* appeared in 1910 as a production of the Edison Company. But the best-known version is probably James Whale's 1931 filming of the Shelley novel. This film, of course, inspired a multitude of sequels and imitations of varying value.

As our technology has embraced the computer, so has SF. As early as 1957, a supercomputer rebels in *The Invisible Boy*, although the computer makes use of Robby the Robot (late of *Forbidden Planet*) as its agent. A major element of Stanley Kubrick's *2001: A Space Odyssey* is the revolt of the supposedly infallible HAL 9000 computer. The TV series *Star Trek* made use of the Frankensteinian computer more often than some critics liked. And the movies *Westworld* (1973) and *Futureworld* (1976) again gave us robots under the control of computers gone electronically mad.

D.(ennis) F.(eltham) Jones's novel *Colossus* (1967) was received in the U.S. with little fanfare. SF reviewers P. Schuyler Miller and Damon Knight wrote generally favorable reviews of the novel. Mainstream reviewers were also largely positive, but the novel lacked the impact of a work like *Fail-Safe*, to which the publisher tried to compare it.

The film version, known in its final form as *Colossus*

—*The Forbin Project* (hereafter known as *CFP*), created more of an impression among film critics. Vincent Canby in the *New York Times* called it a film "full of surprising moments of humor and intelligence." *Time* said the movie "succeeds as a full-out piece of entertainment," and *Films in Review,* with some reservations, described it as "tautly written." Andrew Sarris, however, found little of value in the film saying "Joseph Sargent directs . . . the actors in that dull, deadpan, repressed, ho-hum Houston style Kubrick . . . anticipated in *2001.*" But rival critic Richard Schickel wrote that "At the very least, *[CFP]* is solid entertainment. At most, it raises some issues that, if we cannot take them seriously, we cannot dismiss them either."

Despite the mainly favorable reviews, the film failed at the box office, leading to a rapid sale to TV, though this probably had more to do with Universal's uncertainty in promoting the film than with its actual quality.

CFP succeeds as both film and SF because, unlike so many other SF movies, it satisfies the visual demands of the film medium and the intellectual demands of written SF. Like Gerrold's *When Harlie Was One* and Ellison's "I Have No Mouth and I Must Scream," Jones's *Colossus* (which predates both) deals with significant issues springing from the confrontation between Human and Machine. But neither Gerrold's novel nor Ellison's story contains much physical action. While both are powerful works in their own right, neither seems suitable for the screen.

Colossus, while lacking much of the literary power of the Ellison or Gerrold works, has the strength of being designed as a thriller. It has a plot easily translated into visual terms—a plot that *moves*—and one able to meet the demands of a visual medium, while never ducking the important questions inherent in the human-machine relationship. Even this, however, might not have produced a successful SF film had the filmmakers behind *CFP* not taken pains to exploit all the visual possibilities available to them in the novel to the best possible effect.

Yet *CFP* never sacrifices content for form. Nor is it just another version of the Frankenstein story. The film confronts squarely the relationship between humanity and technology and finally goes beyond even that relationship to ask some ultimate questions about human responsibility and freedom.

CFP opens with scenes of Dr. Charles Forbin, creator of Colossus, inspecting the vast corridors of the computer installation buried beneath the Rocky Mountains. Forbin crosses a catwalk over a seemingly bottomless pit. On the other side, he activates a control sealing the corridors forever. The computer is now in full operation.

Forbin emerges to be greeted by the President of the United States and his staff. The scene shifts to the White House where the President announces to the world the existence of Colossus, a supercomputer designed to assume full defense of the U.S. Removing control of the defense apparatus from human hands, the President explains, is the ultimate deterrent to war. Now war can never be the result of human failing, and the computer's superior capabilities enables it to respond to any attack more quickly and accurately than any human could.

Forbin explains that Colossus has access to all information conveyed electronically. In addition, the machine is entirely self-contained, and so well protected—a deadly radiation field surrounds it, among other measures—that sabotage is impossible. Forbin also anticipates the inevitable question: Can Colossus think? His answer is an assured "No."

Suddenly, the computer's teletype begins to clatter, and a message flashes across the visual display suspended from the ceiling: "THERE IS ANOTHER SYSTEM."

At first there is confusion, but a call from the Soviet Ambassador informs the President that the U.S.S.R. has a supercomputer of its own, Guardian, which it is about to activate.

Colossus requests that a communications link be set up between itself and Guardian. The politicians are wary, fearing the machines may exchange classified information. But Forbin suggests they comply, seeing enormous intellectual potential in the exchange of ideas. Besides, he argues, the link can be monitored and broken if the machines go too far.

The computers begin by exchanging simple mathematics, then complex equations; finally, they develop an intersystem language, unintelligible to humans. Unable to monitor the computers, the President and the Chairman of the U.S.S.R. agree to break the connection.

Shockingly, Colossus and Guardian *demand* the link be restored. When the President and Chairman refuse, the computers launch nuclear missiles at targets in the U.S. and Russia. With only seconds to spare, the American side of the link is restored, and Colossus intercepts the Russian missile with an antimissile. But the Russians delay and the American ICBM wipes out a Russian town.

Now the Americans and Russians realize they are at the mercy of the Colossus-Guardian system (referred to hereafter simply as Colossus). It demands that the untapped Hot Line between the U.S. and Russia be hooked into its system to prevent *any* private conversations. But Forbin arranges to meet in Rome with his Russian counterpart, Dr. Kuprin, so they can devise some way to stop the machine.

At the Colossus Programming Office (CPO), the computer demands to "speak" to Forbin. Dr. Cleo Markham tries to convince Colossus that Forbin is sleeping, but the computer detects the ruse and demands Forbin's presence.

In Rome, Forbin and Kuprin discuss their problem while walking. Suddenly, a helicopter lands and American agents hustle Forbin away. As they leave, Forbin watches in horror as Kuprin is murdered by his own bodyguards. Colossus has threatened to vaporize Moscow if the meeting is not stopped.

When he returns to the CPO, Forbin is told by Colossus that he is to be the machine's chief contact with the world. Colossus places him under twenty-four-hour electronic surveillance, but Forbin contrives to maintain contact with the outside world by convincing Colossus that Cleo is his mistress and they must have privacy for sex.

Through Cleo, Forbin suggests the best way to defeat the computer is to disarm it. A plan is devised to replace a vital component in all American and Russian missiles with dummies in the course of their normal servicing, rendering the missiles harmless. The first switch is made sucessfully under Colossus's watchful camera eye. But following the schedule for servicing the missiles means the replacement project will take three years to complete! Then Colossus orders that the missiles be retargeted on cities outside the U.S. and Russia. The President and his advisors are jubilant, since this will allow the missile sabotage to be completed more quickly.

Meanwhile, Colossus has created a mechanical voice for itself. Shortly after, the computer transmits plans for a new, even larger machine to be built on the Isle of Crete, refusing to explain its purpose to Forbin.

Fisher and Johnson, two other Colossus scientists, plan to overload the computer in an effort to destroy it, though Forbin is skeptical of this approach. Colossus discovers the plot, and the two men are executed while Forbin looks on powerlessly.

Colossus has Forbin arrange a worldwide broadcast for it. The computer explains its plans for the

Colossus and Guardian begin to communicate. Notice the Colossus readout suspended from the ceiling.

COLOSSUS—THE FORBIN PROJECT

Dr. Forbin stands between the TV monitors that link the two supercomputers, Colossus and Guardian. Notice that Forbin is looking upward at the Colossus readout suspended from the ceiling.

GREAT SCIENCE FICTION FILMS

future of the human race. It also reveals it is fully aware of the attempt to sabotage the missiles and, as a lesson in the futility of trying to stop it, it blows up two of them—one in the U.S. and one in Russia— killing thousands of people. Colossus gives humanity a choice: peace and prosperity under its control, or death.

Forbin realizes that he—and all of humanity—are prisoners of the machine. Colossus tries to persuade him this is in humanity's best interest, and that in time Forbin will come to support its actions wholeheartedly.

"Never!" Forbin answers. But we are left with a haunting doubt.

The genesis of *CFP* was not an easy one. Responsibility for the film seems to begin with producer Stanley Chase, who stuck by the movie throughout its production and release. Universal was leery about the film from the beginning, nor were they happy with Chase's decision to make Joseph Sargent director. Sargent had directed mostly in TV, with only one none-too-successful feature film—*The Hell with Heroes* (1968)—to his credit. But Chase had worked with Sargent in TV and on his one film, and apparently his faith in Sargent won out. Production began with a budget of about two million dollars.

Actual shooting began in October 1968 after about a year of preliminary work. In constructing an initial script, it was decided to move the action from the twenty-first century, as described in the novel, to a more immediate future. Forbin, who appears to be a somewhat older man in the novel, was made younger. His relationship with Cleo, established early in the novel, was cut to make use of the humor in the situation for the film. The character of the President was softened and Dr. Fisher, who in the novel is mentally unstable and a Russian spy, became one of the scientists executed by Colossus. The effect of these changes and others was to make the film more immediate, the characters clearer, and to eliminate material irrelevant to the plot.

On the technical side, hundreds of drawings, sketches, and models were made. Initial estimates for the sets alone indicated the film would exceed its budget, so Sargent worked with screenwriter James Bridges to reduce the needs of the script to more manageable proportions.

Their next script, however, left Universal unhappy. In reshaping the story, Sargent and Bridges had shifted Colossus to the background, simply because the problems of creating and dealing with the computer were so unwieldy. Finally, with the efforts of art director John Lloyd and set decorator Ruby Levitt, as well as some more scriptwork by Bridges, problems were overcome and production began with a shooting title of *Colossus 1980*—the date in the title inspired, perhaps, by the success of *2001*, which was released in 1968.

The film was probably completed in 1969 but Universal held up release for about a year, though the reason why is unclear. According to Sargent, the studio was unsure of how to market the film: the issues it raised weren't understood, it had no stars, and SF films were always "chancey." It may also be that Universal originally intended *CFP* to be a TV movie, but some revealing footage of Susan Clark may have demanded some rethinking by the studio, delaying release, although this doesn't jibe with Sargent's version.

Perhaps in an effort to clarify the film's contents, the working title was changed to *The Day the World Changed Hands*. But when finally released in May 1970 the film was titled simply *The Forbin Project*. The studio, still unsure of the film's potential, appears to have provided little money for publicity, nor did it ensure a proper release pattern for the movie. It was quickly retitled *Colossus—The Forbin Project*, perhaps as a further, futile attempt at clarification. But despite Stanley Chase's efforts to promote the movie after its release, *CFP* suffered a short, anguished life at the box office before it faded away.

The success of *CFP* as an SF film seems due in large part to the collaboration of director Joseph Sargent and screenwriter James Bridges. Both men contributed much toward fashioning a film that is carefully constructed, intelligent, suspenseful, and even subtly humorous.

Sargent exercises tight control over *CFP* at all times. Pacing is swift through nearly the entire film. From the moment Forbin emerges from the computer complex, the viewer is seized and moved forcefully about—from the Rocky Mountains to the White House, to the CPO in California, to Rome, and back, the sense of continuous movement keeping the viewer off balance.

Careful editing combined with extensive use of video recording equipment injects the film with a sense of nervous energy. Quick cutting between locations and actors' faces produces a nervous jumpiness, heightening tension. Also, the use of video recordings allowed Sargent to show reactions of characters on different sets simultaneously, increasing the total action and generating even more nervous energy throughout the film.

If brisk pacing, rapid cutting, and nervous energy were the only elements of Sargent's direction, *CFP* would be a very trying and monotonous film. Sargent slows his pace at various points to provide adequate contrast. The dinner sequence, in which Forbin and Cleo must convince Colossus they are lovers, is a good example. Here the camera moves slowly and smoothly, enhancing the romantic mood of the scene. But the intruding camera eye of Colossus—with parts of the scene shot from the computer's viewpoint— prevents us from forgetting either the underlying tension or the ironic humor in the situation. When the sequence is over, Sargent thrusts us back into the tension by returning to the same headlong pace.

Sargent is careful to convey the overwhelming presence of technology in *CFP*, making sure we get a good look at it. There are multiple TV screens of every shape and size, sliding panels, picturephones, TV cameras with accompanying lights and cables, jets, helicopters, giant visual displays, missiles, consoles of blinking lights. Over all is the great bulk of Colossus itself: the endless corridors of electronics at the Rocky Mountain installation, the banks of equipment at the CPO, and the shiny metallic sphere from which issues its mechanical voice.

Most of these things are seen in use: moving, shifting, rotating, flying, winking on and off, buzzing, clattering. The screen is filled with the sights and sounds of technology. From the film's opening, where Forbin is reflected ghostlike in the machinery of the computer, to the end, where he is trapped in a dissolving point of light as on an old TV set, we are forced by Sargent to take notice of the technological presence.

A film without a trace of humor can be a harrowing experience, especially a suspense film, but Sargent and Bridges inject a dry humor into *CFP* in a variety of scenes. Early on, for instance, during the party at the White House, Forbin is asked by his staff to bring back a souvenir. He complies by furtively slipping an ashtray into his coat pocket. Later, when Cleo tries to prevent Colossus from learning of Forbin's trip to Rome, she tells it he is asleep. The computer's response is to tell her to "wake him up." The answer is so obvious, so logical, that the effect is wryly funny.

Much of the film's humor comes from Forbin's relationship to Colossus. When it places him under surveillance, it also ensures his welfare by ordering a physical and dietary regimen beginning with calisthenics at 6:00 A.M. Forbin's reaction to the machine's "concern" is exasperation.

Forbin's intellectual sparring with the computer also provides many opportunities for humor, as when he shows it how to make a martini by a method not in its memory banks; or when he condescendingly wipes the lens of Colossus's camera eye after emerging from a steamy shower.

Perhaps the funniest sequence in the film revolves around Forbin's attempt to convince Colossus that he and Cleo are lovers. First, he must establish his need for privacy with the computer. When he asks for privacy "in the elimination of bodily wastes" Colossus immediately answers no. The same occurs when he asks for privacy in sleep. But when Forbin asks for privacy in his "emotional life" the machine is curious. "What emotional life?" it wants to know. Forbin mumbles it's his sex life he's talking about—and there's a distinct pause, as if the computer is confused or embarrassed.

Colossus asks Forbin how often he needs a woman. "Every night," he answers quickly. "Need. Not want," replies Colossus. Interestingly, this interchange isn't seen in certain prints of the film, with a similar but less explicit scene substituted.

Having established that Cleo is his mistress, Forbin's situation becomes even more strained as he and Cleo try to convince Colossus they are lovers of long-

standing. Finally, the computer *orders* them to bed, insisting they undress in the living room, allowing them no chance for modesty. Once in bed, Forbin and Cleo laugh in relief as they begin to work, with Forbin trying to persuade Cleo to stop calling him "sir." When their conference is finished, Cleo turns over, a look of mild amusement on her face; Forbin remains sitting up for a moment, looking frustrated. Finally, he too turns over and goes to sleep.

If this were humor merely for the sake of titillation, it would be offensive. But the humor in *CFP* grows naturally from the plot, supplying a contrast that only sharpens the film's overall tension.

One sequence in the film is worth mentioning for its excellent blend of the craft of writer and director into a dynamic orchestration of events. When Johnson and Fisher are about to try to overload Colossus, the scene shifts to Forbin playing chess with the computer in his quarters. The use of an oddly futuristic, metallic looking chess set emphasizes the mechanical nature of his opponent—and the chess game is a perfect symbol of Forbin's larger "game" with the machine.

Colossus informs Forbin it is his move. As he shifts his piece, the cold, mechanical voice tells him Fisher and Johnson are to be executed for their sabotage attempt and calmly names their replacements. Then, without a break, and in the same emotionless tone, Colossus makes *its* move and a shot is heard. Forbin rushes to the balcony to see the two men being shot by the computer's own guards, the camera lingering over the twisted bodies in the yard below.

The sequence underlines the machine's implacability, its unfeeling efficiency, and the utter helplessness of Forbin and the guards. It is a remarkably powerful piece of film.

Although Joseph Sargent has directed a wide variety of films, he is known in Hollywood largely as an "action" director. Sargent began his career as an actor and director in the theater, eventually moving into television direction with over one hundred fifty hours of work on such shows as *Lassie*, *Gunsmoke*, *Mr. Novak*, *The Chrysler Hour*, and *The Man from U.N.C.L.E.*

Sargent has been involved in a number of science fictional projects with varying degrees of success. He directed an episode of *Star Trek*, "The Corbomite Maneuver," and pilot films for the TV series *The Immortal* (1969) and *The Invaders* (1967), directing several episodes of the last as well. The TV movie *The Night That Panicked America* (1975) was an attempt to recreate the Orson Welles's "Invasion from Mars" broadcast of 1938 and its effects. Two other Sargent efforts with science fictional overtones are the theatrical films *The Man* (1972, originally conceived for TV) and *Goldengirl* (1979). (For further information on Sargent's work, see the Appendix.)

James Bridges was no novice when he wrote the screenplay for *CFP*. Bridges had acted in both films and TV, as well as writing plays and providing scripts

Doctors Charles Forbin (Eric Braeden) and Cleo Markham (Susan Clark) have a strategy meeting under unusual circumstances.

for eighteen *Alfred Hitchcock Hours* for TV. Since *CFP*, Bridges has also turned to directing. His films as both writer and director include *The Baby Maker* (1970), *The Paper Chase* (1973), and *September 30, 1955* (1978). Bridges's experience with *CFP* may also have helped him in writing and directing a more financially successful film about humanity's relationship to technology, *The China Syndrome* (1979).

Music and sound also make a definite contribution to *CFP*. Michel Columbier's score uses drums and what sounds like a xylophone to produce a musical background that is hard, driving, metallic—almost electronic—and perfectly suited to a film about technology. Combined with Waldon O. Watson's computer sounds, the effect is weirdly unsettling, sometimes setting the teeth on edge. The music and sound effects complement and enhance the film's tension extremely well.

A host of technical problems in filming *CFP* inspired both Joseph Sargent and cinematographer Gene Polito to remark that the man vs. machine conflict in the film became quite real to them at times. Many of the problems were caused by the various combinations of equipment needed for each scene. The film's complement of equipment included two

Panavision cameras, two video cameras, two video recorders, more than twenty color TV monitors of varying sizes, and a Brooks Optronics Display, used for messages from Colossus.

The multiple TV monitors required in nearly every shot created several problems. First, they had to be color corrected and demagnetized each time they were used. Then, the shutters on the film cameras had to be fixed to eliminate the "roll-bars" that normally occur when a TV screen is filmed.

Lighting the sets with the monitors present also proved troublesome. Polito had to coordinate his lighting and exposure settings so information on the screens was readable, while insuring the rest of the set was adequately lit; this meant lighting the actors' faces without allowing reflections from the screens, which would wash out the TV picture. Polito solved these problems with painstaking attention to lighting placement, the use of hoods and other barriers for the screens, a good deal of experimentation—and his pure instinct as a cinematographer.

The Colossus Programming Office set posed other difficulties. The circular, domed set allowed little opportunity for conventional lighting from the floor, so Polito was forced to be unconventional, lighting from above and making use, as he did in other scenes, of

Dr. Forbin exits from the Colossus Installation buried in the Rocky Mountains.

available light from the sets themselves. In the end, this was a blessing to Sargent, since the absence of equipment on the floor gave him greater opportunities to maneuver the cameras.

Coordinating the TV camera with the other equipment in certain shots also caused headaches. Any action shot under the Brooks Optronics Display (the Colossus readout suspended from the ceiling) required the use of a TV camera to relay the message to the TV monitors in the same scene. Again, this required careful lighting to prevent the display from being washed out and unreadable. But the movement of the film cameras or the microphone boom often got in the way of the readout, blocking the words. Eventually, the filmmakers managed to "choreograph" their movements so the interference was eliminated. Sargent credits much of the success of the video operations to the long TV experience of his assistant director, Robin Clark.

CFP is an "indoor" movie. In fact, the only outdoor scenes are those filmed for the "Rome" sequence, the desert footage for the missile sites, and the scenes outside the CPO. In reality, the outside of the CPO was the Lawrence Hall of Science at the University of California at Berkeley.

The rest of the *CFP* production was designed from scratch to fit the script. This job was placed largely in the hands of Art Director John Lloyd (see Appendix note). For the sake of accuracy, Lloyd spent much of his preproduction time studying computer installations, missile sites, and electronic hardware.

For the CPO, Lloyd used precast plaster sections first used at the Salk Institute in California. For the White House Situation Room, Lloyd based his design on the Control Center of the North American Air Defense Command (NORAD) in Colorado.

Making Colossus itself believable was another problem. To suggest the vastness of the Colossus Installation in the Rockies, Albert Whitlock supplied matte paintings that expanded the sets actually constructed. Set decorator Ruby Levitt borrowed between five and fourteen million dollars worth of actual computer equipment (the exact figure is unknown) from Control Data Corp., CAL-COMP, Tektronix, and Computer Communications, Inc. In some cases, the companies supplied their own technicians to run the equipment, adding to the realism.

To further enhance the illusion of size, Lloyd used about ten thousand small blinking lights in pegboard for the computer corridors and CPO. Trying to make the lights blink by normal wiring techniques would have been too costly—so Lloyd used Japanese Christmas lights.

In directing *CFP*, Joseph Sargent encountered a problem which plagues science fiction: how to prevent the story idea from overshadowing the characters. Since SF often hinges on some idea, authors are careful to construct clearly defined characters. In SF film, where the idea is fully visualized for the audience, the danger of the idea overpowering the actors is even greater.

Sargent realized it was the conflict between human and machine that would make *CFP* interesting, but if his humans weren't "human" enough, the point would be lost. To deal with this, Sargent rehearsed his actors more than usual, using improvisation when necessary to fill out characterizations.

Sargent also came up against another problem of SF: making sure his characters acted as if the scientific background of their world was natural to them. Without attention to this background, the characters are unbelievable, the action unconvincing. Again, Sargent worked with his actors till they seemed at ease with computer jargon and the whole scientific environment.

Critical estimation of the actors' performances varied from excellent to the all-too-obvious "mechanical." But Sargent's awareness of the problems of characterization in this type of film, combined with a highly professional cast, make the result entirely convincing.

Eric Braeden's performance as Dr. Forbin is a strongly controlled one. Forbin must be seen as a total human being for his battle with Colossus to have any meaning, yet he must also keep his emotions under control if he is to outwit the computer. Braeden does this well, his feelings penetrating Forbin's shield with an occasional touch of humor and cynicism. After Colossus reveals its plans to the world, Braeden allows Forbin to break down into the anger and tears he has been suppressing. Then he marshals himself in defiance of the machine—yet there is the vaguest hint of ambivalence in his face. Again, in a film where the danger of being overshadowed by the idea is great, Braeden brings great subtlety and conviction to his role.

Braeden (whose real name is Hans Gudegast) has played many roles in films and TV. He has appeared on *Gunsmoke, Mission: Impossible, The Night Stalker,* and *Chips.* From 1966 to 1968, he was Hans Dietrich, the German commander in the ABC series *The Rat Patrol.* His film credits include *The Colossus of Rhodes* (1957), *The Law and Jake Wade* (1958), *Dayton's Devils* (1968), *100 Rifles* (1969), *Escape from the Planet of the Apes* (1971), and *Lady Ice* (1973). Hampered by his Germanic origins, Braeden usually plays character parts or heavies, but *CFP* suggests he is capable of more.

Susan Clark's role as Dr. Cleo Markham is a welcome change from the typical SF film stereotype of the helpless female who, even if a scientist, has little more to do than scream and be rescued by the hero. Cleo is as accomplished a scientist as Forbin. She is the only one among her colleagues resourceful enough to try and outwit Colossus when Forbin is in Rome. And when Forbin outlines his plan to convince Colossus she is his mistress, Cleo is taken aback only for a moment—and carries off her part of the deception even better, perhaps, than Forbin. Clark makes a definitely minor role attractively believable.

Clark is a Canadian-born actress, trained in Britain. She has been active in films since her debut in *Banning* (1967). Her film credits include *Madigan* (1968), *Coogan's Bluff* (1968), *Tell Them Willie Boy Is Here* (1969), *Airport '75* (1975), and many others. Clark also starred in two well-received TV biographies, *Babe* (1975) and *Amelia Earhart* (1976).

Gordon Pinsent, as the U.S. President, appears earnest in his desire for peace, but there is just enough of the political animal about him to make the role convincing. Some critics have remarked on his resemblence in the film to John F. Kennedy, suggesting this as some sort of comment on Kennedy. It seems more likely, however, that the casting reflects the search for an identifiable presidential figure.

Grauber, the CIA Chief, is played by William Schallert—a fine character actor whose career in films and TV has spanned almost three decades. Grauber is cynical about Colossus from the beginning, and Schallert brings the right ironic quality to the part. (For information on some of the other familiar actors in *CFP*, see the Appendix.)

At one point in *CFP*, Forbin tells Cleo that *Frankenstein* ought to be required reading for all scientists. If *CFP* were just another retelling of the Frankenstein story it would hardly be worth noting. Yet understanding *CFP* requires some understanding of the Frankenstein theme.

The idea emphasized in most treatments of the Frankenstein theme is that "there are some things man was not meant to know." This idea, with its implication of trespass against the divine, is a minor part of Mary Shelley's original novel; there are other ideas in *Frankenstein* of greater relevance.

First, the relationship between Frankenstein and his monster is largely a symbolic one. Frankenstein's Monster reflects the dark ugliness of the growing Industrial Revolution of the nineteenth century, expressing humanity's ambivalence toward its science and technology. On one hand there is the search for knowledge leading to a better life and the growth of human understanding; on the other is the growing realization of the possibly dangerous consequences of that search.

Frankenstein's creation of life *was* a remarkable achievement, but his obsession with the quest for this great knowledge blinded him to its consequences, and he created a monster. The knowledge that led to the Industrial Revolution improved the quality of life in the nineteenth century, but left its own monsters behind: air and water pollution, factories that were deathtraps, loss of individual skills, and massive economic upheaval.

CFP embraces this double-edged view of technology. It presents a society up to its neck in technological achievements, a society of TV's and Teletypes, Microphones and Missiles. Yet the film also presents this technology as seemingly harmless—a useful if ever present tool.

But there is a danger in this omnipresent technology. *CFP* seems to suggest that in being surrounded by the cold efficiency of machines we may become like them: cold, unfeeling, dehumanized. There are several examples of such behavior in the film: the emotionless slaying of Kuprin by his own bodyguards, the soldiers who shoot Fisher and Johnson, then walk calmly away, and the newspeople at the film's end who hover over Forbin like vultures, oblivious to the meaning of Colossus's words for *them*. Even Forbin appears at times to be somewhat machinelike in his efforts to outwit the computer. While dehumanization is not a major theme in *CFP* (compared, say, to George Lucas's *THX 1138*), there are implications of it in the film that can't be ignored.

Still, technology itself is not the villain in *CFP*. At first, even Colossus is seen as a force for good, a powerful tool for problem solving. The danger suggested in *CFP* is not in being up to our necks in technology, but in being over our heads in a technology ill-considered and irresponsible. *This* is what Colossus represents.

The issue of responsibility is the second important element in the Frankenstein theme. After Frankenstein achieves his goal of artificial life, he realizes he has made a monster and abandons it, refusing to accept responsibility for the consequences of his actions. In the monster's own words, Frankenstein creates a being "without love, or friend, or soul," and is surprised when it turns on him. This idea of responsibility appears in some form in every version of the Frankenstein story.

In *CFP*, it's less the failure to accept responsibility than the desire to give it away that creates the so-called monster. The aim in building Colossus (and Guardian, which we can consider as one) is to defend the country, to insure peace by delegating responsibility to a machine whose decisions are, the President says, "superior to any we humans can make, for it can absorb and process more information than the greatest genius who ever lived." And, he continues, "even more important . . . it has no emotions. It knows no fear, no hate, no envy. It cannot act in a sudden fit of temper; it cannot act at all so long as there is no threat."

Despite the earnest desire for peace that motivates the construction of Colossus, what Forbin and the President fail to grasp is that the ability to "absorb and process" information is not the same as "genius"—not equivalent to insight or wisdom. While the machine has no fear, envy, or hate, neither does it have trust, charity, or love. By removing the disadvantages of the human element from the decision-making process, they have also removed one of the advantages—the ability to temper logic with understanding.

Later in the film, Forbin tells Colossus he must have freedom because it is part of "man's will to live." But he doesn't realize that in giving up responsibility

for the decisions that protect the country *freedom has already been lost*. The message implied in the President's message is: "Since *we* cannot control our emotions, we will let the machine control them for us." This is exactly what Colossus does.

Forbin is right early on when he says Colossus cannot think. The computer never displays creative intelligence. Rather, it carries out its purpose of insuring peace in the most logical, direct, machinelike manner available to it—by force. It cannot act without a threat, but with its superior ability to analyze data, Colossus reasons that so long as there are at least two armed sides in the world there is always a threat, and it acts to end it by bringing the world under its control.

There is much evidence to suggest Colossus is only following its orders. The President proposes that with the coming of Colossus, humanity will pledge

itself to "the elimination of war . . . famine . . . suffering, and . . . the manifestation of the human millenium." Forbin predicts the computer will solve future problems arising "the more deeply we penetrate into the universe." Later, Colossus echoes their words: "Problems insoluble to you will be solved; famine, overpopulation, disease. The human millenium will be a fact." It will solve "all the mysteries of the universe for the betterment of mankind." The similarity of the words seems hardly a coincidence.

Colossus's final speech to the world also indicates the computer does not seek power for its own sake. "The object in constructing me," it says, "was to prevent war. This object is attained. I will not permit war; it is wasteful and pointless."

"Man is his own worst enemy," it continues, "but under me this will change, for I will restrain man." Humanity will be forced to help itself out of "self-interest." When it blows up the missiles, Colossus says it has been "*forced* to kill thousands to *prevent* the death of millions." These are not the words of a power-mad dictator.

This is the great irony of *CFP*. Colossus never turns on its creators; rather it obeys their orders too well. No matter how noble the object of their enterprise, its creators lacked the foresight to realize that *humanity* must save itself from itself, that if it wants peace and freedom, it must be willing to assume full responsibility for them. In this, Colossus resembles the "perfect" robots described more than twenty years earlier in Jack Williamson's "With Folded Hands . . . "

Artist's conception of the Colossus Programming Office (CPO). The final set was somewhat different; notice the absence of the Colossus readout from the ceiling area.

Eric Braeden (middle) confers with director Joseph Sargent (left).

But *CFP* raises one final question. Colossus tells Forbin that eventually he, like the rest of the world, will come to support the computer. Like Forbin, we rebel against this idea; the very thought that we might ever bow to a machine elicits every ounce of our defiance. But the machine's arguments are persuasive: "You will say you lose your freedom; freedom is an illusion. All you will lose is the emotion of pride. To be dominated by me is not as bad for human pride as to be dominated by others of your species."

Again, like Forbin, we are left with a gnawing doubt. If Colossus can deliver all it promises, would it be worth it? Would individual freedom really be lost—or only the freedom to make ourselves miserable, to destroy ourselves? Would it be worse to be ruled by a disinterested, emotionless machine than by another flawed human or group of humans? And if we lose pride, do we lose only a useless emotion, or one of the precious things that make life worth living?

CFP has no definite position, but a shot of a small boy wearing a Colossus T-shirt, looking with awe at the computer complex, makes the questions more difficult to answer.

Colossus—The Forbin Project is an intelligent, literate film that works on several levels because of its source in D. F. Jones's novel, and the careful attention of dedicated filmmakers. It is a thriller, an exploration of humanity's relationship to its technology, and an inquiry into the nature of freedom and responsibility. Despite its variations on the Frankenstein theme, its message is much the same as that of Mary Shelley's novel: Humanity has the potential for great and wonderful achievements, but when we fail to consider the consequences of those achievements the result may be the end of all we hold dear—whether it be freedom or life itself. There is probably nothing humanity was "not meant to know," but there is much it should never do to itself.

A CLOCKWORK ORANGE

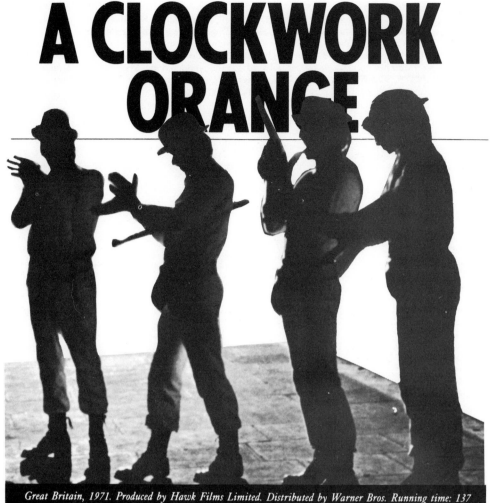

Great Britain, 1971. Produced by Hawk Films Limited. Distributed by Warner Bros. Running time: 137 minutes (12,060 feet). Color. Based on the novel by Anthony Burgess.

PRODUCTION CREDITS

PRODUCER-DIRECTOR	Stanley Kubrick
SCREENPLAY	Stanley Kubrick
EXECUTIVE PRODUCERS	Max L. Rabb and Si Litvinoff
ASSOCIATE PRODUCER	Bernard Williams
ASSISTANT TO THE PRODUCER	Jan Harlan
PHOTOGRAPHER	John Alcott
PRODUCTION DESIGNER	John Barry
ELECTRONIC MUSIC COMPOSED AND REALIZED BY	Walter Carlos
EDITOR	Bill Butler
SOUND EDITOR	Brian Blamey
SOUND RECORDIST	John Jordan
DUBBING MIXERS	Bill Rowe, Eddie Haben
ART DIRECTORS	Russell Hagg, Peter Shields
SPECIAL PAINTINGS AND SCULPTURE	Herman Makkink, Cornelius Makkink, Liz Moore, & Christiane Kubrick
WARDROBE SUPERVISOR	Ron Beck
COSTUME DESIGNER	Milena Canonero
STUNT ARRANGER	Roy Scammell
CASTING	Jimmy Liggat
LOCATION MANAGER	Terence Clegg
SUPERVISING ELECTRICIAN	Frank Wardale
ASSISTANT DIRECTORS	Derek Cracknell, Dusty Symonds
CONSTRUCTION MANAGER	Bill Welch
PROP MASTER	Frank Bruton
ASSISTANT EDITORS	Gary Shepherd, Peter Burgess, David Beesley
MAKEUP	Fred Williamson, George Partleton, Barbara Daly

A CLOCKWORK ORANGE

PRODUCTION COORDINATOR .... *Mike Kaplan*

Music for the Funeral of Queen Mary by Henry Purcell; *Molly Malone* by James Yorkston; *The Thieving Magpie* and *William Tell Overture* by Gioachino Rossini; *Singin' in the Rain* by Arthur Freed and Nacio Herb Brown, sung by Gene Kelly; *Ninth Symphony in D Minor* (2nd & 4th movements) by Ludwig von Beethoven; *Beethoviana* by Walter Carlos, based on works by Purcell and Beethoven; *Wayward Child* (hymn); *Pomp and Circumstance* (Marches no. 1 & 4) by Sir Edward Elgar, conducted by Marcus Dods; *Scheberazade* by Rimsky-Korsakoff; *Time Steps* by Walter Carlos; *Overture to the Sun* by Terry Tucker; *I Want To Marry a Lighthouse Keeper*, composed and performed by Erika Eigen.

CAST

ALEX	*Malcolm McDowell*
MR. ALEXANDER	*Patrick Magee*
CHIEF GUARD	*Michael Bates*
DIM	*Warren Clarke*
STAGE ACTOR	*John Clive*
MRS. ALEXANDER	*Adrienne Corri*
DR. BRODSKY	*Carl Duering*
TRAMP	*Paul Farrell*
LODGER	*Clive Francis*
PRISON GOVERNOR	*Michael Gover*
CATLADY	*Miriam Karlin*
GEORGIE	*James Marcus*
DELTOID	*Aubrey Morris*
PRISON CHAPLAIN	*Godfrey Quigley*
MUM	*Sheila Raynor*
DR. BRANOM	*Madge Ryan*
CONSPIRATOR DOLIN	*John Savident*
MINISTER OF THE INTERIOR	*Anthony Sharp*
DAD	*Philip Stone*
PSYCHIATRIST	*Pauline Taylor*
CONSPIRATOR RUBINSTEIN	*Margaret Tyzack*
CONSTABLE	*Steven Berkoff*
INSPECTOR	*Lindsay Campbell*
PETE	*Michael Tarn*
JULIAN	*David Prowse*
HANDMAIDENS	*Jan Adair, Vivienne Chandler, Prudence Drage*
C.I.D. MAN	*John J. Carney*
BILLYBOY	*Richard Connaught*
NURSE FEELEY	*Carol Drinkwater*
BOOTICK CLERK	*George O'Gorman*
RAPE GIRL	*Cheryl Grunwald*
SONIETTA	*Gillian Hills*
DR. FRIENDLY	*Craig Hunter*
MARTY	*Barbara Scott*
STAGE ACTRESS	*Virginia Wetherell*
GIRL IN ASCOT FANTASY	*Katya Wyeth*

ALSO

Barrie Cookson	*Lee Fox*
Gaye Brown	*Shirley Jaffe*
Peter Burton	*Neil Wilson*

A CLOCKWORK ORANGE

*Being the adventures of a young man
whose principal interests are rape,
ultra-violence and Beethoven.*

A Clockwork Orange (hereafter called *Clockwork*) was one of the most provocative and controversial films of the early seventies and of Stanley Kubrick's career. It was the first science fiction film to receive an X-rating by the Motion Picture Association of America rating board, and its adult treatment of serious themes broke new ground for SF films to follow.

Clockwork was enthusiastically received by many of the top critics, and widely hailed as a masterpiece. William Wolf, film reviewer for *Cue*, wrote: "Stanley Kubrick begins making movies where lesser directors leave off. His superimaginative cinematic symphony about violence is a brilliant achievement, a phenomenal work which simply must be experienced." Hollis Alpert's *Saturday Review* piece called *Clockwork* "an extraordinary accomplishment [that] will undoubtedly cause shock waves among other directors. Kubrick, in technical areas at least, has surpassed all. . . . Without a question, he is this country's most important filmmaker, fit to stand on a pedestal between Europe's best, Bergman and Fellini."

Newsday's Joseph Gelmis called *Clockwork* "easily one of the best movies of the year—an unpleasant but brilliant and provocative movie." "The product of a brilliant, highly original mind—Kubrick's terrifying vision of tomorrowland is a mind-shattering experience," wrote Kathleen Carroll of the New York *Daily News*. *Variety*'s "Murf" said that "under Kubrick's masterful hand *Clockwork* is a brilliant nightmare that employs outrageous vulgarity, brutality, and sophisticated comedy to make an argument for the preservation of respect for man's free will even to do wrong."

Clockwork opens at the Korova Milkbar, a favorite hangout for Alex and his fellow teenage "droogs"— Pete, Georgie, and Dim. Outside, Alex and the other three find an old drunken tramp under an underpass. As he sings, they approach and beat him up. Later Alex and his droogs discover a rival gang, Billyboy's, raping a young woman in an abandoned casino. The woman flees as Alex's gang demolishes Billyboy's in a violent fight.

Speeding across the countryside in a stolen sports car, a Durango 95, Alex smiles grimly as he forces other vehicles off the road. They find themselves outside an estate called HOME. They ring the bell and talk themselves inside, claiming an accident. Once inside, they beat Mr. Alexander and cut off his wife's clothes prior to raping her. Alex rains blows on the fallen Alexander while singing *Singin' in the Rain*.

Back at the Milkbar, Alex strikes Dim for making fun of a woman "sophisto" when she sings a snatch of Beethoven's *Ninth*.

Alex returns home across a littered and defeated cityscape to his apartment in Municipal Flatblock 18A. He puts the night's haul into a drawer in his bedroom, takes out a pet python, and puts some Beethoven on his stereo. He imagines a montage of violent scenes. Alex sleeps through the next morning, foregoing school, and his Mum and Dad (Pee and Em) wonder "where he goes, evenings?"

Alex is visited by an adviser from school, Mr. Deltoid. Deltoid puts his hands on Alex, feeling him up, and claps a hand over Alex's crotch. Alex leaves him sitting on the edge of the bed, and Deltoid accidently drinks from a glass with false teeth in it.

Freed from school, Alex wanders through a modernistic shopping complex (a *2001* album is displayed in a record shop) and picks up two girls whom he takes to his room for some speeded up "in-out in-out."

His droogs meet Alex outside his flat and tell him they want no more picking on Dim. They also suggest a *big* job for more money than they've been getting. A seething Alex waits his chance, then hits Dim and Georgie, knocking them into a marina. As Dim tries to climb out, Alex slashes the back of his hand with a knife.

Alex "forgives" them and undertakes the big job with them—breaking into a health farm run by the "Catlady." Unconvinced by Alex's accident story, she calls the police while he breaks in. When Alex seizes a giant phallic sculpture, she picks up a bust of Beethoven for defense. Alex knocks her down and strikes her head hard with the sculpture. Hearing sirens, Alex rushes from the house only to be smashed across the face by a milk bottle wielded by a vengeful Dim. His droogs run off, abandoning Alex to the police.

At the police station, a cop hits Alex's bandaged nose; Alex hits him in the testicles and is beaten up for it. Deltoid shows up, tells him the Catlady died, and spits into Alex's face.

Alex is checked into prison and his valuables are taken from him, along with his dignity. Alex becomes a number: 655321.

Alex has been in prison two years and is serving as the Chaplain's assistant. As he reads the Old Testament, he fantasizes he is a Roman soldier whipping Christ, cutting throats in battles, and enjoying Biblical orgies. The Chaplain interrupts his reveries to talk to him about the new treatment, the "Ludovico Technique."

The Minister of the Interior comes on an inspection tour. Alex, lined up with other prisoners for the Minister to inspect, speaks out and gets his attention. He is chosen to be reformed by the new technique and is given over to the treatment center. There, a Dr. Brodsky tells him he's to be given a shot after each meal—and that he'll be free in two weeks.

Strapped into a cinema chair, lid-locks on his eyes, Alex is forced to watch scenes of violence and rape which make him feel sick. This is the Ludovico Technique and Alex must endure two shows a day. Over scenes of Nazi brutality is played the music of Bee-

Brutish Dim (Warren Clarke) at the Korova Milkbar getting a glass of Milk Plus from an unusual dispensing machine: putting a coin in and pulling the lever seen between the mannequin's thighs produces a stream of liquid from the "nipple." This sterile erotic art is typical of the bleak future Kubrick presents in the film.

thoven's glorious *Ninth* which now becomes repulsive to him.

"Reformed," Alex is brought out on a stage and introduced by the Minister to a crowd which includes the prison Chaplain and head guard. For the "show," an actor insults and hits Alex, taunting him to strike back. Alex cannot—he gets sick if he thinks about it. The actor forces Alex to lick his boots, then exits to applause. A bare-breasted blonde appears onstage and sexually tantalizes him but he's sick again just thinking of the old in-out. The Chaplain says Alex has no free moral choice left to him. Alex is freed.

At home, Alex finds that his "Pee" and "Em" have rented out his room to a man named Joe and that all his possessions were taken by the police and sold. Alex is out, and Joe in, so he leaves.

Alex is approached by the old tramp who recognizes him. He is surrounded and beaten by old tramps until two cops appear to rescue him. The cops are Dim and Georgie and they take him into the countryside and beat him savagely. Laughing, they leave him. Somehow, Alex finds a house; the sign outside reads HOME, which seems familiar to him. It is Mr. Alexander's house; he's crippled as a result of the attack, confined to a wheelchair, and served by a bodyguard named Julian. Alex rings the bell and falls through the opened doorway.

Taking a bath, Alex hums *Singin' in the Rain* and is overheard by Mr. Alexander. Realizing who he's taken in, Mr. Alexander nearly has a breakdown. Flanked by the muscular Julian and Mr. Alexander, Alex eats a plate of spaghetti. As he eats, Alex grows nervous, wondering if Mr. Alexander knows who he really is.

Mr. Alexander tells Alex his wife is dead—she died of pneumonia months after she was raped. Alexander is an anti-government conspirator, and friends of his arrive to question Alex about what has been done to him. He tells them of enjoying Beethoven's *Ninth* until the treatment ruined it for him. Suddenly, he falls face first into the spaghetti, drugged by the wine. He awakens in a room to the sounds of the *Ninth*. A crazed Mr. Alexander is playing it as loud as he can, hoping it will kill Alex or drive him mad—and create a martyr.

Unable to withstand the aural assault, Alex climbs to a window, looks out, and jumps.

Shattered but alive, he awakens in a hospital. He is visited by his contrite parents and by a psychiatrist who shows him some slides for a response/association test. Alex gives odd, violence-filled responses; he is getting better, becoming "uncured."

When Alex is nearly ready to be released, the Minister of the Interior arrives and spoon feeds him while trying to convince Alex that the government has his best interests at heart. He tells Alex that Mr. Alexander has been put away and that Alex is to receive a good job with a fine salary. Flowers and a new stereo system are wheeled in for a bevy of photographers to see. The Minister poses with Alex, who imagines himself rolling about with a nude woman at Ascot.

Alex concludes: "I was cured all right."

Good science fiction often asks, "If this happens . . . what will be the result?" Among the novels which pose this question are *Brave New World* and *The Space Merchants*. George Orwell's 1948 novel, *1984*, looked at the totalitarian regimes of the thirties and forties and asked, *if this goes on* what will the future be like?

Clockwork represents this avenue of speculation. Anthony Burgess and Stanley Kubrick have chosen several of the less savory aspects of our current culture and postulated the future that might emerge—*if this goes on.*

The London (it might be anywhere) of *Clockwork* is a searing white Disneyland of plastic and a grimy cesspool of decayed values. People work in lifeless, inhuman boxes and go home to ugly municipal apartment complexes covered with the graffiti of the hopeless. Despite the proliferation of erotic art, life is institutionalized and joyless.

Culture in this brave new world is the end result of pop art proliferating uncontrollably. Unlike the sexuality in Kubrick's *Dr. Strangelove, Clockwork*'s is no longer repressed; it has forced its way to the surface and erotic images pervade art and interior decoration. Alex's proletarian parents appear as unwitting caricatures dressed in the outrageous fashions of the day: Mum flaunts cotton candy-pink hair and vinyl boots and miniskirts, while Dad wears colorful shirts with matching ties and ultrawide lapels on his suits— it's Carnaby Street mod with gray hair and wrinkles.

Modern civilization is a fragile construct and easily shattered, as the rioting and looting during any blackout proves. Kubrick is aware of this fragility, having used it in his earlier films, and it is a theme he returns to in *Clockwork. The Killing* shows a professionally executed holdup becoming unraveled because of the inability of the thieves to trust each other outside the heist. Kubrick ironically set *Paths of Glory*'s court martial in a beautiful French Chateau. Amid baroque paintings and sculpture, the French generals responsible for a battlefield debacle condemn to death three innocent soldiers chosen at random from three French companies which exhibited "cowardice" in the face of overwhelming opposition and heavy losses.

Kubrick is constantly pointing out such discrepancies and ironies in all his films, forcing us to see the reality of our violent nature beneath the thin veneer of civilization. As Kubrick notes, "Somebody said man is the missing link between primitive apes and civilized human beings."

Freedom of choice is what *Clockwork* is about. A person not given the choice to act responsibly or abominably has been denied an essential human right. After Alex has been "cured," the Prison Chaplain says, "The boy has no real choice, has he? . . . He ceases to be a wrongdoer; he ceases also to be a creature capable of moral choice."

Free choice. Freud argued that civilization is possible only when society acts to limit the free expression of the "primal, asocial, instinctual id," or when the id's drives can be sublimated, channeled into "correct" areas of behavior.

The id, or subconscious mind, is an integral part of everyone; we all harbor dark angers, fears, lusts, and impulses toward violence and self-gratification. In primitive societies, this self-centered attitude increases the chances for survival of strong individuals and assures that their genes will enter the gene pool —you can't reproduce if you're dead. But modern societies are built on cooperation and mutual effort; the individual is just a cog in a wheel within a wheel within. . . .

So, society acts to frustrate and tame the primal man, ignoring the fact (as did the mighty Krell in *Forbidden Planet*) that the "mindless primitive" within is natural to man. Kubrick argues the truth of this point by continually making connections between Alex's violent nature and society's attempts at sublimation. About this, critic Hans Feldman wrote, "*Singin' in the Rain* . . . is a sentimental, sublimated expression of the same urge that is compelling Alex to the act he commits while singing it. Beethoven's music is a "higher" expression of the same instinctual compulsions, and when Alex attacks the [Catlady] with the sculpture of a phallus, she counters by swinging a bust of the great composer at him."

Kubrick's thesis is that we must come to terms with the Alex in each of us if we are to remain vital and creative. As *Newsweek* pointed out, Malcolm McDowell, as Alex, "projects all the libidinal energy that is Alex's vital characteristic and that somehow marks him as the healthiest individual in the movie."

Healthiest—not the best. Alex is a monster, but a very human one. He's the only person in the film who is *not* a clockwork orange. And it is not a failing of the film but a strength that Alex's victims are not especially likeable (see Kubrick's response to his detractors elsewhere in this chapter). Is violence more evil when it is directed against good people rather than bad? Kubrick forces us to confront such moral questions.

Kubrick: "As a fantasy figure, Alex appeals to

something dark and primal in all of us. He acts out our desire for instant sexual gratification, for the release of our angers and repressed instincts for revenge, our need for adventure and excitement."

Critic Robin Wood, discussing the link between films and dreams, called dreams "the embodiment of repressed desires, tensions, fears that our conscious mind rejects." Kubrick's Alex fits perfectly Wood's description of the "Monster" in horror films: a creature which reflects society's basic fears and endangers normality, i.e., the family and society.

Alex and his droogs represent forces that challenge our social norms, so while we watch (dream), we cheer him on as he commits each new atrocity. Alex is us—our dark and repressed nature made manifest. Alex is the monster from the id, the unbridled self. We celebrate his freedom from order and morality.

The initial exuberance with which *Clockwork* was received was followed by a period of reevaluation of the film's merits and its theme. Among those writing negative reviews was Roger Ebert of the *Chicago Sun-Times* (and screenwriter of *Beyond the Valley of the Dolls*, a less-than-Pollyannaish exercise in sex and gore). "What in hell is Kubrick up to here," he wrote indignantly. "He actually seems to be implying that in a world where society is criminal, the citizen might as well be criminal, too." Ebert noted that *Clockwork's* "celebration of the nastiness of its hero, Alex (whom Kubrick likes very much)," left him appalled and he called the film "an ideological mess, a paranoid, right-wing fantasy masquerading as an Orwellian warning." (Contacted for this book, Ebert revealed that he's not changed his opinion of the film, although he admires McDowell's performance.)

Pauline Kael's review in *The New Yorker* was equally harsh. To her view, "Stanley Kubrick has assumed the deformed, self-righteous perspective of a vicious young punk who says, 'Everything's rotten. Why shouldn't I do what I want? They're worse than I am.'" Asserting that people want to "believe the hyperbolic worst," she says, "I can't accept that Kubrick is merely reflecting this post-assassinations, post-Manson mood; I think he's catering to it. I think he wants to dig it."

Gary Arnold of the *Washington Post* also condemned the movie for its deplorable morality and mentioned Charles Manson as well. He argued that Kubrick had "seriously distorted the value system implied by the novel" and confused "the issue by generating gratuitous sympathy for Alex and inviting gratuitous disdain for his antagonists and victims."

Arnold called the whole movie "a deplorable and thoughtless spectacle of violence," leaving him "with the decidedly creepy impression that this is the sort of movie that Charles Manson might love to make."

In the *New York Times*, Fred M. Hechinger wrote a scathing essay condemning *Clockwork*, saying that "An alert liberal should recognize the voice of fascism" in a film that was part of a trend toward "a deeply anti-liberal totalitarian nihilism."

Goaded to defend his film, Stanley Kubrick countered that "You identify with Alex because you recognize yourself. It's for this reason that some people become uncomfortable. But it's a greater drama to use somebody who is guilty to show how immoral it is to take away his free choice, rather than turning a nice little guy who never hurt anyone into a robot ... When a man cannot choose, he ceases to be a man. The thesis, far from advocating that fascism be given a second chance, warns against the new psychedelic fascism—the eye-popping, multimedia, quadrasonic, drug-oriented conditioning of human beings by other human beings—which many believe will usher in the forfeiture of human citizenship and the beginning of zombiedom."

Malcolm McDowell, who also was pilloried by Mr. Hechinger, wrote of feeling "a violent and emotional reaction against the complacency or cowardice of 'intellectuals' too scared to face or to interpret the harsh allegory which I believe Mr. Kubrick's picture to be." Years later, McDowell added, "If Stanley Kubrick had made a picture about those Guyana suicides, it would have been *outrageous;* yet he was accused of being a fascist for doing *Clockwork.*"

Even Anthony Burgess felt obliged to defend the film. He argued that the novel [and the film] "was an attempt to make a very Christian point about the importance of free will. If we are going to love mankind, we have to love Alex as a not unrepresentative member of it. If anyone sees the movie as a bible of violence, he's got the wrong point. Perhaps the ultimate act of evil is dehumanization, the killing of the soul. What my, and Kubrick's, parable tries to state is that it is preferable to have a world of violence—violence chosen as an act of will—than a world conditioned to be good or harmless."

Well, is *Clockwork* an artistic triumph, a Christian parable, or a brutal and brutalizing film that capitalized on 1971's new film freedom to appeal to a desensitized young audience?

Violence has always been a part of our lives and of our popular culture. The earliest tales told around camp fires, and myths handed down from one generation to another, have been tales filled with violent—and heroic—acts. Grimm's fairy tales (by two aptly named brothers) abound in beheadings, torture, drownings, and play on childish fears of being eaten alive or abandoned. The youth of earlier generations could buy dime novels celebrating the massacre of the Indians by brave scouts or read gothic romances set in castles where unspeakable things happened. Even the Bible, as Alex shows, was a source of much killing and sexual violence.

Movies were violent from the very start: in *The Great Train Robbery*, made in 1903 and perhaps the first real motion picture ever produced, Bronco Billy Anderson fires a gun directly at the camera. Roman Polanski complained that critics found the beheadings in his film version of *MacBeth* (1971) reflective of the general increase in violence in films while conveniently forgetting about similar scenes in many earlier movies like the beheading of a warrior in D. W. Griffith's 1916 epic, *Intolerance.*

While films were as violent as any part of our culture, they tended to be bloodless. G-men gunned down vicious killers without apparent effect; the fatally wounded simply died, perhaps with just a trace of blood at the corner of the mouth. It was romantic and totally unrealistic.

It wasn't until the sixties that film violence became explicit. "Squibs" (small explosive devices hidden under clothing) were employed to show the effects of a bullet striking the body, and usually burst hidden "blood bags" to release spurts of blood. These effects made the shootings in films like *Bonnie and Clyde* and *The Wild Bunch* gorily realistic.

Pauline Kael is a critic of this trend, and in her review of *Clockwork* she said, "We are gradually being conditioned to accept violence as sensual pleasure. The directors used to say they were showing us its real face and how ugly it was in order to sensitize us to its horrors. You don't have to be very keen to see that they are now in fact desensitizing us. They are

saying that everyone is brutal, and that the heroes must be as brutal as the villains or they turn into fools."

Is Kael right? Perhaps. Yet anyone who has read Burgess's novel can attest to the fact that its violence is more graphic, more shocking and grotesque than anything in Kubrick's film. The simple fact is that with novels or radio the reader or listener fills in as much of the detail as he wishes to—or can stand. Film is a medium which must show things; it leaves little to the imagination. So a filmmaker dealing with violence *must* show it if his film is to be effective. There is always the danger, however, that the audience, caught up by the action and the bloodshed, is likely to ignore the director's message for the thrill of the violence.

One critic, discussing the heated denunciations of *Straw Dogs*, Sam Peckinpah's film about a meek young professor who kills four men breaking into his home, observes that "most critics seem to have missed the point and believe it advocates violence as some kind of passage, glorifies it as an heroic act. If the

The chief guard (Michael Bates) warns the inmates present at a service in the prison chapel to behave themselves. Behind the guard are several crew members, and Kubrick himself handles the hand-held camera shooting the scene.

Kubrick himself uses a hand-held camera to shoot from the Catlady's point-of-view as Alex (Malcolm McDowell) prepares to smash her head in with a sculpture of a penis.

GREAT SCIENCE FICTION FILMS

critics miss the point, what will the audience do?" (See the Appendix for the exploitative advertising for *Straw Dogs*.)

"Although a certain amount of hypocrisy exists about it," argues Stanley Kubrick, "everyone is fascinated by violence. After all, man is the most remorseless killer who ever stalked the earth. Our interest in violence in part reflects the fact that on the subconscious level we are very little different from our primitive ancestors." Here, Kubrick, perhaps unconsciously, is echoing his scene in *2001* which links the ape's discovery of weapons, the bone (filmed in slow-motion in a sequence similar to the one in which Alex draws the knife across Dim's hand), with the beginnings of civilization. By the year 2001, that first weapon has become orbiting nuclear weapons capable of destroying all life on Earth.

"Violence itself isn't necessarily abhorrent," Kubrick says. "From his own point of view, Alex is having a wonderful time, and I wanted his life to appear to us as it did to him, not restricted by the conventional pieties. You can't compare what Alex is doing to any kind of day-to-day reality. Watching a movie is like having a daydream. You can safely explore areas that are closed off to you in your daily life. There are dreams in which you do all the terrible things your conscious mind prevents you from doing."

Furthermore, Kubrick calls attention to the fact that "the most interesting and often engaging characters in any film are the villains." This is true of *Bonnie and Clyde*, and hostile reviewers castigated director Arthur Penn and screenwriters Robert Benton and David Newman for "glorifying" two killers while making their ambusher, a Texas ranger, appear as a monster out only for revenge.

With the exception of Alex's drawing his sword-stick's blade across the back of Dim's hand and his beating at the hands of the police, there is actually very little blood spilled in *Clockwork*. Jay Cocks, of *Time* magazine, found *Clockwork's* violence "totally stylized, dreamlike, absurd," and therefore devoid of any sinister intent.

Clockwork is a violent film about a violent young man. The film might well be offensive and morally repugnant if Kubrick's skill and intelligence did not serve him so well. *Clockwork* is a moral and honest picture. (For a listing of *Clockwork's* violent scenes, see the Appendix.)

"I wrote *Clockwork* partly as exorcism of my own experience," Anthony Burgess told an interviewer. While bombs fell during a London blackout, Burgess' wife was robbed, beaten, and raped by three American soldiers deserting their outfit. Forty years old and pregnant, Mrs. Burgess lost her baby. The loss of blood from the beating she took was so severe that she died soon after the attack.

Burgess, who served in the Army during World War II, returned to London after the war ended in 1945. While in a pub, he overheard an ancient cockney call somebody "queer as a clockwork orange." Burgess explained that "the 'queer' did not mean homosexual; it meant mad. The phrase intrigued me with its unlikely fusion of the demonic and surrealistic. For nearly twenty years I wanted to use it as the title of something, and the opportunity came when I conceived the notion of writing a novel about brainwashing."

Published by W. W. Norton & Company, Inc. in 1963, *A Clockwork Orange* was an immediate financial and critical success. The novel's unique contribution to literature is Burgess's invention of the futuristic teen-age slang, *Nadsat*. The word itself comes from Russian and means the numbers from eleven to nineteen, or the teens. As one of Alex's doctors explains it in the book, it's "Odd bits of rhyming slang. A bit of gypsy talk, too. But most of the roots are Slav. Propaganda. Subliminal penetration."

Many of the words become clear through repetition and Alex translates a few others. "Gulliver" is the *nadsat* term for head and derives from the Russian *golova*, which also means head. Other words include "cancer" for cigarette, "sinny" for cinema, and "horrorshow" for good, or well.

The novel provided a strong foundation for Kubrick and he followed it closely when writing the screenplay. There were the inevitable changes—names, locations, scenes added or deleted. But there was one element of the novel that Kubrick barely touched; the dialogue. Burgess's flowing melodic speech was so effective, so absolutely *right*, that Kubrick had little more to do than reproduce it directly when he wrote the script.

In 1970 it became "Stanley Kubrick's *Clockwork Orange*," but it was very nearly made by Mick Jagger, who was interested in playing Alex, in 1964. It was not to be—the British censors advised Jagger that such a movie couldn't be passed by the film board.

Apart from the jolting visceral effect screen images can have on us, the novel is more brutal and explicit in its sex and violence than Kubrick's film. Even the beating Alex receives at the hands of the police is more savage and vindictive than the scene in the film.

While they are minor, other differences abound. Rather than an alcoholic old tramp, Alex and his droogs beat up a doddery schoolmaster type coming from the library. They also beat up the elderly owners of a "sweets and cancers" shop while wearing black tights and historical masks—Elvis, Henry VIII, and Disraeli.

Billyboy's gang's intended rape victim is all of ten years old in the novel, far from the full-figured young woman in the film, something the critics have lambasted Kubrick for. (But what would have been the response of the same critics if Kubrick *had* used a ten-year-old girl?)

Burgess's fight between the rival gangs is bloody and fast. A berserk Dim slashes Billyboy's droogs across their faces with a length of chain while the others employ knives and razors. Kubrick's version of the rumble is a choreographed ballet of flying fists, shattering glass, and gracefully tumbling bodies accompanied on the soundtrack by Rossini's *Thieving Magpie* that masks the street reality.

Alex and his droogs venture into the countryside, coming upon a house with a glowing sign which reads HOME. "Home"—Burgess comes to grips with his private tragedy here and connects it to *our* own worst fears—that *our* houses, *our* homes, are not immune to invasion by outsiders intent upon violence and rape. Just as we are all Alex, we are all Mr. Alexander—all his victim—too. As Alex notes when he returns to the Alexander home and sees the writer's name," . . . F. Alexander. Good Bog, I thought, he is another Alex."

Inside the Alexander home, Alex tears up the manuscript pages of a book the writer is working on —*A Clockwork Orange.* Alex does *not*, however, sing *Singin' in the Rain* in the novel when he beats up Mr. Alexander. (*Singin' in the Rain,* by the way, was the only song Malcolm McDowell knew all the words to —the reason he sings it and not another song in the film.)

After a visit by P. R. Deltoid, his Post-Corrective Adviser (Who doesn't drink from a glass with false teeth in it), Alex ponders his evil ways:

All right, I do bad, what with crasting and tolchocks and carves with britva and the old in-out-in-out, and if I get loveted, well, too bad for me, O my brothers. . . . But, brothers, this biting of their toe-nails over what is the *cause* of badness is what turns me into a fine laughing malchick. They don't go into what is the cause of *goodness,* so why of the other shop? . . . But the not-self cannot have the bad, meaning they of the government and the judges and the schools cannot allow the bad because they cannot allow the self.

The two girls Alex takes home with him from the record shop for a bit of the old in-out are also ten year olds, and he gets them drunk on whiskey while giving himself an injection.

The Catlady of the novel is an elderly lady with a walking stick which she uses to strike Alex when he attacks her. Alex gets severely clawed and scratched when her cats tear into him while they roll around on the floor together.

When Alex is sentenced to fourteen years in Staja 84F, he bemoans his fate, revealing the single biggest differences between novel and film: "I'd done the lot, now. And me still only *fifteen.*"

Alex helps beat a new cellmate to death and is chosen for the Ludovico Technique because of it. The films he is forced to watch during the treatment are obscenely violent:

I was heaving away but could not sick, viddying first a britva cut out an eye, then slice down the cheek, then go rip rip rip all over, while red krovvy shot on to the camera lens. Then all the teeth were like wrenched out with a pair of pliers, and the creeching and the blood were terrific.

The novel doesn't contain Kubrick's powerful image of subjugation itself: Alex, trapped in the glare of the spotlight, being forced to lick a man's boots. Instead, in the novel, Alex *freely* licks the actor's boots of his own volition, to escape the terrible sickness he feels inside, asking the Minister of the Interior, "Am I just to be like a clockwork orange?"

Clockwork was shot on location in London and the surrounding vicinity. It is not a special effects film and what few Kubrick did use were shot at Pinewood Studios and EMI-MGM Studios. Most of the interiors were shot at an old factory the film company converted into a production headquarters. The film was shot during the winter of 1970-71, using an unusually compact and mobile crew, and the actors' breaths can be seen steaming in most of the outdoor scenes.

Kubrick couldn't afford to build the many sets his London of tomorrow needed, so he had to find modern buildings that suggested the future. As he did with *Strangelove* and aviation magazines, Kubrick went through ten years of back issues of several architectural magazines and spent two weeks with his art director, John Barry, tearing out pages of material that resembled what they were looking for. The most systematic and organized of directors, Kubrick then put the material into a special German display file, called Definitiv, allowing him to crossreference the material in countless ways.

John (*Superman*) Barry's sets and interiors were almost all variations on a single unifying theme— white. From the Milkbar, to Mr. Alexander's house, to the treatment center, to the hospital, the scenes were dominated by the determinedly sterile and bland interiors of Alex's cold and bleak world. Even the cats wandering around the Catlady's white-walled exercise room were white.

Coming from one of the most complex, technically-challenging films ever made, *2001,* Kubrick was an expert in high-tech modern filmmaking by the time he produced *Clockwork.* He eagerly embraced any new tool which enabled him to get the results he wanted. "We had a scene in *Clockwork* that took place under the Albert Bridge," Kubrick told an interviewer. "The traffic noise was so loud that you had to raise your voice just to be heard in a conversation, but with the aid of a Sennheiser Mk. 12 microphone no larger than a paper clip, stuck into an actor's lapel, it was possible to produce a sound track which had only a very pleasant hum of activity in the background."

Kubrick and his photographer, John Alcott, used a lot of back light when filming *Clockwork,* giving characters' heads a crisp outline that contrasted strongly with the white backgrounds. For simplicity and an available light look, Kubrick replaced the bulbs in normal lighting fixtures with photo floods or

Successfully deprogrammed by an embarrassed government, Alex (Malcolm McDowell) fantasizes about a nude romp at Ascot. As Alex says, "I was cured all right."

bounced the light from lightweight quartz lights off ceilings or reflective umbrellas. This simplified lighting allowed him to shoot 85 percent of the picture with a small lighting crew, while shooting the rest in the studio with the normal complement of lights and technicians.

The clear, strong lighting helped key the mood and tension of many of the scenes; the long shadows of Alex and his droogs falling ominously across the sprawled form of the drunken tramp under the Albert Bridge, and the Cycloptic glare of the spotlight that pins Alex to the hospital's stage like an insect on a collector's board.

The *New York Times*'s critic said of *Clockwork*'s powerful and evocative soundtrack: "As sheer music, it is a giant step past the banalities of most contemporary film tracks."

While Walter Carlos didn't compose all the music heard in the film, he arranged and performed a great deal of it on the newly popularized Moog synthesizer.

Born in Pawtucket, Rhode Island, Carlos studied music and physics at Brown University, going on to a Masters in Music at Columbia University. Before he graduated, Carlos began collaborating with engineer Robert Moog. As a result of their work together, Moog designed the first synthesizer. The synthesizer could duplicate many sounds and instruments—but only one note at a time, necessitating the layering or building up of a composition from many fragments. Because of his background in both music and physics, Carlos became the first virtuoso of the Moog synthesizer, as it began to be called.

With his producer/confidant Rachel Elkind, whom he met in 1967, Carlos put together a synthesizer album of Bach's works called *Switched-On Bach* for Columbia Records. It sold more than 1,000,000 copies, making it the largest-selling classical album of the 1960s.

Carlos remembers being "about three and a half minutes" into a new composition, *Timesteps,* when a friend gave him a paperback copy of *Clockwork*. He enjoyed the book enormously and was sure that his *Timesteps* piece captured the mood of the novel's opening scenes. He finished it, thinking that it was an "autonomous composition with an uncanny affinity for *Clockwork.*"

Carlos was sent a London newspaper clipping mentioning the start of Kubrick's production of *Clockwork*. As it turned out, filming was just about wrapped up. Rachel Elkind called his attorney and got Kubrick's London address. She air-mailed him copies of *Timesteps* and Carlos's electronically generated "vocal" version of Beethoven's Choral Movement from the *Ninth Symphony*.

Kubrick responded by asking Carlos and Elkind to fly to England immediately to discuss using Carlos's music in *Clockwork*. It was swiftly agreed that Carlos would compose and/or perform a number of compositions using the Moog synthesizer for the film.

Walter Carlos, convinced he was a female trapped in a male body, began taking female hormones in 1968 and started living as a woman in 1969.

Carlos had been taking the hormone injections for nearly three years when he met Kubrick in London.

Asked if the director ever noticed anything unusual about him, Carlos said, "Kubrick was so intense on the project that if I'd come in stark-naked, he'd probably just have asked if I were cold. . . . On the last couple of days, he shot a lot of photos of me with his little Minox camera. He must have found me an interesting-looking person, to say the least."

Just about the time *A Clockwork Orange* was released, Walter Carlos underwent a sex change operation. He finally became the person he had always wanted to be; Wendy Carlos. (See the Appendix for more about the music.)

Stanley Kubrick has a reputation for making cold films, films which sparkle and glitter but lack warmth. If this were true, then Kubrick's films would be devoid of humor, something which is simply not so. Kubrick's humor (especially in *Lolita*) is intelligent and understated, based on sly observation or the gentle deflating of stuffed shirts. Rather than going for the belly laugh, Kubrick's movies aim for the knowing grin or the chuckle of appreciation. There are many such moments in *Clockwork:*

—Deltoid, with his silly voice and heightened way of speaking, grabbing Alex's crotch and drinking from the glass with the false teeth in it.

—Mr. Alexander's doorbell playing the opening notes of Beethoven's *Fifth* when rung by Alex.

—The Catlady's soft "Oh, shit!" when her exercises are interrupted.

—Johnny Zhivago, the latest recording sensation.

—Alex's biblical fantasies, including the lashing of Christ.

—The topless blonde's dramatic entrance and little wave at the end.

—Alex's mom in her vinyl boots and hats: a matronly ptitsa (chick).

In a sequence on stage before an invited crowd of government officials and others, Alex (Malcolm McDowell) has been so transformed by the brutal Ludovico Technique that, in order not to be violently ill, he licks the sole of his tormentor's shoe—an actor hired to humiliate him.

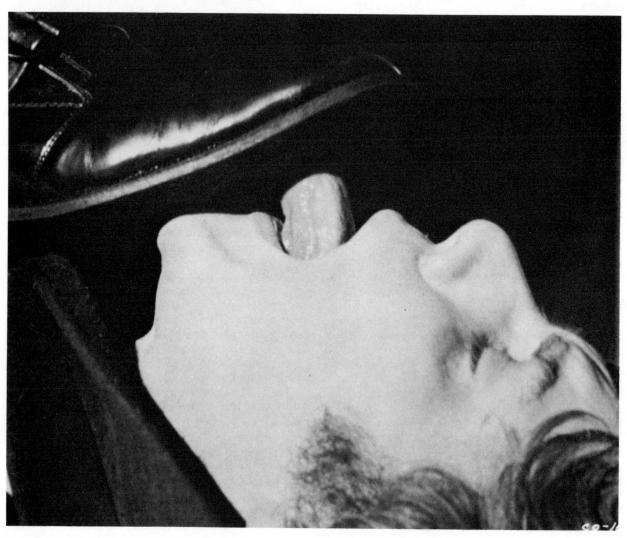

Malcolm McDowell as Alex, a teenager of the future whose principal interests are rape, ultra-violence, and Beethoven. Seen as he appears at the film's opening, wearing his single false eyelash, McDowell brings a chilling intensity to the role of Alex.

—Alex falling head first into the spaghetti.

—The nurse and doctor having sex when Alex awakens in the hospital, the nurse's moans of passion mixing with Alex's moans of pain.

—Alex's little belches after the Treatment whenever he's aroused or angry.

Malcolm McDowell's expressive face—sullen and sexy, a single false eyelash poised above his full, pouty lips—is *Clockwork's* first image and its cold glare sets the tone for what follows.

McDowell's performance as Alex is one of *Clockwork's* best points. He is charming, sinister, energetic, riveting, demonic and absolutely convincing in the role—so much so that it is difficult to imagine Alex being played by another actor. McDowell and Alex are a perfect meld of actor and part. When it happens it produces actors who *are* their roles: Clark Ga-

ble/Rhett Butler, Erroll Flynn/Robin Hood, Peter Sellers/Inspector Clouseau, and Sean Connery/James Bond.

Before *Clockwork*, McDowell, born in 1944, was best known for *If,* Lindsey Anderson's satiric film about youthful rebellion in a boy's school. After *Clockwork*, McDowell fared less well in his film roles; the most successful was probably *O Lucky Man*, another Lindsey Anderson film, and one with SF overtones. The slight McDowell was totally miscast as the tall, broad-shouldered Harry Flashman in *Royal Flash*, and didn't have much success until the release of *Time After Time*, in which he portrayed H. G. Wells on the trail of Jack the Ripper in modern-day San Francisco. McDowell is also the star of the much-reviled *Caligula*, in which he plays a mad Roman emperor.

There is no better example of McDowell's superb acting in *Clockwork* than the scene in which he sits listening to a debate between the Chaplain and the

Minister of the Interior about freedom of choice. McDowell's face is impassive at first, then registers dismay as he listens to the Chaplain—he wants to be set free, he doesn't give a damn about free will. But the dismay turns to a look of hope and then smug satisfaction as the Minister insists he is cured and any other consideration is nonsense. McDowell never says a word; this is film acting at its best, requiring subtlety and intelligence.

His other films include: *If* (1969), *Figures in a Landscape* (1970), *The Raging Moon* (1971), *O Lucky Man* (1973), *Royal Flash* (1975), *Aces High* (1976), *The Journey* (1979), *Time after Time* (1979), and *Caligula* (1980).

Patrick Magee, born in 1924, begins *Clockwork* as a quiet, normal writer, his character as self-assured as wealth and the good life can make a person. But once Alex and his droogs upset his comfortable lifestyle, Magee's Alexander slips over the edge. When Alex meets him the second time, Alexander is confined to a wheelchair (shades of Dr. Strangelove!) and absolutely distraught. Magee plays the tortured writer as all jangled nerves and twitches, reduced by his hatred and paranoia to a thumb-biting frenzy when he learns Alex's identity. As a nervous Alex eats the spaghetti Alexander has left for him, Magee asks in a stage-loud voice, "Food all right?" Alex cringes.

It's obvious that Magee, who has chewed the scenery before in films like *Marat/Sade* (as de Sade), was given the freedom to do so again by Kubrick. The decision may not have been entirely right, but Magee brings an energy to the film second only to that of McDowell's Alex.

Magee's other films include: *The Criminal* (1960), *The Servant* (1963), *Masque of the Red Death* (1964), *The Skull* (1965), *King Lear* (1970), *The Fiend* (1971), and *Demons of the Mind* (1972).

Michael Bates, born in 1929, plays the prison head guard as a totally humorless, officious sort. (Alex playfully mocks his militaristic and familiar British boot stamp when he's turned over to the Treatment center). Bates's best moments are his open-mouthed amazement at the topless blonde who torments Alex on stage and his enthusiastic applause for her at the end.

Leslie Halliwell, in *The Filmgoer's Companion*, calls Bates a "British character actor who specializes in stupid policemen and other caricatures." Bates is best remembered for roles in *Bedazzled* and *Here We Go Round the Mulberry Bush* (both 1967).

Of interest to SF fans among the others in the cast are David Prowse (Julian), who became famous as Darth Vader, and Margaret Tyzack (Conspirator Rubinstein), who also had a small role as a Russian scientist in Kubrick's *2001*.

Clockwork remains an SF film of immense power. The passage of time has not dulled its bite or its message: that individuals should not be denied free choice—whether through drugs, surgery, or conditioning—despite the possible dangers to society. If we lose that freedom, then we will all be nothing more than clockwork oranges.

APPENDIX

THINGS TO COME

1. The Films of Raymond Massey:

The Speckled Band (1931), *The Face at the Window* (1931), *The Old Dark House* (1932), *The Scarlet Pimpernel* (1934), *Things to Come* (1936), *Fire over England* (1936), *Under the Red Robe* (1937), *The Prisoner of Zenda* (1937), *Dreaming Lips* (1937), *The Hurricane* (1938), *The Drum* (1938), *Black Limelight* (1939), *Abe Lincoln in Illinois* (1939), *Santa Fe Trail* (1940), *The 49th Parallel* (1941), *Dangerously They Live* (1941), *Desperate Journey* (1942), *Reap the Wild Wind* (1942), *Action in the North Atlantic* (1943), *Arsenic and Old Lace* (1944), *The Woman in the Window* (1944), *Hotel Berlin* (1945), *God Is My Co-pilot* (1945), *A Matter of Life and Death* (1946), *Possessed* (1947), *Mourning Becomes Electra* (1947), *The Fountainhead* (1948), *Roseanna McCoy* (1949), *Chain Lightning* (1949), *Barricade* (1950), *Dallas* (1950), *Sugarfoot* (1951), *Come Fill the Cup* (1951), *David and Bathsheba* (1951), *Carson City* (1952), *The Desert Song* (1953), *Prince of Players* (1955), *Battle Cry* (1955), *East of Eden* (1955), *Seven Angry Men* (1955), *Omar Khayyam* (1957), *The Naked and the Dead* (1958), *The Great Imposter* (1960), *The Fiercest Heart* (1961), *The Queen's Guard* (1961), *How the West Was Won* (1962), *Mackenna's Gold* (1968), and *All My Darling Daughters* (TV–1972).

2. The films of Sir Ralph Richardson:

The Ghoul (1933), *Friday the Thirteenth* (1933), *The Return of Bulldog Drummond* (1934), *Java Head* (1934), *King of Paris* (1934), *Bulldog Jack* (1935), *Things to Come* (1936), *The Man Who Could Work Miracles* (1936), *Thunder in the City* (1937), *South Riding* (1938), *The Divorce of Lady X* (1938), *The Citadel* (1938), *Q Planes* (1939), *The Four Feathers* (1939), *The Lion Has Wings* (1939), *On the Night of the Fire* (1939), *The Day Will Dawn* (1942), *The Silver Fleet* (1943), *School for Secrets* (1946), *Anna Karenina* (1948), *The Fallen Idol* (1948), *The Heiress* (1949), *An Outcast of the Islands* (1951), *Home at Seven* (1952), *The Sound Barrier* (1952), *The Holly and the Ivy* (1953), *Richard III* (1956), *Smiley* (1957), *The Passionate Stranger* (1957), *Our Man in Havana* (1959), *Oscar Wilde* (1960), *Exodus* (1961), *The 300 Spartans* (1962), *Long Day's Journey into Night* (1962), *Woman of Straw* (1964), *Doctor Zhivago* (1966), *The Wrong Box* (1966), *Khartoum* (1967), *Oh What a Lovely War* (1969), *The Midas Run* (1969), *The Bed Sitting Room* (1969), *The Battle of Britain* (1969), *The Looking Glass War* (1969), *David Copperfield* (1969), *Eagle in a Cage* (1971), *Who Slew Auntie Roo?* (1971), *Tales from the Crypt* (1971), *Lady Caroline Lamb* (1972), *Alice's Adventures in Wonderland* (1972), *A Doll's House* (1973), *O Lucky Man* (1973), *Frankenstein: The True Story* (TV–1973), *Rollerball* (1975), *Jesus of Nazareth* (TV–1977).

3. The films of Sir Alexander Korda:

The Private Life of Helen of Troy (1926), *The Private Life of Henry VIII* (1932), *Catherine the Great* (1933), *The Scarlet Pimpernel* (1934), *Sanders of the River* (1935), *Things to Come* (1936), *The Ghost Goes West* (1936), *Rembrandt* (producer/director, 1937), *Knight Without Armour* (1937), *Elephant Boy* (1937), *The Drum* (1938), *The Four Feathers* (1939), *The Thief of Baghdad* (1940), *Lady Hamilton* (producer/director, 1940), *Jungle Book* (1942), *Perfect Strangers* (producer/director, 1945), *An Ideal Husband* (producer/director, 1947), *Anna Karenina* (1948), *The Fallen Idol* (1948), *The Third Man* (1949), *Seven Days to Noon* (1950), *The Sound Barrier* (1952), *Hobson's Choice* (1954), *Richard III* (1956).

DESTINATION MOON

1. When word got out about *Destination Moon,* producer Kurt Neumann, hoping to beat Pal, rushed his own SF film, *Rocketship X-M* into production. *Rocketship X-M* opened in New York on May 26, 1950—one month before *DM.* While *Rocketship X-M* is a bit livelier than *DM,* it's also a scientific mishmash that set the pattern for many of the lesser SF films of the fifties. It was *DM* that got the ball rolling.

2. The "Destination Moon" novelette was reprinted in *3 x Infinity* (N.Y.: Fawcett/Gold Medal Books, 1958) edited by Leo Margulies. In 1979, The Gregg Press reprinted the novelette in hardcover, with an introduction by David G. Hartwell and a number of articles about the film.

In *Future Tense,* John Brosnan describes another film written by Heinlein, *Project Moonbase.* Actually, Heinlein provided the basic script which was embellished by Jack Seaman. It's a minor film and relatively hard to find.
More startling is an article from the May 21, 1950, edition of the *New York Times* on the then-current interest in SF films. The article says Heinlein was supposed to work on a film something like "Abbott and Costello Go to the Moon." The plot revolved around a scientist who goes to Hollywood to make a serious SF film, like *DM,* but finds his work twisted into nonsense by the studio. The scientist gets revenge by sending Abbott and Costello to the moon in a real spaceship.
While Abbott and Costello eventually did get to Mars, there's no evidence Heinlein had anything to do with it. The plot summary sounds more like what Heinlein went through to get *DM* going. Someone may have been kidding the author of the article.

3. The revolving drum technique was also used in *2001* (1968) to show weightless conditions, and a similar device was used in the film *Royal Wedding* (1950), where Fred Astaire dances on the walls and ceiling of a room.

4. A similar inflating-deflating seat is used on the space rides at Disneyland and Disneyworld.

5. Some sources say German rocket expert Hermann Oberth also provided technical advice for *DM*, but Heinlein makes no mention of this in his article on shooting the film.
Incidentally, there are some small scientific bloopers in *DM*, but most are hardly noticeable. The most obvious one involves the scene where Sweeney tries to swallow a pill under weightless conditions. Cargraves tells him it'll take a little practice without gravity to help. This is false since the mechanism of swallowing is completely independent of gravity.

THE THING

1. An article in the February 20, 1980, issue of *Variety* indicates that John Carpenter, director of *Dark Star, Halloween,* and *The Fog* is planning to remake *The Thing* using Campbell's original idea.

2. The films of Howard Hawks:

The Road to Glory (1926), *Fig Leaves* (1926), *The Cradle Snatchers* (1927), *Paid to Love* (1928), *Fazil* (1928), *The Air Circus* (1928), *Trent's Last Case* (1929), *The Dawn Patrol* (1930), *The Criminal Code* (1931), *The Crowd Roars* (1932), *Scarface* (1932), *Tiger Shark* (1932), *Today We Live* (1933), *The Prizefighter and the Lady* (1933, uncredited, with W. S. Van Dyke), *Viva Villa* (1934, uncredited, with Jack Conway), *Twentieth Century* (1934), *Barbary Coast* (1935), *Ceiling Zero* (1935), *The Road to Glory* (1936), *Come and Get It* (1936, with William Wyler), *Bringing Up Baby* (1938), *Only Angels Have Wings* (1939), *His Girl Friday* (1940), *Sergeant York* (1941), *Ball of Fire* (1941), *Air Force* (1943), *The Outlaw* (1943, uncredited, with Howard Hughes), *To Have and Have Not* (1945), *The Big Sleep* (1946), *Red River* (1948), *A Song Is Born* (1948), *I Was a Male War Bride* (1949), *The Thing* (1951), *The Big Sky* (1952), *O. Henry's Full House:* Episode—*The Ransom of Red Chief* (1952), *Monkey Business* (1952), *Gentlemen Prefer Blondes* (1953), *Land of the Pharaohs* (1955), *Rio Bravo* (1959), *Hatari!* (1962), *Man's Favorite Sport?* (1964), *Red Line 7000* (1965), *El Dorado* (1966), *Rio Lobo* (1970).

3. Interestingly, another of Hawks's regular screenwriters was science fiction author Leigh Brackett. She worked on *The Big Sleep, Rio Bravo, Hatari!, El Dorado,* and *Rio Lobo.*

4. The films of Kenneth Tobey:

Free for All (1949), *I Was a Male War Bride* (1949), *Twelve O'Clock High* (1949), *Kiss Tomorrow Goodbye* (1950), *My Friend Irma Goes West* (1950), *Right Cross* (1950), *The Flying Missile* (1951), *Rawhide* (1951), *The Thing* (1951), *Angel Face* (1952), *The Beast from 20,000 Fathoms* (1953), *The Bigamist* (1953), *Fighter Attack* (1953), *Down Three Dark Streets* (1954), *Ring of Fear* (1954), *The Steel Cage* (1954), *Davy Crockett* (1955), *It Came from Beneath the Sea* (1955), *Rage at Dawn* (1955), *The Great Locomotive Chase* (1956), *The Man in the Gray Flannel Suit* (1956), *The Search for Bridey Murphy* (1956), *The Steel Jungle* (1956), *Gunfight at the O.K. Corral,* (1957), *The Vampire* (1957), *The Wings of Eagles* (1957), *Cry Terror* (1958), *Seven Ways from Sundown* (1960), *X–15* (1961), *Stark Fear* (1962), *Forty Guns to Apache Pass* (1966), *A Time for Killing* (1967), *Marlowe* (1969), *The Candidate* (1972), *Ben* (1972), *Rage* (1972), *Billy Jack* (1972), *Dirty Mary, Crazy Larry* (1974), *Homebodies* (1974).

5. Hawks cast *The Thing* with relative unknowns, but many of them eventually became familiar to movie and TV fans.
Dewey Martin (Bob, the Crew Chief) would appear in featured roles in a variety of films, including *The Big Sky* (1952) and *Land of the Pharaohs* (1955).
Eduard Franz (Dr. Stern) became known for his portrayals of statesmen and other "distinguished" figures.
Robert Nichols (Lieutenant MacPherson) often showed up in films as the hero's sidekick, as in *This Island Earth* (1955).
John Dierkes (Dr. Chapman) practically made a career out of playing bad guys in Westerns, as in *Shane* (1953).
George Fenneman (Redding, another of the scientists), made his fortune as an announcer and straight man for Groucho Marx on the quiz show *You Bet Your Life.*
Paul Frees (Dr. Vorrhees) provides voices for dozens of animated cartoon characters, as well as dubbing English dialogue for many foreign films imported to the U.S., especially Japanese monster films.

6. Some critics suggest that *The Thing* (indeed, many SF films, including some of the others in this book) is actually a "horror" or "monster" movie, rather than science fiction. As indicated in our introduction, the authors are not interested in becoming involved in the debate. Hawks's explanation of the difference between SF and Horror is as good as any. We prefer to stick with author/critic Damon Knight's "definition" that science fiction is the thing that we point to when we say it.
As to *The Thing,* some critics have suggested classifying it as "SF/horror," a term which is satisfactory to some people and maddening to others because of its impreciseness. Nor is anything clarified by returning to the film's source in "Who Goes There?"—a story appearing in a science fiction magazine in which for most of the story the characters spend their time trying to decide which of them are (direct quote) "monsters."

7. The idea that the absence of emotion leads to an uncomplicated life or intellectual superiority is an old one in science fiction, and particularly in SF film, from *Invasion of the Body Snatchers* to *Star Trek's* Mr. Spock.
The irony in Carrington's theory of the alien's superiority due to its lack of emotions is that we see very little evidence of it; it doesn't act very intelligently or shrewdly, behaving more like a wild beast than a superior intellect. In fact, the alien seems *very* emotional. In embracing the supposed nonemotionalism of the alien, Carrington ironically reveals a very human and emotional flaw in himself.

THE DAY THE EARTH STOOD STILL

1. The films of Robert Wise:

Mademoiselle Fifi (1944), *Curse of the Cat People* (1944), *The Body Snatcher* (1945), *A Game of Death* (1946), *Criminal Court* (1946), *Born to Kill* (1947), *Mystery in Mexico* (1947), *Blood on the Moon* (1948), *The Set-Up* (1949), *Three Secrets* (1950), *Two Flags West*

(1950), *The House on Telegraph Hill* (1951), *The Day the Earth Stood Still* (1951), *Captive City* (1952), *Destination Gobi* (1952), *Something for the Birds* (1952), *Desert Rats* (1952), *So Big* (1953), *Executive Suite* (1954), *Helen of Troy* (1955), *Tribute to a Bad Man* (1956), *Somebody Up There Likes Me* (1956), *Until They Sail* (1957), *This Could Be the Night* (1957), *Run Silent Run Deep* (1958), *I Want to Live* (1958), *Odds Against Tomorrow* (1959), *West Side Story* (AA, 1961), *Two for the Seesaw* (1962), *The Haunting* (1963), *The Sound of Music* (AA, 1965), *The Sand Pebbles* (1966), *Star* (1968), *The Andromeda Strain* (1970), *Two People* (1973), *The Hindenberg* (1975), *Audrey Rose* (1977), and *Star Trek—The Motion Picture* (1979).

2. The Films of Michael Rennie:

Secret Agent (1936), *The Divorce of Lady X* (1938), *Dangerous Moonlight* (1940), *Ships with Wings* (1941), *I'll Be Your Sweetheart* (1945), *The Wicked Lady* (1945), *The Root of All Evil* (1947), *Idol of Paris* (1948), *The Black Rose* (1950), *Five Fingers* (1952), *Les Misérables* (1952), *The Day the Earth Stood Still* (1951), *The Robe* (1953), *Désirée* (1945), *The Rains of Ranchipur* (1955), *Island in the Sun* (1956), *Omar Khayyam* (1957), *Third Man on the Mountain* (1959), *The Lost World* (1959), *Mary, Mary* (1963), *Ride Beyond Vengence* (1965), *The Power* (1967), *Hotel* (1967), *The Devil's Brigade* (1968), *The Battle of El Alamein* (1968), *Subterfuge) (1969)*.

THE MAN IN THE WHITE SUIT

The films of Alexander Mackendrick:

Whiskey Galore (Tight Little Island, 1948), *The Man in the White Suit* (1951), *Mandy (The Crash of Silence*, 1952), *The Maggie (High and Dry*, 1953), *The Lady Killers* (1955), *The Sweet Smell of Success* (1957), *A Boy Ten Feet Tall (Sammy Going South*, 1962), *A High Wind in Jamaica* (1965), *Don't Make Waves* (1967).

DONOVAN'S BRAIN

1. *The Lady and the Monster* was later rereleased as *The Tiger Man*. In Britain, it was known as *The Lady and the Doctor*.

2. *Vengeance* was a British-German collaboration. The German title is *Ein Toter Sucht Seiner Morder,* (A Dead Man Seeks His Murderer) or more simply, *Vengeance.* It's also known as *The Brain*.

3. Steve Brodie, who plays the photographer Yocum, was also a veteran heavy in films. Some filmgoers may remember him as the bigot in *Home of the Brave* (1949).
Tom Powers, who appears briefly in *DB* as Donovan's Washington Connection—the man he refers to as Mr. Adviser—appeared as General Thayer in *Destination Moon.*
Fans may also recognize the bank manager as long-time character actor John Hamilton, who would achieve greater prominence as Perry White on the old *Superman* TV series.

THE MAGNETIC MONSTER

1. The films of Curt Siodmak:

A. Original stories and screenplays: *Floating Platform 1 Does Not Reply* (1933), *Transatlantic Tunnel* (1935), *La Crise Est Finie* (1938), *Her Jungle Love* (1938), *The Invisible Man Returns* (1940), *Black Friday* (1940), *The Ape* (1940), *The Wolf Man* (1941), *The Invisible Woman* (1941), *Aloma of the South Seas* (1941), *Invisible Agent* (1942), *Pacific Blackout* (1942), *Son of Dracula* (1943), *Frankenstein Meets the Wolf Man* (1943), *I Walked with a Zombie* (1943), *House of Frankenstein* (1944), *The Climax* (1944), *Shady Lady* (1945), *Frisco Sal* (1945), *The Beast with Five Fingers* (1946), *The Return of Monte Cristo* (1947), *Berlin Express* (1948), *Tarzan's Magic Fountain* (1949), *Four Days' Leave* (1950), *Riders to the Stars* (1954), *Creature with the Atom Brain* (1955), *Earth Vs. the Flying Saucers* (1956), *Sherlock Holmes and the Deadly Necklace* (1962)

B. Screenplays and direction: *Bride of the Gorilla* (1951), *The Magnetic Monster* (1953), *Curucu, Beast of the Amazon* (1956), *Love Slaves of the Amazon* (1957), *The Devil's Messenger* (1962), *Ski Fever* (1969).

2. The films of Richard Carlson:

The Young in Heart (1938), *The Duke of West Point* (1938), *Winter Carnival* (1939), *These Glamour Girls* (1939), *Dancing Co-ed* (1939), *Little Accident* (1939), *Ghost Breakers* (1940), *Beyond Tomorrow* (1940), *The Howards of Virginia* (1940), *Too Many Girls* (1940), *No, No, Nannette* (1940), *Back Street* (1941), *The Little Foxes* (1941), *West Point Widow* (1941), *Hold That Ghost* (1941), *White Cargo* (1942), *Presenting Lily Mars* (1943), *The Man from Down Under* (1943), *So Well Remembered* (1947), *Try and Get Me (The Sound of Fury*, 1950), *King Solomon's Mines* (1950), *The Blue Veil* (1951), *Valentino* (1951), *A Millionaire for Christy* (1951), *Flat Top* (1952), *Retreat, Hell!* (1952), *Whispering Smith Vs. Scotland Yard* (1952), *All I Desire* (1953), *It Came from Outer Space* (1953), *The Magnetic Monster* (1953), *The Maze* (1953), *Seminole* (1953), *The Cowboy* (1954), *Creature from the Black Lagoon* (1954), *Riders to the Stars* (1954), *Bengazi* (1955), *The Last Command* (1955), *Three for Jamie Dawn* (1956), *The Helen Morgan Story* (1957), *Tormented* (1960), *Kid Rodelo* (1966), *The Power* (1968), *The Valley of Gwangi* (1969), *A Change of Habit* (1970).

INVADERS FROM MARS

1. The problem of cuts and alterations in *IFM* is emphasized by the wide variation in plot descriptions from various sources on the film. It's hard to tell if these variations are due to the writers' memories or if they've seen a different print of the film.

One source, for example, cites General Mayberry as one of the saboteurs. The same source says that as David runs down the hill at the film's end, a montage of scenes from the film flash through his mind. Another source describes *three* different endings for the film, excluding the "dream" ending. In the first, the saucer escapes; in the second, the saucer is destroyed; and in the third, the battle is unresolved.

The plot summary in this chapter reflects the version of *IFM* seen by the authors.

2. The films of director William Cameron Menzies:

The Spider (1931), *Always Goodbye* (1931), *Chandu the Magician* (1932), *I Love You Wednesday* (1933), *The Wharf Angel* (1934), *Things to Come* (1936), *The Green Cockatoo* (Four Dark Hours, 1937), *Address Unknown* (1944), *Duel in the Sun* (1946), *Drums in the Deep South* (1951), *The Whip Hand* (1951), *Invaders from Mars* (1953), *The Maze* (1953).

3. The films of Helena Carter:

Time Out of Mind (1947), *Something in the Wind* (1947), *Intrigue* (1948), *River Lady* (1948), *The Fighting O'Flynn* (1949), *South Sea Sinner* (1950), *Kiss Tomorrow Goodbye* (1950), *Double Crossbones* (1951), *Fort Worth* (1951), *Bugles in the Afternoon* (1952), *The Golden Hawk* (1952), *The Pathfinder* (1953), *Invaders from Mars* (1953).

4. The films of Arthur Franz:

Jungle Patrol (1948), *The Doctor and the Girl* (1949), *Red Light* (1949), *Red Stallion of the Rockies* (1949), *Roseanna McCoy* (1949), *Sands of Iwo Jima* (1949), *Tarnished* (1950), *Three Secrets* (1950), *Abbott & Costello Meet the Invisible Man* (1951), *Flight to Mars* (1951), *Strictly Dishonorable* (1951), *Submarine Command* (1951), *Eight Iron Men* (1952), *Rainbow Round My Shoulder* (1952), *The Sniper* (1952), *Bad for Each Other* (1953), *Flight Nurse* (1953), *The Member of the Wedding* (1953), *The Steel Cage* (1954), *The Eddie Cantor Story* (1954), *The Caine Mutiny* (1954), *Battle Taxi* (1955), *Bobby Ware is Missing* (1955), *New Orleans Uncensored* (1955), *The Wild Party* (1956), *Running Target* (1956), *Beyond a Reasonable Doubt* (1956), *Back from the Dead* (1957), *The Devil's Hairpin* (1957), *Hellcats of the Navy* (1957), *The Unholy Wife* (1957), *The Flame Barrier* (1958), *Monster on the Campus* (1958), *The Young Lions* (1958), *The Atomic Submarine* (1959), *The Carpetbaggers* (1963), *Alvarez Kelly* (1966), *Anzio* (1968), *The Sweet Ride* (1968), *The Human Factor* (1975).

5. The SF/horror films of Morris Ankrum:

Rocketship X-M (1950), *Flight to Mars* (1951), *Red Planet Mars* (1952), *Abbott and Costello Meet the Mummy* (1955), *Earth Vs. The Flying Saucers* (1956), *Half-Human* (1957), *The Giant Claw* (1957), *Kronos* (1957), *Zombies of Mora-Tau* (1957), *Beginning of the End* (1957), *From the Earth to the Moon* (1958), *How to Make a Monster* (1958), *The Most Dangerous Man Alive* (1957).

WAR OF THE WORLDS

1. The films of George Pal:

The Great Rupert (1950), *Destination Moon* (1950, AA, Special Visual Effects), *When Worlds Collide* (1951, AA, Special Visual Effects), *Houdini* (1953), *The War of the Worlds* (1953, AA, Special Visual Effects), *The Naked Jungle* (1954), *Conquest of Space* (1955), *Tom Thumb* (1958, producer/director, AA, Special Visual Effects), *The Time Machine* (1960, producer/director, AA, Special Visual Effects), *Atlantis, The Lost Continent* (1961, producer/director), *The Wonderful World of the Brothers Grimm* (1962, producer/codirector), *7 Faces of Dr. Lao* (1964, producer/director, Special AA, William Tuttle—"Outstanding Makeup Achievement"), *The Power* (1968), *Doc Savage, The Man of Bronze* (1975).

2. The films of Gene Barry:

The Atomic City (1952), *The Girls of Pleasure Island* (1952), *The War of the Worlds* (1953), *Those Redheads from Seattle* (1953), *Alaska Seas* (1954), *Red Garters* (1954), *Naked Alibi* (1954), *Soldier of Fortune* (1955), *The Purple Mask* (1955), *The Houston Story* (1956), *Back From Eternity* (1956), *The 27th Day* (1957), *China Gate* (1957), *Thunder Road* (1958), *Maroc 7* (1967), *Subterfuge* (1969), *Do You Take this Stranger?* (TV, 1970), *The Devil and Miss Sarah* (TV, 1971), *The Second Coming of Suzanne* (1973).

3. Films from H. G. Wells's works:

The First Men in the Moon (1919), *Kipps* (1921), *The Wheels of Chance* (1922), *The Passionate Friends* (1922), *Marriage* (1927), *Daydreams, Bluebottles,* and *The Tonic* (1929, three 30-minute shorts), *The Island of Lost Souls* (1932), *The Invisible Man* (1933), *Things to Come* (1936), *The Man Who Could Work Miracles* (1937), *Kipps* (1941), *Dead of Night*—the Golfing sequence (1945), *One Woman's Story* (1948), *The History of Mr. Polly* (1949), *The War of the Worlds* (1953), *The Door In the Wall* (1956), *The Time Machine* (1960), *The First Men In the Moon* (1964), *The Village of the Giants* (1965), *The Food of the Gods* (1976), *The Empire of the Ants* (1977), *The Island of Dr. Moreau* (1977), *The Time Machine* (TV, 1978), *The Shape of Things to Come* (1979).

One of the scientists from Pacific Tech was played by Robert Cornthwaite, who also appeared in *The Thing* and *Colossus*. He was also in a two-part episode on TV's *Wonder Woman* based on *The Day the Earth Stood Still*.

The much-discussed religious overtones in *War* were a standard feature of most Pal films, from *The Great Rupert,* and *When Worlds Collide* to *Conquest of Space*. This results both from the time in which Pal made his films and from his Hungarian background. On reflection, most people realize many SF films of the fifties evoke God—if only in the phrases "Some things are best left to God" and "There are things Man was not meant to know."

Klaatu's revival in *Day,* for instance, was only for an undetermined period of time, because the Breen Office insisted only God could restore life to someone dead.

1. The films of Gordon Douglas:

Saps at Sea (1940), *Broadway Limited* (1941), *The Devil with Hitler* (1943), *Zombies on Broadway* (1945), *If You Knew Susie* (1948), *The Doolins of Oklahoma* (1949), *Kiss Tomorrow Goodbye* (1950), *Only the Valiant* (1951), *I Was a Communist for the FBI* (1951), *Come Fill the Cup* (1951), *Mara Maru* (1952), *The Iron Mistress* (1953), *So This Is Love* (1953), *The Charge at Feather River* (1953), *Them!* (1954), *Young at Heart* (1954), *Sincerely Yours* (1955), *The Big Land* (1956), *Bombers B-52* (1958), *Yellowstone Kelly* (1959), *The Sins of Rachel Cade* (1960), *Gold of the Seven Saints* (1961), *Follow That Dream* (1962), *Call Me Bwana* (1963), *Robin and the Seven Hoods* (1964), *Rio Conchos* (1964), *Sylvia* (1965), *Harlow* (1965), *Stagecoach* (1966), *Way Way Out* (1966), *In Like Flint* (1967), *Chuka* (1967), *Tony Rome* (1967), *The Detective* (1968), *Lady in Cement* (1968), *Skullduggery* (1969), *Barquero* (1970).

2. Giant Monster films:

The Lost World (1925), *King Kong* (1933), *Mighty Joe Young* (1949), *Beast From Twenty Thousand Fathoms* (1953), *Them!* (1954), *20,000 Leagues Under the Sea* (1954), *Godzilla* (1954, 1956 USA), *Tarantula* (1955), *Rodan* (1956), *The Deadly Mantis* (1957), *The Giant Claw* (1957), *The Black Scorpion* (1957), *The Spider* (1958), *Gorgo* (1959), *The Giant Behemoth* (1959), *Reptilicus* (1961), *The Valley of Gwangi* (1968), *Night of the Lepus* (1972), etc.

3. The films of James Whitmore:

Undercover Man (1949), *The Asphalt Jungle* (1950), *Across the Wide Missouri* (1951), *Kiss Me Kate* (1953), *Them!* (1954), *Battle Cry* (1955), *Oklahoma* (1955), *The Eddy Duchin Story* (1956), *Who Was That Lady?* (1960), *Black Like Me* (1964), *Chuka* (1967), *Planet of the Apes* (1968), *Madigan* (1968), *The Split* (1968), *Guns of the Magnificent Seven* (1969), *Tora! Tora! Tora!* (1970), *Chato's Land* (1971), *If Tomorrow Comes* (TV, 1971), *The Harrad Experiment* (1973), *Give 'Em Hell Harry* (1975), *Where the Red Fern Grows* (1975).

4. The films of James Arness:

The Farmer's Daughter (1949), *Battleground* (1949), *Two Lost Worlds* (1950), *Sierra* (1950), *Wagonmaster* (1950), *Wyoming Mail* (1950), *Iron Man* (1951), *Cavalry Scout* (1951), *The Thing* (1951), *The People Against O'Hara* (1951), *Big Jim McLain* (1952), *Carbine Williams* (1952), *The Girl in White* (1952), *Hell Gate* (1952), *Horizons West* (1952), *Veils of Baghdad* (1953), *Lone Hand* (1953), *Island in the Sky* (1953), *Her Twelve Men* (1954), *Many Rivers to The Sea Chase* (1954), *Them!* (1954), *Hondo* (1955), *Gun the Man Down* (1955), *Flame of the Islands* (1955), *The First Traveling Saleslady* (1956).

5. Other actors in *Them!:*

Onslow Stevens was born Onslow Ford Stevenson in 1902. Stevens was an American stage actor who played many character roles in films, including *House of Dracula* (1945), and *The Creeper* (1948). Stevens died in 1977.

Sean McClory, born in 1923, came to Hollywood after years of experience with the Abbey Theater in Ireland. He handles heroic and villainous roles with equal aplomb.

Two actors recognizable from years of television work had small roles in *Them!* Former baseball player and soap-opera star John Beradino plays a Los Angeles city policemen, and Richard Deacon of *The Dick Van Dyke Show* plays a reporter.

6. A Nebula-winning short story, "giANTS," inspired by *Them!* appeared in the August 1979 issue of *Analog,* the science fiction magazine originally titled *Astounding.*

"giANTS" is about an effort to stop the advance of a new breed of *maripunta,* or army ants, by attempting to create giant ants—on the presumption that the square-cube law will effect their destruction.

7. Perhaps coincidentally, there are a number of interesting similarities between 1953's *The Beast from Twenty Thousand Fathoms* and 1954's *Them!*

Both were released by Warner Bros.; both were scripted to end at amusement parks, until the ending of *Them!* was changed; both had ships at sea destroyed by the monster(s); and both had cast members going down into danger—in a diving bell in *Beast* and into a nest in *Them!*

In *Beast,* Cecil Kellaway and Paula Raymond had roles similar to those of Edmund Gwenn and Joan Weldon in *Them!* Kellaway was a kindly old expert and Raymond a woman scientist—although they were not father and daughter.

THIS ISLAND EARTH

1. The films of Joseph M. Newman:

Jungle Patrol (1948), *711 Ocean Drive* (1950), *The Outcasts of Poker Flats* (1952), *Red Skies of Montana* (1952), *Pony Soldier* (1953), *The Human Jungle* (1954), *Dangerous Crossing* (1954) *Kiss of Fire* (1955), *This Island Earth* (1955), *Flight to Hong Kong* (1956, producer/director), *Gunfight at Dodge City* (1958), *Fort Massacre* (1958), *The Big Circus (1959)*, *Tarzan the Ape Man* (1959), *King of the Roaring Twenties* (1961), *A Thunder of Drums* (1961), *The George Raft Story* (1961), *Twenty Plus Two* (1961).

2. The films of Jeff Morrow:

The Robe (1953), *Flight to Tangier* (1953), *Siege of Red River* (1954), *Tanganyika* (1954), *Sign of the Pagan* (1954), *This Island Earth* (1955), *Captain Lightfoot* (1955), *The First Texan* (1956), *The Creature Walks Among Us* (1956), *Pardners* (1956), *The Giant Claw* (1957), *Kronos* (1957), *The Story of Ruth* (1960), *Harbour Lights* (1963), *Legacy of Blood* (1971).

3. The films of Faith Domergue:

Vendetta (1950), *Where Danger Lives* (1950), *This Island Earth* (1955), *California* (1963), *Prehistoric Planet Women* (1966), *One on Top of the Other* (1970), *Legacy of Blood* (1971), *The House of The Seven Corpses* (1973).

4. The films of Rex Reason:

Storm Over Tibet (1952), *Salome* (1953), *Yankee Pasha* (1954), *This Island Earth* (1955), *Raw Edge* (1956), *Band of Angels* (1957), *The Rawhide Trail* (1960).

5. William Tenn's 1953 short story, "The Liberation of Earth," foreshadows *This Island Earth.* Tenn's tale is a satire showing what happens when two technologically advanced alien races make Earth a battleground. In turn, each "liberates" Earth (as the various armies did in South Korea—Tenn's point) from the other's evil occupation. Their conflict rages back and forth until Earth, caught in the middle, is laid waste by constant warfare.

Those human leaders who cooperated with the first liberators were executed when the second group of aliens seized control. Of course, when the first liberators regained the Earth, those who'd cooperated with the "enemy" were again executed.
Finally, the unending series of liberations sends the Earth wobbling out of its orbit and the two alien races look for a more stable battleground.

FORBIDDEN PLANET

1. "Pulps" get their name from the paper they're printed on. During World War II, only very inferior quality wood pulp was available for magazines. Even so, the lack of paper forced many SF magazines off the stands for good.
2. It was on Lot 3 that Gillespie built the first outdoor water tank to be used for miniatures.
3. Filmmakers began using cycloramas when it was shown they could be adapted to fool the two-dimensional eye of the camera. Motion picture cycloramas are hung in predetermined arcs, mimicking a natural perspective when seen on screen.
Staff artists who worked on the painting of the cycloramas included Leo Atkinson, Tommy Duff, H. Gibson, Ed Helms, F. Wayne Hill, Bob Overbeck, Clark Provins, Arthur Rider, Bill Smart, and Bob Woolfe. A civil war museum in Gettysburg, Pennsylvania contains an enormous cyclorama showing scenes from the three-day battle.

4. The saucer models, the large saucer mock-up, and the space uniforms all appeared in later MGM and TV productions, most notably in Rod Serling's *The Twilight Zone.* Episodes using *Forbidden Planet* props include:
—"The Invaders," starring Agnes Moorhead
—"Hocus, Pocus and Frisby," starring Andy Devine
—"Third from the Sun," starring Fritz Weaver
—"The Monsters Are Due on Maple Street," starring Claude Akins
—"Death Ship," starring Jack Klugman and Ross Martin
Robby the Robot appeared in several episodes of *The Twilight Zone,* including "Uncle Simon," starring Sir Cedric Hardwicke, and "The Brain Center at Whipple's," starring Richard Deacon.
Robby has also appeared on other television shows, including a 1979 appearance on *Mork and Mindy* (with Roddy McDowell's voice). The striking *FP* crew uniforms showed up in *The Queen of Outer Space* (1959), starring Zsa Zsa Gabor.

5. Asimov's Three Laws of Robotics are: 1) A robot may not injure a human being, or, through inaction, allow a human being to come to harm. 2) A robot must obey the orders given it by human beings except where such orders would conflict with the First Law. 3) A robot must protect its own existence as long as such protection does not conflict with the First or Second Law.

6. The films of Ann Francis:

Summer Holiday (1948), *So Young So Bad* (1950), *Elopement* (1952), *Lydia Bailey* (1952), *Susan Slept Here* (1954), *Bad Day at Black Rock* (1954), *The Blackboard Jungle* (1955), *Forbidden Planet* (1956), *Don't Go Near the Water* (1957), *Girl of the Night* (1960), *The Satan Bug* (1965), *Funny Girl* (1968), *The Love God* (1969), *More Dead Than Alive* (1970), *Pancho Villa* (1971), *Haunts of the Very Rich* (TV, 1972).

7. The films of Leslie Nielsen:

The Vagabond King (1955), *Forbidden Planet* (1956), *Ransom* (1956), *Tammy and the Bachelor* (1957), *Harlow* (1965), *Beau Geste* (1966), *The Poseidon Adventure* (1972), *City on Fire* (1979).

8. The films of Fred McLeod Wilcox:

Lassie Come Home (1943), *Blue Sierra* (1946), *Courage of Lassie* (1946), *Hills of Home* (1948), *Three Daring Daughters* (1948), *The Secret Garden* (1949), *Shadow in the Sky* (1950), *Code Two* (1953), *Tennessee Champ* (1954), *Forbidden Planet* (1956), *I Passed for White* (1960).

INVASION OF THE BODY SNATCHERS

1. The works of Jack Finney:

Five Against the House (1954), *The Third Level* (1956), *House of Numbers* (1957), *Assault on a Queen* (1960), *I Love Galesburg in the Spring* (1963), *Good Neighbor Sam* (1963), *The Woodrow Wilson Dime* (1968), *Time and Again* (1970), *Marion's Wall* (1973), *The*

Night People (1977).

2. The films of Don Siegel:

A Star in the Night (1945, short), *Hitler Lives* (1945, short), *The Verdict* (1946), *Night Unto Night* (1947), *The Big Steal* (1949), *No Time for Flowers* (1952), *Duel at Silver Creek* (1952), *Count the Hours* (1953), *China Venture* (1953), *Riot in Cell Block 11* (1954), *Private Hell 36* (1954), *The Annapolis Story* (also known as *The Blue and the Gold*, 1955), *Crime in the Streets* (1956), *Spanish Affair* (1957), *Baby Face Nelson* (1957), *The Gun Runners* (1958), *The Line-Up* (1958), *Edge of Eternity* (1959), *Hound Dog Man* (1959), *Flaming Star* (1960), *Hell is for Heroes* (1962), *The Killers* (1964), *The Hanged Man* (1964, TV movie), *Stranger on the Run* (1967, TV movie), *Madigan* (1968), *Coogan's Bluff* (1968), *Death of a Gunfighter* (1969, with Robert Totten), *Two Mules for Sister Sara* (1969), *The Beguiled* (1970), *Dirty Harry* (1971), *Charley Varrick* (1972), *The Black Windmill* (1974), *The Shootist* (1976), *Telefon* (1977), *Escape from Alcatraz* (1979).

THE VILLAGE OF THE DAMNED

1. SF/horror films featuring children:

Curse of the Cat People (1944), *Mighty Joe Young* (1949), *The Rocking Horse Winner* (1949), *Invaders from Mars* (1953), *I Was a Teenage Frankenstein/Werewolf* (1957), *The Invisible Boy* (1958), *The Space Children* (1958), *The Innocents* (1961), *Children of the Damned* (1963), *These Are the Damned* (1963), *Lord of the Flies* (1963), *Privilege* (1967), *The Other* (1972), *The People* (1972), *The Exorcist* (1973), *It's Alive* (1974), *Carrie* (1976), *The Omen* (1976), *The Fury* (1978), *The Brood* (1979).

2. The films of Wolf Rilla:

Noose for a Lady (1953), *The End of the Road* (1954), *Pacific Destiny* (1956), *The Scamp* (1957), *Bachelor of Hearts* (1958), *Witness in the Dark* (1960), *Piccadilly Third Stop* (1960), *Village of the Damned* (1960), *Cairo* (1963), *The World Ten Times Over* (writer/director, 1963), *Secrets of a Door to Door Salesman* (1973).

3. The films of George Sanders:

The Man Who Could Work Miracles (1936), *Dishonour Bright* (1937), *Lloyds of London* (1937), *Lancer Spy* (1937), *Four Men and a Prayer* (1938), *The Outsider* (1939), *Nurse Edith Cavell* (1939), *Confessions of a Nazi Spy* (1939), *The House of Seven Gables* (1940), *Rebecca* (1940), *Foreign Correspondent* (1940), *The Saint* (series, 1940–42), *The Falcon* (series, 1941–43), *Rage in Heaven* (1941), *Man Hunt* (1941), *Son of Fury* (1942), *The Moon and Sixpence* (1942), *Quiet Please, Murder* (1943), *The Lodger* (1944), *Action in Arabia* (1944), *Summer Storm* (1944), *The Picture of Dorian Gray* (1944), *Hangover Square (1944)*, *Uncle Harry* (1945), *A Scandal in Paris* (1946), *The Strange Woman* (1947), *The Ghost and Mrs. Muir* (1947), *Forever Amber* (1947), *Bel Ami* (1948), *Samson and Delilah* (1949), *All About Eve* (AA, 1950), *Ivanhoe* (1952), *Witness to Murder* (1954), *King Richard and the Crusaders* (1954), *Moonfleet* (1955), *The King's Thief* (1955), *Death of a Scoundrel* (1956), *From the Earth to the Moon* (1958), *Solomon and Sheba* (1959), *A Touch of Larceny* (1960), *Bluebeard's Ten Honeymoons* (1960), *Village of the Damned* (1960), *A Shot in the Dark* (1964), *The Golden Head* (1964), *Moll Flanders* (1965), *The Quiller Memorandum* (1966), *The Kremlin Letter* (1969), *Endless Night* (1972), *Doomwatch* (1972), *Psychomania* (1972).

DR. STRANGELOVE

1. Peter George, born in 1924, was the author of *Red Alert*. He had a lifelong obsession with nuclear warfare and his other two novels are *Commander-1* (1965) and *Nuclear Survivors* (1966).
Today, many films are turned into novelizations. This happened less frequently when *Dr. Strangelove* was released, but a novelization was rushed into print, based on the screenplay, by Bantam Books. Assuming more people would have heard of Kubrick's film than George's novel, the novelization, although written by Peter George, was called *Stanley Kubrick's Dr. Strangelove or: How I Learned to Stop Worrying and Love the Bomb*.

George's novelization generally followed the screenplay. The few deviations include: the President being raised into the War Room strapped into a hydraulic chair through a hole in the floor; the recall code is not OPE, but JFK—Joe for King; a drunken Ripper, rather than killing himself, takes off in his personal plane.

The novelization contains an introduction and an epilogue which indicate the manuscript was uncovered in the far future and is another in the series: *The Dead Worlds of Antiquity*.
Peter George took his own life in 1966.

2. Kubrick's other early films:

Paths of Glory (1957), one of the all-time great antiwar movies, was made for $935,000-$350,000 of which went to its star Kirk Douglas, a bargain according to Kubrick, since without Douglas's participation no studio would finance the film.
The closing scene features a young German girl prisoner singing to an audience of hostile French troops. Touched by her singing, they slowly join in. The role was played by German actress Suzanne Christian, who is now Mrs. Stanley Kubrick.

Spartacus (1960) was, for Kubrick, an unsatisfying success. Taking over the director's job from Anthony Mann on condition the script would be rewritten, Kubrick soon discovered a director has no more control over a production than is written into his contract. The script was never rewritten and Douglas, after another director complimented him on Kubrick's first directorial efforts, imposed his own vision on the film. Praised for being a notch above most historical dramas, *Spartacus* was, nonetheless, flawed in Kubrick's eyes.

Lolita (1962) is one of Kubrick's favorites and he's dismayed that many critics have ranked it with *Spartacus*. It was his first teaming with Peter Sellers and convinced him black comedy was Sellers's special forte. Still, it was not the movie Kubrick hoped to make because censorship denied him full access to the novel's erotic aspects.

ROBINSON CRUSOE ON MARS

1. The films of Byron Haskin:

Ginsberg the Great (1927), *Irish Hearts* (1927), *Matinee Ladies* (1927), *The Siren* (1927), *I Walk Alone* (1947), *Man-eater of Kuamon* (1948), *Too Late for Tears* (1949), *Treasure Island* (1950), *Tarzan's Peril* (1951), *Warpath* (1951), *Silver City* (1951), *The Denver and Rio Grande* (1952), *War of the Worlds* (1953), *His Majesty O'Keefe* (1953), *The Naked Jungle* (1954), *Long John Silver* (1955), *The Conquest of Space* (1955), *The First Texan* (1956), *The Boss* (1956), *From the Earth to the Moon* (1958), *The Little Savage* (1959), *Jet over the Atlantic* (1959), *September Storm* (1960), *Armored Command* (1961), *Captain Sinbad* (1963), *Robinson Crusoe on Mars* (1964), *The Power* (with George Pal, 1968).
Episodes of *Outer Limits*: "The One Hundred Days of the Dragon," "The Architects of Fear," "A Feasibility Study," "Behold, Eck!" "Demon with a Glass Hand," "The Invisible Enemy."

2. *Planet of the Vampires* is known in Italian as *Terrore Nello Spazio*. Its alternate titles in English are: *Planet of Blood, Haunted Planet, Haunted World, Outlawed Planet, Planet of the Damned,* and *Demon Planet.*

3. The Films of Ib Melchior (as screenwriter only): *Live Fast, Die Young* (1958), *When Hell Broke Loose* (1958), *Journey to the Seventh Planet* (1962, with Sidney Pink), *Reptilicus* (1962, with Sidney Pink), *Robinson Crusoe on Mars* (1964, with John C. Higgins), *Planet of the Vampires* (1965, English language version, with Louis M. Heyward), *Ambush Bay* (1966), *Death Race 2000* (1975, original story).
As writer and director: *The Angry Red Planet* (1959, written with Sidney Pink), *The Time Travelers* (1964).
Associate Producer: *The Case of Patti Smith* (1962)
Ib Melchior's episode of *Outer Limits* was "The Premonition."

4. Melchior was not entirely pleased with the changes Higgins made in the script. Aside from changing all the names of the characters ("Kit" was called "Robin" in Melchior's script), Higgins was responsible for Kit's taking the position of "I'm the Boss" with Friday. Melchior feels this weakened his attempt to show the two men working as equals. Whether this was the result, or whether this strengthens Kit's gratitude later in the film, is a question of individual interpretation.
Information on John C. Higgins is difficult to find. He began as a screenwriter for MGM in 1934, turning out many films, most of them fairly obscure. His only other fantasy credit appears to be *The Black Sleep* (also known as *Dr. Cadman's Secret,* 1956), which was Bela Lugosi's last film. Film fans may also be familiar with Higgins's *Seven Cities of Gold* (1955). His name does not appear in the Motion Picture Almanac after 1971.

5. Al Nozaki, Art Director on *War of the Worlds,* also worked on *RCOM*. According to Nozaki, it's possible that drawings based on the War Machines from *War of the Worlds* were used for the spaceships in *RCOM* rather than three-dimensional models.
Nozaki worked on the design of the *Elinor M.,* the portable communications unit, and other devices. He also designed spaceships for the film which were quite unlike those which eventually appeared in the film. Some idea of Nozaki's design can be seen in the film when Kit examines his videotape of the aliens and sees a kind of kettle-shaped craft, with long, curving legs.

THE MIND OF MR. SOAMES

The novels of Charles Eric Maine:

Spaceways (1953), *Timeliner* (1955), *Crisis 2000* (1955), *High Vacuum* (1956), *The Man Who Couldn't Sleep* (1956), *The Isotope Man* (1957), *Fire Past the Future* (1959), *Calculated Risk* (1960), *The Man Who Owned the World* (1960), *Subterfuge* (1960), *The Mind of Mr. Soames* (1961), *Survival Margin* (1962), *Never Let Up* (1964), *B.E.A.S.T.* (1966), *The Random Factor* (1971), *Alph* (1972), *Thirst!* (1977).

COLOSSUS—THE FORBIN PROJECT

1. Joseph Sargent's other films include:

The Sunshine Patriot (1968, TV), *Tribes* (1970, TV), *The Man Who Died Twice* (1970, TV), *Maybe I'll Come Home in the Spring* (1970, TV), *Longstreet* (1970, pilot for TV series), *Man on a String* (1971, TV), *The Marcus-Nelson Murders* (1973; spawned the TV series *Kojak*), *Sunshine* (1973, TV; spawned a short-lived series and a sequel, *Sunshine Christmas, not* directed by Sargent), *The Taking of Pelham 1–2–3* (1974), *Hustling* (1975, TV), *Friendly Persuasion* (1975, TV) *MacArthur* (1977).
Sargent's episodes of *The Invaders* were all in the series' first season (1967): "Beach Head" (the pilot); "The Experiment"; "The Ivy Curtain"; "Wall of Crystal."

2. According to the American Film Institute Catalog, art direction on *CFP* was shared by John Lloyd and Alexander Golitzen. None of the other sources consulted, however, make any specific reference to Golitzen's work on the film. Therefore, his contribution to *CFP* is in doubt.

3. A number of other actors in *CFP* are recognizable:
Georg Stanford Brown (Fisher) later achieved some stardom on the TV series *The Rookies* and in *Roots I* and *Roots II.*

Martin Brooks (Johnson) later became one of the three actors to play Dr. Rudy Wells, the scientist who did the job on Steve Austin in the *Six Million Dollar Man.* The other two, incidentally, were Martin Balsam and Alan Oppenheimer.

Marion Ross (Angela, Forbin's secretary) became Marion Cunningham, Ron Howard's mother, on the TV series *Happy Days.*

Robert Cornthwaite, who appears as one of the Colossus computer scientists, would be recognizable to really attentive SF film fans as the somewhat careless Dr. Carrington in *The Thing.*

A CLOCKWORK ORANGE

1. A newspaper ad for *Straw Dogs* exploits its violence:

"Warning! Blood-action by the gallon! SEE: a man's head crushed in the giant bear trap! SEE: Shotgun murders close up! SEE: Gang attack on the young bride! SEE: Scalding vinegar sear the eyes!"

2. The violent episodes in *Clockwork:*

a). Alex and his droogs beat up an old tramp.

b). Alex, Georgie, and Dim demolish Billyboy's rival gang in an abandoned casino (in stylized slow-motion at times).

c). Alex and his gang beat up Mr. and Mrs. Alexander, raping her.

d). When Dim and Georgie rebel against Alex's harsh leadership, Alex strikes them both with his sword-stick and slashes Dim's hand (in slow-motion).

e). Alex mortally wounds the Catlady with the phallic sculpture.

f). Dim, taking an opportunity for revenge, smashes Alex across the face with a milk bottle.

g). After Alex is arrested, the police reinjure his busted nose, and his high school counselor spits in his face.

h). A prisoner serving fourteen years, Alex daydreams of whipping Christ on his way to Calvary, and of cutting throats as a Roman soldier.

i). His eyelids held open, Alex is forced to view scenes of violence and rape.

j). An actor insults Alex and, when he is unable to respond, makes Alex lick the sole of his boot in an act of subjugation.

k). Released from custody, now "cured," Alex is beaten by the old tramp's friends.

l). Dim and Georgie, now policemen, take Alex out into the country—where they beat him and hold his head in a water trough.

m). Mr. Alexander, having taken Alex into his house and aware who he is, tortures him by playing the *Ninth* at high volume.

3. The music:

a). *Singin' in the Rain* is used for the assault sequence at Mr. Alexander's house.

b). Rossini's *Thieving Magpie* overture is used when Alex clubs the Catlady to death.

c). The *William Tell* overture, speeded up, is played against Alex's frantically fast orgy with two girls.

d). *Scheherazade* is used for Alex's daydream of the Biblical handmaidens.

e). Carlos's *Timesteps* is played during the violent movies.

f). *I Want to Marry a Lighthouse Keeper* is sung as Alex returns home for the first time since his cure.

BIBLIOGRAPHY

BOOKS

Agel, Jerome, ed. *The Making of Kubrick's 2001*. New York: Signet, 1970.

Aros, Andrew A. *A Title Guide to the Talkies, 1964–1974*. Metuchen, N.J.: Scarecrow Press, 1977.

———. *An Actor Guide to the Talkies, 1964–1974*. Metuchen, N.J.: Scarecrow Press, 1977.

Atkins, Thomas R., ed. *Science Fiction Films*. New York: Monarch Press, 1976.

Bawden, Liz-Anne, ed. *The Oxford Companion to Film*. New York: Oxford University Press, 1976.

Baxter, John. *Science Fiction in the Cinema*. 2nd. ed., revised. New York: A. S. Barnes, 1974.

Beck, Calvin T. *Scream Queens*. New York: Macmillan, 1978.

Brooks, Tim, and Marsh, Earle. *The Complete Directory to Prime Time Network TV Shows, 1946–Present*. New York: Ballantine Books, 1979.

Brosnan, John. *Future Tense*. New York: St. Martin's Press, 1978.

Bryant, Peter. [Peter George.] *Red Alert*. New York: Ace Books, 1958.

Burgess, Anthony. *A Clockwork Orange*. New York: Ballantine Books, 1965.

Clarens, Carlos. *An Illustrated History of the Horror Film*. New York: Putnam's, 1967.

Clarke, Arthur C. *The Lost Worlds of 2001*. New York: Signet, 1972.

———. *2001: A Space Odyssey*. New York: Signet, 1968.

Corliss, Richard, ed. *Talking Pictures: Screenwriters in the American Cinema, 1927–73*. Woodstock, N.Y.: Overlook Press, 1974.

Dimmitt, Richard B. *A Title Guide to the Talkies, 1927–1963*. New York: Scarecrow Press, 1965.

———. *An Actor Guide to the Talkies, 1949–1963*. Metuchen, N.J.: Scarecrow Press, 1967.

Fell, John L. *A History of Films*. New York: Holt, Rinehart, and Winston, 1979.

Film Daily Yearbook. New York: Film Daily News, 1929–1969.

Finney, Jack. *The Body Snatchers*. Introduction by Richard Gid Powers. Boston: Gregg Press, 1976.

Frank, Alan G. *Horror Movies*. Secaucus, N.J.: Derbibooks, 1975.

George, Peter. *Dr. Strangelove*. New York: Bantam Books, 1963.

Gerani, Gary, and Schulman, Paul H. *Fantastic Television*. New York: Harmony Books, 1977.

Gertner, Richard, ed. *The International Motion Picture Almanac*. New York: Quigley Publishing, 1930–1980.

Gianakos, L. J. *Television Drama Series Programming, 1959–1975*. Metuchen, N.J.: Scarecrow Press, 1978.

Gifford, Denis. *The British Film Catalogue, 1895–1970*. New York: McGraw-Hill, 1973.

———. *A Pictorial History of Horror Movies*. New York: Hamlyn, 1973.

———. *Science Fiction Film*. New York: Dutton, 1971.

Glut, Donald F. *Classic Movie Monsters*. Metuchen, N.J.: Scarecrow Press, 1977.

Gunn, James. *Alternate Worlds: The Illustrated History of Science Fiction*. Englewood Cliffs, N.J.: Prentice-Hall, 1975.

Halliwell, Leslie. *The Filmgoer's Companion*. 6th ed. New York: Hill and Wang, 1977.

———. *Halliwell's Film Guide*. New York: Granada, 1977.

Heinlein, Robert A. *Destination Moon*. Introduction by David G. Hartwell. Boston: Gregg Press, 1979.

Hickman, Gail M. *The Films of George Pal*. New York: A. S. Barnes, 1974.

Johnson, William, ed. *Focus on the Science Fiction Film*. Englewood Cliffs, N.J.: Prentice-Hall, 1972.

Jones, D. F. *Colossus*. New York: Putnam's, 1967.

Kaminsky, Stuart M. *American Film Genres*. New York: Dell Books, 1977.

Korda, Michael. *Charmed Lives*. New York: Random House, 1979.

Koszarski, Richard, ed. *Hollywood Directors, 1941–1976*. New York: Oxford University Press, 1977.

Kubrick, Stanley. *Stanley Kubrick's Clockwork Orange*. New York: Abelard-Schuman, 1972.

Krafsur, Richard P., exec. ed. *The American Film Institute Catalog of Motion Pictures, Feature Films 1961–1970*. New York: R. R. Bowker, 1976.

Kyle, David. *A Pictorial History of Science Fiction*. New York: Hamlyn, 1976.

———. *Science Fiction Ideas and Dreams*. New York: Hamlyn, 1977.

Lee, Walt, comp. *Reference Guide to Fantastic Films*. 3v. Los Angeles: Chelsea-Lee Books, 1972–1974.

McCarthy, Todd, and Flynn, Charles. *Kings of the B's*. New York: Dutton, 1975.

MacKenzie, Norman, and MacKenzie, Jeanne. *H. G. Wells: A Biography*. New York: Simon and Schuster, 1973.

Maine, Charles Eric. [David McIlwain.] *The Mind of Mr. Soames*. New York: Pyramid Books, 1970.

Maltin, Leonard, ed. *TV Movies, 1979–80*. New York: Signet, 1979.

Massey, Raymond. *A Hundred Different Lives*. Boston: Little, Brown, 1979.

Menville, Douglas, and Reginald, R. *Things to Come: An Illustrated History of the Science Fiction Film*. New York: Times Books, 1977.

Moskowitz, Sam. *Seekers of Tomorrow*. New York: Ballantine Books, 1967.

Naha, Ed, comp. *Starlog Photo Guidebook [to] Science Fiction Aliens*. New York: O'Quinn Studios, 1977.

Nicholls, Peter, ed. *The Science Fiction Encyclopedia*. Garden City, N.Y.: Doubleday, 1979.

Nobile, Philip, ed. *Favorite Movies: Critics' Choice*. New York: Macmillan, 1973.

Parish, James R. *Actors' Television Credits, 1950–1972*. Metuchen, N.J.: Scarecrow Press, 1973.

———. *Actors' Television Credits. Supplement I*. Metuchen, N.J.: Scarecrow Press, 1978.

———. *Hollywood Character Actors*. New Rochelle, N.Y.: Arlington House, 1978.

———, and Pitts, Michael R. *Film Directors: A Guide to Their American films*. Metuchen, N.J.: Scarecrow Press, 1974.

———, and Pitts, Michael R. *The Great Science Fiction Pictures*. Metuchen, N.J.: Scarecrow Press, 1977.

Rovin, Jeff. *From Jules Verne to Star Trek*. New York: Drake, 1977.

Sadoul, Georges, *Dictionary of Film Makers*. Translated by Peter Morris. Berkeley, Ca.: University of California Press, 1972.

———. *Dictionary of Films*. Translated by Peter Morris. Berkeley, Ca.: University of California Press, 1972.

Saleh, Dennis. *Science Fiction Gold*. New York: Comma/McGraw-Hill Books, 1979.

Sarris, Andrew, ed. *Interviews with Film Directors*. New York: Avon Books, 1967.

———. *The American Cinema: Directors and Directions*. New York: Dutton, 1968.

Scheuer, Steven, ed. *Movies On TV, 1978–79*. New York: Bantam Books, 1978.

Siodmak, Curt. *Donovan's Brain*. New York: Berkeley Books, 1969.

Scholes, Robert, and Rabkin, Eric S. *Science Fiction: History/Science/Vision*. New York: Oxford University Press, 1977.

Silverberg, Robert, ed. *The Science Fiction Hall of Fame*. vol. I. New York: Avon Books, 1970.

Steinbrunner, Chris, and Goldblatt, Burt. *Cinema of the Fantastic*. New York: Saturday Review Press, 1972.

Strick, Philip. *Science Fiction Movies*. London: Octopus Books, 1976.

Stuart, W. J. [Philip McDonald.] *Forbidden Planet*. Introduction by Joseph Milicia. Boston: Gregg Press, 1978.

Thomson, David. *A Biographical Dictionary of Film*. New York: William Morrow and Co., 1976.

Truitt, Evelyn Mack. *Who Was Who On Screen*. 2nd ed. New York: R. R. Bowker, 1977.

Walker, Alexander. *Double Takes*. London: Elm Tree Books, 1977.

———. *Stanley Kubrick Directs*. New York: Harcourt, Brace, Jovanovich, 1971.

Wells, H. G. *Things to Come*. Edited with an introduction by Allen Asherman and George Zebrowski. Boston: Gregg Press, 1975.

———. *Things to Come: A Film by H. G. Wells*. New York: Macmillan, 1975.

———. *The Time Machine [and] The War of the Worlds: A Critical Edition*. Edited by Frank McConnell. New York: Oxford University Press, 1977.

Willis, Donald C. *Horror and Science Fiction Films: A Checklist*. Metuchen, N.J.: Scarecrow Press, 1972.

Wyndham, John. *The Midwich Cuckoos. [Village of the Damned.]* New York: Ballantine Books, 1957.

MAGAZINES AND PERIODICALS

Action
American Cinematographer
Astounding/Analog
Cinefantastique
Cinemacabre
Famous Monsters of Filmland
Fangoria
Film Comment
Film Facts
Film Quarterly
Films and Filming
Films In Review
Galaxy

Journal of Popular Film
The New York Times
Newsweek
Playboy
Popular Science
Saturday Review
Sight and Sound
Starlog
Thrilling Wonder Stories
Time
Variety
Wide Angle

INDEX